Van Gogh

Into the Undergrowth

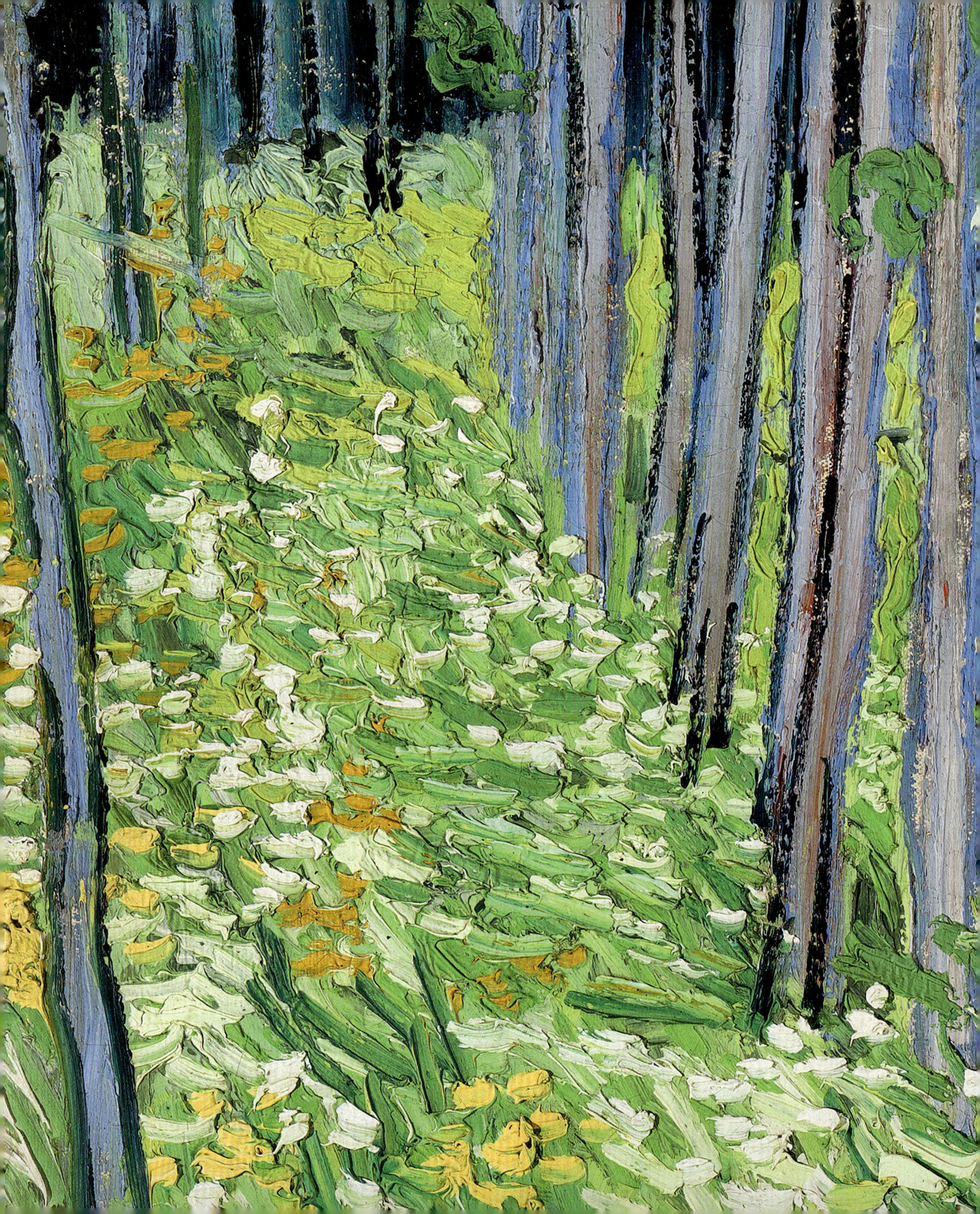

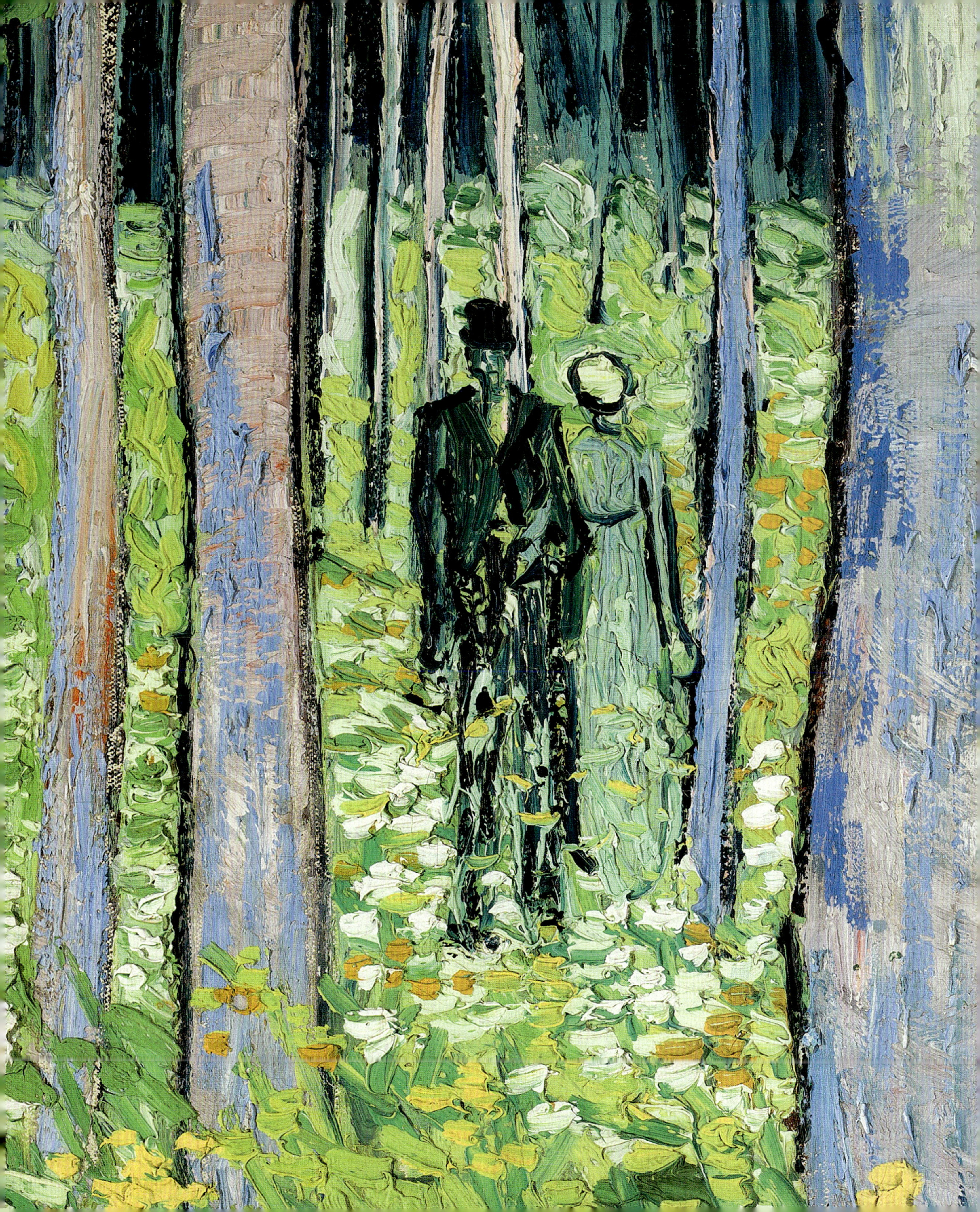

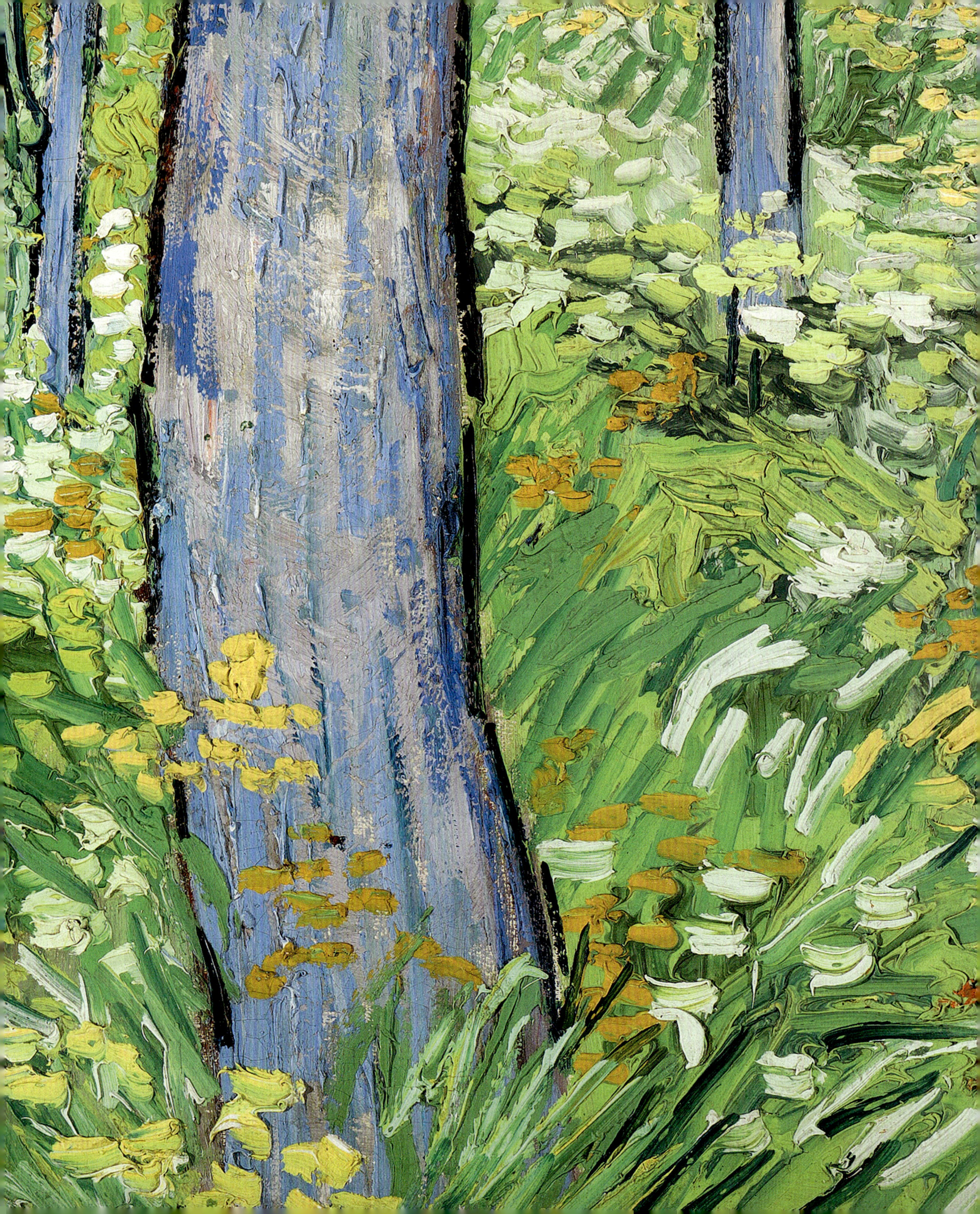

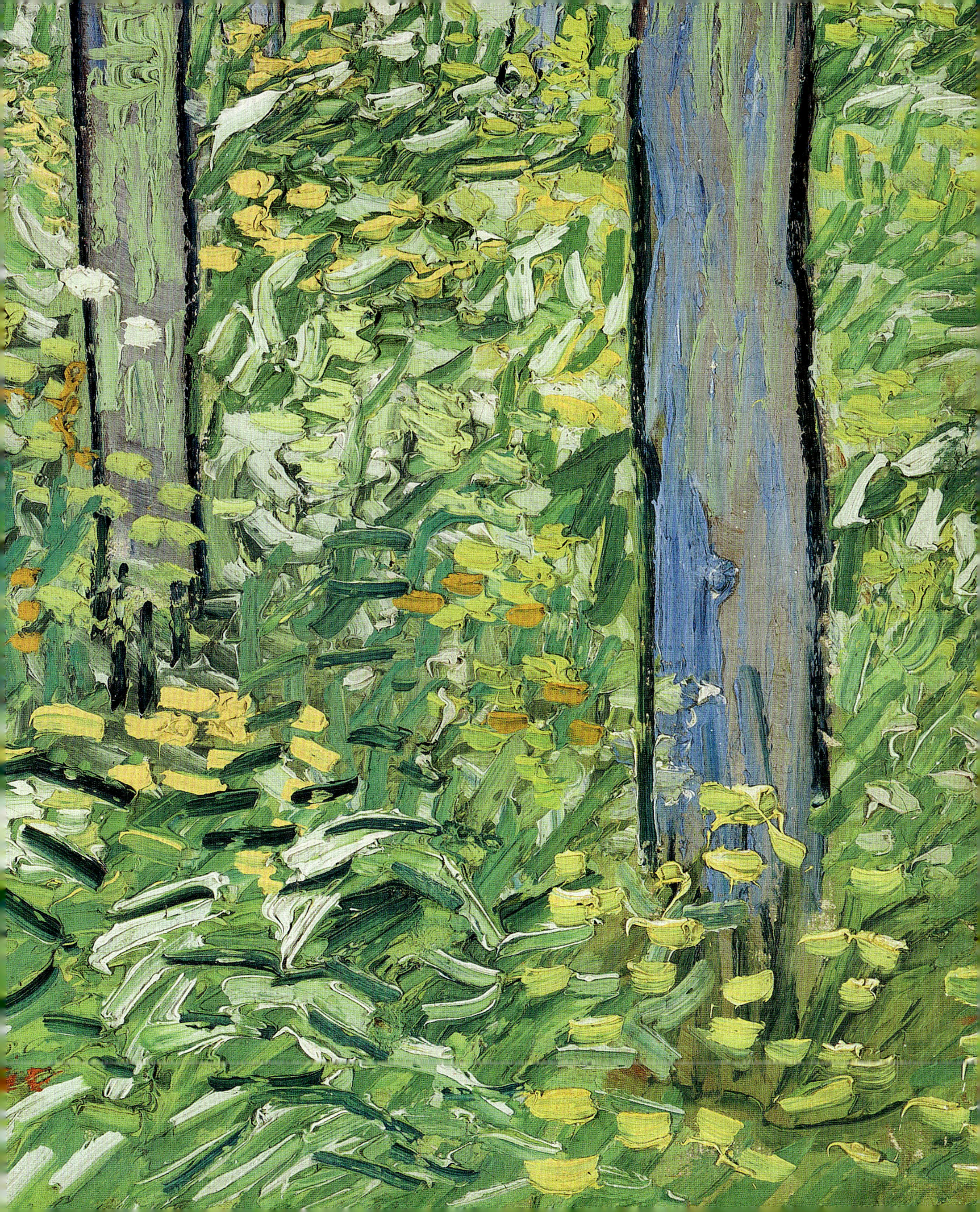

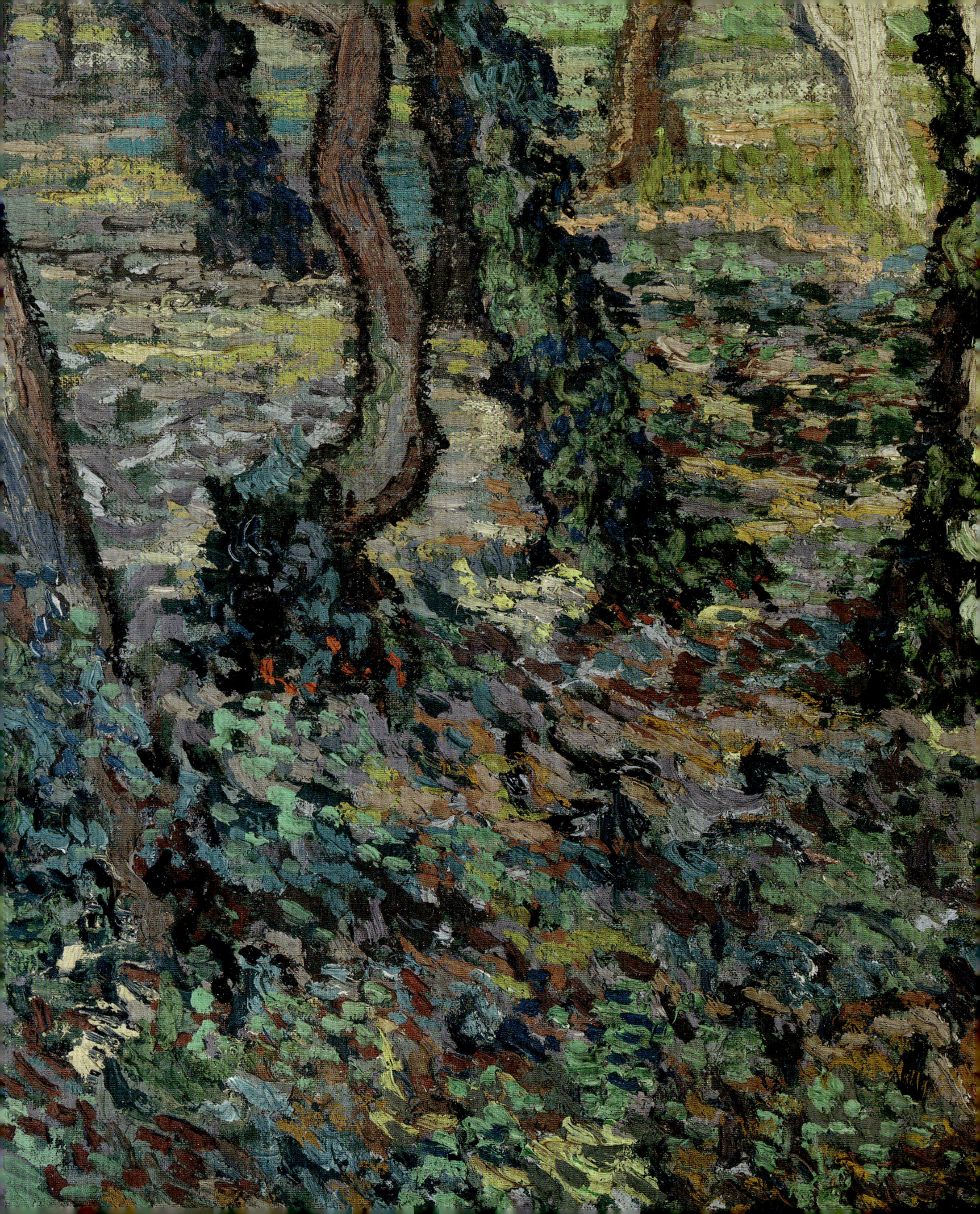

Van Gogh

Into the Undergrowth

Cornelia Homburg
Simon Kelly
Laura Prins
Jenny Reynaerts

Cincinnati Art Museum
in association with
D Giles Limited, London

cincinnati art museum

Van Gogh: Into the Undergrowth was organized with the generous support of the Harold C. Schott Foundation.

This exhibition is supported by Christie's and an indemnity from the Federal Council on the Arts and Humanities.

The Cincinnati Art Museum expresses gratitude for the support provided by ArtsWave, the Ohio Arts Council, the City of Cincinnati, as well as our members.

This catalogue accompanies the exhibition *Van Gogh: Into the Undergrowth* on display at Cincinnati Art Museum from October 15, 2016 to January 8, 2017

First published jointly in 2016 by GILES
An imprint of D Giles Limited
4 Crescent Stables, 139 Upper Richmond Road,
London SW15 2TN, UK
www.gilesltd.com

ISBN: 978-0-931537-45-5 (softcover edition)
ISBN: 978-1-907804-84-7 (hardcover edition)

For the Cincinnati Art Museum:
Julie Aronson, Curator
Kristi Nelson, Exhibition Project Manager
Anne Buening, Managing Editor
Connie Newman, Retail Coordinator

For D Giles Limited:
Copy-edited and proof-read by Jodi Simpson
Designed by Caroline and Roger Hillier, The Old Chapel Graphic Design
Produced by GILES, an imprint of D Giles Limited, London
Printed and bound in China

Library of Congress Cataloging-in-Publication Data

Names: Homburg, Cornelia. | Cincinnati Art Museum, organizer, host institution.
Title: Van Gogh : into the undergrowth / Cornelia Homburg, Simon Kelly, Laura Prins, and Jenny Reynaerts.
Other titles: Van Gogh (Cincinnati Art Museum)
Description: Cincinnati, OH : Cincinnati Art Museum in association with D Giles Limited, 2016. | Includes bibliographical references and index.
Identifiers: LCCN 2016011165| ISBN 9780931537455 (pbk.) | ISBN 9781907804847 (hardcover)
Subjects: LCSH: Gogh, Vincent van, 1853-1890--Exhibitions. | Landscapes in art--Exhibitions.
Classification: LCC ND653.G7 A4 2016 | DDC 759.9492--dc23 LC record available at http://lccn.loc.gov/2016011165

All measurements are in inches and centimeters;
height precedes width.

Front cover: Vincent van Gogh (1853–1890), *Undergrowth with Two Figures* (detail), June 1890, oil on canvas, 19½ × 39¼ in. (49.5 × 99.7 cm), Cincinnati Art Museum, Bequest of Mary E. Johnston, 1967.1430, F 773

Back Cover: Vincent van Gogh (1853–1890), *Tree Trunks in the Grass*, late April 1890, oil on canvas, 28⁹⁄₁₆ × 36 in. (72.5 × 91.5 cm), Collection Kröller-Müller Museum, Otterlo, KM 100.189, F 676

Frontispiece: Vincent van Gogh (1853–1890), *Tree Trunks with Ivy* (detail), July 1889, oil on canvas, 19¹⁵⁄₁₆ × 25½ in. (49 × 64.7 cm), Collection Kröller-Müller Museum, Otterlo, KM 100.398, F 747

pages 76 and 77: Vincent van Gogh (1853–1890), *River Bank in Springtime* (detail), April–May 1887, oil on canvas, 19 × 22½ in. (48.3 × 57.2 cm), Dallas Museum of Art, gift of Mr. and Mrs. Eugene McDermott in memory of Arthur Berger, 1961.99, F 352

Contents

Director's Foreword

Vincent van Gogh's *Undergrowth with Two Figures*, painted during the final month of his life in Auvers-sur-Oise near Paris, is unquestionably one of the most beloved paintings in the Cincinnati Art Museum's permanent collection. When the picture travels for international exhibitions, as it is often called upon to do, its whereabouts become the first question for many museum visitors. It represents the finest qualities of the artist's *sous-bois* works and is an endless source of fascination for scholars and casual observers alike.

On behalf of the Cincinnati Art Museum's curators, staff, and trustees, I am proud to present to you at long last the study that Van Gogh's important painting deserves. Through the exhibition and catalogue *Van Gogh: Into the Undergrowth*, we hope to contextualize a less-examined body of Van Gogh's work and thereby to deepen our understanding of the artist. I am grateful to our colleague museums who have made rare and essential loans to help us in this pursuit. Notably, the Van Gogh Museum in Amsterdam has been a generous key partner from the outset.

Van Gogh: Into the Undergrowth would not have happened without the collaborative leadership of a remarkable group of researchers and curators: Dr. Julie Aronson, who brought the project to a successful conclusion during a time of staff transition; Dr. Kristi Nelson, who served as a stellar project manager and advisor; Dr. Esther Bell, who originated and led the project during her excellent tenure at the Cincinnati Art Museum; and Anne Buening, whose tireless efforts underpin every aspect of the exhibition and catalogue. I would also like to express my deep gratitude to our funders for their generous support, especially the Harold C. Schott Foundation. Special thanks for operational support go to ArtsWave, the Ohio Arts Council, and the City of Cincinnati, as well as our members.

It is my hope that *Van Gogh: Into the Undergrowth* will provide you with new evidence to inform our understanding of Van Gogh's tragic genius and yet another clue to his unique vision. I invite you to continue your study of Van Gogh and the course of history through the artists and writers who have the great gift of changing how we see our world.

Cameron Kitchin
Louis and Louise Dieterle Nippert Director
Cincinnati Art Museum

Fig. 1
Vincent van Gogh (1853–1890), *Self-Portrait*, 1890, oil on canvas, 22½ × 17¼ in. (57.2 × 43.8 cm), National Gallery of Art, Washington, Collection of Mr. and Mrs. John Hay Whitney, 1998.74.5 , F 626

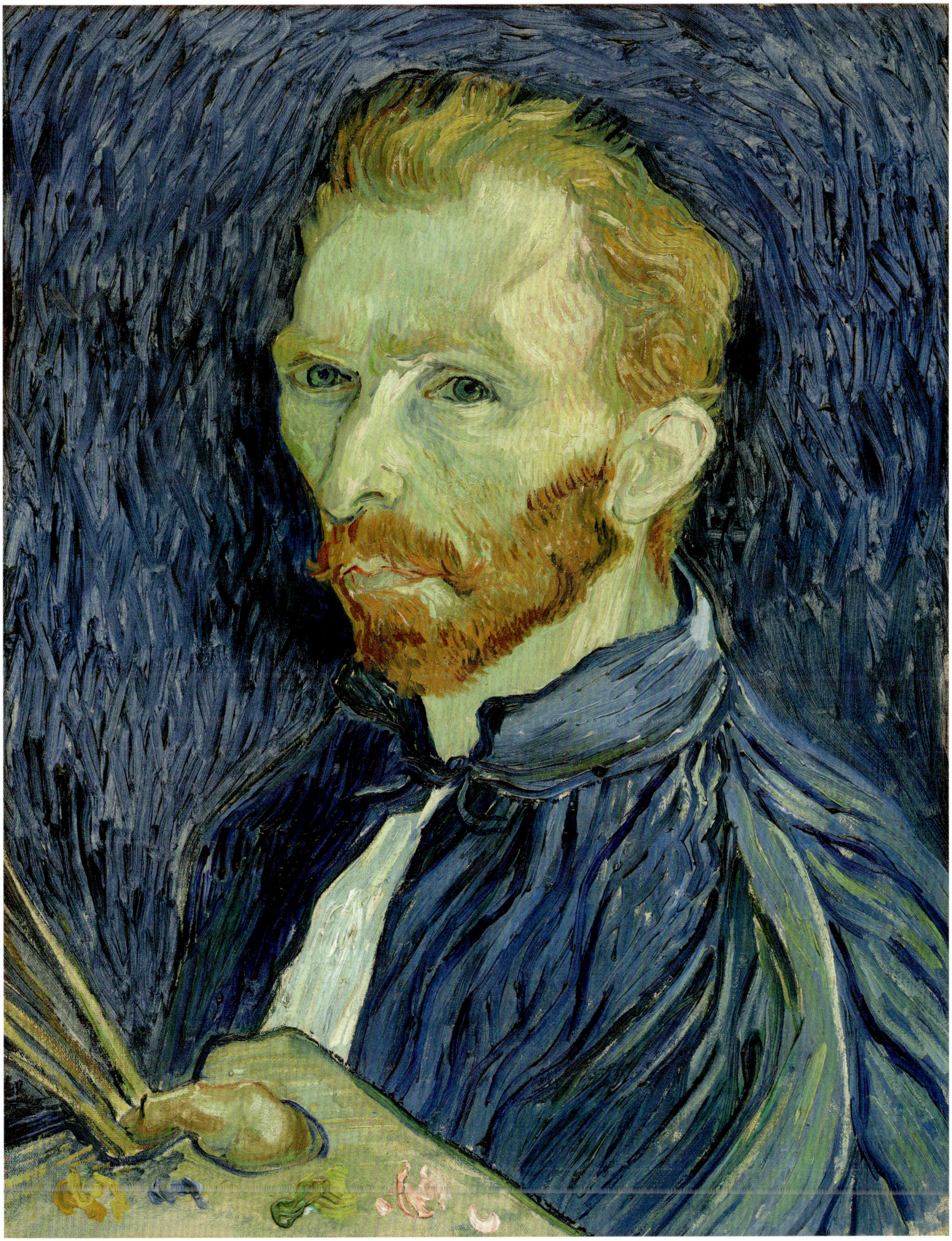

Acknowledgments

Van Gogh: Into the Undergrowth is one of a series of noteworthy exhibitions—including *Thomas Gainsborough and the Modern Woman* of 2011—to illuminate a remarkable work or group of works in the collections of the Cincinnati Art Museum. The project originated with former Curator of European Paintings, Drawings, and Sculpture Esther Bell, now Curator in Charge of European Paintings at the Fine Arts Museums of San Francisco. When approached for the third time in as many years for the loan of *Undergrowth with Two Figures*, Esther entered into a congenial conversation with the Van Gogh Museum in Amsterdam that has resulted in the loan of two of the artist's major pictures to the current exhibition. This exhibition is the manifestation of Esther's curatorial vision, and we are deeply indebted to her for the conceptual development of the checklist, for giving shape to the catalogue, and for conducting a number of productive discussions with the lenders in the early stages of this exciting project.

There are many people who have made significant contributions to the success of this exhibition and its accompanying publication. With a curatorial vacancy in European paintings, we faced a number of challenges, surmounted by the skillful project management of Kristi Nelson, Professor Emerita of Art History at the University of Cincinnati. A small team of key Art Museum staff has worked hand in hand with Dr. Nelson and, once I assumed responsibility for the presentation of this exhibition, with me. This project would not have been possible without the expertise and dedication of Director of Collections and Exhibitions Susan Hudson, Associate Registrar Jennifer Eckman, and Curatorial Assistant Anne Buening. I am grateful every day for Anne's skills in publications management, her ability to anticipate needs, and her cheerful assistance, without which I would be utterly helpless.

Our catalogue authors—Cornelia Homburg, senior Van Gogh specialist and independent scholar; Simon Kelly, Curator and Head of the Department of Modern and Contemporary Art at the Saint Louis Art Museum; Jenny Reynaerts, Senior Curator of Eighteenth- and Nineteenth-Century Painting at the Rijksmuseum, Amsterdam; and Laura Prins, independent scholar—have provided fresh insights into this special aspect of landscape painting and brought us a deeper knowledge of *Undergrowth with Two Figures*. Others have also made a significant impact on the quality of this publication, notably copyeditor Anita Buck with her phenomenal attention to detail, and Dan Giles, Allison McCormick, and Sarah McLaughlin of our publishing partner, D Giles Ltd.

We would like to express our appreciation to the following individuals for providing research assistance, support with loans, help with the location of works of art, and other aid essential to this project. First and foremost among them are our colleagues Axel Rüger, Nienke Bakker, Maite van Dÿk, and the library staff of the Van Gogh Museum, Amsterdam. We also thank: Leo Jansen; Marieke Jooren; Teio Meedendorp; Monique Hageman; Niels de Boer; Olaf Tans; Lloyd DeWitt, Art Gallery of Ontario; Edward Jacobs and Liesbeth Helmus, Centraal Museum, Utrecht; Rachel Rees, Allison Whiting, and Amy Indyke, Christie's, New York; William Griswold and Per Knutås, Cleveland Museum of Art; Olivier Meslay, Heather MacDonald, and Martha MacLeod, Dallas Museum of Art; Dieter Schwarz, Kunstmuseum Winterthur; Thomas Campbell, Keith Christiansen, Susan Stein, and Emily Foss, The Metropolitan Museum of Art, New York; Guy Cogeval, Isabelle Cahn, and Isolde Pludermacher, Musée d'Orsay, Paris; Jean-Luc Martinez, Musée du Louvre, Paris; Akiko Mabuchi, Yusuke Kawase, and Hiroyo Hakamata, The National Museum of Western Art, Tokyo; Josephina de Fouw and Suzanne Veldink, Rijksmuseum, Amsterdam; Christina Williams, Ann Lynch, and Jamie Burchfield, Sotheby's, New York; Stephen Ongpin, Stephen Ongpin Fine Art, London; Lisette Pelsers, Liz Kreijn, and André Straatman, Stichting Kröller-Müller Museum, Otterlo; Joan Greer, University of Alberta; and Mercedes Kleinfeld, University of Bonn.

As with every exhibition, the entire museum staff has mobilized to bring this exhibition to fruition and has worked assiduously with professionalism and camaraderie. Exhibition Designer Chrystal Roggenkamp merits special recognition for an elegant display that is certain to enhance the visitor experience and understanding of these intimate works of art. My heartfelt thanks also go out to our director, Cameron Kitchin, for embracing this project, and to the following members of the team, with an apology to those whose names do not appear here: Cynthia Amnéus; Amy Burke; Rob Deslongchamps; Jill Dunne; Carol Edmondson; Kim Flora and the Design and Installation crew; Jennifer Hardin; Emily Holtrop and the Learning and Interpretation Department; Victoria Karloff; Galina Lewandowicz; David Linnenberg; Will Love and the Security staff; Kirby Neumann and the Development Department; Kristin Spangenberg; Jessica Stringfield; Serena Urry; and Terri Weiler. The graphic design firm BLDG also merits our gratitude for their fine work with us on this project.

Last, but most importantly, I would like to convey our deepest gratitude for the generosity of our lenders:

Ananda Foundation N.V.
Art Gallery of Ontario
P. and N. de Boer Foundation
Centraal Museum, Utrecht
Cleveland Museum of Art
Dallas Museum of Art
Kunstmuseum Winterthur
The Metropolitan Museum of Art, New York
Musée d'Orsay, Paris
Musée du Louvre, Paris
The National Museum of Western Art, Tokyo
Parkview
Stichting Kröller-Müller Museum, Otterlo
Van Gogh Museum, Amsterdam

Julie Aronson
Curator of American Paintings, Sculpture, and Drawings

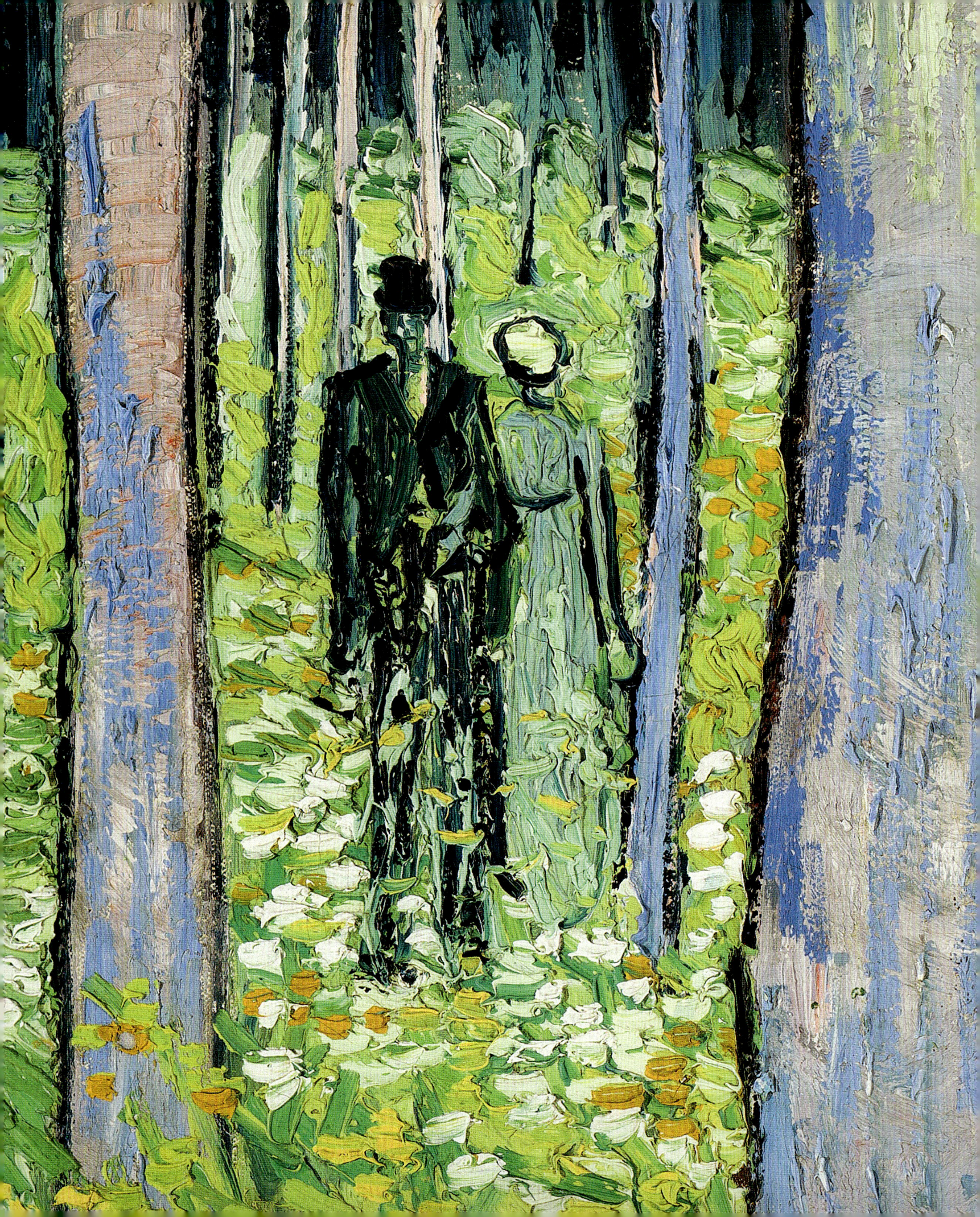

Undergrowth with Two Figures

A Brief History

Laura Prins

FOR THE LAST SEVENTY DAYS OF HIS LIFE, Vincent van Gogh lived in Auvers, a village northwest of Paris, where he began to regain some of his confidence as an artist. In a letter of 11 June 1890 to Joseph and Marie Ginoux, his friends from Arles, Van Gogh even showed a sense of pride and optimism: "They have twice written an article about my paintings, once in a Paris newspaper and the other time in Brussels, where I had exhibited, and now, lately, again in a newspaper of my own country, Holland, and that means that a lot of people have been to see my paintings and that I've sold on better terms. And it isn't over."[1] Van Gogh had once dreamed of the yellow house in Arles being a collective studio, where he, Paul Gauguin, Émile Bernard, and others would change the course of modern art. This dream had burst like a bubble, however, after the ill-fated ear incident just before Christmas 1888, when Gauguin's visit to Arles revealed an incompatibility of the artists' temperaments. Gauguin had left for good and Van Gogh had come and gone from the Arles hospital, followed by a voluntary admission to the Saint-Rémy asylum for a year. While he did continue to create numerous impressive paintings, Van Gogh's spirit had changed. Burdened by his dependence on his brother Theo, Vincent no longer believed that he would ever be able to support himself. But it was too late to change course: Van Gogh could only continue to work as he did. "I think it'll be more advantageous to work than not to work, *despite all the bad luck that's to be foreseen with paintings*," Van Gogh wrote to Theo, just when he arrived in Auvers, literally sick and tired of the asylum.[2]

With the benefit of hindsight, the modest pride Vincent expressed to the Ginouxes is both endearing and distressing. Indeed, all was not over, but Van Gogh, thirty-seven years old at that time, could not carry on for long. Until his suicide, he worked like one possessed, as if there were no time to waste. It was in this period that he created the peculiar yet breathtaking masterpiece *Undergrowth with Two Figures*, one of the twelve ambitious panoramic landscapes he created during the last six weeks of his life.

Vincent van Gogh (1853–1890),
Undergrowth with Two Figures
(cat. 9, detail)

The Long Way to Cincinnati

After Vincent's death, followed by the death of his brother six months later, Theo's widow became responsible for an enormous number of paintings and drawings. Jo van Gogh-Bonger (1862–1925) made sure that the hard work of her late brother-in-law and the unwavering support of her late husband finally paid off. She arranged to have the works exhibited all over Europe and the United States, sold parts of the collection, and published a selection of the letters between the devoted brothers. All this exposure contributed to Van Gogh's unprecedented international reputation. After Jo's death, her son Vincent Willem (1890–1978)—nicknamed "the Engineer"—took over the management of Van Gogh's heritage. While the core of the collection still belongs to the family, exhibited yet kept secure in the Van Gogh Museum, Amsterdam, a large number of Vincent's marvelous paintings ended up—sometimes as the solitary Van Gogh—in museum collections all over the world.

Undergrowth with Two Figures could have been in an American collection in 1913, when it was exhibited at the three venues of the Armory Show, on offer for $10,600 (fig. 2).[3] It was only sixteen years later, however, that the Boston-based collector Gilbert Fuller (1882–1960) bought the painting from the French dealer Paul Rosenberg, who had in turn bought it from (or via) Leicester Galleries in London in 1927, where the painting was exhibited.[4] It is interesting to note how the response of the English public changed in only three years, as Oliver Brown, director of Leicester Galleries, wrote to Vincent Willem van Gogh: "Everyone admires the Van Gogh's [*sic*] with enthusiasm, whereas on the former occasion [i.e., the exhibition of 1923], they were either puzzled or hostile."[5] On 9 February 1927, Brown informed Vincent Willem that most paintings had been sold for the requested price, including *Undergrowth with Two Figures* for 6,000 Dutch guilders.[6]

The collector Fuller kept *Undergrowth with Two Figures* for more than ten years, proudly lending it on a few occasions to museum exhibitions.[7] In 1943, Fuller sold it through the Howard Young Galleries to art dealer Germain Seligman for $23,400.[8] That same year Germain's cousin and partner Georges Seligmann hoped for a huge profit when he tried to sell the work to one of The Procter & Gamble Company heirs, Mary E. Johnston (1890–1967), who had only recently started to collect modern paintings. On a visit to Seligmann's gallery, Johnston had admired the Van Gogh *sous-bois*. Seligmann was happy to reserve the work for her; he wrote later: "You know how much I myself like this Van Gogh; I felt lucky in being able to acquire it: its marvelous depth, the religious almost Gothic feeling that emanates from it, the brilliancy, transparency of the colors, and the originality of the composition make this picture quite unique in its way in the history of painting."[9] To drive the deal home, Seligmann was willing, so he wrote, to lower "the original price of $45,000" significantly and was wily in applying pressure, telling Johnston that a certain Mrs. Charmion Weygand had expressed interest as well. Mrs. Weygand had "brought in Mrs. Matthews who said she was enchanted with the painting." But Johnston was not impressed, and rightly so; she kindly let Seligmann know that she could not "even consider the 'Sous Bois' by Van Gogh . . . even at your reduced amount."[10] About a year later, the painting was still in Seligmann's possession. Johnston then saw her opportunity and bought the painting, after some savvy negotiation, together with Picasso's *Still Life with Glass and Lemon* (Cincinnati Art Museum), for a total of $41,000.[11]

For years, the Van Gogh appears to have been a private pleasure of Johnston. Although she did lend it to exhibitions, she did so anonymously, at the same time that she publicly showed off

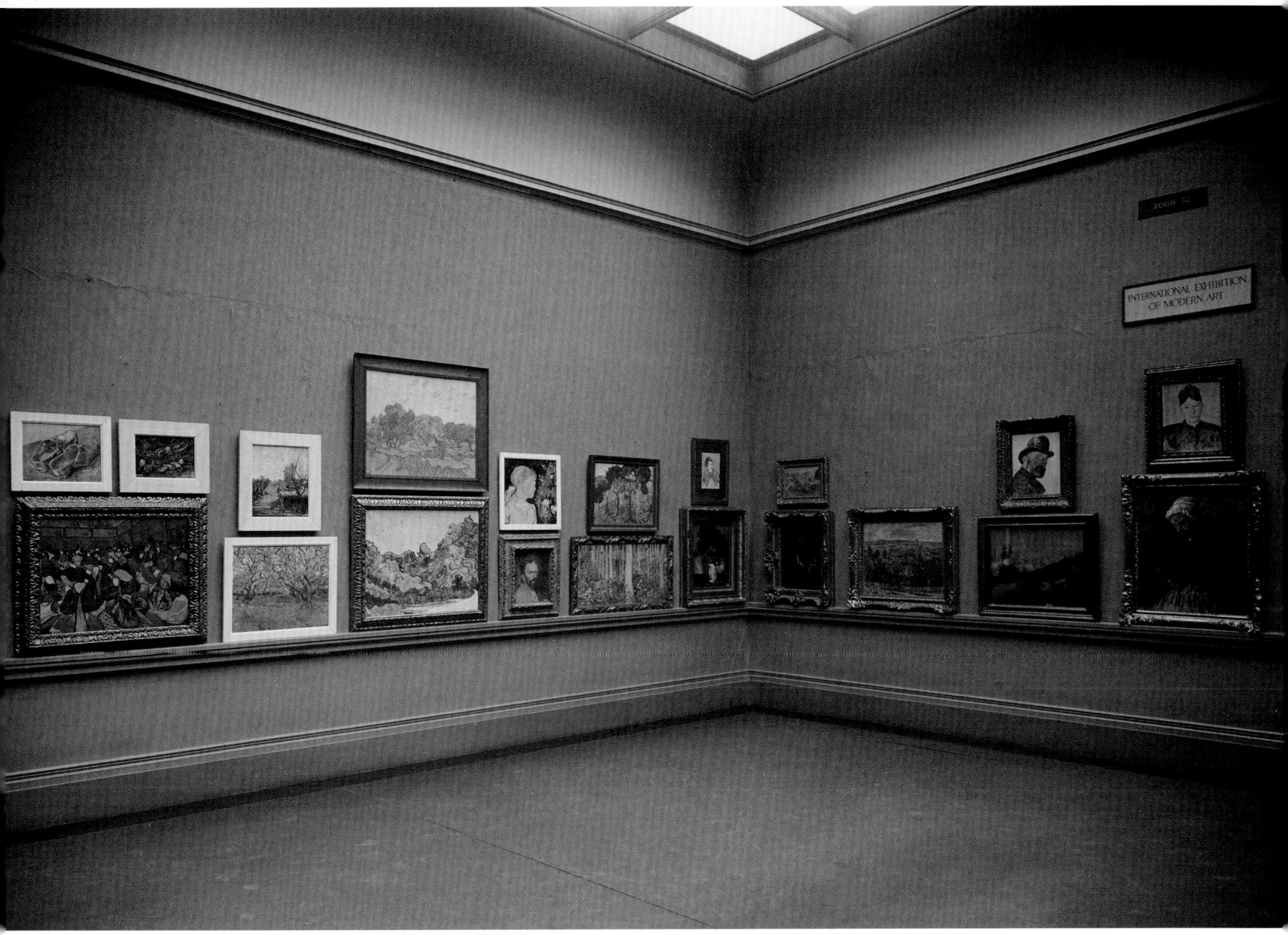

Fig. 2
Exhibition view of Room 52,
International Exhibition of
Modern Art / Armory Show,
The Art Institute of Chicago,
24 March–16 April 1913,
The Art Institute of Chicago,
Institutional Archives, 00143400-02

her collection of twentieth-century paintings.[12] Before Johnston died in 1967, she made sure her entire collection was kept intact and accessible to the public at the Cincinnati Art Museum.[13] To this day, Van Gogh's *Undergrowth with Two Figures* remains a highlight of the Museum collections.

Revealing Its True Colors

Undergrowth with Two Figures is certainly "quite unique," to quote Seligmann's smooth words. The size, approximately 50 by 100 centimeters, is not standard. Van Gogh had cut these canvases himself from a roll he ordered from Tasset et L'Hôte. Analysis of the weft threads has shown that the fabric on which the Cincinnati work was painted was cut from the beginning (or end) of the canvas roll.[14] This painting was also one of the first double squares Van Gogh made, as revealed in a letter of 17 June 1890. The size was probably inspired by the artist Charles François Daubigny, whose widow still lived in Auvers, because a week earlier Van Gogh had expressed the "idea for doing a more important canvas of *Daubigny's* house and garden."[15] Daubigny was known for his rectangular landscapes (fig. 3), so it was not surprising that Van Gogh honored the Barbizon painter's garden in two double-square paintings around 10 July.[16] Another inspiration must have been the artist Pierre Puvis de Chavannes, whose large decorative panel *Inter artes et naturam* (fig. 4) Van Gogh had seen in Paris when he visited Theo and his young family.[17] Vincent explained to his sister that "by looking at it for a long time one would think one was present at an inevitable but benevolent rebirth of all things that one might have believed in."[18] It is tempting to read between the lines a reference to Van Gogh's revival as an artist.

Undergrowth with Two Figures does not have a panoramic feel to it, nor does it breathe the same optimism that Puvis's panel aroused in Van Gogh (see also cat. 9). Instead, the double-square size intensifies the density of the forest, in which the rhythmic composition of the poplars—typical of artificially planted forests in northern France (and the Netherlands)—against a dark blue background prevents a grand view. The composition with the ostensibly endless pattern of trees and lush vegetation, within which the ghostlike couple appear insignificant in relation to Mother Nature, seemed to be Van Gogh's version of Puvis, the panel he summarized to his sister as "All humanity, all nature simplified, but how it could be, if it isn't already."[19] Nature's infinite strength, even if it felt almost claustrophobic like this *sous-bois* scene, always comforted the troubled artist.

Van Gogh described his painting to Theo as "undergrowth, violet trunks of poplars which cross the landscape perpendicularly like columns. The depths of the undergrowth are blue, and under the big trunks the flowery meadow, white, pink, yellow, green, long russet grasses and flowers."[20] One color, however, seems to have disappeared from the painting: the pink in the "flowery meadow." When conservator Per Knutås researched the painting in 2009, he not only discovered that it needed a thorough cleaning, he also saw tiny remnants of pink in certain areas. Van Gogh is known to have used the red Geranium Lake pigment in his French oeuvre. In Van Gogh's day, this paint had only recently become available on the market, and it was well known to artists even then that the color may fade when exposed to light.[21]

When Knutås realized that some of what now appeared to be white flowers must once have been pink, he was eager to find out what the painting originally looked like. He contacted Gregory Dale Smith, conservation scientist at the Indianapolis Museum of Art, and Jeff Fieberg, associate professor of chemistry at Centre College in Danville, Kentucky, and together they scrupulously

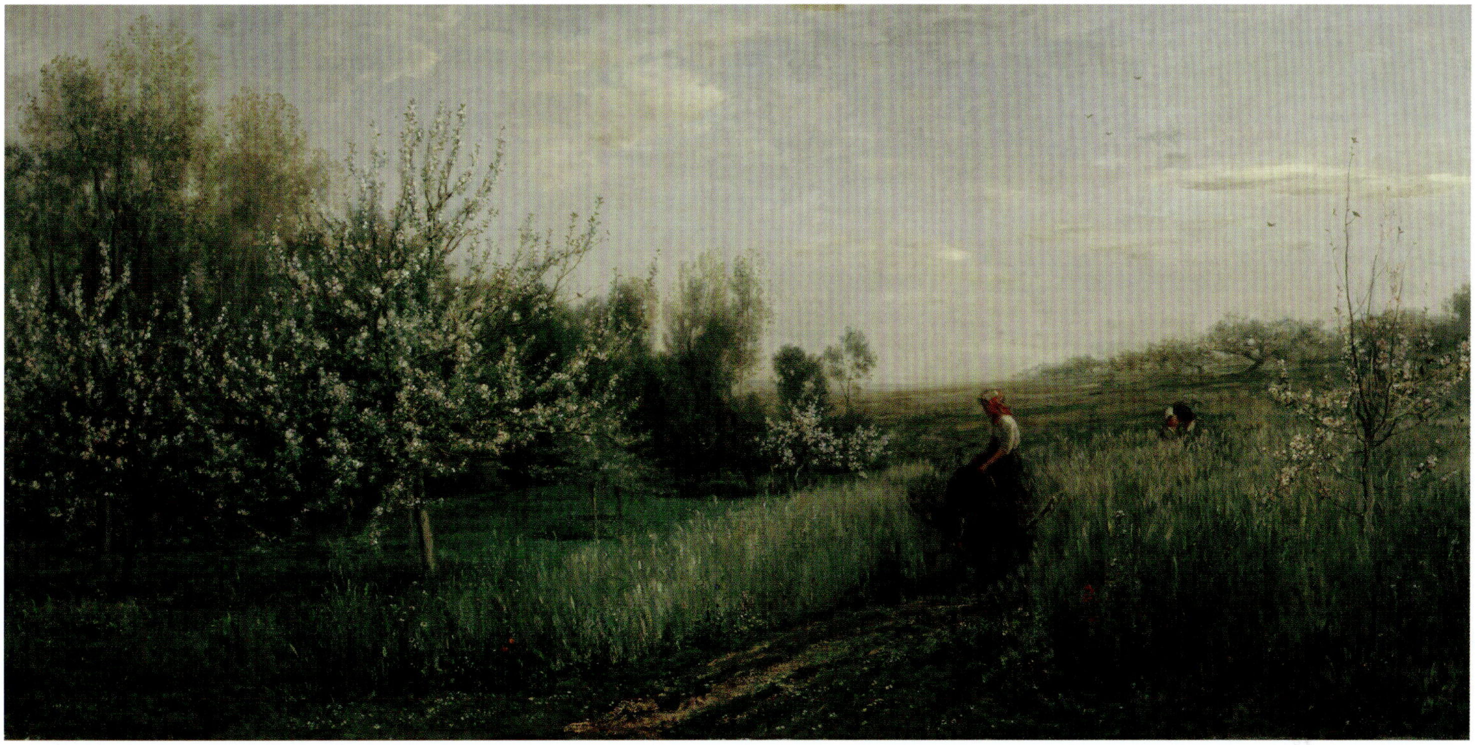

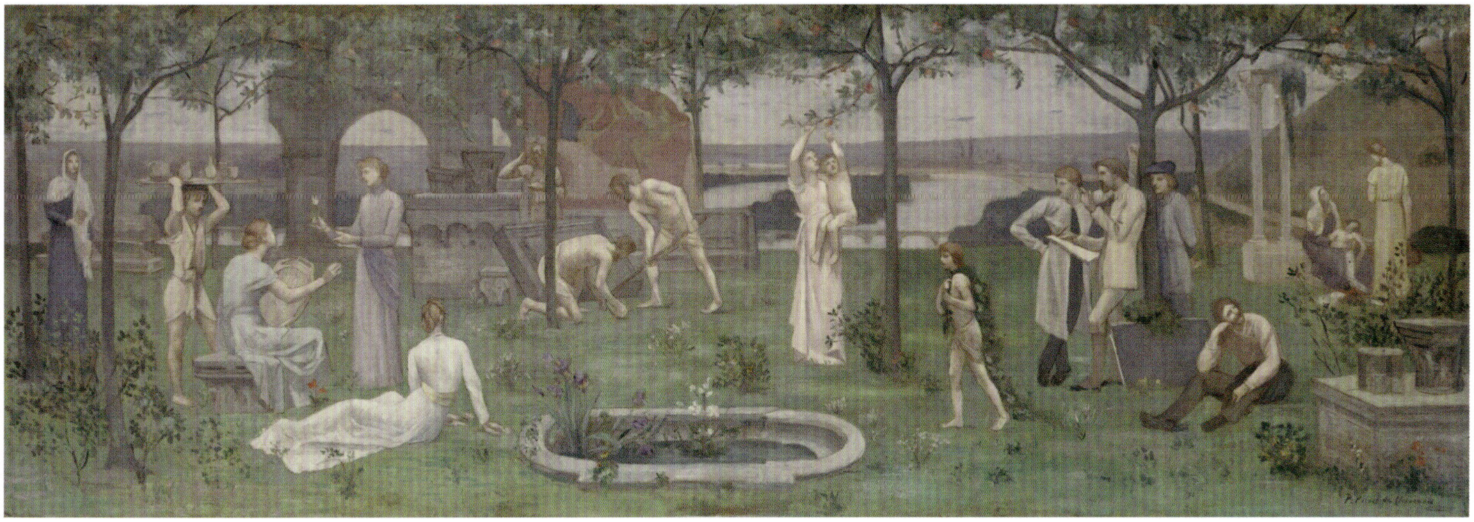

Fig. 3 (top)
Charles François Daubigny (1817–1878), *Spring (Le printemps)*, 1857, oil on canvas, 37¹³⁄₁₆ × 76 in. (96 × 193 cm), Musée d'Orsay, Paris, France, RF 76

Fig. 4 (bottom)
Pierre Puvis de Chavannes (1824–1898), *Inter artes et naturam (Between Art and Nature)*, ca. 1890–95, oil on canvas, 15⅞ × 44¾ in. (40.3 × 113.7 cm), The Metropolitan Museum of Art, Gift of Mrs. Harry Payne Bingham, 1958, 58.15.2

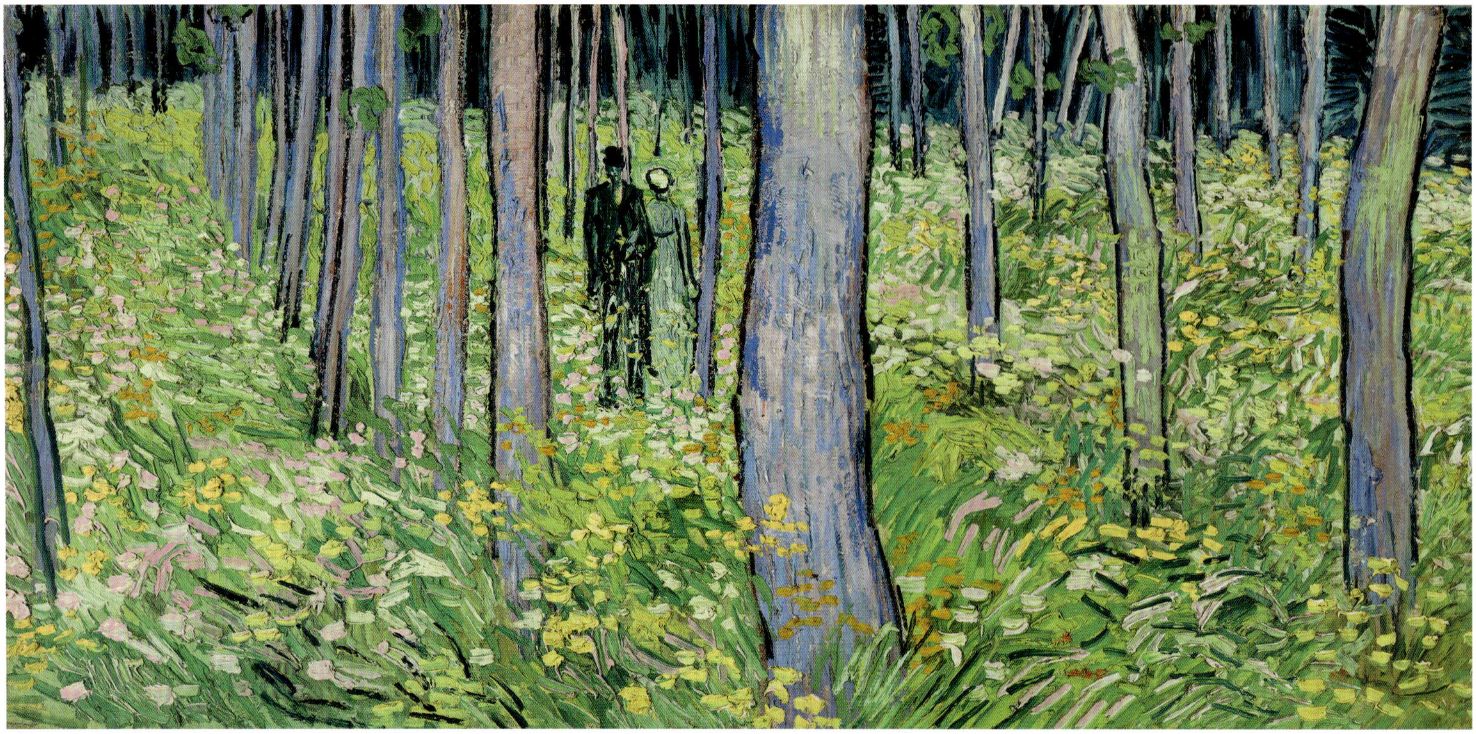

Fig. 5
Vincent van Gogh (1853–1890), *Undergrowth with Two Figures*, with digitally restored pink flowers

analyzed the composition of the white flowers. The technique of Raman spectroscopy allowed them to investigate the painting without destroying any part of it: using laser light to read the compounds of the paint layers, they examined 387 daubs of white to determine which were originally pink. With these results, they were able to make a careful reconstruction of the painting's original appearance (fig. 5).[22] Although a reconstruction like this remains open to speculation and is not complete—the trunks have traces of pink as well—it does show that the painting was much more vibrant when Van Gogh finished it. Unfortunately, we can never in actuality reconstruct the original state of the painting. However, the recent restoration, which mainly consisted of cleaning the entire paint surface, did manage to reveal what exciting and fresh colors were lying hidden under the dirty varnish and wax that had penetrated from the lining. There is no better way to honor this Cincinnati painting than by focusing in this exhibition on the importance of the subject of undergrowth to Van Gogh's oeuvre, and to those of the artists preceding him.

Notes

I would like to give a special thanks to Monique Hageman of the Van Gogh Museum, who helped and inspired me with her infinitive love of provenance research. I also thank Teio Meedendorp and Hans Luijten of the Van Gogh Museum and Olaf Tans.

1 Vincent van Gogh to Joseph and Marie Ginoux, 11 June 1890, letter 883.

2 Vincent van Gogh to Theo van Gogh and Jo van Gogh-Bonger, on or about 21 May 1890, letter 874.

3 See catalogue of the 1913 Armory Show. The painting was sent to many exhibitions: nine in Germany, including the 1912 Sonderbund; one in Amsterdam; four in the United States, including the 1913 Armory Show; two in Switzerland; one in Paris; and two in London. F 773 was not exhibited in the 1905 show at the Stedelijk Museum, Amsterdam, as incorrectly recorded in both the 1928 and 1970 editions of J.-B. de la Faille's catalogue raisonné, *The Works of Vincent van Gogh: His Paintings and Drawings*, rev. ed. (Amsterdam: Meulenhoff International; New York: Reynal, 1970).

4 In the revised catalogue raisonné of De la Faille (*Works of Vincent van Gogh*, 1970 ed.), the provenance has been recorded incorrectly, because of the memoirs of Oliver Brown, who recalled that he sold "A Man and a Woman Walking in a Wood" to a "well-known French dealer for under £1,000" at his 1923 exhibition. Brown's memoir, published in 1968, is quoted in Susan A. Stein, ed., *Van Gogh: A Retrospective* (New York: Hugh Lauter Levin Associates, Inc., 1986), 353. The "well-known French dealer" was wrongly identified as Wildenstein. See also Walter Feilchenfeldt, *Vincent van Gogh: The Years in France: Complete Paintings 1886–1890* (London: Philip Wilson, 2013; first published in German, 2009), 264. Feilchenfeldt has corrected the provenance.

5 Oliver Brown to Ir. Vincent Willem van Gogh, 16 December 1926, Van Gogh Museum, Amsterdam (Vincent van Gogh Foundation). In this same letter, Brown therefore requested having more paintings on view in his 1926 Van Gogh exhibition, "For instance, 'A man and a woman walking in the wood', no. 36 in the [1923] exhibition." Vincent Willem granted this request. Through this correspondence we also know that the painting was still in the family collection in 1926, and not sold in 1923; see note 4.

6 Oliver Brown to Ir. Vincent Willem van Gogh, 9 February 1927, Van Gogh Museum, Amsterdam (Vincent van Gogh Foundation).

7 Such as *Exhibition of French Painting of the Nineteenth and Twentieth Centuries* (Fogg Art Museum, Harvard University, Cambridge, MA, 6 March–6 April 1929), no. 90, and *Art in New England: Paintings, Drawings, Prints from Private Collections in New England* (Museum of Fine Arts, Boston, 9 June–10 September 1939), no. 57.

8 Son of French art dealer Jacques Seligmann. See invoice of Howard Young Galleries, 16 February 1943 (copy in the Cincinnati Art Museum curatorial files), and inventory books in the records of Jacques Seligmann & Co., box 282, folder 6, no. 7205, Jacques Seligmann & Co. Records, 1904–1978, bulk 1913–1974, Archives of American Art, Smithsonian Institution, http://www.aaa.si.edu/collections/jacques-seligmann--co-records-9936.

9 Georges Seligmann to Mary E. Johnston, 30 June 1943, Jacques Seligmann & Co. Records, general correspondence, box 52, folder 31.

10 Mary E. Johnston to Georges Seligmann, 7 July 1943, Jacques Seligmann & Co. Records, box 52, folder 31.

11 Correspondence between Georges Seligmann and Mary E. Johnston, 1943–44 (box 52, folder 31) and between Georges Seligmann and Mrs. Charmion Weygand, 1943–44 (box 101, folder 13), Jacques Seligmann & Co. Records.

12 Johnston's collection was exhibited in *Cincinnati's New Collectors*, Cincinnati Modern Art Society, November 1945. "Cincinnati's New Collectors at Cincinnati Modern Art Soceity," *ARTnews* 44 (15–30 November 1945): 14–15.

13 The Mary E. Johnston collection was bequeathed to the Cincinnati Art Museum in 1967, but formally entered the permanent collection in 1972; see *The Mary E. Johnston Collection*, exh. cat. (Cincinnati: Cincinnati Art Museum, 1972).

14 Ella Hendriks et al., "Automated Thread Counting and the Studio Practice Project," in *Van Gogh's Studio Practice*, ed. Marije Vellekoop et al. (Amsterdam: Van Gogh Museum; Brussels: Mercatorfonds, 2013), 178–79.

15 Vincent van Gogh to Theo van Gogh, 17 June 1890, letter 889.

16 F 777 (Rudolf Staechelin Collection, on permanent loan to the Kunstmuseum, Basel, 2002) and F 776 (Hiroshima Museum of Art, Japan, see fig. 15).

17 Puvis de Chavannes created the large panel as decoration for Musée des Beaux-Arts, Rouen. A smaller replica of the painting is in the Metropolitan Museum of Art, New York (inv. 58.15.2).

18 Vincent van Gogh to Willemien van Gogh, 5 June 1890, letter 879.

19 Ibid.

20 Vincent van Gogh to Theo van Gogh and Jo van Gogh-Bonger, 2 July 1890, letter 896.

21 See esp. Muriel Geldof et al., "Van Gogh's Geranium Lake," in Vellekoop, *Van Gogh's Studio Practice*, 268–89.

22 Gregory Smith, "Conservation Science: Van Gogh and the Case of Geranium Lake," *IMA Magazine* (August–October 2012): 4–7. Thanks also to Per Knutås for allowing me access to his notes.

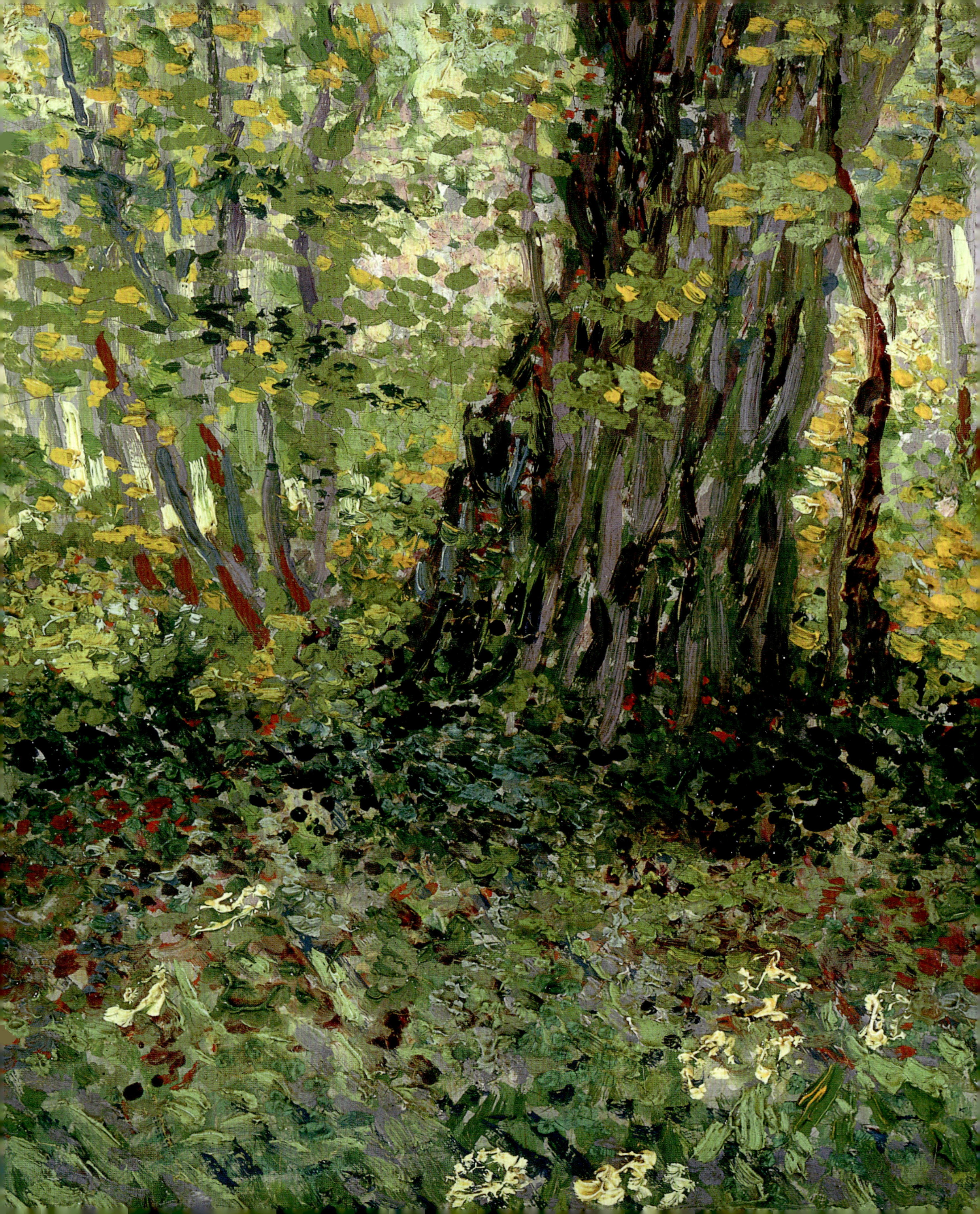

"The Great Revolution"

Van Gogh, the Barbizon School, and Constructing an Avant-Garde

Simon Kelly

Think of Barbizon, that's a wonderful story.
Vincent van Gogh to Theo van Gogh, 15 October 1883

Modern art is discussed in Manette Salomon, *and some artist or other speaking of "what will remain" says: what will remain are "the landscape artists"—that had a grain of truth, because Corot, Daubigny, Dupré, Rousseau—Millet as a landscape painter, that lasts.*
Vincent Van Gogh to Theo van Gogh, 5 and 6 September 1889

AMONG HIS IMPRESSIONIST AND POST-IMPRESSIONIST PEERS, Van Gogh was exceptional in the extent of his interest in the work of the Barbizon painters.[1] From his early years, when he began to collect print imagery, until the last week of his life, when he was inspired by the work of Charles François Daubigny, Van Gogh remained fascinated by these artists, who, from the 1830s, had established a colony in the village of Barbizon some thirty-five miles (fifty-six kilometers) to the southeast of Paris. At a time of rapid industrialization and modernization, their work, for him, embodied a sense of deep attachment to the land and nature. As he wrote in Nuenen on 4 April 1885: "I'm definitely convinced that a painter of peasant life can do no better than follow the example of Barbizon dwelling and living right in the midst of what one is painting for it's new and different outside each day."[2] Over the years, Van Gogh developed a deep ideological and spiritual connection with these artists: Jean-François Millet, Théodore Rousseau, Jean-Baptiste-Camille Corot, Charles François Daubigny, Narcisse Virgile Diaz de la Peña, Karl Bodmer, and Jules Dupré.[3] He was especially close to Millet, or *père* Millet, as he described him. Van Gogh was an artist very well versed in artistic tradition: for him, Millet and the landscape painters of the Barbizon School were crucial painters in an evolving nineteenth-century avant-garde artistic tradition that he himself sought to continue. This essay examines Van Gogh's complex relationship—generally deeply admiring and, occasionally, critical—with these painters.

Vincent van Gogh (1853–1890), *Undergrowth* (cat. 5, detail)

Van Gogh's engagement with the Barbizon painters coincided with a period—the 1870s and 1880s—that witnessed remarkable increases in the commercial value of their output. In 1889, for example, Millet's *Angelus* sold for the enormous sum of 553,000 francs, a sale record for any modern painting. As has been noted by Nicholas Green, this commercial development was closely tied to the idea of "dealing in temperaments" and the emergence of an extensive biographical discourse around the Barbizon artists.[4] Biographer-critics, as well as friends of the artists—particularly Alfred Sensier, Frédéric Henriet, and Henri Dumesnil—all produced in-depth empirical biographies that encouraged new interest in these artists' personalities and, by extension, their painting. This period also witnessed the new and expanded dissemination of Barbizon work in both print and photographic form. Van Gogh was familiar with all these developments, initially as a result of his early years as an art dealer with the Goupil company. He closely monitored the fortunes of the Barbizon painters at auction and on the art market, diligently read all the new biographies of these artists,[5] and collected a large archive of reproductions of their work, experiencing their imagery predominantly in the print medium.[6] Van Gogh's engagement with the Barbizon painters therefore depended on his wholehearted immersion with a new, modern art market system, even if he himself sometimes questioned the very tenets of this newly sophisticated capitalistic framework.[7] It is important to remember that he saw the Barbizon painters as enjoying their market success largely posthumously. For Van Gogh, their lifetime careers were ones of outsider struggle and neglect, as they sought to develop a new and pioneering avant-garde visual language.

Van Gogh's involvement with the Barbizon School has, of course, often been discussed. The recent volumes of Van Gogh's correspondence by Leo Jansen, Hans Luijten, and Nienke Bakker—particularly the more in-depth online version—are invaluable in highlighting the extent of Van Gogh's engagement with the Barbizon painters.[8] Chris Stolwijk too has thoughtfully explored these relationships.[9] Louis van Tilborgh has provided a rich and comprehensive examination of Van Gogh's relationship with Millet.[10] In general, however, less attention has been given to Van Gogh's fascination with the other Barbizon artists—Corot, Rousseau, Daubigny, Diaz de la Peña, Dupré, and Bodmer. All these artists were primarily landscape painters, and indeed the Barbizon School was principally a school of landscape painting. This essay argues that not only Van Gogh's avant-garde figural paintings of peasant life, but also his avant-garde landscapes—from his close-up *sous-bois* to his panoramic views of wheatfields and open plains—drew heavily on the Barbizon example. How then did the Barbizon painters impact Van Gogh's work and, indeed, his very sense of his own identity?

The Idea of Barbizon

Van Gogh first discussed the idea of Barbizon in his letters in 1880, writing to his brother Theo of his "great and ardent desire to come to . . . Barbizon" where, more than any other place, one might have the "opportunity to fall in with some more advanced artist who would be for me truly a Heaven-sent angel."[11] Despite these words, there is, perhaps surprisingly, no evidence that Van Gogh ever visited Barbizon but, nonetheless, it is of interest to see here his early association between the village and avant-garde, "advanced" art.[12] Three years later, in July 1883, he would reaffirm this idea, describing the Barbizon artists as "the leaders" of "the great revolution in art."[13] For Van Gogh, Barbizon art acquired its radicalism by way of its contrast with an Other, namely the polished, academic art of such painters as William-Adolphe Bouguereau. In contrast to the idealized decadence of such art, the Barbizon "revolution" was grounded in a close and intense study of the natural world. During Van Gogh's time in the remote Dutch region of Drenthe in the fall of 1883, Barbizon was very much on his mind. He focused on the benefits of the country as opposed to the corruption of the city, and noted, "Think of Barbizon, that's a wonderful story." For Van Gogh, Barbizon was a narrative of painters who had left urban life for the country, as he had, "to renew myself in nature."[14] The revivifying effects of nature were for him contrasted with the degenerative effects of the city. In the weeks to come, Van Gogh would write of the Barbizon artists' work: "Not only do I understand them as people but, in my view, everything, even the tiniest most intimate particulars, sparkles with life."[15] For Van Gogh, the ideal of Barbizon inspired his decision to explore remote areas of the Netherlands such as Drenthe, as well as Nuenen, seeking rural experiences similar to those of his Barbizon mentors. The model of Barbizon as an avant-garde artistic colony, moreover, remained a persistent influence into the late 1880s. As has been argued by Elizabeth Childs, the Barbizon community of artists served as a potent paradigm for Van Gogh as he sought to develop his Studio of the South in Arles in 1888.[16]

Van Gogh also connected the Barbizon painters with radical politics. In 1884, he wrote of his identification with "the generation of [18]48 . . . the revolutionaries, Michelet—and also the peasant painters of Barbizon." The 1848 Revolution had, indeed, empowered the peasantry and expanded universal suffrage.[17] For Van Gogh, implicitly, Barbizon images of peasant life gave visual form to the hopes and ideals of this revolution.

At the same time, he emphasized the avant-garde importance of the Barbizon artists' pure landscape painting. In 1889, he remembered a passage from the Goncourt brothers' novel of bohemian artistic life, *Manette Salomon*, in which the Barbizon painter Chassagnol was asked which artists would last, and he replied, "The landscapists . . . the landscapists."[18] Van Gogh affirmed, "That had a grain of truth, because Corot, Daubigny, Dupré, Rousseau—Millet as a landscape painter, that lasts."[19] He then noted the avant-garde connection between the Barbizon artists and the Impressionists: "When Corot says on his deathbed: in a dream, I saw landscapes with completely pink skies, it was charming; then—very good—in Monet, Pissarro, Renoir, we see those completely pink skies, so the landscape painters do last well, that was damned true."[20] In Van Gogh's narrative, Corot's dream had come to fruition in the more colorful work of the Impressionists.

Jean-François Millet

Van Gogh's admiration for the Barbizon School was focused above all on the artist Jean-François Millet, whom he referenced in his correspondence more than any other painter. In 1875, Van Gogh had a transformative experience at the Hôtel Drouot as he watched a sale of ninety-five of Millet's pastels that had belonged to the collector Émile Gavet. He wrote at the time that he felt as though he were walking on "holy ground" when he entered the gallery to see these pastels.[21] Around the same time, Van Gogh also saw the landscape *The Church at Gréville* (Musée d'Orsay, Paris) that had just entered the Luxembourg, the state museum of contemporary art, as Millet's first work in this institution.[22] Van Gogh visited the Luxembourg regularly on Sundays during his time in Paris. In the following years, he would remain fascinated by Millet. Around 1880, as Van Gogh sought to develop his skill as a figurative painter, he produced a series of ten drawings after Millet's series of images of working peasants, *Les travaux des champs* (*Labors of the Fields*). Only one of these early copies survives: *Reaper with Sickle* (Uehara Museum of Modern Art, Shimoda, F 1674).[23] At this time, Van Gogh also made drawings after *The Angelus* (a work he had first referenced in 1874, Kröller-Müller Museum, Otterlo, F 834), *The Sower* (Van Gogh Museum, Amsterdam, F 830), and *The Diggers* (Kröller-Müller Museum, Otterlo, F 829).

Van Gogh's view of Millet was shaped and transformed by his reading of Alfred Sensier's biography soon after it came out in 1881.[24] Sensier's biography developed two key constructs around Millet's identity that made a deep impact on Van Gogh: first, Millet as a pious peasant painter, and second, Millet as a controversial, avant-garde artist. As has often been noted, the first construct in fact distorted the reality of Millet's life;[25] it was, however, an image deeply attractive to Van Gogh, himself the son of a pastor, and he would repeatedly reference the "religious" quality of Millet's work.[26] Perhaps less well known is Sensier's second construct of Millet as a radical artist, immersed in nature and caring little for the world of the city and commerce. In 1882, Van Gogh spoke of a charcoal self-portrait of Millet (fig. 6), reproduced in Sensier, that fed into this identity. Here, Millet represented himself as a meditative figure, wearing a shepherd's cap. For Van Gogh, this summed up his image of the artist. He wrote: "There's a portrait of Millet by Millet that I find beautiful, no more than a head with a kind of shepherd's cap on top. But the looking—with half-closed eyes—the intense looking of a painter—how beautifully that's caught..."[27] In later correspondence in 1885, Van Gogh further developed this image of Millet's selfless devotion to his art, quoting the artist's interest in being close to nature—symbolized by his wearing of clogs—and, in contrast to Hague School artists such as Jozef Israëls and Anton Mauve, having little time for fashionable finery and city luxury.[28] Despite Millet's enormous posthumous commercial recognition and the considerable sales that Millet had enjoyed in his final years, Van Gogh maintained a view of Millet as an artist selflessly devoted to his work who experienced little lifetime commercial success. When *The Angelus* made its sale record in 1889, he even contrasted this success with the "black famine" that had surrounded Millet.[29]

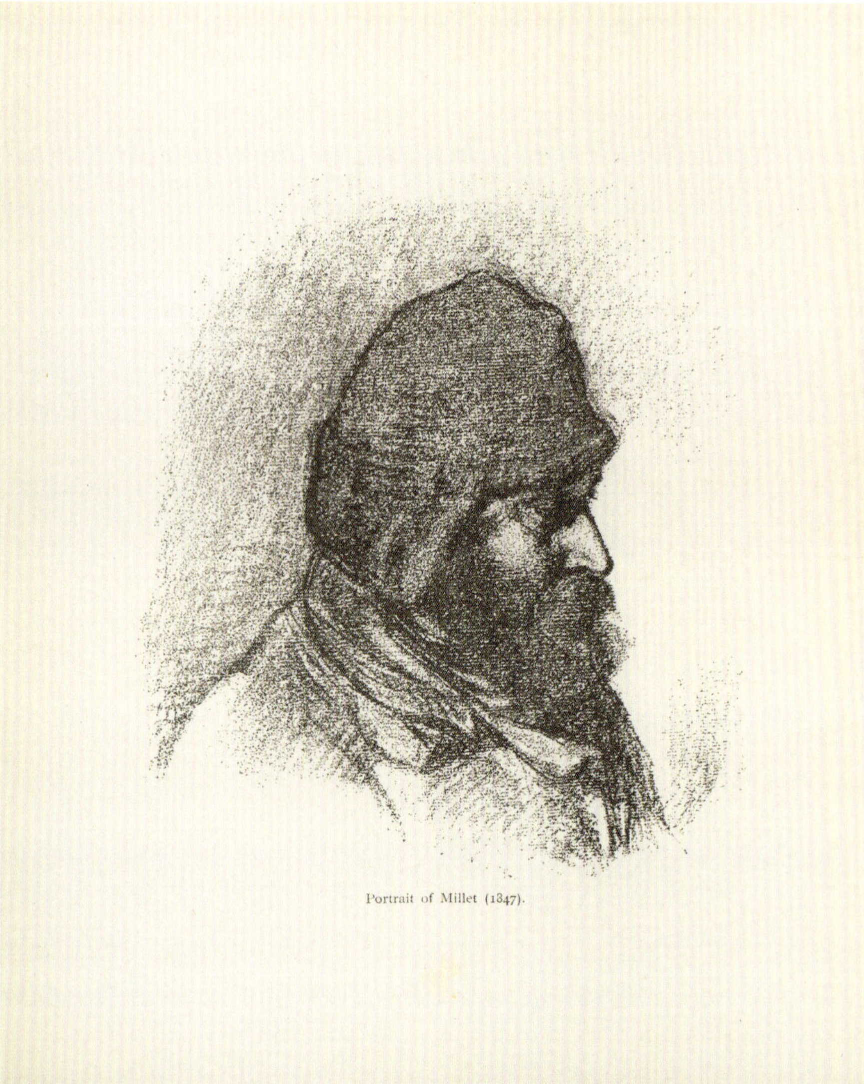

Fig. 6
Jean-François Millet (1814–1875), *Portrait of Millet*, 1847, in Alfred Sensier, *Jean-François Millet: Peasant and Painter* (Boston: James R. Osgood and Company, 1881), p. 75, Mary R. Schiff Library and Archives, Cincinnati Art Museum

Van Gogh's view of Millet's radicalism was at its height during his time in Nuenen,

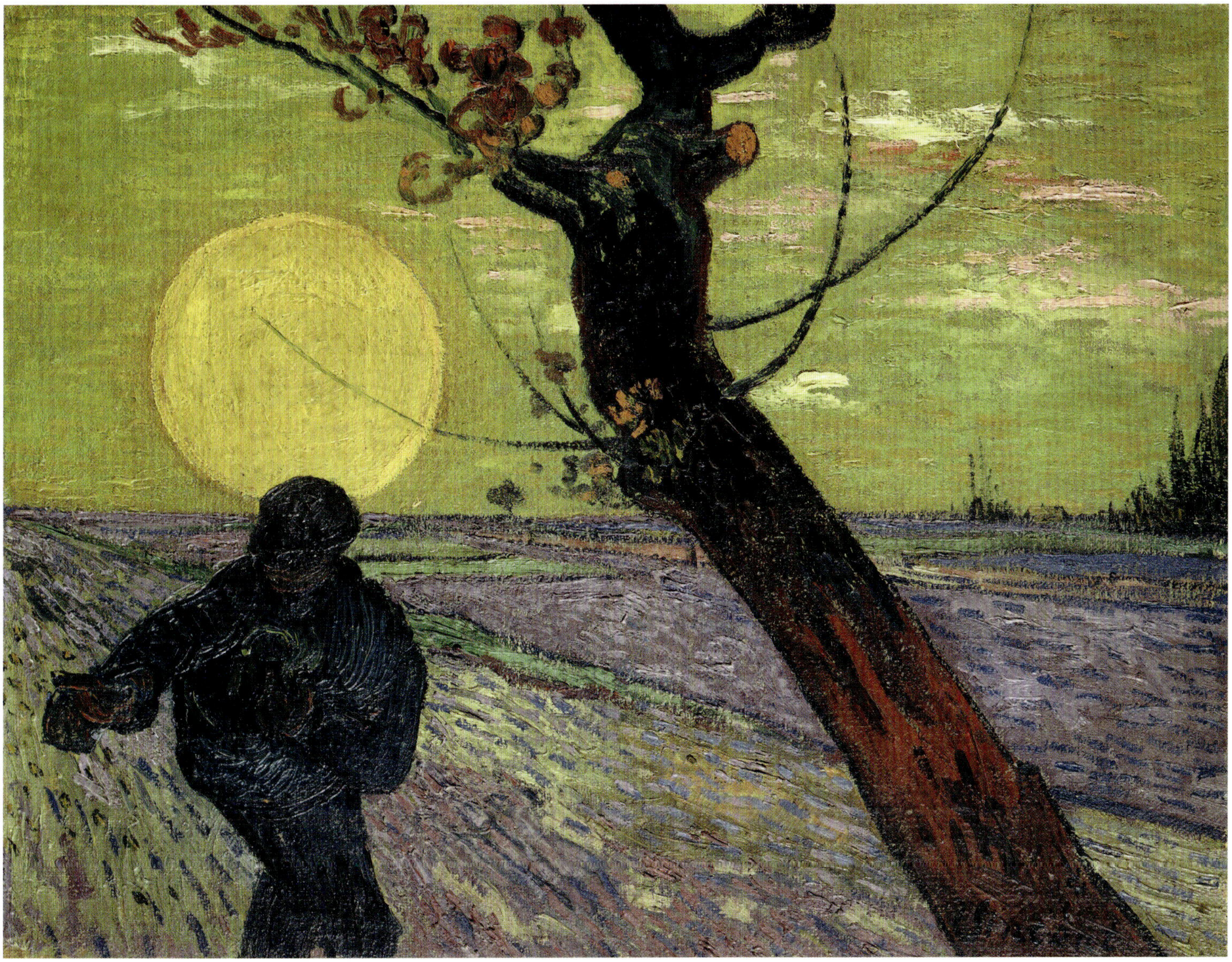

1883 to 1885, when he focused on peasant painting, particularly *The Potato Eaters* (Van Gogh Museum, Amsterdam, F 82). In February 1884, Van Gogh affirmed that it was "Millet, not Manet" who was the "essential modern painter" who "had opened the path to many."[30] For Van Gogh, the painting of rural life was central to the painting of modernity. As he noted on 14 July 1885, the painting of the peasant had started as a "genre" but "with Millet in the van as the eternal master, it's the very heart of modern art."[31] The elder master's impact lessened in the following years, 1886 to 1888, as Van Gogh moved to Paris and explored more urban subject matter, as well as a heightened palette. Subsequently, Van Gogh's letters from the South of France in the summer of 1888 once again frequently reference Millet's work. For the first time, Van Gogh was critical of the elder artist's painting, citing his "lack of color" and even describing the "sower" as "a colorless gray."[32] Van Gogh now produced a group of sower paintings, inspired by Millet's subject, but with newly intense colors, highlighting his interest in complementary contrasts.[33] This is particularly evident in *The Sower with Setting Sun* (fig. 7), a subject frequently represented by Millet, in which

Fig. 7
Vincent van Gogh (1853–1890), *The Sower with Setting Sun*, November 1888, oil on canvas, 28¾ × 36¼ in. (73 × 92 cm), Foundation E. G. Bührle Collection, Zurich, Given by the heirs of Emil Bührle to the Foundation E. G. Bührle Collection, 49 (1960), F 450

Van Gogh transforms the elder artist's work into a more abstracted composition, the bright yellow halo of the sun complementing the violet of the striding figure. Van Gogh also flattens and crops the central tree form, reflecting the impact of Japanese prints, another crucial influence at this time. Even as his formal approach diverged from that of Millet, however, Van Gogh would remain wedded to the significance of the morality of the elder artist's "character."[34]

Van Gogh's engagement with Millet focused on Millet's work as a figural painter. At the same time, however, as has less often been noted, Van Gogh was also deeply affected by Millet's output as a pure landscape painter, a crucial aspect of Millet's oeuvre, especially in his final decade. Van Gogh would probably have been familiar with Millet's desolate late masterpiece, his 1870 Salon painting *Novembre*, his largest landscape and the culmination of his landscape practice. This work was destroyed in Berlin during World War II, which perhaps accounts for its relative neglect today. We certainly know that Van Gogh saw a smaller painting with a similar high horizon, *The Plain of Chailly with Harrow and Plough* (fig. 8). This was the only landscape by Millet that he ever copied, producing a large-scale copy in early 1890 (Van Gogh Museum, Amsterdam, F 632) after Alfred Delaunay's reproductive print.[35] Van Gogh's copy changed Millet's autumnal landscape into a snow-covered field: the tint of his field has also changed over time from purple to blue-green.

Van Gogh knew well Millet's late pastel landscapes that also became a crucial element of the elder artist's output. Again, these contained experimental compositions, often with the same high horizon lines and serving as variants on the paintings. Van Gogh had seen many of these pastels in the Hôtel Drouot exhibition in 1875.[36] He saw many of the same works at Millet's large-scale retrospective at the École des Beaux-Arts in 1887.[37] Van Gogh's turn toward landscape compositions with high horizons following his arrival in the South of France in 1888 is generally related to the influence of Japanese prints but can equally be ascribed to the impact of Millet's late landscapes.[38]

Perhaps the best-known aspect of Van Gogh's engagement with Millet is the late color copies he made after the elder artist's prints. During his time at Saint-Rémy in the fall of 1889, without adequate models and wanting to improve his mastery of the human form, Van Gogh again turned to Millet's prints, this time as models for a series of figural studies.[39] On one occasion, he produced a copy, *First Steps, after Millet* (The Metropolitan Museum of Art, New York, F 668), after a reproductive photograph.[40] Van Gogh was sensitive to the accusation that he might be producing copies, and considered these pictures as essentially private studies rather than exhibition paintings. He described them as "translations" from black-and-white prints to the medium of color in paint; they served especially as a continued vehicle for his exploration of complementary colors, as in the vibrant color palette of *La méridienne* (Musée d'Orsay, Paris, F 686). When he sent these works to Theo in the spring of 1890, Theo considered them to be "perhaps the finest things you have done."[41]

Jean-Baptiste-Camille Corot

Van Gogh's engagement with Corot was long-standing, and he first referenced the artist in a very early letter from 1873, the first time that he mentioned a Barbizon painter.[42] We know moreover that in 1875 Van Gogh even made a drawing after a Corot Ville d'Avray landscape, his first known copy after a Barbizon artist.[43] Van Gogh deeply empathized not only with Corot's art, but with his

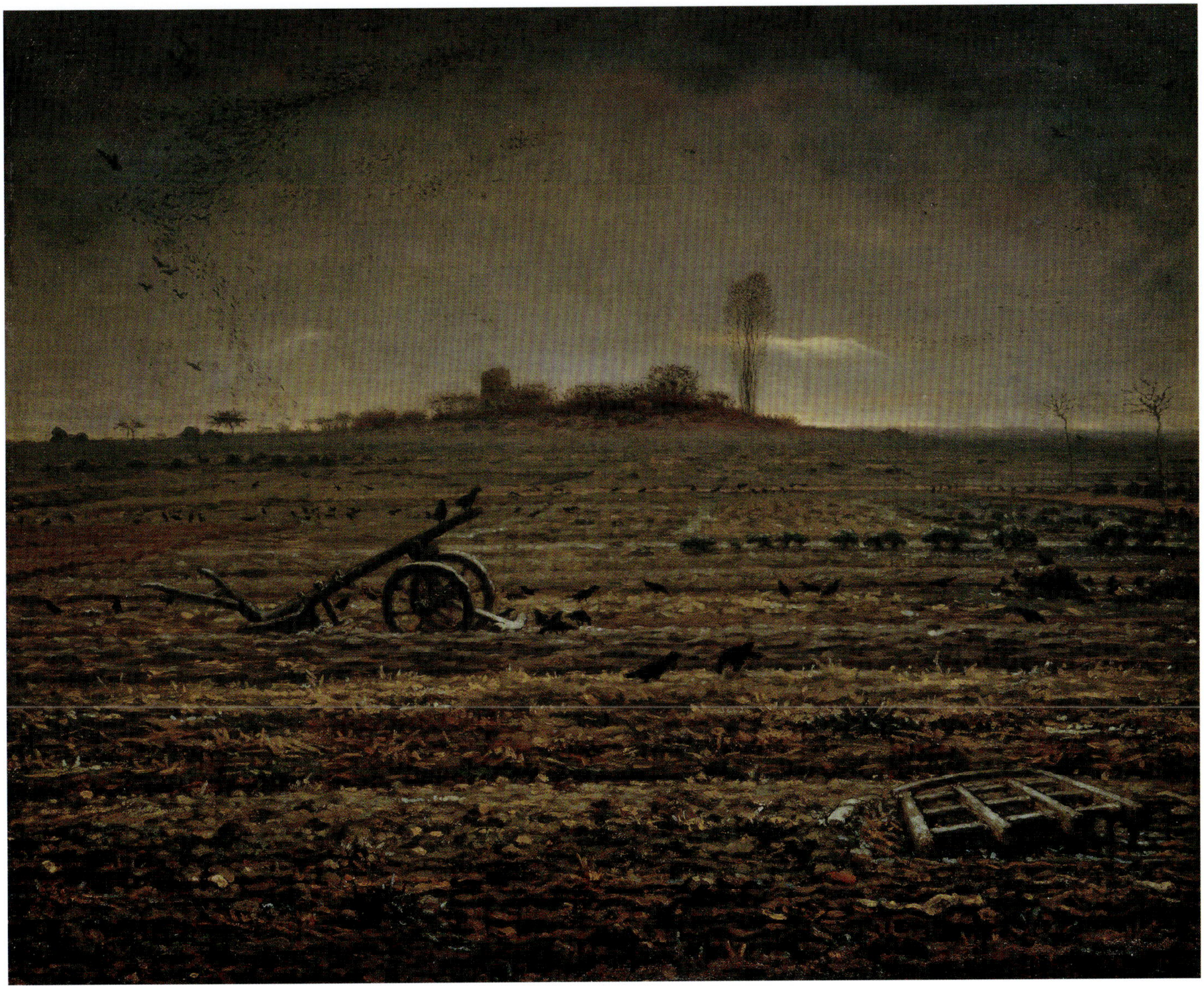

Fig. 8
Jean-François Millet (1814–1875), *The Plain of Chailly with Harrow and Plough*, 1862, oil on wood, 23⅝ × 28¾ in. (60 × 73 cm), Österreichische Galerie Belvedere, Vienna, 2450

persona. In early 1875, he hung a portrait of Corot cut from the *Illustrated London News* on the wall of his London lodgings (fig. 9).[44] Around 1883, he read Henri Dumesnil's biography of Corot, a memoir by a long-time friend of the painter that highlighted the artist's "sincerity" and "honesty."[45] Van Gogh was deeply affected by this construct, even offering Corot's character as an ideal for his more volatile father.[46]

Van Gogh's engagement with the work of Corot was particularly intense during the spring and summer of 1875, soon after his arrival in Paris. Before this time, he had certainly seen Corot's work in the Goupil galleries, but his experience of Corot was transformed by the remarkable group of works on view in Paris in the wake of the artist's death in February 1875. He referenced seeing three "very beautiful" works by Corot at the Paris Salon (where these were surrounded by black ribbons).[47] More significantly, he also saw Corot's posthumous retrospective, which took place in the prestigious establishment setting of the École des Beaux-Arts. The exhibition contained a spectacular grouping of 226 objects that showcased the extensive variety of the artist's work, from plein-air studies to figural works to monumental Salon paintings. Of all the works on view, it was the moody large-scale religious landscape painting *Christ in Gethsemane* (*Christ au jardin des oliviers*) (fig. 10) that made the greatest impact on the Dutch painter, a choice that itself reflected Van Gogh's serious and meditative personality.[48] In describing *Christ in Gethsemane*, he focused on

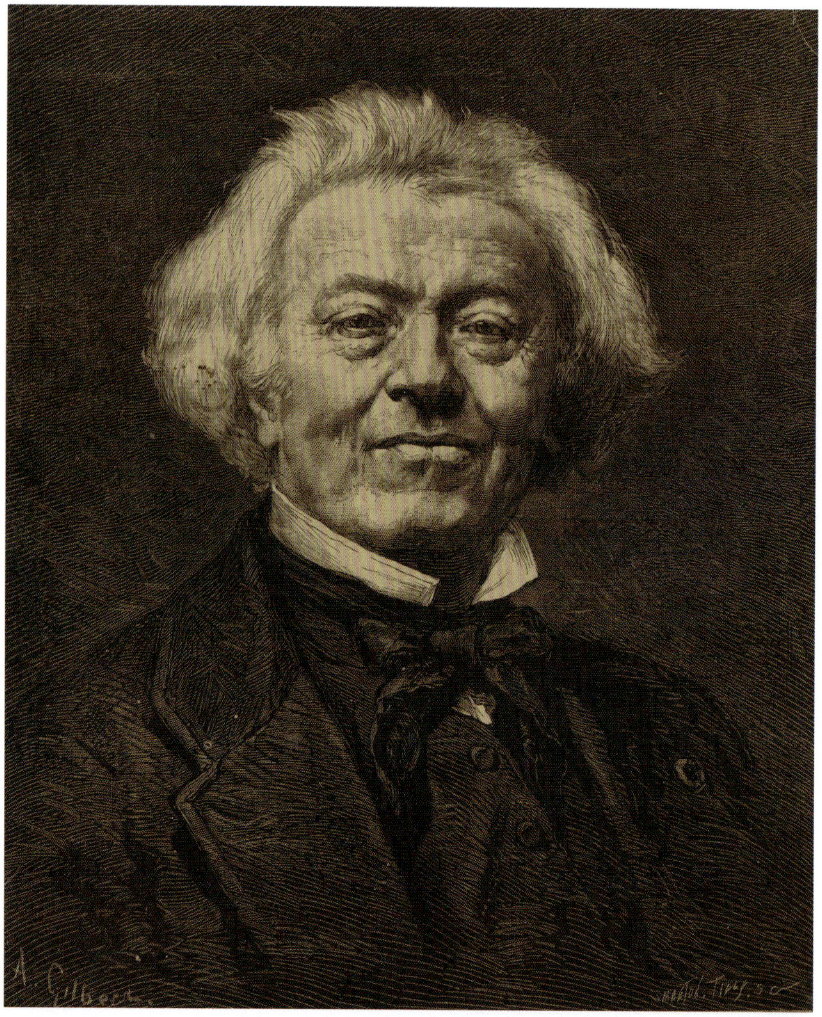

Fig. 9
Burn Smeeton (fl. 1840–1870s) and Auguste Tilly (d. 1898) after Achille Isidore Gilbert (1828–1899), *The Late M. Corot, French Painter*, wood engraving, 9½ × 7¹³⁄₁₆ in. (24.2 × 19.8 cm), Van Gogh Museum, Amsterdam (Vincent van Gogh Foundation), t172V/1962

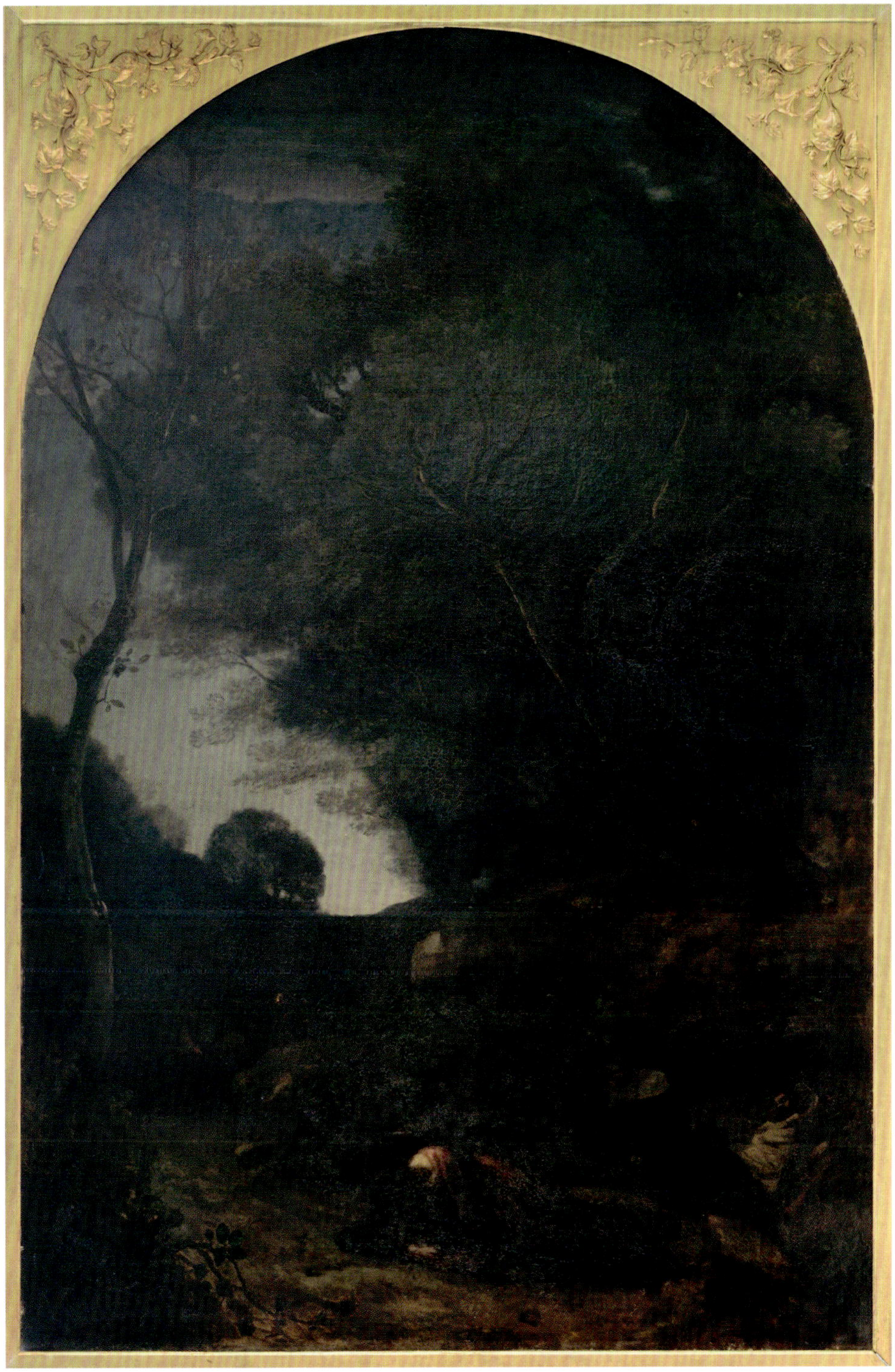

Fig. 10
Jean-Baptiste-Camille Corot
(1796–1875),
Christ in Gethsemane
(*Christ au jardin des oliviers*), 1849,
oil on canvas,
95¼ × 61⁷⁄₁₆ in. (242 × 156 cm),
Collection Musées de Langres,
Property of the State, R610

the landscape, noting "on the right, the olive trees dark and against the darkening blue sky" as well as the twinkling evening star.[49] Van Gogh never forgot this painting and, some fourteen years later, remembered it as a model of "sublime" religious painting, combining gravitas with an avant-garde sensibility.[50] Perhaps inspired by this memory of Corot's work, he would himself experiment with a religious painting on this same theme in 1889 before ultimately scraping it off the canvas. In Saint-Rémy in the same year, he would also describe the "silvery-grey" of Corot's palette as a model for his exploration of this tone in his paintings of olive trees.[51]

Fig. 11
Auguste-Paul-Charles Anastasi (1820–1889) after Théodore Rousseau (1812–1867), *Oven in Les Landes*, 1847, lithograph from the scrapbook of Vincent van Gogh, Van Gogh Museum, Amsterdam (Vincent van Gogh Foundation), t1487.10V1963

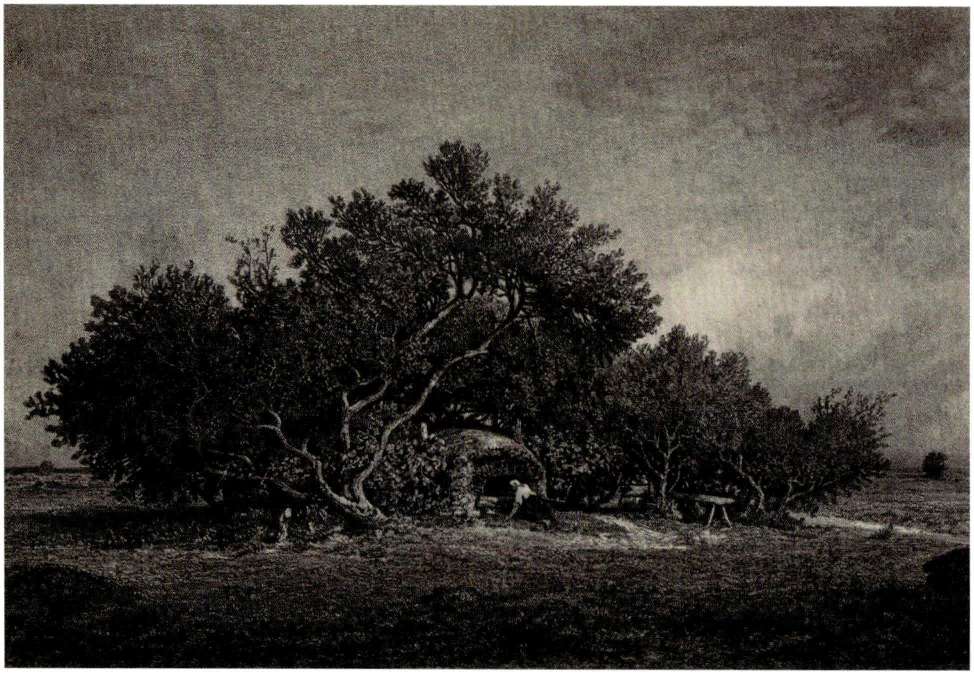

Théodore Rousseau and Karl Bodmer

Although much has been written about Van Gogh's admiration for Millet, much less has been said about his interest in the work of Théodore Rousseau, Millet's close friend. We have seen Van Gogh's drawn copies after Millet in 1880. It is less well known that, at the same time, he also made two small watercolors and a large sepia drawing, all now lost, after Rousseau's *Oven in Les Landes* (fig. 11), a view of rural life in the region of Landes. Van Gogh was particularly interested in this image, which he knew from Auguste-Paul-Charles Anastasi's reproductive print. He hung the print on the wall of his lodgings in The Hague in 1878 and, in the fall of 1883, compared the ovens in the Drenthe region to the one in the print.[52] Rousseau's image showed the serpentine trunk and branches of a tree and its dense foliage encircling the oven.[53] Van Gogh's three copies allowed him to study tree form and foliage, just as his studies after Millet enabled him to study the human form. This early study of a twisting southern tree could even have been at the back of Van Gogh's mind when he started to paint his olive trees in the South in 1889.

Van Gogh almost certainly read Sensier's biography of Rousseau—a kind of companion to the Millet biography—and he respected this landscape painter's deep engagement with nature. In 1882, he was impressed by Rousseau's grand and richly colorful *La descente des vaches*—a "large sketch"—which he saw in an impressive exhibition in The Hague of Barbizon paintings drawn from Dutch private collections.[54] In Van Gogh's most in-depth discussion of Rousseau's work, in 1883, he wrote of two paintings by the artist—pendant forest views of overarching trees at sunset (*Edge of the Forest of Fontainebleau, Setting Sun*, fig. 12) and in the early morning (*The Forest of Fontainebleau: Morning*, Wallace Collection, London), both of which he had seen, the former in the Luxembourg and the latter in Richard Wallace's collection during his time in London. He emphasized the importance of the artist's subjective engagement with nature and described the "dramatic effect" of these works, noting that they were "more than nature, more like a revelation."[55] Van Gogh's words represented a defense of the intensity of Rousseau's engagement with nature against charges of the artist's mannerism. The larger painting, in the Luxembourg, had indeed created considerable controversy when first shown at the 1850 Salon, largely because of the artist's very gestural and sketchy impasto; Rousseau used this rugged effect to mimic the texture of bark, particularly in the rendering of his foreground tree trunks. Van Gogh may have remembered this effect when he came to make his own subsequent paintings of tree trunks.

Van Gogh admired Rousseau's understanding of the Forest of Fontainebleau, agreeing with his brother, who had affirmed that Rousseau's group of works at the 1889 Exposition Universelle showed this "knowledgeable side" so that, in his pictures, "one can recognize all the species of tree with real heather and real ferns at their feet."[56] In the same exchange, Van Gogh wrote of the similar quality of intense engagement that he found in the work of Karl Bodmer, who had lived and worked at Barbizon from the late 1840s. He had always admired Bodmer's view of the Forest of Fontainebleau in the Luxembourg, *Paysage et cerfs* (*Landscape with Deer*) (Hôtel de Ville, Dordogne), also acquiring a print after this painting. Now he wrote of Bodmer: "Was he not able to study nature as a hunter, a savage, did he not love it and know it with experience of an entire long manly life . . . not that *from the point of view of colour* I'm *always* an admirer of Bodmer, but I admire and I like the man who knew all the forest of Fontainebleau, from the insect to the wild boar and from the stag to the lark. From the tall oak and the lump of rock to the fern and the blade of grass."[57] Bodmer's deep understanding of nature embodied that exceptional insight into flora and fauna that for Van Gogh was emblematic of the Barbizon artists.

Fig. 12
Théodore Rousseau (1812–1867), *Edge of the Forest of Fontainebleau, Setting Sun* (*Sortie de fôret à Fontainebleau, soleil couchant*), ca. 1850, oil on canvas, 55⅞ × 77^15/16 in. (142 × 197 cm), Musée du Louvre, Paris, RF 112

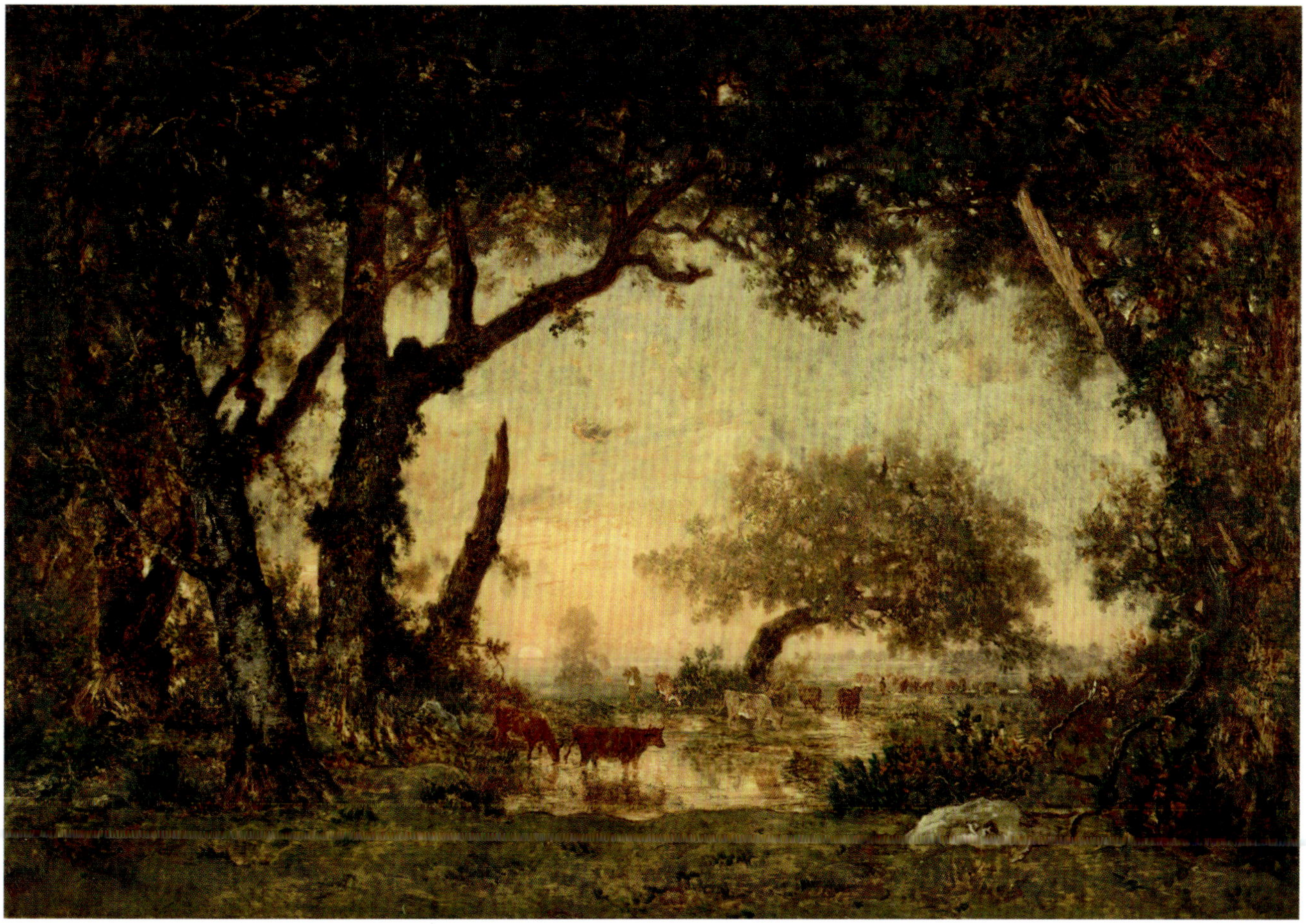

Narcisse Virgile Diaz de la Peña and the *Sous-Bois* Tradition

In an 1888 letter, Van Gogh compared himself to Diaz de la Peña, as he considered them both artists willing to produce work for the marketplace, an opinion that itself complicates the traditional view of Van Gogh as an artist little interested in the sale of his paintings.[58] Diaz produced a wide range of work but was especially known as a painter of the Forest of Fontainebleau and its *sous-bois*. Of all Barbizon artists, Diaz developed the greatest specialty in *sous-bois*, producing hundreds of these. In 1863, the critic and dealer Arthur Stevens

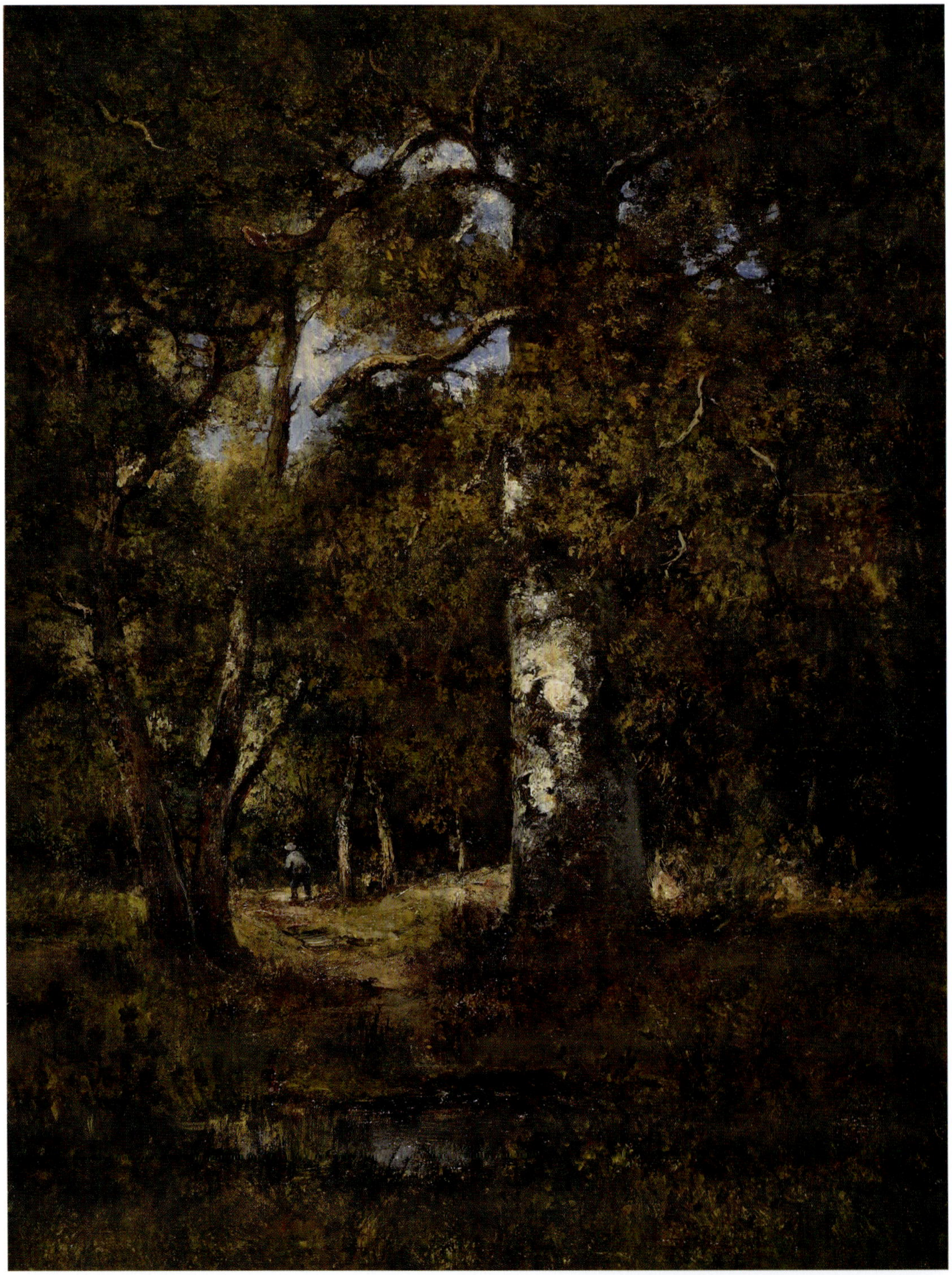

Fig. 13
Narcisse Virgile Diaz de la Peña (1807–1876),
Forest with a Great Sunny Oak and Fisherman at a Pond, n. d.,
oil on canvas,
24 1/16 × 18 1/8 in. (61.1 × 46 cm),
Photo courtesy of Schiller & Bodo European Paintings, New York

recounted a conversation between Rousseau and Diaz: "Rousseau said one day to Diaz: 'No one has painted a dessous de bois like you.' 'Stop,' said Diaz, 'I know one path in landscape but you, Rousseau, you know them all!'"[59]

Often, Diaz used a compositional format of overarching trees, almost like a stage set, frequently animating his scenes with individual figures: such a format was close to that in Rousseau's *Edge of the Forest of Fontainebleau, Setting Sun* (fig. 12). Diaz also, however, developed a specialty of close-up studies or "études" of individual tree trunks (fig. 13). These fragmentary views represent a kind of subgenre of the *sous-bois*: Diaz had shown them in some number—as studies of beech and oak trees—as early as his first auction of paintings in 1849.[60] Often, they created an immersive environment with little sense of spatial recession and no opening for the sky. In such works, Diaz often cropped his tree forms. On occasion too, he also painted these close-up compositions on a larger scale, as in his *Forest of Fontainebleau* from 1868 (cat. 16), a work which itself can be seen as a reprise of Rousseau's well-known 1861 Salon painting *The Rock Oak* (private collection). Diaz's various kinds of *sous-bois* were well known and commercially successful in Paris of the 1870s and 1880s and would have been visible to Van Gogh in galleries such as Durand-Ruel, or Boussod & Valadon.[61] Critics—for example, Philippe Burty and Jules Claretie—also promoted Diaz as a forest painter of dappled light and color.[62] This view of Diaz as a colorist was one that Van Gogh himself also recognized. On 13 October 1885 he praised Diaz as "a painter to his core," comparable to Rubens.[63] He noted in particular Diaz's ability to use color to express form.[64]

Diaz's prominence as a *sous-bois* painter offers valuable context for Van Gogh's own *sous-bois* paintings. *Trees and Undergrowth* (Van Gogh Museum, Amsterdam, F 309a)—one of a group painted on the outskirts of Paris in 1887—has an effect of dappled light and chiaroscuro contrast reminiscent of the *sous-bois* of Diaz. As with Diaz, Van Gogh here created a painting in which the viewer is immersed within the forest and where there is little sense of spatial recession. Van Gogh's paintings of undergrowth, such as *A Corner in the Garden of the Asylum at Saint-Rémy* (see fig. 44), produced two years later in July 1889 in the garden at Saint-Rémy, also relate to Diaz.[65] Shortly before beginning these pictures, Van Gogh noted that, even though he might forget the capital itself, he "couldn't forget all those beautiful Barbizon canvases then, and it seems unlikely and anyway unnecessary to do better than that."[66] In these works, in contrast to his Paris *sous-bois*, Van Gogh concentrated on rendering the surfaces of tree trunks, rather than attempting to evoke an overall effect of atmospheric light. Such an approach can be compared with the Barbizon tradition, embodied by Rousseau and Diaz, of close-up tree views and the creation of a facture that mimicked natural textures. In a view of spring 1890, Van Gogh focused even more specifically on rendering the texture of the bark of a pine tree.[67]

Jules Dupré: "Crazy"

Van Gogh also greatly admired the work of Jules Dupré. In the spring of 1885, he read a biographical article on Dupré in *La Vie Moderne* that emphasized this artist's intense, almost spiritual engagement with nature.[68] Van Gogh remained fascinated with the idea of Dupré as a pioneering avant-garde artist, committed to his work and scorning commerce. Later, in the South of France, Van Gogh referenced the Goncourt brothers' description of Dupré as "crazy," a description that may further have enhanced his identification with Dupré, given his awareness of his own mental instability.[69]

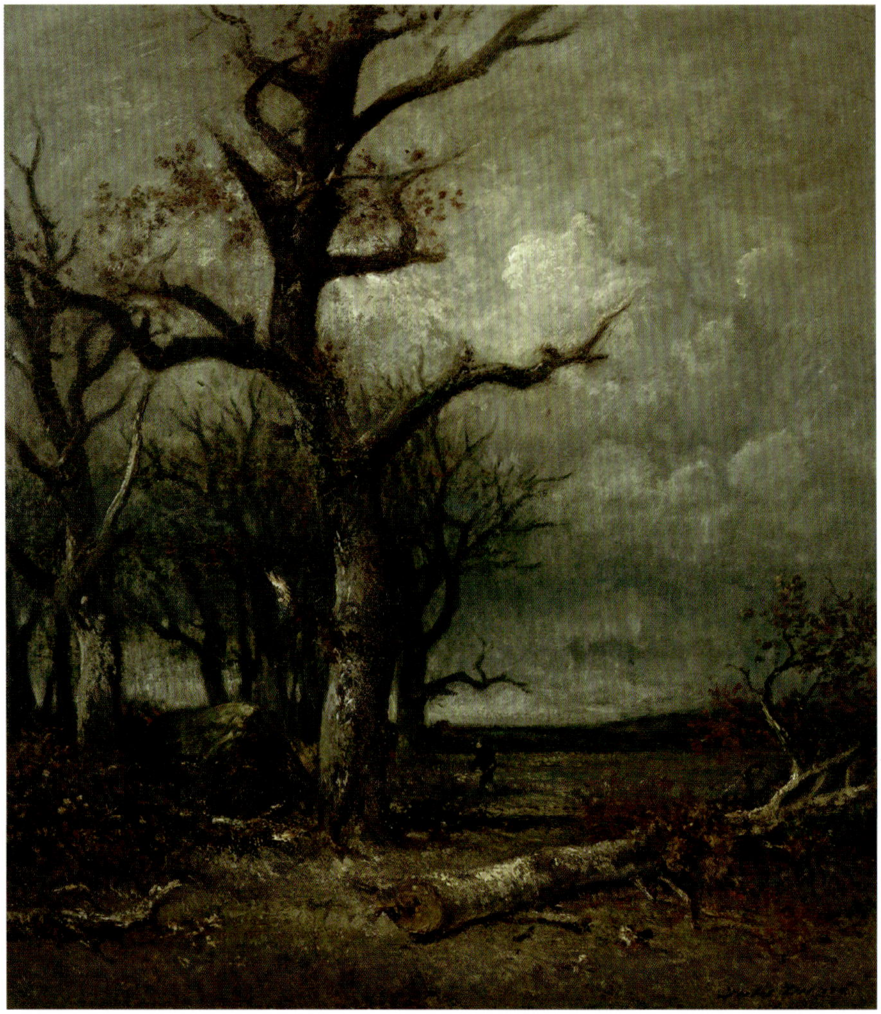

Fig. 14
Jules Dupré (1811–1889),
Autumn, ca. 1865,
oil on canvas, 41 15/16 × 36 13/16 in.
(106.5 × 93.5 cm),
The Mesdag Collection,
The Hague, hwm 122

In the summer of 1883, Van Gogh praised Dupré's ability to invest a tree with a sense of human emotion, as in *Autumn* (fig. 14).[70] Here, he argued that the artist was tapping into a traditional idea of the pathetic fallacy: he seems to have associated this ability with the Barbizon artists, ascribing to Corot the same ability to invest human emotion into the natural form of a tree.[71] Van Gogh's interest in Dupré was particularly evident during his visit to the remote region of Drenthe in the fall of 1883. On one occasion, he compared a view at twilight to *Evening,* a painting by Dupré (The Mesdag Collection, The Hague) "with two huts in it on which the mossy roofs stand out surprisingly deep in tone against a hazy, dusty evening sky."[72] On another, decaying roots were "absolutely melancholic and dramatic . . . just like Jules Dupré."[73] On yet another, an intense evening scene reminded him of Dupré's "sublime" palette.[74] Van Gogh's own dark, sonorous colors in his own landscapes now also strongly reflected the impact of Dupré.

Van Gogh was especially intoxicated by the color of Dupré's work and, in the fall of 1885, wrote poetically and at length of the artist's coloristic power: "Jules Dupré is like Delacroix in landscape, for what enormous diversity of mood he expressed in symphonies of color. . . . an autumn landscape with foliage from deep wine red to vivid green, from bright orange to dark havana. . . . I've always idolized Jules Dupré. . . . for he's a real colorist."[75] As Van Gogh's own color palette lightened in the late 1880s, Dupré's influence would diminish, but Van Gogh remained fascinated by his persona.

Charles François Daubigny

Van Gogh read Frédéric Henriet's biography of Daubigny, possibly as early as 1877.[76] In his early years, he was particularly attracted to the poetry of Daubigny's prints, not only those with the artist's own compositions, but also Daubigny's reproductive images after Jacob van Ruisdael's *The Bush* and *The Ray of Sunlight*. Van Gogh was drawn to Daubigny's personality—identifying strongly in 1883 with the artist's recorded belief that his strongest works were those not produced for the market.[77] His interest in Daubigny culminated with his move in the spring of 1890 to the small town of Auvers, north of Paris, especially well known as the site of Daubigny's house and studio. Daubigny had died twelve years earlier, but his widow continued to live in the house and it remained largely unchanged from the time of his death. Van Gogh's decision to move to Auvers may, indeed, have been informed by the site's connection with Daubigny. In the spring of 1890, Van Gogh produced a series of views of the fields at Auvers. These reflect the influence of Daubigny, who had also painted the same fields extensively in works such as the 1877 *Auvers, Landscape with Plough* (Toledo Museum of Art, Ohio). Van Gogh also produced three paintings of Daubigny's garden: a close-up sketch of plants and flowers and two large, double-size, more panoramic views with the artist's house behind. This was indeed the only subject that Van Gogh would produce on this scale in two variants. Each of these works had variations in color and iconography: the cat that appears in the foreground left of the Basel *Daubigny's Garden* (Kunstmusuem Basel, F 777) is, for example, painted over in the Hiroshima painting (fig. 15). Van Gogh referenced the latter work in a letter of 23 July 1890 as "one of my most deliberate canvases."[78] Only four days later, he shot himself; this may have been his final painting.[79]

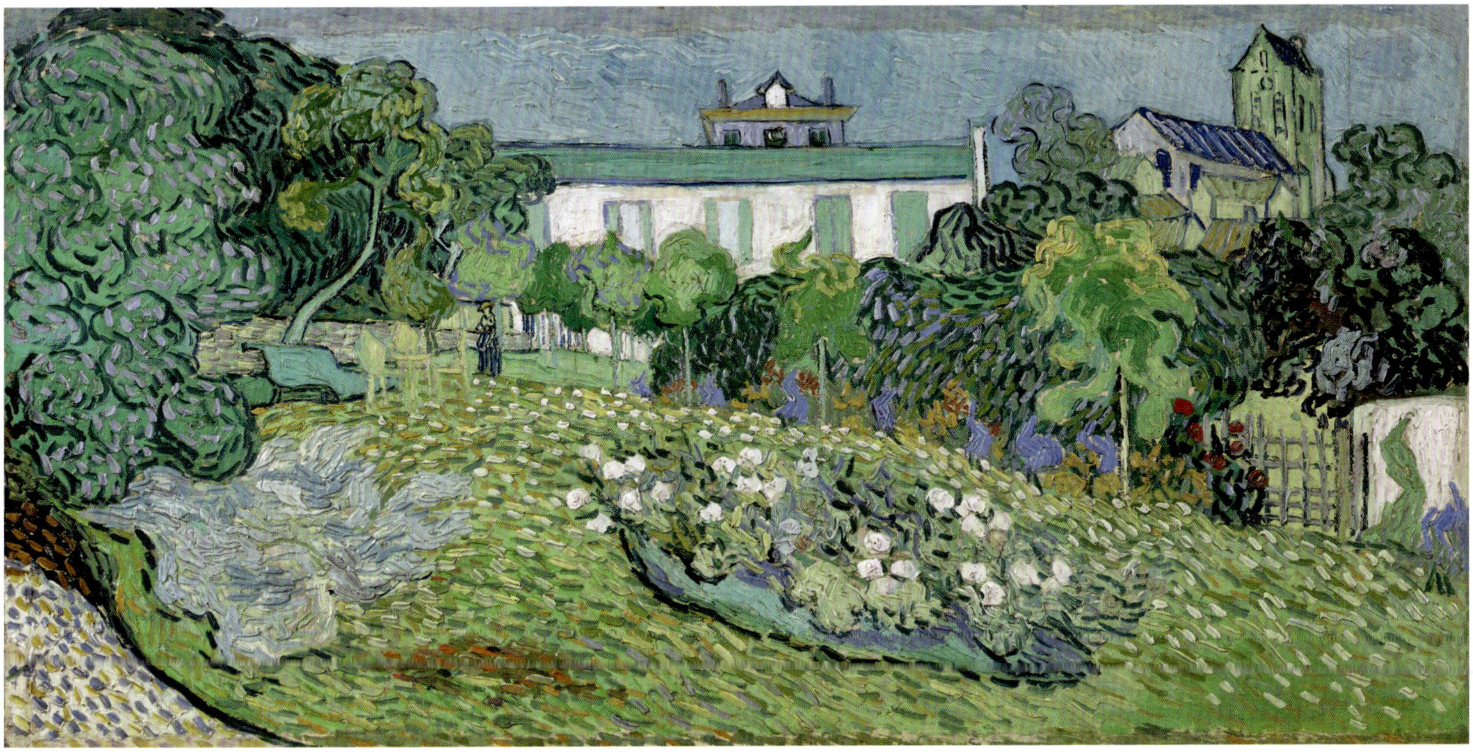

Fig. 15
Vincent van Gogh (1853–1890),
Daubigny's Garden, 1890,
oil on canvas,
20¾ × 41 in. (53.2 × 103.5 cm),
Hiroshima Museum of Art, Japan,
F 776

Conclusion

Van Gogh's engagement with the Barbizon artists developed from his key viewing experiences in Paris in 1875 to his early copies after Millet and Rousseau to his paintings of the early 1880s, when he was very much formally and ideologically influenced by the elder painters. The direct impact of Barbizon art was greatest on his work up until 1885. Perhaps surprisingly, Van Gogh continued to argue for the avant-garde significance of Barbizon painting thereafter, even after his experience with the contemporary traditions of Impressionism and Neo-Impressionism in Paris moved his art in a very different coloristic direction. Van Gogh's return to peasant and rural imagery in the South of France initiated a spectacular revival of Barbizon-type subjects, although in a completely new color register. Van Gogh now drew on Barbizon painters for their iconographic and moral importance, as well as their compositional tropes and experiments with mimetic facture. The remarkable series of twenty-one painted copies after Millet is the greatest testimony to the continuing resonance of this artist's example. In a final culminating moment, Van Gogh's move to Auvers offered an opportunity for spiritual identification and closeness with the ghost of Daubigny.

Van Gogh was deeply aware of the history of art, and admired work ranging from the Dutch seventeenth-century tradition to Dürer to contemporary Japanese prints.[80] Barbizon painting, however, arguably made a more consistent and long-term impact on his work than any other artist group, or any single artist. Throughout his career, Van Gogh's figural peasant paintings—at the center of his output—depended on Millet's example. In Van Gogh's landscapes, the oscillation between renderings of near and far, of proximity and distance, was also deeply dependent on his Barbizon forebears. Van Gogh saw the Barbizon artists as experimental avant-garde outsiders, whose innovation ensured that their output enjoyed an "eternal youth."[81] Within this context, the greatest tribute that he paid to their work was to radicalize and subvert it, thus creating new kinds of imagery that would have equal importance for future avant-garde generations.

Notes

1 Perhaps Pissarro showed the greatest comparable interest in the Barbizon painters. At the 1887 Millet retrospective, he very much admired the elder artist's drawings, although he was more critical of his paintings. Renoir was a great admirer of the landscapes of Corot.

2 Vincent van Gogh to Theo van Gogh, 4 April 1885, letter 489.

3 The latter was the only major Barbizon painter who lived on into the 1880s. The term "Barbizon School" seems to have been first used (in its French version, "L'École de Barbizon") in 1866 by the French writer Hector de Callias. It was first used in English by the Scottish art writer David Croal Thomson in 1888, and it was he who was largely responsible for disseminating the term. Van Gogh clearly thought of the artists working at Barbizon as a coherent group, even though he did not use the term "Barbizon School."

4 See Nicholas Green, "Dealing in Temperaments: Economic Transformations of the Artistic Field in France during the Second Half of the Nineteenth Century," *Art History* 10 (March 1987): 59–78.

5 "I would rather read the life of père Millet or T. Rousseau or Daubigny." Vincent van Gogh to Theo van Gogh, 20 August 1882, letter 258.

6 The prints on the wall of Van Gogh's Montmartre lodgings in the summer of 1875 included Corot (*Evening* [*resting place*]), Bodmer (*Fontainebleau*), Troyon (*Morning*), Dupré (*Evening*), Millet (*The Four Times of Day*), and Daubigny (*Dawn* [*cock crowing*]). Vincent van Gogh to Theo van Gogh, 6 July 1875, letter 37.

7 See Simon Kelly, "'A big, good enterprise': Vincent van Gogh and His Markets," in *Becoming Van Gogh*, ed. Timothy Standring (New Haven: Yale University Press, 2012), 55–70.

8 Leo Jansen, Hans Luijten, and Nienke Bakker, eds., *Vincent van Gogh: The Letters* (London: Thames & Hudson; Brussels: Mercatorfonds, 2009), online at http://www.vangoghletters.org. Van Gogh referenced Millet in 182 letters, more than any other artist. He also quoted Corot in 81 letters, Daubigny in 59, Dupré in 56, Rousseau in 47, Diaz in 19, and Bodmer in 16. He cited Breton in 99 letters. By way of context, he referenced Rembrandt in 112 letters, Delacroix in 100, Ruisdael in 42, Dürer in 20, and Hokusai in 6. These numbers provide quantitative insight into the importance of the Barbizon painters to Van Gogh relative to other artists and artistic traditions.

9 See, e.g., Chris Stolwijk, "Van Gogh and the Pictorial Genre of Evening and Night Scenes," in *Van Gogh and the Colors of the Night*, ed. Sjraar van Heugten, Joachim Pissarro, and Chris Stolwijk (Amsterdam: Van Gogh Museum; New York: Museum of Modern Art; Brussels: Mercatorfonds, 2008), 22–28; and Stolwijk, "How Nature Speaks: Holland, 1881–85," in *Van Gogh and Nature*, ed. Richard Kendall, Sjraar van Heugten, and Chris Stolwijk (New Haven: Yale University Press, 2015), 27–65.

10 See Louis van Tilborgh, "The Same but Different: Van Gogh and His Mentor Millet," in *Van Gogh & Millet*, ed. Louis van Tilborgh et al., exh. cat. (Amsterdam: Van Gogh Museum, 1988; Paris: Musée d'Orsay, 1999), 9–24.

11 Vincent van Gogh to Theo van Gogh, 24 September 1880, letter 158.

12 This seems to be confirmed by a later letter in which he remarked that he had never seen the house of Millet ("I've never seen the little house where Millet lived": Vincent van Gogh to Theo van Gogh, 14 July 1885, letter 515). Van Gogh did visit Courrières, the birthplace of Jules Breton, in northern France, as well as Ville-d'Avray, the birthplace of Corot, in the Paris suburbs.

13 Vincent van Gogh to Theo van Gogh, 29 July 1883, letter 389: "the great revolution in art of which Millet, Daubigny, Breton, Troyon, Corot are the leaders."

14 Vincent van Gogh to Theo van Gogh, 15 October 1883, letter 396.

15 At the same time, he was aware of the changes brought on by tourism in Barbizon during the course of the century, noting that the Drenthe region had a sense of remoteness that the artist "scarcely finds even now in present-day Barbizon." Vincent van Gogh to Theo van Gogh, 31 October 1883, letter 401.

16 See Elizabeth C. Childs, "Seeking the Studio of the South: Van Gogh, Gauguin and Avant-Garde Identity," in *Vincent Van Gogh and the Painters of the Petit Boulevard*, ed. Cornelia Homburg (Saint Louis: Saint Louis Art Museum, 2001), 113–50, esp. 136–40.

17 "The newer men of *today don't want me*, though—that's all right, I DON'T CARE ABOUT THAT—*both* as people *and* as painters, I prefer the generation of around 48 to around 84, but as to 48, *not* the Guizots but the *revolutionaries*, Michelet—and also the *peasant painters of Barbizon*." Vincent van Gogh to Theo van Gogh, 30 September 1884, letter 463.

18 See Jules de Goncourt and Edmond de Goncourt, *Manette Salomon* (1867; Paris: Gallimard, 1996), 225.

19 Vincent van Gogh to Theo van Gogh, 5 and 6 September 1889, letter 800.

20 Ibid. Van Gogh had read this story, which served as the opening words to Philippe Burty's catalogue introduction in the *Exposition de l'oeuvre de Corot á l'École Nationale des Beaux-Arts* (Paris: Typ. Jules-Juteau, 1875), 5. Van Gogh had, in fact, already recounted this story in a letter of spring 1888.

21 "There was a sale here of drawings by Millet, I don't know whether I've already written to you about it. When I entered the room in Hôtel Drouot where they were exhibited, I felt something akin to: Put off thy shoes from off thy feet, for the place whereon thou standest is holy ground" (Vincent van Gogh to Theo van Gogh, 29 June 1875, letter 36). Later, he wrote: "I'm always glad that I saw the collection of drawings by Millet at the Hôtel Drouot" (Vincent van Gogh to Theo van Gogh, 20 August 1883, letter 377).

22 He would later remember this work when seeing a village church in the Dutch landscape in 1883; it possibly informed his later church views, including *The Church at Auvers* (1890, Musée d'Orsay, F 789). In 1887, a second work by Millet, the landscape *Springtime*, entered the Luxembourg. This orchard scene, together with Daubigny's orchard views, probably underpinned Van Gogh's orchard paintings in the South of France in the spring of 1888.

23 For these studies, see Marije Vellekoop, "Van Gogh in the Borinage: From Evangelist to Artist, 1880," in *Van Gogh: The Birth of an Artist*, ed. Sjraar Van Heugten (New Haven: Yale University Press, 2015). Most of his drawings after these prints have been lost and this has undoubtedly served to marginalize the significance of this early engagement with Millet's art.

24 See Alfred Sensier and Paul Mantz, *La vie et l'oeuvre de Jean-François Millet* (Paris: A. Quantin, 1881).

25 See Neil McWilliam, "Mythologising Millet," in *Barbizon: Malerei der Natur, Natur der Malerei*, ed. Christoph Heilmann, Andreas Burmester, and Michael Zimmermann (Munich: Klinkhardt & Biermann, 1999), 438–47. Sensier's was a somewhat distorted image, since we know that Millet was agnostic, and also a highly cultivated man from well-off yeoman, rather than peasant, stock.

26 "Millet though, is the *religious* type." Vincent van Gogh to Theo van Gogh, 16 October 1883, letter 397. In 1883, Van Gogh would affirm that Millet had a "gospel" and that there was little distinction between his work and a "good sermon" (Vincent van Gogh to Theo van Gogh, on or about 21 September 1883, letter 388). In 1890, he also noted that Millet painted a "something on high" (Vincent van Gogh to Willemien van Gogh, 19 February 1890, letter 856).

27 Vincent van Gogh to Theo van Gogh, 26–27 November 1882, letter 288. This drawing is reproduced in Sensier and Mantz, *La vie et l'oeuvre de Jean-François Millet*, 110.

28 "On reading Sensier, what he said about the start of his [Millet's] career struck me so much that although I don't remember it *literally*, I remember the sense of it, that is, 'that [i.e., indifference] would be bad enough for me if I needed fine shoes and the life of a gentleman—but—*because I go around in clogs, I shall manage*'. . . .

. . . In my view this means that *as a human being* he [Millet] has shown painters a way that Israëls and Mauve, say, who live quite luxuriously, do *not* show . . . Millet is—PÈRE *Millet*, that is, counsellor and guide in *everything*, for the younger painters." Vincent van Gogh to Theo van Gogh, 13 April 1885, letter 493.

29 Vincent van Gogh to Theo van Gogh, 2 July 1889, letter 785.

30 Vincent van Gogh to Theo van Gogh, 3 February 1884, letter 428.

31 Vincent van Gogh to Theo van Gogh, 14 July 1885, letter 515.

32 "Can we now paint the sower with color, with simultaneous contrast?" Vincent van Gogh to Theo van Gogh, 28 June 1888, letter 634.

33 Ibid. Van Gogh's move away from Millet's palette is evident in his 19 June 1888 letter to Émile Bernard, letter 628, in which he remembered his earlier Nuenen works: "In those days, I was enthusiastic about grey."

34 Vincent van Gogh to Émile Bernard, 8 October 1889, letter 809.

35 Van Gogh asked his brother Theo for the Delaunay print in 1889. He drew vertical lines on the print to assist in his copy, and there is also a grid beneath the surface of the painting.

36 The 1875 Gavet sale included seven views of expansive open plains

including *L'hiver, plaine de Chailly* (*Winter, The Plain of Chailly*, Glasgow Museums, inv. 35.542) and *La plaine de Barbizon, effet de neige* (*Winter*, Calouste Gulbenkian Museum, Lisbon, inv. 89). It also included two close-up views: *Les coucous, fleurs de printemps* and *Fleurs de printemps* (both Museum of Fine Arts, Boston: *Primroses*, inv. 17.1523 and *Dandelions*, inv. 17.1524, respectively). In addition, it contained many mountain views of Auvergne and Normandy marines. See *Vente Gavet*, 11–12 June 1875 auction catalogue (Getty Research Institute).

37 The 1887 show featured 218 paintings, pastels, watercolors, drawings, and prints. These included the painting titled in the catalogue as *La plaine au petit jour* (*The Plain at Daybreak*) (no. 35, bis, now known as *The Plain of Chailly with Harrow and Plough*, fig. 8); and the two large-scale pastels, *La plaine au petit jour* (no. 83, now known as *Winter, the Plain of Chailly*, Glasgow Museums) and *La plaine de Barbizon, effet de neige* (no. 88, Calouste Gulbenkian Museum, Lisbon). In his catalogue introduction (which Van Gogh probably read), Mantz described the pastel, *L'hiver* (*Winter, the Plain of Chailly*, Glasgow Museums) as "only two actors, the earth and the sky . . . sadness . . . by its melancholy sentiment, this pastel evokes the memory of the beautiful landscape, November, exhibited in 1870" ["Deux acteurs seulement la terre et le ciel . . . tristesse . . . par le sentiment mélancolique, ce pastel évoque le souvenir du beau paysage, Novembre, expose en 1870"]. See Paul Mantz, "Jean-François Millet," in *Catalogue descriptif des peintures, aquarelles, pastels, dessins rehaussés, croquis et eaux-fortes de J-F. Millet réunis à L'École des Beaux-Arts* (Paris: A. Quantin, 1887), 30.

38 See Noelle C. Paulson, "High Horizons," in *Van Gogh: Up Close*, ed. Cornelia Homburg (New Haven: Yale University Press, 2012), 224–35.

39 As in 1880, he turned to the ten prints of *Les travaux des champs* as his source. He also produced larger paintings after other prints such as *The Four Times of the Day*. For a detailed examination of these copies, see Sjraar van Heugten, Philip Conisbee, and Louis van Tilborgh, "Van Gogh's Copies after Millet" in *Van Gogh & Millet*, 85–153, and Cornelia Homburg, *The Copy Turns Original: Vincent van Gogh and a New Approach to Traditional Art Practice* (Amsterdam and Philadelphia: John Benjamins, 1996).

40 This photograph, with Van Gogh's pencil squaring-up added, is in the Van Gogh Museum, Amsterdam. Van Gogh owned other photographs after Millet's work—Theo had sent him a roll of photographs—although these cannot be identified. These probably came from the Braun stock: 94 photographs after Millet's work were listed in the Braun 1887 catalogue of photographs for sale. See *Catalogue general des photographies inalterables au charbon et heliogravures faites d'apres les originaux peintures, fresques, dessins et sculptures des principaux musées d'Europe, des galeries et collections particulieres les plus remarquables* (Paris: A. D. Braun & Cie, 1887), 469–70.

41 Theo van Gogh to Vincent van Gogh, 3 May 1890, letter 867.

42 Van Gogh inquired about Vernier's lithographs after Corot. Vincent van Gogh to Theo van Gogh, mid-January 1873, letter 3.

43 Vincent van Gogh to Theo van Gogh, 13–18 April 1875, letter 32. The sketch is included in the letter.

44 Vincent van Gogh to Theo van Gogh, 6 March 1875, letter 30.

45 See Henri Dumesnil, *Corot: Souvenirs intimes* (Paris: Rapilly, 1875).

46 "WHEN you speak with Pa, think at the same time of *Corot*, say, you'll then automatically avoid some of the extremes into which Pa lapses much too much. . . . There are other upright lives, more in a milder spirit, in the character of Corot": Vincent van Gogh to Theo van Gogh, 21 September 1883, letter 388. Van Gogh referenced various aspects of Corot's life from Dumesnil that further supported this image in three subsequent letters to Theo on 15 October 1883 (letter 396), 16 December 1883 (letter 414), and 4 January 1884 (letter 419). He also noted that Corot had "serenity if anyone did."

47 The Corot pictures were *Women Cutting Wood* (location unknown), *Pleasures of the evening (danse antique)* (Hammer Collection, Los Angeles), and *Biblis* (location unknown).

48 Van Gogh's interest in Corot's religious landscapes is further suggested by a visit he made to the elder artist's birthplace at Ville d'Avray in the summer of 1875. There, he was impressed by a series of Corot's large-scale religious paintings: *Saint Jerome* and four pictures on the transept walls of the church.

49 See Vincent van Gogh to Theo van Gogh, 31 May 1875, letter 34. This work dates from 1849 and is now considerably darkened.

50 Vincent van Gogh to Émile Bernard, 26 November1889, letter 822. He went on: "In his work, you feel Homer, Aeschylus, Sophocles too, sometimes, as well as the Gospels, but how sober and always giving due weight to modern, possible sensations common to us all." He remembered how the viewing of this painting in 1878 had "moved me deeply."

51 Vincent van Gogh to Émile Bernard, 8 October 1889, letter 809.

52 "I'll hang up The oven by T. Rousseau . . . which I got from you." Vincent van Gogh to Theo van Gogh, 9–10 January 1878, letter 139. "The ovens are more or less like the ones in T. Rousseau's Communal oven; stand in the gardens under old apple trees or among the celery and cabbages." Vincent van Gogh to Theo van Gogh, 14 September 1883, letter 386.

53 Anastasi's print showed Rousseau's image as it was in 1847 (perhaps after a watercolor) when the foliage was much more dense; there were no background church and cottages and no children in the foreground. Rousseau later extensively revised his painting (now in the Leipzig Museum of Fine Arts), lessening the density of the foliage. Van Gogh probably never saw the actual painting; it was in the Frédéric Hartmann collection until it was auctioned in Paris in 1881, when it attracted much attention, and was discussed in the *Gazette des Beaux-Arts*.

54 "There are many beautiful things there by Dupré, Corot, Daubigny, Diaz, Courbet, Breton, Jacque & c. I especially liked the large sketch by T. Rousseau from the Mesdag collection, a drove of cattle in the Alps." It is unclear if Van Gogh is referencing the sketch or large-scale finished painting, both of which were in The Mesdag Collection. See Vincent van Gogh to Theo van Gogh, 15 and 16 July 1882, letter 246. The exhibition included ten works by Corot, three by Rousseau, four by Dupré, eight by Diaz, and five by Daubigny.

55 Vincent van Gogh to Theo van Gogh, 11 July 1883, letter 361.

56 Theo van Gogh to Vincent van Gogh, 5 September 1889, letter 799. Van Gogh responded that he thought Theo's letter was "really good," especially for his references to Rousseau and Bodmer. Vincent van Gogh to Theo van Gogh, 10 September 1889, letter 801.

57 Vincent van Gogh to Theo van Gogh, 2 September 1889, letter 798; for Bodmer, see Richard Kendall, "Van Gogh, Nature and Science," in Kendall et al., *Van Gogh and Nature*, 72–74.

58 "I feel that he [Gauguin]'s more Millet than I am, but I'm more Diaz than he is, and like Diaz, I'll try to please the public so that some sous may come into the community." Vincent van Gogh to Theo van Gogh, 4 or 5 October 1888, letter 697.

59 Rousseau disait un jour a Diaz: "Personne n'a peint un *dessous de bois* comme toi.- p. 81: Laisse donc, repondit Diaz, je connais UN chemin dans le paysage, mais toi, Rousseau, tu les connais TOUS!" See Arthur Stevens, *Le Salon de 1863* (Paris: La Librairie des Arts, 1866), 80–81. Stevens's volume was originally published in installments as "Un Étranger au Salon" in *Le Figaro* in 1863. The author used the pseudonym of J. Graham.

60 See the 1849 sale ("Études et esquisses de N. Diaz"). Similar études appeared regularly in his later sales: the 1863 sale indeed contained a separate section for fifteen *études d'après nature*; these included "*étude de hêtre*" and "*étude de chêne*." For Diaz's *sous-bois*, see Simon Kelly, "'This dangerous game': Rousseau, Diaz and the Uses of the Auction in the Marketing of Landscape," in *Soil and Stone: Impressionism, Urbanism, Environment*, ed. Frances Fowle and Richard Thomson (Burlington, VT: Ashgate, 2003), 33–48. For a full sense of the extent of Diaz's production of Forest of Fontainebleau views, see Pierre Miquel and Rolande Miquel, *Narcisse Diaz de la Peña (1807–1876)*, vol. 2, *Catalogue raisonné de l'oeuvre peint* (Paris: ACR Édition, 2006).

61 Many *sous-bois* indeed appear in the stock books of Goupil and Boussod & Valadon from the 1870s and 1880s (693 paintings by Diaz in total, with large numbers of *sous-bois*; and 212 paintings by Rousseau, with a few *sous-bois*). See Galerie Boussod, Valadon & Co. Stock Books, Dieterle family records of French art galleries, 1846–1986, Series II, Boussod, Valadon & Co. ledgers, 1879–1919, Getty Research Institute.

62 See Philippe Burty, "N. Diaz," in *Maîtres et petits maîtres* (Paris: G. Charpentier, 1877); and Jules Claretie, "N. Diaz de la Peña," in *Exposition des oeuvres de N. Diaz de la Peña* (Paris: Jules Claye, 1877).

63 Van Gogh's words responded to his view of Diaz's *Nymph and Cupid* (Amsterdam Museum, Amsterdam), then in the Fodor collection in Amsterdam. See Vincent van Gogh to Theo van Gogh, 13 October 1885, letter 535.

64 Diaz was also important to Van Gogh as mentor to Adolphe Monticelli, another painter who became an important influence in the mid-1880s as he explored new approaches to color.

65 See Jennifer Thompson, "Sous-bois," in Homburg, *Van Gogh: Up Close*, 202–11.

66 Vincent van Gogh to Theo van Gogh, 25 June 1889, letter 783.

67 Van Gogh hoped to render the olive and pine trees of the South as a counterpoint to Barbizon painters who had already specialized in the rendering of oak trees, as in the case of Rousseau and Bodmer, or apple or willow trees, as with Daubigny. In the spring of 1890 he wrote, "Well, the day is probably not far off when people will paint the olive tree in every way as they have painted the willow and the Dutch pollard willow, as they have painted the Norman apple tree since Daubigny and Cesar de Cock." Vincent van Gogh to Joseph Jacob Isaäcson, 25 May 1890, letter RM21.

68 Vincent van Gogh to Theo van Gogh, 28 April 1885, letter 496: "I was glad to find some biographical particulars of Jules Dupré in the No. of La Vie Moderne—I've sometimes thought that *Mistigris* (the shrewdest of landscape painters), who appears in Balzac's Comédie humaine, could *perhaps* have been Dupré in his youth."

69 Vincent van Gogh to Theo van Gogh, 22 July 1888, letter 645.

70 "Israëls put it perfectly in the case of a Jules Dupré (Mesdag's large one) [*Autumn*]: 'It's just like a figure painting.' It's that dramatic quality . . ." Vincent van Gogh to Theo van Gogh, 11 July 1883, letter 361.

71 ". . . in Corot every tree-trunk is drawn and modelled with attention and love as though it were a figure. And a tree-trunk by Corot is something altogether different from one by De Bock." Vincent van Gogh to Theo van Gogh, 26 August 1881, letter 171.

72 Vincent van Gogh to Theo van Gogh, 14 September 1883, letter 386. Van Gogh had seen this painting in the summer of 1882 under the title *Evening* (*Avondstond*) at the exhibition in the Hague Academy.

73 Vincent van Gogh to Theo van Gogh, 7 October 1883, letter 393.

74 "That same irritatingly tedious spot—in the evening as a poor little figure moves through the twilight—when that vast, sun-scorched earth stands out dark against the delicate lilac tints of the evening sky, and the very last fine dark blue line on the horizon separates earth from sky—can be as sublime as in a J. Dupré." Vincent van Gogh to Theo van Gogh, 16 September 1883, letter 387.

75 Vincent van Gogh to Theo van Gogh, 28 October 1885, letter 537.

76 Vincent van Gogh to Theo van Gogh, 30 October 1877, letter 133: "Looked through that book at Uncle's, the engraved oeuvre of C. Daubigny." Frédéric Henriet's *C. Daubigny et son oeuvre gravé* (Paris, 1875) also contained a biography of Daubigny, in addition to a listing of his prints.

77 Van Gogh also admired Daubigny's work as a colorist, describing an early morning scene in the summer of 1883 as reminiscent of him because of its vivid color, and especially its luminous green. Vincent van Gogh to Theo van Gogh, 22 June 1883, letter 356.

78 Vincent van Gogh to Theo van Gogh, 23 July 1890, letter 902.

79 The croquis of the painting that Vincent included in his letter to Theo of 23 July 1890 includes the cat walking across the foreground. Van Gogh, however, painted out the cat in the final painting. He must have made this change between July 23 and 27.

80 For Van Gogh's interest in Dutch art, see Joseph J. Rishel, "Vincent and the North: Five Case Studies Up Close," in Homburg, *Van Gogh: Up Close*, 98–119.

81 "I believe more than ever in the eternal youth of the school of Delacroix, Millet, Rousseau, Dupré, Daubigny, just as much as in the current one [Impressionism] or even the artists to me." Vincent van Gogh to Theo van Gogh, 31 May and 6 June 1889, letter 777.

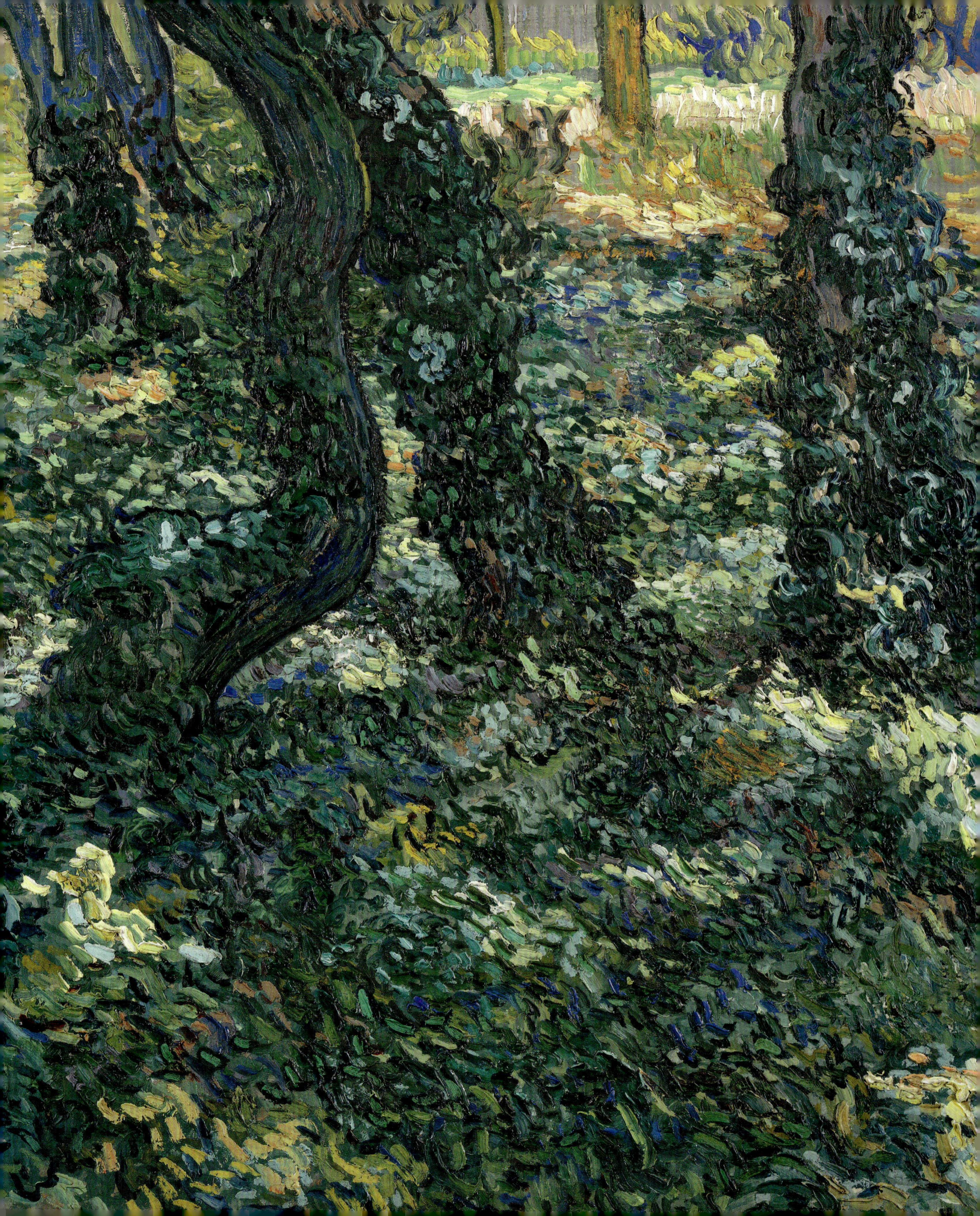

Tree Lovers

Development and Meaning of the *Sous-Bois* Genre

Jenny Reynaerts

IN A DRAWING BY JEAN-BAPTISTE-CAMILLE COROT dating from around 1840, a young man leans against a huge oak (fig. 16), a giant of a tree in the Forest of Fontainebleau. The forest had been the royal hunting ground for centuries, and to preserve game stocks few trees had ever been felled. This gave the forest authenticity and history—as well as immense trees.[1]

Corot's companion looks diminutive beside the tree, and the contrast reflects the insignificance of man in nature. At the same time, though, he draws strength from it. In the 1830s, when the Barbizon School came into being in this setting, painters sought the direct expression of an intimate and personal sense of nature.[2] It gave rise to a subgenre in landscape painting: the *sous-bois*. This term can be interpreted in a number of ways. The translations *undergrowth*, *kreupelhout* (Dutch), and *Unterholz* (German) encompass both tree trunks and the forest floor with plants and tree roots, but exclude studies of complete trees.[3] Nineteenth-century French artists, however, also used *sous-bois* in titles of pictures of trees or spinneys with a solitary figure, as in Corot's *Le petit cavalier sous bois*, a *cliché-verre* of 1854 (see fig. 53). In these works, the viewpoint is low and the trees dominate. A cropped composition and the absence of a horizon create the illusion of proximity and fidelity to nature. This essay examines the rise and transformation of the painting genre in light of both types.

Nature Explored in Close-Up

The development of the *sous-bois* motif reflects the changing perception of nature in the nineteenth century. Significant paradigm shifts in natural science were visualized in landscape painting. At the end of the eighteenth century people began to discover and embrace the intrinsic value of nature, instead of regarding it simply in terms of ownership, exploitation, or fear of the wilderness. This change was rooted in the views of the eighteenth-century Swiss philosopher Jean-Jacques Rousseau, who defined nature as innocent and contrasted it with the corruption of

Vincent van Gogh (1853–1890), *Undergrowth* (cat. 7, detail)

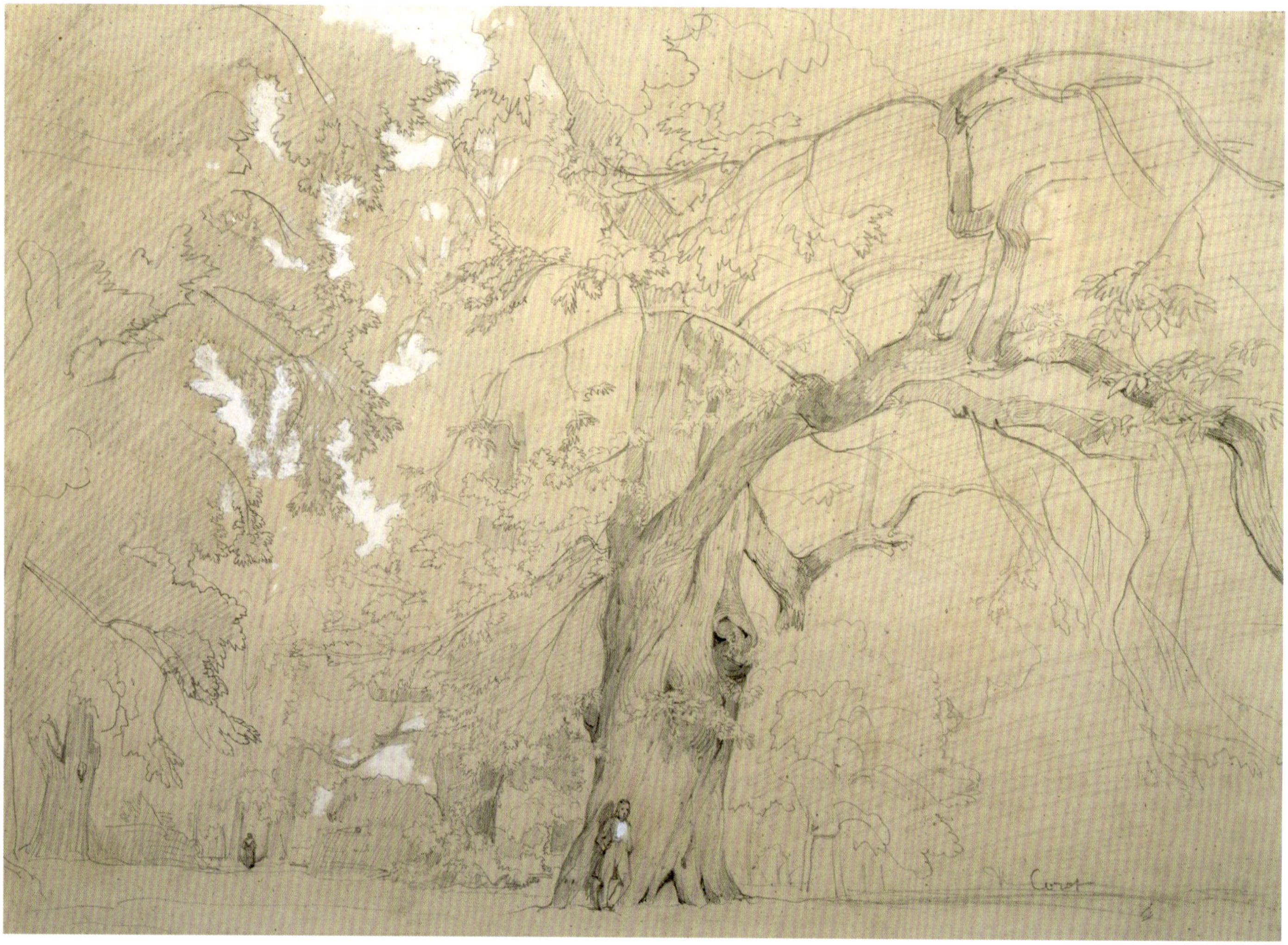

Fig. 16
Jean-Baptiste-Camille Corot (1796–1875),
Young Man in front of a Great Oak, ca. 1840,
graphite heightened with white gouache on buff wove paper,
11½ × 15$^{11}/_{16}$ in. (29.2 × 39.8 cm),
The Museum of Fine Arts, Houston, Museum Purchase funded by the Houston Alumnae Chapter of Delta Delta Delta Sorority in honor of Laura Lee Blanton, 97.209

man-made society. In *Émile, or On Education* (1762), Rousseau advocated education for boys based on personal development, preferably in the open air.

In his last work, the autobiographical essays *Reveries of the Solitary Walker* (published posthumously in 1782), Rousseau blended scientific analysis with the subjective experience of nature.[4] In the seventh walk he described how at a low point in his life he retreated to an island in Lake Bienne near Geneva, his birthplace, and day after day studied the plant kingdom at close quarters, losing himself in nature to emerge reborn. "The more sensitive the observer's soul, the more he delights in the ecstasy aroused in him by this harmony [of nature]. On such occasions, a sweet and deep reverie takes hold of his senses and he loses himself with delicious intoxication in the immensity of this beautiful system with which he feels at one."[5]

The conflicting combination of scientific analysis of the natural order and untrammeled instinctive experience, coupled with changes in the landscape brought about by advancing industrialization, underlies the subsequent rise of landscape painting in the nineteenth century. Fascinated landscape painters followed developments in botany and in the burgeoning sciences of geology and meteorology. The discoveries of such scientists as Johann Wolfgang von Goethe, the explorer Alexander von Humboldt, the meteorologist Luke Howard, and the geologist Charles Lyell brought to light new physical processes and showed nature as an interplay of forces, constantly moving and changing. Underlying their discoveries was always a quest for the relationship between man and nature, synthesis and harmony.[6]

Artists and writers explored this relationship in a more empathetic manner. In the 1840s, by way of experiment, Henry David Thoreau tested Rousseau's ideas by withdrawing into the woods near Walden Pond in Concord, Massachusetts. "I went to the woods because I wished to live deliberately, to front only the essential facts of life, and see if I could not learn what it had to teach, and not, when I came to die, discover that I had not lived."[7]

The French landscape painters of the first half of the nineteenth century similarly distanced themselves from the city. Corot and fellow painters like Charles Jacque, Jules Dupré, Narcisse Virgile Diaz de la Peña, and Théodore Rousseau regularly spent the summer in Barbizon, a village near the Forest of Fontainebleau—Jacque and Rousseau actually settled there permanently—and learned about the forest by painting it.[8]

In Ornans, Gustave Courbet made a direct link between his painting and the rocky countryside of the Franche-Comté, where he was born. "To paint a region you have to know it. And I know my region, I paint it. This *sous-bois*, it's near my home, this river, it's the Loue, this one the Lison; these rocks, they are the rocks of Ornans and Puits Noir. Go and see, and you will recognize all my pictures."[9] Inspired by the early Barbizon painters, Courbet sought new creative energy and self-expression in the landscape. He revealed just how much the natural landscape governed his art in the painted landscape on his easel in the programmatic work of 1855, *The Painter's Studio*: *A Real Allegory of a Seven Year Phase in My Artistic (and Moral) Life*.[10]

Empathy with nature in general and the personal landscape in particular also mobilized defenders, who, running counter to the process-driven and inevitable change identified by scientists, wanted to conserve nature in its raw state and protect it from the changes made by human agency. Thoreau's experiment arose from his distaste for man's unnatural existence, brought about by the opportunities of industrialization. Later in the century it was chiefly town-dwellers who saw unspoiled nature as a place of escape and seclusion.[11] The need to preserve places like these grew in line with the changes brought by economic progress in the second half of the nineteenth century and, like the scientific discoveries, was one of the drivers in the rise of landscape painting.[12]

A *sous-bois* is the ultimate image of this double identification—identification of and with nature. By standing so close that the gaze goes no further than undergrowth or the surrounding trees, artist and viewer alike are able to lose themselves in nature. Personal experience and natural history coincide.[13]

The Study of Nature

Although the forestscape originated in seventeenth-century Netherlandish painting, and the painter Otto Marseus van Schrieck even introduced the term *sottobosco* for his still lifes of plants, insects, and reptiles in a woodland setting, the genre truly began to flourish only at the end of the eighteenth century.[14] Romantic sensibility and the need for truthful analytical nature study together led to the practice of working outdoors on color sketches and drawings, which inevitably meant that artists learned about individual elements of the landscape.

Around 1800 the first guidebooks for landscape painters began to appear, all of them hammering home the importance of this pictorial exploration of details in nature. The studies, often in watercolor or oils, were combined in the studio to create a composed landscape, as a rule a *paysage historié*, lending veracity and realism to the synthetic composition. Although he was certainly not the first practitioner of the *plein air* oil sketch, it was Pierre Henri de Valenciennes, the author of the first guide for young landscape painters, who formalized the practice.[15] He wrote that every study must show evidence of natural light. Artists consequently had to make a note of the weather—bright sunshine or cloud, morning or evening light—at the time the detail was recorded so that there would be no incongruities in the finished work. This applied to clouds, trees and smaller plants. Valenciennes's studio was full of such oil sketches (fig. 17).[16]

Valenciennes often returned to the same spot to sketch it in bright light or with a cloudier sky, a clue to what was important in this study of nature: authenticity, expressed in precise observation and rendition of the natural light. Valenciennes was an inspired teacher in Paris, where he taught at the Académie des Beaux-Arts, and earlier, in the international artists' colony in Rome, where his students Jean Victor Bertin and Achille Etna Michallon disseminated his ideas at the Académie de France.[17]

In an attempt to reconcile this academic study of the landscape with the ideas of contemporary science, the German physician, physiologist, and amateur painter Carl Gustav Carus wrote *Neun Briefe über die Landschaftmalerei* (Nine Letters on Landscape Painting), which appeared between 1815 and 1824.[18] These letters were inspired by Goethe's scientific discoveries, particularly in geology, and by Caspar David Friedrich's paintings. Carus wrote that artists had to try to depict natural processes in their landscapes, and this would lead of its own accord to a new true-to-life form of painting that he described with the neologism "Erdleben-Bildkunst," earth-life art.[19] By this he meant depicting geological processes through the strata in rock, or the seasons through the changing colors of leaves. At the same time, artists had to be open to the varying moods that the landscape evoked in them. This also applied to elements of nature: "They exert an effect in

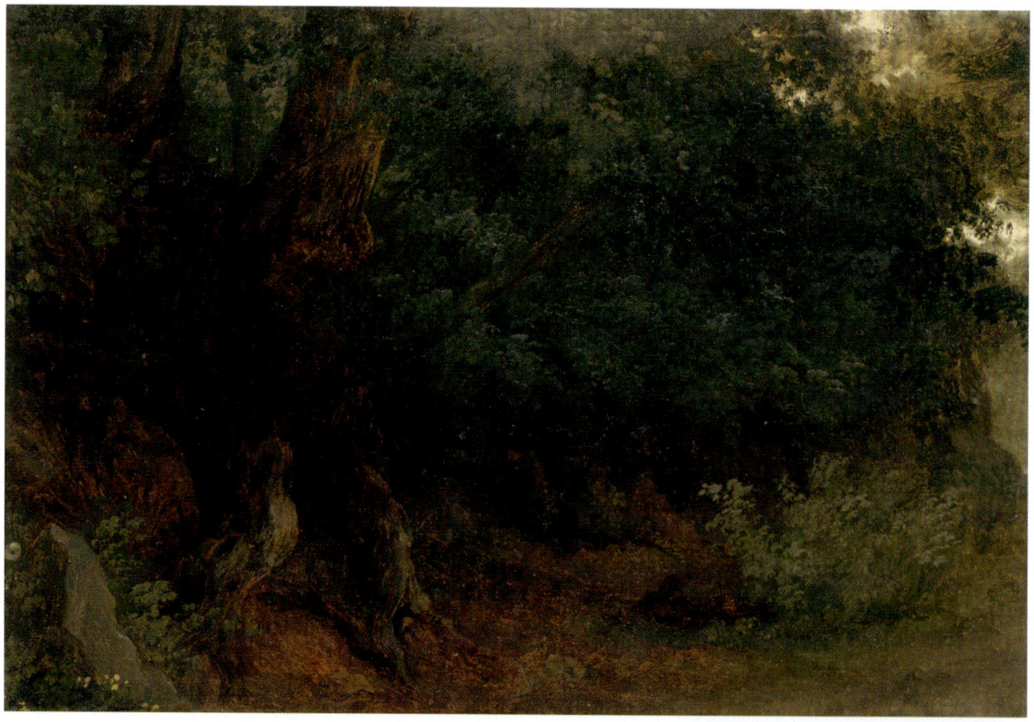

Fig. 17
Pierre Henri de Valenciennes (1750–1819), *Tronc d'arbre, racines et feuilles* (*Tree Trunk, Roots, and Foliage*), 1775–1819, oil on cardboard, 9⁹⁄₁₆ × 13 in. (23 × 33 cm), Musée du Louvre, Paris, France, RF 2921

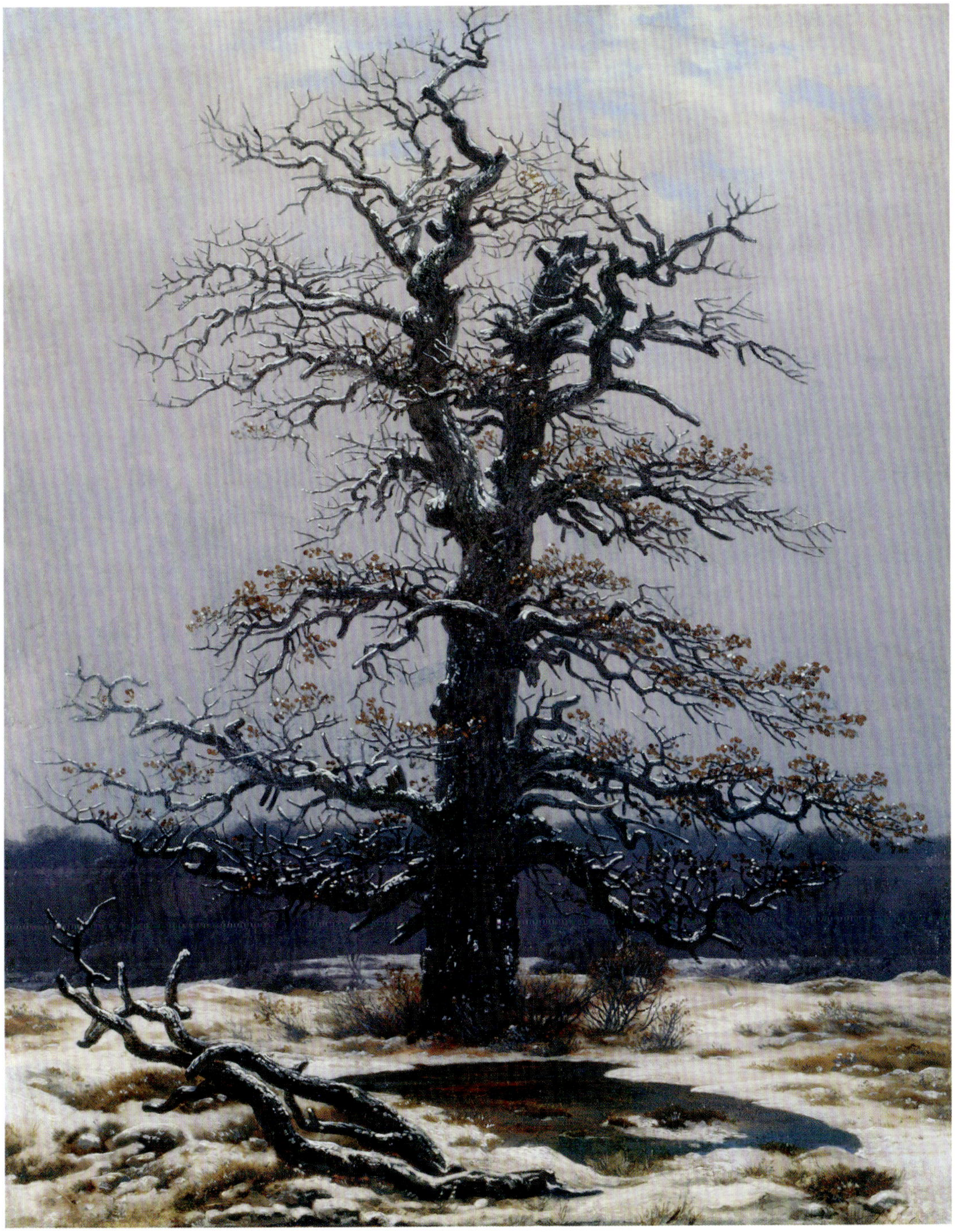

Fig. 18
Caspar David Friedrich (1774–1840), *Oak in the Snow*, 1827–28, oil on canvas, 17⁵⁄₁₆ × 13⁹⁄₁₆ in. (44 × 34.5 cm), Wallraf-Richartz Museum and Fondation Corboud, Cologne, WRM 2666

keeping with the sense of life that manifests itself in them. If they are unorganized, the effect will be chilling; if emergent, stimulating; if complete and perfect, calming. . . . The dense vegetation that covers a valley floor evokes a sense of the luxuriant vitality of life; a mature tree in full leaf invites tranquil contemplation; and a yellowed or lifeless tree indicates melancholy."[20]

Although Friedrich's work inspired Carus's theories, the painter himself did not put them into practice. Friedrich used his nature studies chiefly as an aide-mémoire for constructed compositions that reflected his own interpretation of nature (fig. 18). His trees are vehicles of mood, not accurate depictions of natural processes following the rules of "earth-life art."[21]

How a Topic Became a Genre

The discovery of nature and the new nature study was a European phenomenon. In England, as early as the end of the eighteenth century, theories of the picturesque prompted a Romantic approach to nature. Predecessors like Richard Wilson and Thomas Gainsborough often painted a landscape in its own right rather than as a mise-en-scène for a mythological or biblical subject. Wilson, who trained in sketching from nature in Italy, was in fact the first artist to take as his motif his own landscape—in his case that of Wales—albeit often as a commission from the owner of the land. This choice was surprising, but stylistically Wilson was a follower of Claude Lorrain, and he painted predominantly from a panoramic perspective.[22] One of Wilson's students, fellow Welshman Thomas Jones, was in Rome at the same time as Valenciennes and, like him, painted directly in oils in the open air.[23] John Constable followed in their footsteps. He did not go to Italy but preferred the landscape of his native Suffolk and the views around his home in Hampstead. Constable created a large reservoir of close-up oil studies, many of which he annotated with observations of nature. He also showed these works at the Royal Academy, among them *A Study of Trees from Nature* in 1822 and *A Study of Trees, a Sketch* in 1823.[24] It is difficult to identify precisely which works these were, but his *Study of Tree Trunks* of around 1821 gives an impression (fig. 19).

The oil sketch was thus rapidly promoted from the studio wall to the exhibition gallery, reflecting the growing appreciation of the sketch in general. The positive reception given in France to Constable's work and that of the young English painter Richard Parkes Bonington during this period is well known, and it is likely that the effect of their direct observations of nature was discussed in Italy, too.[25] From around 1800 Rome developed into a hotspot of the new

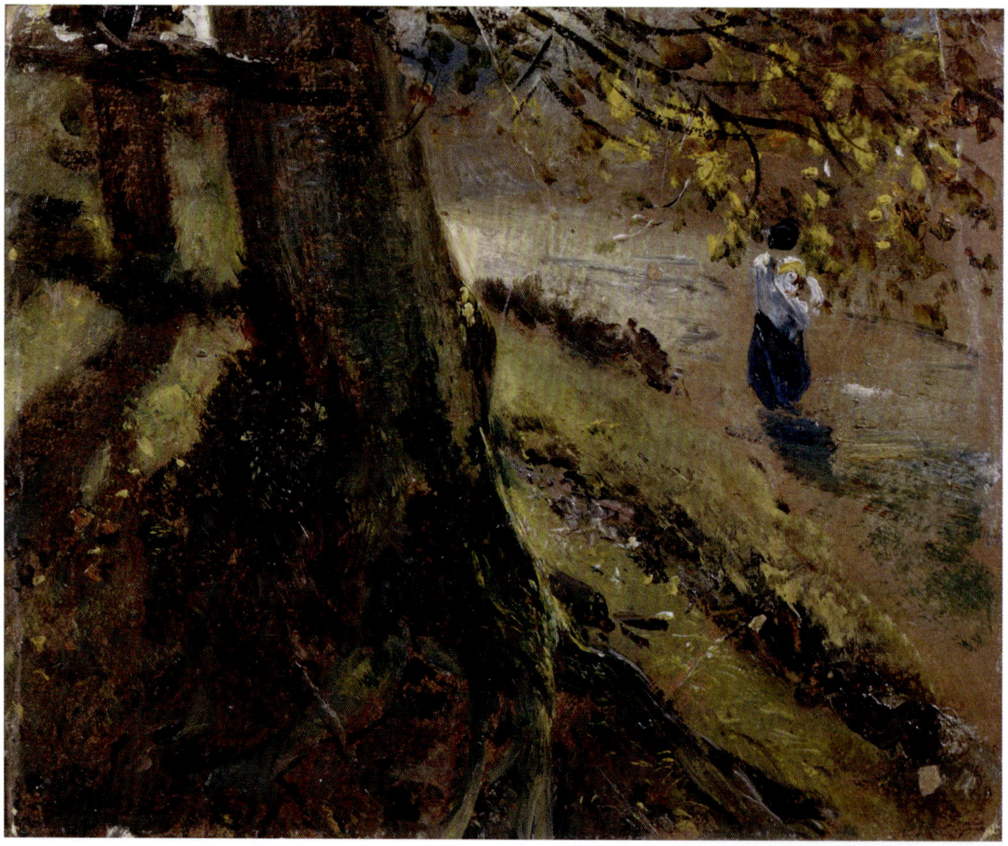

Fig. 19
John Constable (1776–1837),
Study of Tree Trunks, ca. 1821,
oil on paper,
9¾ × 11½ in. (24.8 × 29.2 cm),
Victoria and Albert Museum,
London, Given by Isabel Constable,
323-1888

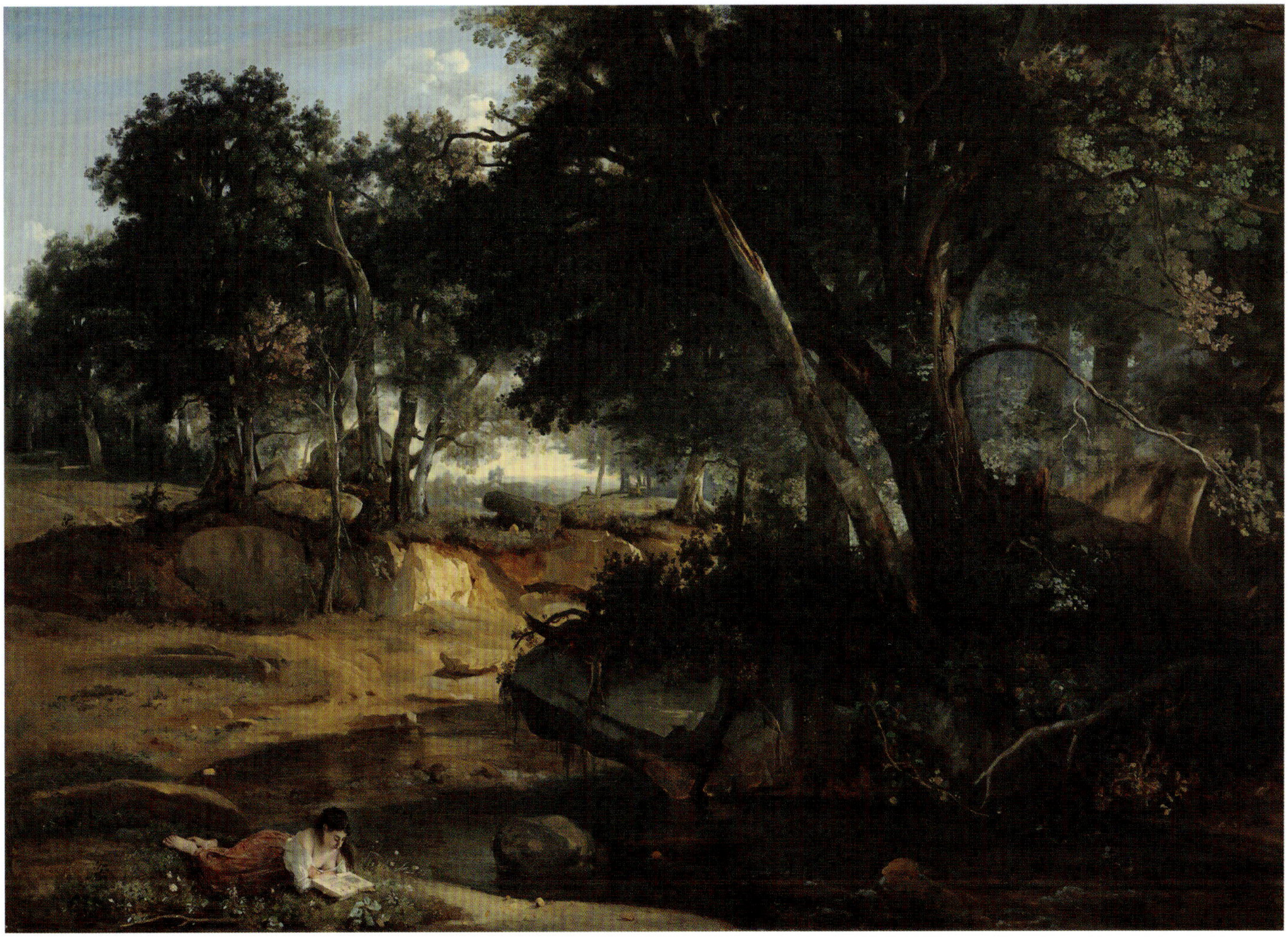

landscape painting. Oil studies from nature were very popular there, particularly among artists who took up residence in the Roman Campagna every summer. Most of them had trained as history painters and regarded sketching nature *en plein air* as relaxation. In their free time they created landscape paintings in their own right, often *vedute* (topographical views), but also close-up studies of nature.[26]

If there was one artist who assimilated and incorporated Valenciennes's lessons, it was Corot. He had first seen Bonington's work in 1821 and regarded it as a decisive influence on his decision to become a painter.[27] As a student of Michallon and Bertin, Corot was familiar with painting outdoors before he went to Rome, where he lived from 1825 to 1828.[28] In Italy Corot broadened his experience in painting in the open air, but unlike his fellow painters, who according to academic rules confined themselves to preliminary studies, he changed the traditional relationship between sketch and finished work and continued this practice when he returned to France. In contrast to the sketches of trees and tree trunks Constable had exhibited ten years earlier, Corot's tree studies of the 1830s, such as *Forest of Fontainebleau*, were large—a gallery-appropriate size (fig. 20).[29] Although Corot traveled throughout France and beyond, his painting is associated above all with the Barbizon School. He went to the village before he set off for Italy, and again in the first spring after his return. From then on he regularly worked there in the summer.

Fig. 20
Jean-Baptiste-Camille Corot (1796–1875),
Forest of Fontainebleau, 1834,
oil on canvas,
69⅛ × 95½ in. (175.6 × 242.6 cm),
National Gallery of Art, Washington, Chester Dale Collection, 1963.10.109

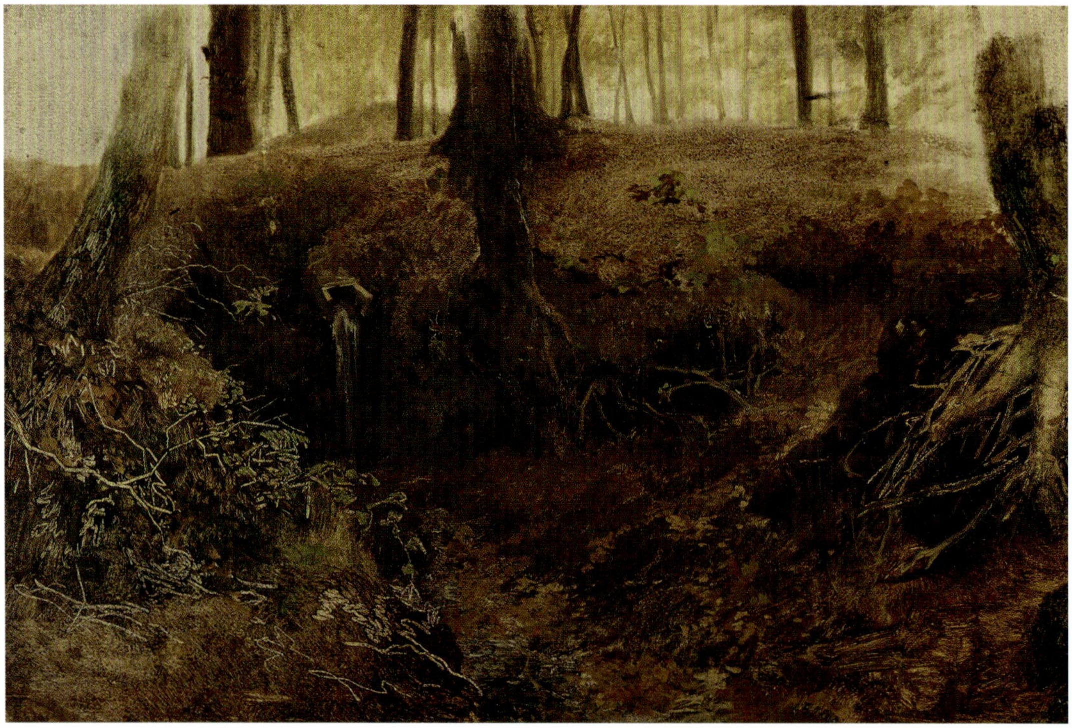

Fig. 21
Matthijs Maris (1839–1917),
The Origin: Woodland View in Oosterbeek, ca. 1860,
oil on canvas,
22 1/16 × 27 15/16 in. (56 × 71 cm),
Collection of the Gemeentemuseum, The Hague,
inv. nr 0333781

Théodore Rousseau, another pioneer of the *plein air*, initially used his oil studies to compose Romantic landscapes with a panoramic viewpoint, made in the studio. In 1836 he submitted *The Descent of the Cattle in the High Jura Mountains* (The Mesdag Collection, The Hague) to the Salon. This daring composition of cows in a wood with no view or vista was rejected, and although artists admired it, this work and similar later paintings met with considerable adverse criticism. In 1841 Rousseau withdrew from the Salon for several years to develop his own style. Settled in Barbizon, he made one woodland view after another, now from a low vantage point. By 1849, when he started to show at the Salon again, the tide had turned and his work was praised.[30]

In this period the Barbizon School became an international magnet for young artists interested in the new landscape art. In line with the new ideas, they all painted forest views from the *sous-bois* perspective: a cropped composition of trees with or without a very high horizon, the light filtered through the leaves and the focus on the lowest tier of shrubs, undergrowth, rocks, and earth.

The constant pilgrimage of young artists to Barbizon meant that the *sous-bois* as a genre spread worldwide. Specialists emerged—like the Barbizon painter Diaz de la Peña (cat. 16), of whom the critic Jules Claretie wrote: "Nobody has better understood the law of light, the magic and, say, the folly of the sun in leaves and undergrowth."[31] The genre was widely appreciated and was picked up by artists ranging from the American Arthur Parton of the Hudson River School to the Russian Ivan Shishkin, a member of The Wanderers (*Peredvizhniki*), as well as by photographers.[32] The Dutchman Matthijs Maris, who first visited Barbizon in 1860 and later worked in the Dutch artists' colony of Oosterbeek, is a good example. In *The Origin: Woodland View in Oosterbeek* (fig. 21), Maris virtually crawls on the ground. The title is both metaphor and factual reference to the nearby estate De Oorsprong—The Origin—where he made the work.[33] The immersion in nature through a *sous-bois* made the genre permanently popular and successful.

Animated Nature

One of Théodore Rousseau's most impressive *sous-bois* is the unfinished *Massacre of the Innocents*, which he began in 1847 (fig. 22). It expresses the artist's outrage at the felling of ancient oaks in the Forest of Fontainebleau, which he saw as an act of vandalism. Rousseau's felled trees are like the fallen on a battlefield; the title is worthy of a history painting. An almost identical work, possibly of the same scene, was painted by Jules Dupré, who worked with Rousseau in Barbizon (*L'abattage des arbres*, 1840, Musée des Beaux-Arts, Dijon).

This "pathetic fallacy," the term John Ruskin coined in *Modern Painters* (1836) to describe the attribution of human emotions and character traits to nature, was a typical Romantic phenomenon and certainly contributed to the growing popularity among artists of woodland, trees, and the *sous-bois* in this period.[34] With their anthropomorphic appearance and the history they contained within them, trees were ideal subjects for identification with a person.

This idea became a veritable trope in the 1850s as a result of the popularity of *Fontainebleau in Autumn* (cat. 10), a painting by Karl Bodmer. It was disseminated in a lithograph by Eugéne Leroux; Vincent van Gogh owned one.[35] The oak Bodmer painted acquired its own identity in 1865 in Claude Monet's series of paintings *The Bodmer Oak*. Pathetic fallacy had been a trend in Fontainebleau for some time. In the wake of the Barbizon School the forest was transformed from a rural spot near Paris to *the* weekend destination for mid-nineteenth-century Parisians. Despite Rousseau's protests, the ancient forest had been largely tamed; paths and walks had been

Fig. 22
Théodore Rousseau (1812–1867),
The Massacre of the Innocents, 1847,
oil on canvas,
37⅜ × 57¹¹⁄₁₆ in. (95 × 146.5 cm),
The Mesdag Collection,
The Hague, hwm 293

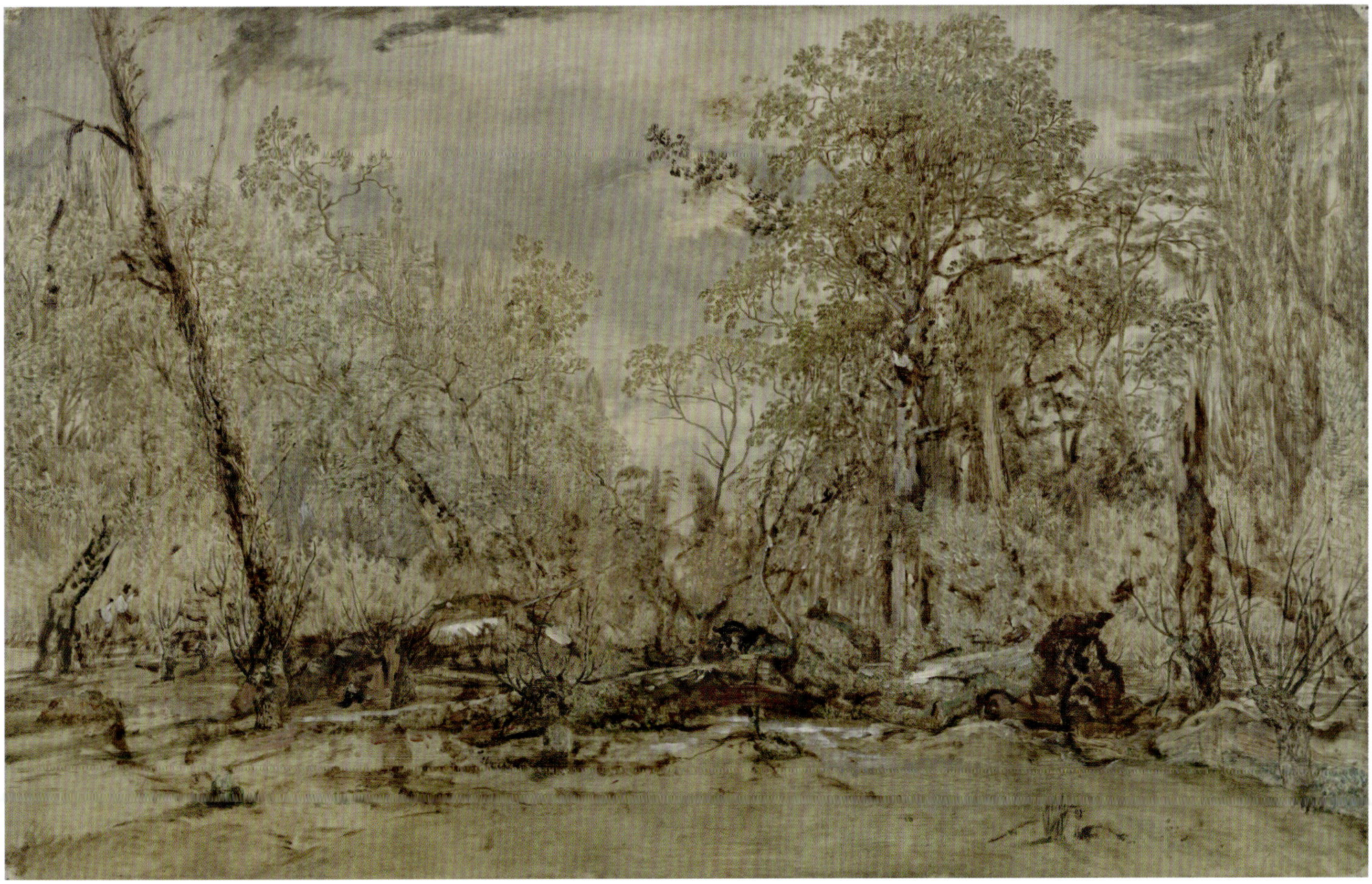

created, and some trees had acquired picturesque names.[36] This metamorphosis resulted from the recurrent paradox of the Romantic perception of nature, which transmutes the wilderness into a park in order to preserve it.

A striking feature of *sous-bois* works is that people appear more often than animals. Like the trees, these figures evolved over time. From the ordinary staffage of shepherds and peasants who, like animals, have a self-evident intimate relationship with nature, the people in these works transform into figures that communicate the experience of the painted landscape and simultaneously take on the role of viewer. The solitary walker is one such frequent figure, wholly bound up in the woods but at the same time the interpreter of the artist's and the public's sense of nature.

In the 1850s Corot worked out the theme in a series of *cliché-verres*. In this new experimental printing technique, in which a design painted or drawn on glass is exposed to the sun and printed on light-sensitive paper, he made a number of dreamy scenes of a narrow country lane, lined and canopied by tall trees. The technique was clearly inspired by Rembrandt's etchings, and one of the scenes is actually titled *Le bûcheron de Rembrandt* (1853). The others range from more anecdotal pictures—*Le petit cavalier sous bois* (1854; see fig. 53), *Les jardins de Horace* (1855), *Dante et Virgile* (1858)—to more general approaches. In *Le songeur* (cat. 13), the solitary dreamer surveys both details and nature as a whole.

Corot's *cliché-verres* heralded his later "lyrical" landscapes, in which the trees are as much the channels of the atmosphere in the painting as the figures beneath them (cat. 12). Compared with the work of the 1830s, the trees have lost their painstaking detail and individuality and blend into the whole. The execution is now about the harmonious tone, and not the defining line. Nonetheless, even though it is expressed differently from Bodmer's sturdy oak, the concept of nature is still the same and the artist is seeking a synthesis between depiction and emotion.[37] "Reality is a part of art; sentiment completes it," as Corot wrote.[38]

The Forest as Laboratory

This preoccupation with the feelings nature stirs in the artist changed with the Impressionists. Monet's allusion to Bodmer's oak is more than an homage to the artist; it is also the identification of a pictorial motif. Monet treated the tree as a study of light and dark patches of color—more akin, in fact, to Valenciennes's academic instruction than the Romantic notions in the mid-century. The composition of *Forêt de Fontainebleau* (cat. 18) is similar to Corot's (fig. 20) and Rousseau's (cat. 14), but Monet's identification of the trees is subordinated to what really fascinated the artist: the filtered light on the forest floor. The balanced lighting of the older painters, who attached greater value to the tonal harmony of the scene, has now made way for contrasts and optical movement. Other Impressionists—Frédéric Bazille, Alfred Sisley, Pierre-Auguste Renoir, and Camille Pissarro—also approached the genre in this way. In their paintings the forest is a theater full of lighting effects, a laboratory for optical experiments.

We know that in the summer of 1887 Vincent van Gogh explored precisely these effects of light and color with Paul Signac, Camille Pissarro, and Pissarro's son Lucien. Elsewhere I have suggested that for Van Gogh the *sous-bois* always functioned as a *tabula rasa*, a new beginning, be it his first paintings in 1882 (cat. 1), experiments with the new French style (cats. 2, 4, and 5), or a nervy and hesitant resumption after his breakdown in 1889 (cats. 6 and 7).[39] It is tempting to think that this applies to every *sous-bois*: a new beginning that commences in the close observation of nature. This is certainly true of landscape painting in Italy around 1800, when experiments and the abandonment of academic rules led to painting *en plein air.* It also applies to the Barbizon painters, especially Corot and Théodore Rousseau, who combined a changed perception of nature with the new techniques and possibilities of painting in the open air. Mary Morton points to a similar tendency in Gustave Courbet in the 1850s, when he chose landscape as his subject because nature offered him an arena "where the artist could enact an original performance-in-paint."[40] And again, in the Impressionist phase around 1865, there were experiments in the forest.

Cézanne described Monet as an eye, "the most prodigious eye of any painter."[41] Monet's perception of lighting and color resulted in the depiction of the forest in its passing manifestations. Cézanne also saw the artist as an instrument, but emphasized the intellectual handling of the optical input. "The artist is nothing but a receptacle for sensations, a brain, a recording device."[42] He was concerned with the translation of the visual and emotional experience of a landscape into a balanced image. "The landscape is reflected, humanized, recorded in me. I have the objective, the project, of fixing it on my canvas."[43] Thus he created his own landscape, determined not by the play of light, as in Monet and Renoir, but by the rhythm of the vertical lines of the trees (cat. 23).[44] This vision can also be found in the later forestscapes by Pissarro, who was cited by Cézanne as an inspiration.

The Enchanted Wood

Studying the plant world brought Jean-Jacques Rousseau comfort and the possibility of returning to himself. Henry Thoreau at Walden even wanted to bring the whole of mankind back to its natural state. Is this possibility of refuge and self-examination the reason why the *sous-bois* became so popular in the nineteenth century? Physically and mentally exhausted, Van Gogh expressed this idea in a letter to his brother from Saint-Rémy: "As for ideas I have no others except to think that a wheat field or a cypress are well worth the effort of looking at them from close at hand, and so on."[45] For painters and viewers alike, the forest view offered both rest and renewed vitality.

We can see a rapid development in Van Gogh's *sous-bois*. Whereas in 1887 he was concerned chiefly with pictorial study and practice in a new way of seeing, in 1889 in the garden of the Saint-Rémy asylum he painted a free interpretation of nature that echoed his own experience (cats. 6 and 7).[46] Van Gogh was keeping pace with a development that occurred in the genre from around 1880.[47] In the later work of Monet (cat. 18) and Renoir (cat. 21), the woodland view took on a metaphysical, almost visionary character.

Both the Monet and the Renoir painting show the forest as a closed world that has little to do with observable reality. In the paintings of Cézanne and of the older Pissarro, and in Gauguin's Breton work (cat. 24), all dating from the 1880s, this seclusion is accentuated by tree trunks that bisect the picture plane. The tree canopy is invisible and the interplay of the lines of the trunks takes place in the foreground or middle ground.

This effect appears at its most extreme in the paintings of Henri Rousseau (Le Douanier). In *Rendezvous in the Forest* (fig. 23) the screen of trees emphasizes the secrecy of the meeting and at the same time acts as a barrier, shutting the viewer out from this other world. The same mysterious, fairytale atmosphere of the impenetrable wood can be found in the work of the

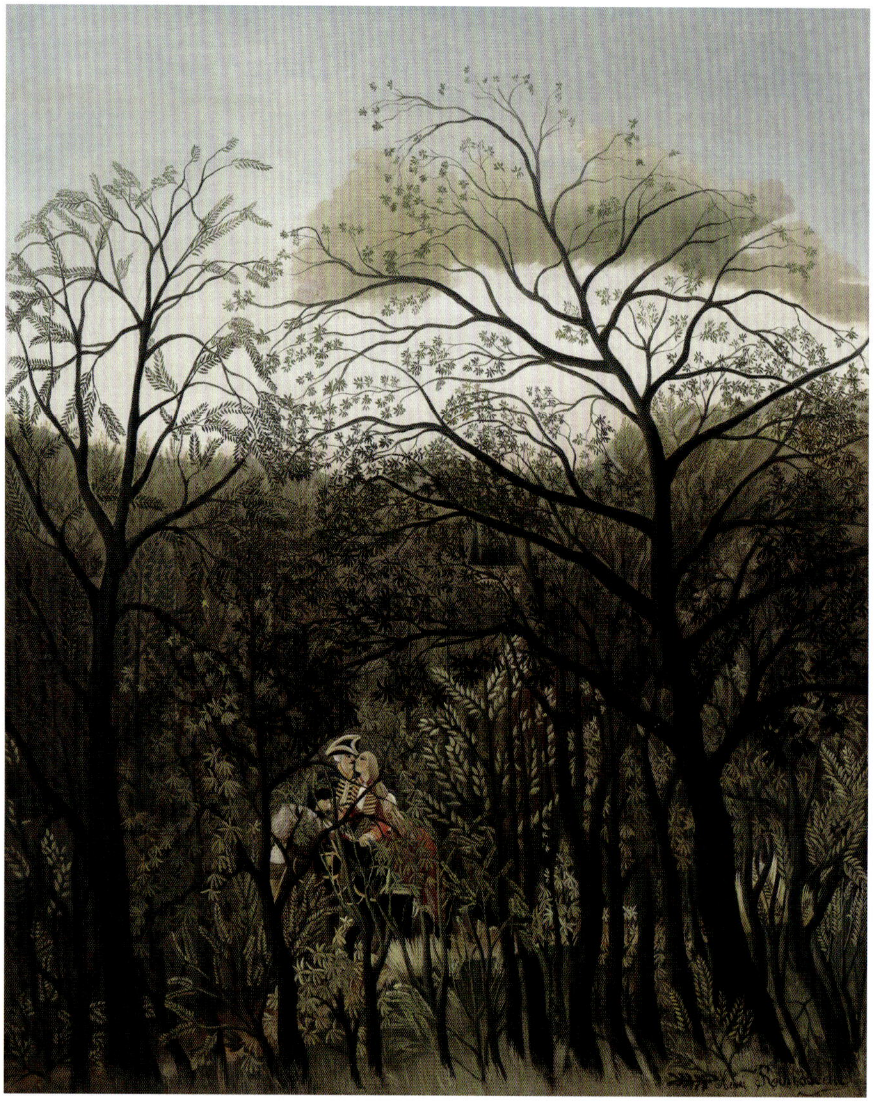

Fig. 23
Henri Rousseau (1844–1910),
Rendezvous in the Forest, 1889,
oil on canvas,
36¼ × 28¾ in. (92 × 73 cm),
National Gallery of Art,
Washington,
Gift of the W. Averell Harriman
Foundation in memory of Marie N.
Harriman, 1972.9.20

Fig. 24 (opposite, top)
Jan Toorop (1858–1928),
The New Generation, 1892,
oil on canvas,
47¹¹⁄₁₆ × 52¼ in. (121.2 × 132.7 cm),
Museum Boijmans van Beuningen,
Rotterdam, inv. 2337 (MK)

Fig. 25 (opposite, bottom)
Vincent van Gogh (1853–1890),
Tree Roots, July 1890, oil on canvas,
19¹³⁄₁₆ × 39⁷⁄₁₆ in. (50.3 × 100.1 cm),
Van Gogh Museum, Amsterdam
(Vincent van Gogh Foundation),
s195V/1962, F 816

French Symbolist painters' group called the Nabis and in Paul Gauguin's writings from Tahiti.[48] Trees surround figures that now play a greater role, but which, turned in on themselves, no longer have a role as intermediaries (cat. 25).

In his later *sous-bois* works, Van Gogh, too, painted tree trunks as columns dominating the small space (cats. 8 and 9).[49] The arrangement of the rows of trees in *Undergrowth with Two Figures* (cat. 9) is reminiscent of the pillars in a church. Here Van Gogh is engaging with Bernard and Gauguin both stylistically and iconographically.

In the 1890s *sous-bois* increasingly depicted such an enigmatic setting. The ancient forest became a jungle, an enchanted wood, or a *hortus conclusus*. Romantic identification with observable nature metamorphosed into alienation and distortion. The Dutch-Javanese Symbolist artist Jan Toorop painted trees as oriental creatures whose roots and branches may be protecting a child—or could be devouring it (fig. 24). Toorop's trees are reminiscent of the writhing roots in *Tree Roots*, what may well have been Van Gogh's last work (fig. 25). They suggest an indefinable fate, like the unfinished state of the painting itself. Toorop, who organized Van Gogh's first exhibition in the Netherlands in 1892, undoubtedly knew *Tree Roots*.

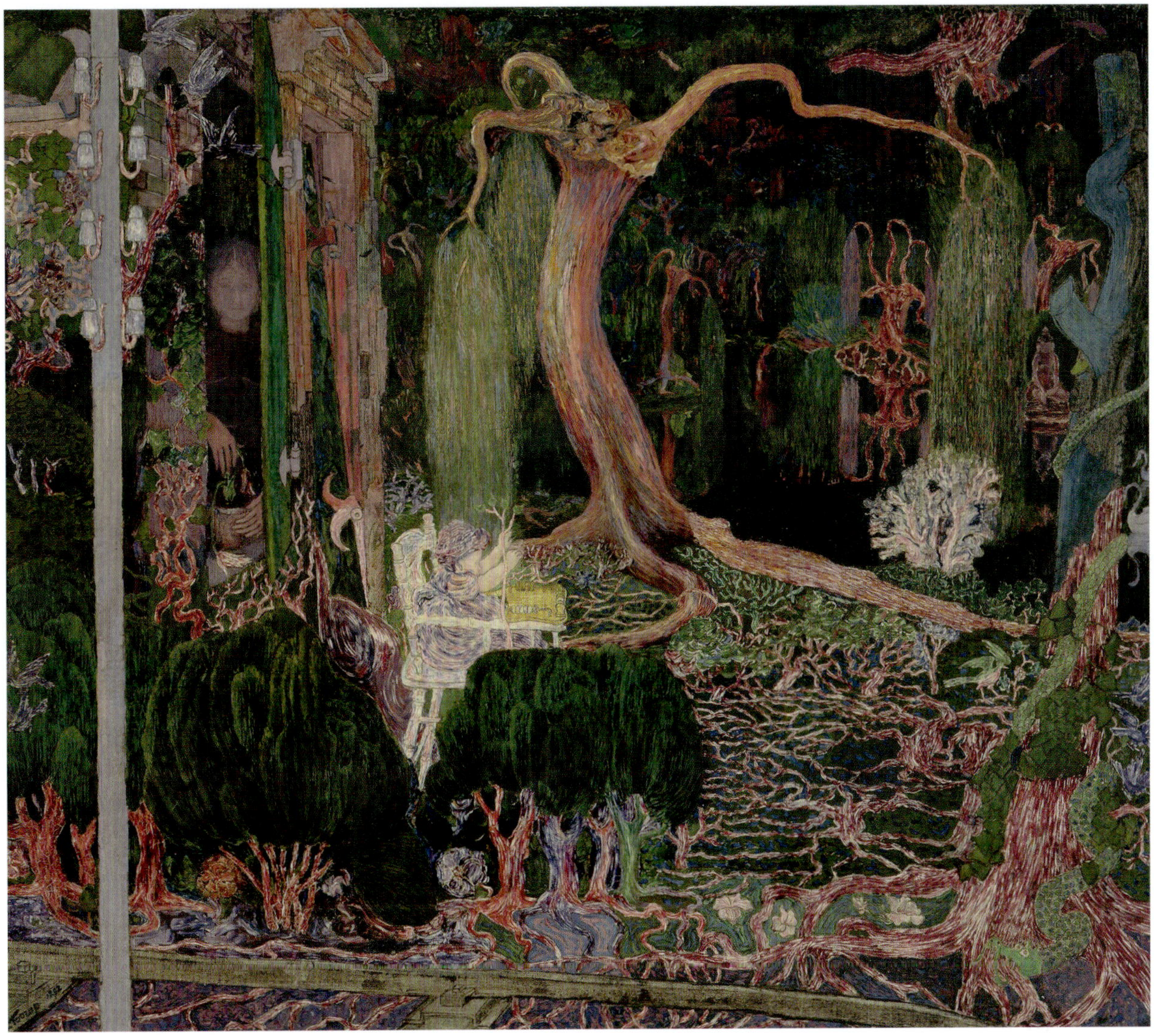

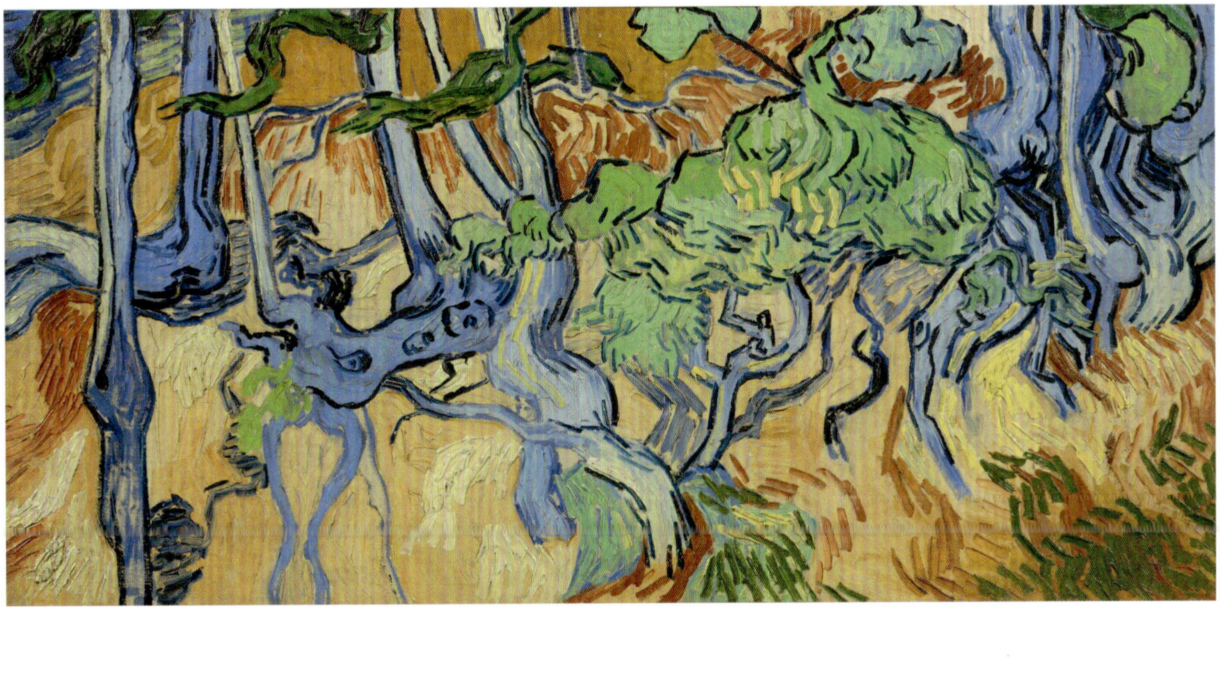

The meaning of the woods in these paintings is ambiguous, as is the relationship between the isolated figures and the trees that surround them. They seem to be absorbed not in nature but in their own psyches. Abandoning recognizable nature, artists struck out on a different path, and the character of the *sous-bois* changed fundamentally.

Conclusion

The *sous-bois* began as the meticulous close-up observation of a tree, a stump, or the forest floor as part of the study of nature for an academically trained painter. The drawing or oil sketch developed into a portrait in its own right—of undergrowth, a tree, a spinney—a typical Romantic expression of the individual, intimate relationship between man and nature. As the genre came into its own, the *sous-bois* served to create a mood or to convey the painter's modern perception. The basis—the academic study—nevertheless long remained a presence in the mature genre, and perhaps for this reason the *sous-bois* continued to be the perfect medium for experiments and new ideas.

Notes

I thank Mercedes Kleinfeld for her bibliographical research and Josephina de Fouw, Joan Greer, Laura Prins, and Suzanne Veldink for their helpful comments.

1 On the history of Fontainebleau and its relationship with the city, see Nicholas Green, *The Spectacle of Nature: Landscape and Bourgeois Culture in Nineteenth-Century France* (Manchester: Manchester University Press, 1990), 153–83.

2 For the most recent scholarship on the Barbizon School, see Vincent Pomarède, ed., *L'École de Barbizon: Peindre en plein air avant l'impressionnisme*, exh. cat. (Lyon: Réunion des Musées Nationaux, 2002).

3 Because of the limited scope of this article, I have decided to leave an analysis of the use of the term in titles and art criticism to another occasion.

4 Guilhem Scherf, ed., *Jean-Jacques Rousseau et les arts*, exh. cat. (Paris: Éditions du Patrimoine, Centre des Monuments Nationaux, 2012), 114–17; Christian Rümelin, ed., *Die Verzauberung der Landschaft zur Zeit von Jean-Jacques Rousseau/Enchantement du paysage au temp de Jean-Jacques Rousseau*, exh. cat. (Cologne: Wienand; Geneva: Musées d'Art et d'Histoire de la Ville de Genève, 2012), 8–21.

5 Jean-Jacques Rousseau, "Septième promenade," in *Les rêveries d'un promeneur solitaire* (1782; repr., Paris: Edition Flammarion, 1964), 126; Jean-Jacques Rousseau, *Reveries of the Solitary Walker*, trans. Russell Goulbourne (1782; repr., Oxford: Oxford University Press, 2011), 71. On the effect of *Les rêveries* on early-nineteenth-century aesthetics, see Margret Stuffmann and Dorit Schäfer, eds., *Camille Corot: Natur und Traum* (Karlsruhe: Staatliche Kunsthalle Karlsruhe, 2012), 369–73.

6 Jenns Eric Howoldt and Uwe Schneede, eds., *Expedition Kunst: Die Entdeckung der Natur von C. D. Friedrich bis Humboldt*, exh. cat. (Hamburg: Dölling und Galitz, 2002), 9–16, 27–36; Bärbel Hedinger, Ines Richter-Musso, and Ortrud Westheider, eds., *Wolkenbilder: Die Entdeckung des Himmels*, exh. cat. (Munich: Hirmer, 2004), 134–210.

7 Henry David Thoreau, *Walden; or, Life in the Woods* (1854; repr., Mineola, NY: Dover Publications, 1995), 59. On Jean-Jacques Rousseau's influence on Thoreau, see Mark J. Temmer, *Art and Influence of Jean-Jacques Rousseau: The Pastorale, Goethe, Gottfried Keller, and Other Essays* (Chapel Hill: University of North Carolina Press, 1973), 93–124. Thoreau's sensual immersion in the woods is analyzed in Victor Carl Friesen, "A Tonic of Wildness: Sensuousness in Henry David Thoreau," in *Empire of the Senses: The Sensual Cultural Reader*, ed. David Howes (Oxford; New York: Berg, 2005), 251–64.

8 See Pomarède, *L'École de Barbizon*, esp. 48–53, 144–45, 174–80, on the *sous-bois*.

9 "Pour peindre un pays, il faut le connaître. Moi je connais mon pays, je le peins. Ces sous-bois, c'est chez moi, cette rivière, c'est la Loue, celle-ci le Lison; ces rochers, ce sont ceux d'Ornans et du Puits noir. Allez-y voir, et vous reconnaîtrez tous mes tableaux." Quoted in André Fermigier, *Courbet: Étude biographique et critique* (1971; repr., Geneva: Skira, 1994), 16.

10 Mary Morton and Charlotte Eyerman, *Courbet and the Modern Landscape* (Los Angeles: The J. Paul Getty Museum, 2006), vii, 4.

11 Greg M. Thomas, *Art and Ecology in Nineteenth-Century France: The Landscapes of Théodore Rousseau* (Princeton: Princeton University Press, 2000); Morton and Eyerman, *Courbet and the Modern Landscape*, 67; Jenny Reynaerts, "Der Ästhetik der Polderlandschaft," in *Der weite Blick: Landschaften der Haager Schule aus dem Rijksmuseum*, exh. cat. (Ostfildern: Hatje Canz, 2008), 49–54.

12 Richard Brettell and Scott Schaeffer, eds., *A Day in the Country: Impressionism and the French Landscape*, exh. cat. (New York: Abradale Press, 1990), 299–304; Reynaerts, "Der Ästhetik der Polderlandschaft," 39–49, on the Dutch situation.

13 Rümelin, *Die Verzauberung der Landschaft*, 10.

14 On Marseus van Schrieck, see Douglas R. Hildebrecht, "Otto Marseus van Schrieck (1619/20–1678) and the Nature Piece: Art, Science, Religion, and the Seventeenth-Century Pursuit of Natural Knowledge" (PhD diss., University of Michigan, 2004).

15 Pierre Henri de Valenciennes, *Élémens de perspective pratique, à l'usage des artistes, suivis de reflexions et conseils à un elève sur la peinture et particulierement sur le genre du paysage* (Paris: L'Auteur, 1800). A modern edition of the second part is published by Rumeur des ages (La Rochelle, 2005).

16 Peter Galassi, *Corot in Italy: Open-Air Painting and the Classical-Landscape Tradition* (New Haven: Yale University Press, 1991), 66; see also Bruno Mantura and Geneviève Lacambre, eds., *Pierre-Henri de Valenciennes, 1750–1819*, exh. cat. (Naples: Electa Napoli, 1996).

17 Galassi, *Corot in Italy*, 41–46; Mantura and Lacambre, *Pierre-Henri de Valenciennes*, 27–30; Gary Tinterow, Michael Pantazzi, and Vincent Pomarède, *Corot*, exh. cat. (New York: The Metropolitan Museum of Art, 1996), 11.

18 Carl Gustav Carus, *Nine Letters on Landscape Painting, Written in the Years 1815–1824*, trans. David Britt, with an introduction by Oskar Bätschmann (Los Angeles: Getty Research Institute, 2002).

19 Howoldt and Schneede, *Expedition Kunst*, 9–14.

20 Carus, *Nine Letters*, 94: "Letter II, Enclosure II. On the Effect of Individual Landscape Objects on the Mind."

21 Howoldt and Schneede, *Expedition Kunst*, 16; Hubertus Gassner, *Caspar David Friedrich: Die Erfindung der Romantik*, exh. cat. (Munich: Hirmer, 2006), 35–38, 196–205, 226.

22 David H. Solkin, *Richard Wilson: The Landscape of Reaction*, exh. cat. (London: Tate Gallery, 1982).

23 Mark Evans, *John Constable: Oil Sketches from the Victoria and Albert Museum* (London: V&A Publications; New York: Harry N. Abrams, 2011), 15; Ann Sumner and Greg Smith, eds., *Thomas Jones (1742–1803): An Artist Rediscovered*, exh. cat. (New Haven: Yale University Press in association with National Museums & Galleries of Wales, Cardiff, 2003), esp. 131–63, 251–71.

24 Charles Robert Leslie, *Memoirs of the Life of John Constable*, 3rd ed. (1845; London: Phaidon Edition, 1995), 49, 78.

25 Pomarède, *L'École de Barbizon*, 54–66; Galassi, *Corot in Italy*, 41, 233n1, second part; Evans, *John Constable*, 33–34.

26 Galassi, *Corot in Italy*, 83–130; Anna Ottavi Cavina, ed., *Paysages d'Italie: Les peintres du plein air (1780–1830)*, exh. cat. (Milan: Electa, 2001), passim.

27 Patrick Noon, ed., *Constable to Delacroix: British Art and the French Romantics*, exh. cat. (London: Tate, 2003), 192.

28 Galassi, *Corot in Italy*, 131–43; Tinterow, Pantazzi, and Pomarède, *Corot*, 13–15.

29 Tinterow, Pantazzi, and Pomarède, (*Corot*, 27n116) identifies *Vue prise dans la forêt de Fontainebleau* (National Gallery of Art, Washington DC, R 255) as the first painting Corot exhibited at the 1831 Salon, but makes clear (p. 88n2) that is it uncertain whether the painting was exhibited in 1831 or 1834. For our argument, however, it is not important.

30 Michel Schulman and Marie Bataillès, *Théodore Rousseau 1812–1867: Catalogue raisonné de l'oeuvre peint* (Paris: Éditions de l'Amateur, 1999), passim; Pierre Miquel and Rolande Miquel, *Théodore Rousseau 1812–1867* (Paris: Somogy, 2010), 86–103, 120–29.

31 "Personne n'a compris mieux que lui la loi de la lumière, la magie, et pour ainsi dire la folie du soleil dans les feuilles et les sous-bois." As quoted in Pierre Miquel and Rolande Miquel, *Narcisse Diaz de la Peña (1807–1876)* (Paris: ACR Édition, 2006), 1:74, see also 1:50–63, 2:6–270 (paysages).

32 Peter Bermingham, *American Art in the Barbizon Mood: A Visual History* (Chicago: University of Chicago Press, 1976), 55–68; David Jackson and Per Hedström, eds., *The Peredvizhniki: Pioneers of Russian Painting*, exh. cat. (Stockholm: Nationalmuseum, 2011), 31–33, 242–49.

33 Frouke van Dijke, Doede Hardeman, and Gerrit Willems, eds., *Holland op zijn mooist: Op pad met de Haagse School*, exh. cat. (Dordrecht: Dordrechts Museum; The Hague: Gemeentemuseum, 2015). For these and similar paintings made at De Oorsprong by the Oosterbeek group, see Cornelia Homburg, ed., *Vincent van Gogh: Timeless Country, Modern City* (Milan: Skira, 2010), 50.

34 John Ruskin, "Of the Pathetic Fallacy," in *The Works of John Ruskin*, vol. 5, *Modern Painters III*, ed. Edward Tyas Cook and Alexander Wedderburn (Cambridge: Cambridge University Press, 2010); Robert Rosenblum, *Modern Painting and the Northern Romantic Tradition: Friedrich to Rothko* (London: Thames & Hudson, 1978), 36.

35 Kathleen Adler, ed., *Van Gogh: The Man and the Earth*, exh. cat. (Milan: ORE Cultura, 2014), 43n12, 44.

36 Green, *The Spectacle of Nature,* 167–78.

37 Stuffmann and Schäfer, *Natur und Traum*, 315, 364–66.

38 "Le réel est une partie de l'art; le sentiment complète." Etienne Moreau-Nélaton, *Corot, raconté par lui-même* (Paris: Henri Laurens, 1924), 1:105.

39 Adler, *Man and the Earth*, 41–53.

40 Morton and Eyerman, *Courbet and the Modern Landscape*, 2.

41 "L'oeil le plus prodigieux depuis qu'il ya des peintres." Werner Busch, ed., "Paul Cézanne, Gespräch mit Joachim Gasquet (um 1900)," in *Landschaftsmalerei* (Berlin: Reimer, 1997), 322–23.

42 "L'artiste n'est qu'un réceptable de sensations, un cerveau, un appareil enrégistrateur." Busch, "Paul Cézanne," 321.

43 "Le paysage se reflète, s'humanise, se pense enrégistrateur en moi. Je l'objective, le projette, le fixe sur ma toile." Busch, "Paul Cézanne," 322.

44 Busch, "Paul Cézanne," 323.

45 Vincent van Gogh to Theo van Gogh, 25 June 1889, letter 783.

46 Cornelia Homburg, ed., *Van Gogh: Up Close*, exh. cat. (New Haven: Yale University Press, 2012), 23–33.

47 Ibid., 78–84, on the related treatment of the subject by Monet, Renoir, and Van Gogh.

48 Paul Gauguin, "Noa noa," in *Oviri, écrits d'un sauvage,* ed. Daniel Guérin (Paris: Gallimard, 1974), 99–130.

49 See also Homburg, *Van Gogh: Up Close*, 236–47.

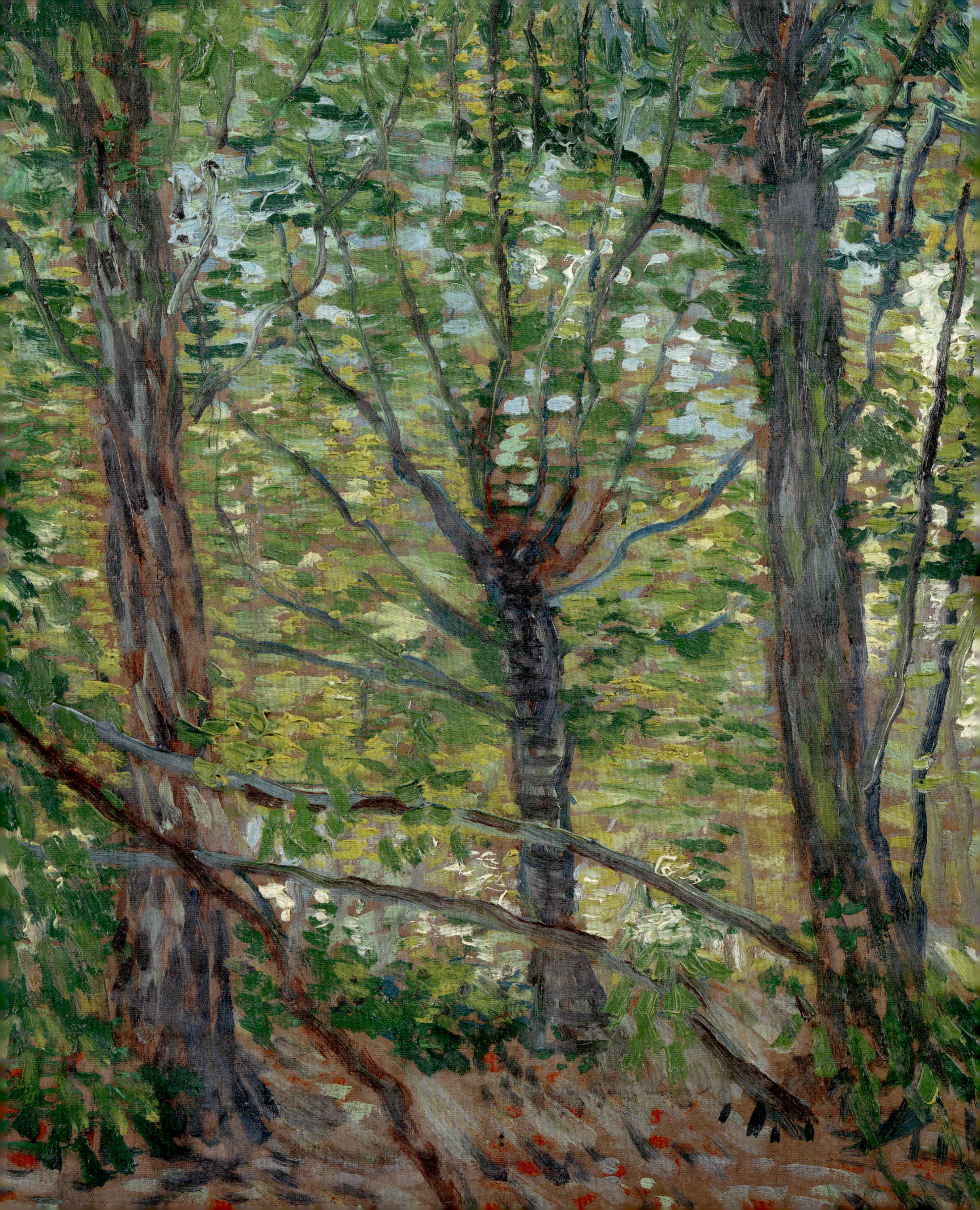

Van Gogh's Nature

Taking Position

Cornelia Homburg

VAN GOGH'S DRAMATIC *UNDERGROWTH WITH TWO FIGURES* (cat. 9) invites the question of how the artist chose his views of nature in order to create a picture. As this exhibition highlights, the *sous-bois* was a recurring theme in Van Gogh's oeuvre, engendered specific models and traditions. In most of his mature work, the artist's depictions of a motif were deliberate, driven by his ambition and interest at a particular time. Throughout his life he was a keen observer and lover of nature, a domain he considered ideal for regaining strength and finding consolation in times of stress or crisis. Yet Van Gogh's choices as an artist were exceedingly selective and very specific, with nature providing the source from which he developed the ideas and direction of his art. While Émile Zola's naturalist dictum that "Art [was] nature seen through a temperament" greatly influenced Van Gogh's thinking,[1] the artist went much further and selected, even manipulated motifs from nature with careful thought and purpose to create a specific expression and craft his own artistic identity.

In the Netherlands, for example, Van Gogh concentrated on representations of nature that enabled him to define himself as a peasant painter. Later on he adjusted his focus by moving to the South of France and sharing the preoccupations of the avant-garde in Paris—especially Japanese art, which he had come to appreciate when living in the French capital. While Van Gogh maintained certain ideas about nature throughout his life, others he reformulated or conceived from scratch to respond to new requirements and challenges that he encountered over the years.

Painter of Peasant Life

In 1884–85, while living with his parents in the village of Nuenen in the southern part of the Netherlands, Van Gogh reached a level of self-confidence that encouraged him to clarify his ambitions as an artist beyond the mastery of painterly skills. He intended to establish himself as a painter of rural life, following in the footsteps of the painters of Barbizon, above all his much-

Vincent van Gogh (1853–1890), *Trees* (cat. 4, detail)

admired model Jean-François Millet (fig. 26). Van Gogh wanted to celebrate the regular and timeless rhythm of the countryside as the basis for his art, as well as for stability in his life:

> Painting and, to my mind, particularly painting peasant life, gives peace of mind, even though one has a lot of scraping along and wretchedness on the *outside* of life. I mean painting is a *home*, . . .
>
> And I was sick of the *boredom* of civilization. It *is* better, one *is* happier if one puts it into effect—but pretty much literally—at least one feels really alive. And it is *something* to be deep in the snow in winter, to be deep in the yellow leaves in the autumn, to be deep in the ripe wheat in the summer, to be deep in the grass in the spring. It is *something* to always be with the mowers and the peasant girls, in summer with the big sky above, in the winter by the black fireplace. And to feel—this has always been so and always will be.[2]

In addition to his deep appreciation of rural life and the empathy he felt for the working classes, Van Gogh was well aware of the enormous success of the Barbizon School and of Millet's fame in particular. Closer to home, he had witnessed the international reputation of Anton Mauve and other members of the Hague School, whose work was inspired by the painters of Fontainebleau, and with whom he had interacted when living in The Hague in 1882–83.[3] He had recognized that their representation of an idyllic countryside that seemed untouched by modern developments, and was characterized by the labors of the fields and the changing seasons, was appreciated by a large public. It became a model through which he could develop his own identity as a painter. Setting his sights in particular on the art market in Paris, where his brother Theo was an art dealer, Van Gogh felt his best chance for success lay in becoming part of this tradition of landscape and peasant painting.

Like Millet, who was portrayed by his biographer as wearing wooden shoes and living among the peasants of Barbizon,[4] Van Gogh did not merely intend to depict rural life in his work, but to immerse himself in his subject by dressing like a worker and seeking out the peasants in their homes. This attitude stood in stark contrast to his own background and living situation. Van Gogh came from a family of clergymen, with uncles who had built successful careers as art dealers or in the navy. He himself was well educated, multilingual, and had lived in England, Belgium, and Paris as part of his training in his younger years. That aspect of his life, however, like views of his village, his family, or the comfortable home that he shared, remained largely unexplored in his paintings.[5]

Despite his awareness of the miserable living conditions of the rural class and the changes to its existence brought about by industrialization, Van Gogh chose to glorify peasant life and emphasize its picturesque aspects.[6] He compared the wretched huts of the laborers with the cozy intimacy of birds' nests,[7] and represented them as a welcoming environment where women tended the garden (see, e.g., *Cottage under the Trees, with a Peasant Woman*, private collection, F 187), a laborer returned home after work (*Cottage with a Man Coming Home*, Soumaya Museum, Mexico City, F 170), and a friendly candle glowed in the window (fig. 27).[8] The artist aimed to infuse his views of nature with a humanizing element and evoke an emotional response in the viewer.[9] Early on he had admired "the lofty quality, the almost religious emotion of Millet," and had declared, "In all of nature, in trees for instance, I see expression and a soul, as it were."[10]

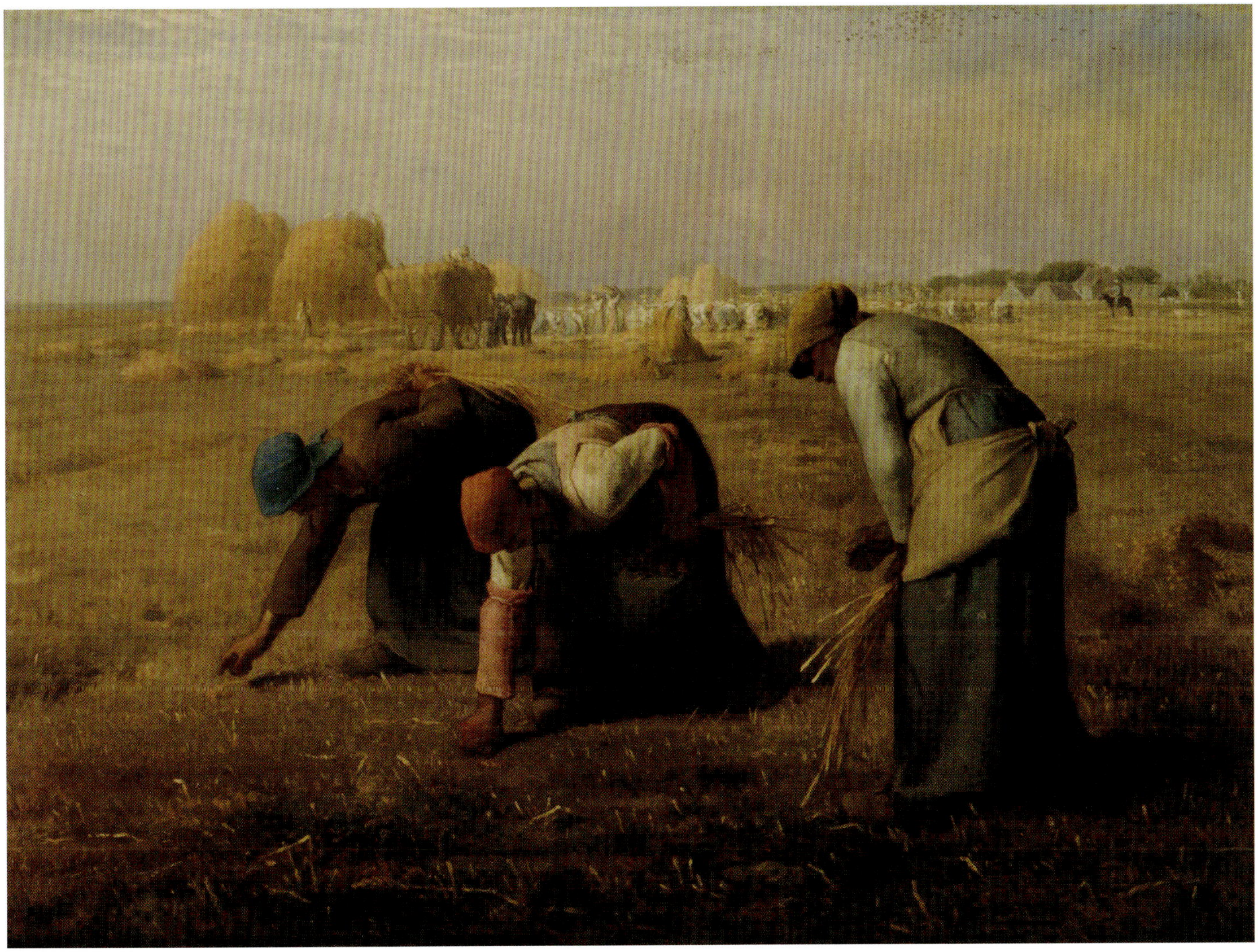

Fig. 26
Jean-François Millet (1814–1875),
The Gleaners, 1857, oil on canvas,
$32^{15}/_{16} \times 43^{11}/_{16}$ in. (83.6 × 111 cm),
Musée d'Orsay, Paris, RF 592

Van Gogh's search for empathy in nature was further amplified by depictions that contained obvious traces of human presence and intervention: fields are worked and gardens tended, and many paintings include figures, sometimes observed, often invented. His tendency to idealize a subject was guided not by his wish to create a perfect image of nature, but rather to instill emotional expression in his work while tying it into established traditions. When Van Gogh sought solutions for such practical matters as the use of color and technique, Millet remained his guiding star. As Van Gogh was living in the countryside, he could find his motifs just beyond his doorstep, but otherwise he had to rely largely on artists' manuals, black-and-white illustrations, and his memory of actual paintings. His reading provided vital inspiration, and Sensier's romanticized biography of Millet, in particular, made a lasting impact.

> How rightly it was said of Millet's figures—*his peasant seems to be painted with the soil he sows!* How accurate and true that is. And how much it comes down to knowing how to make on the palette those colours *that one cannot name* and of which everything fundamentally—actually consists. Perhaps—I dare say *certainly*—the questions of *colours*, and specifically broken—and—neutral—colours, will preoccupy you *once more.*[11]

This reference to Millet's peasants became a much-repeated guideline for Van Gogh's own work and supported his use of earthy colors. Rural life was cast in recognized parameters within which peasants, typified as a class, were rough and primitive, and the countryside was characterized by the changing seasons. The view of laborers ("coarse, flat faces with low foreheads and thick lips, not that sharp look, but full and Millet-like"[12]) in their blue clothes working in the ripe fields could represent the colors of summer,[13] and other hues characterized the rest of the seasons: "The spring is tender green (young wheat) and pink (apple blossom). The autumn is the contrast of the yellow leaves against violet tones. The winter is the snow with the little black silhouettes."[14] Even though Van Gogh spoke of green and pink, yellow and violet, citing the complementary color pairs according to the manuals he read, in his paintings he toned them down, as he could not imagine using pure, "unbroken" color.

Painter of the South

When Van Gogh arrived in Arles in early 1888 after a two-year stay in Paris, his point of view had been transformed and his search for his artistic identity redirected. Paris had not obliterated his love of nature and countryside, but it had changed his frame of reference. In the French capital he had encountered the latest developments in painting and quickly realized that in comparison to the work of the Impressionists and Neo-Impressionists his own oeuvre from the Netherlands looked hopelessly outdated. Van Gogh set out with great determination to acquire a modern vocabulary of brushstroke and color, but he also recognized that he needed a fresh context within which to position his work, and that his much-beloved Millet could not fulfill that role as he had in the past.

In his letters from Arles, the Dutchman defined his artistic position vis-à-vis his Parisian colleagues and friends by establishing specific arguments.[15] While living in the Netherlands, Van Gogh had already known and read about Eugène Delacroix, admiring his work and use of color,

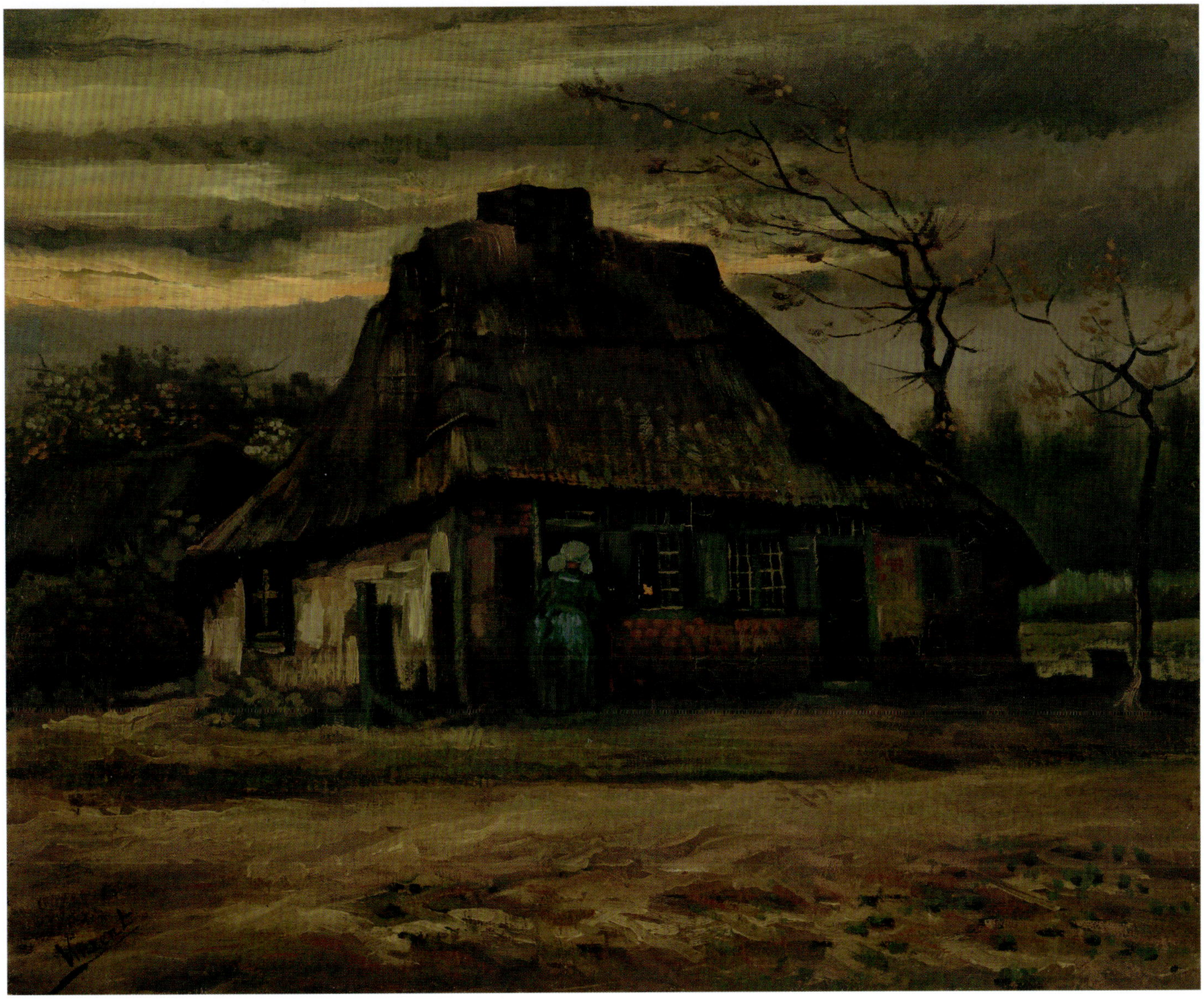

Fig. 27
Vincent van Gogh (1853–1890),
The Cottage, May 1885,
oil on canvas,
25⅞ × 31¼ in. (65.7 × 79.3 cm),
Van Gogh Museum, Amsterdam
(Vincent van Gogh Foundation),
s87V/1962, F 83

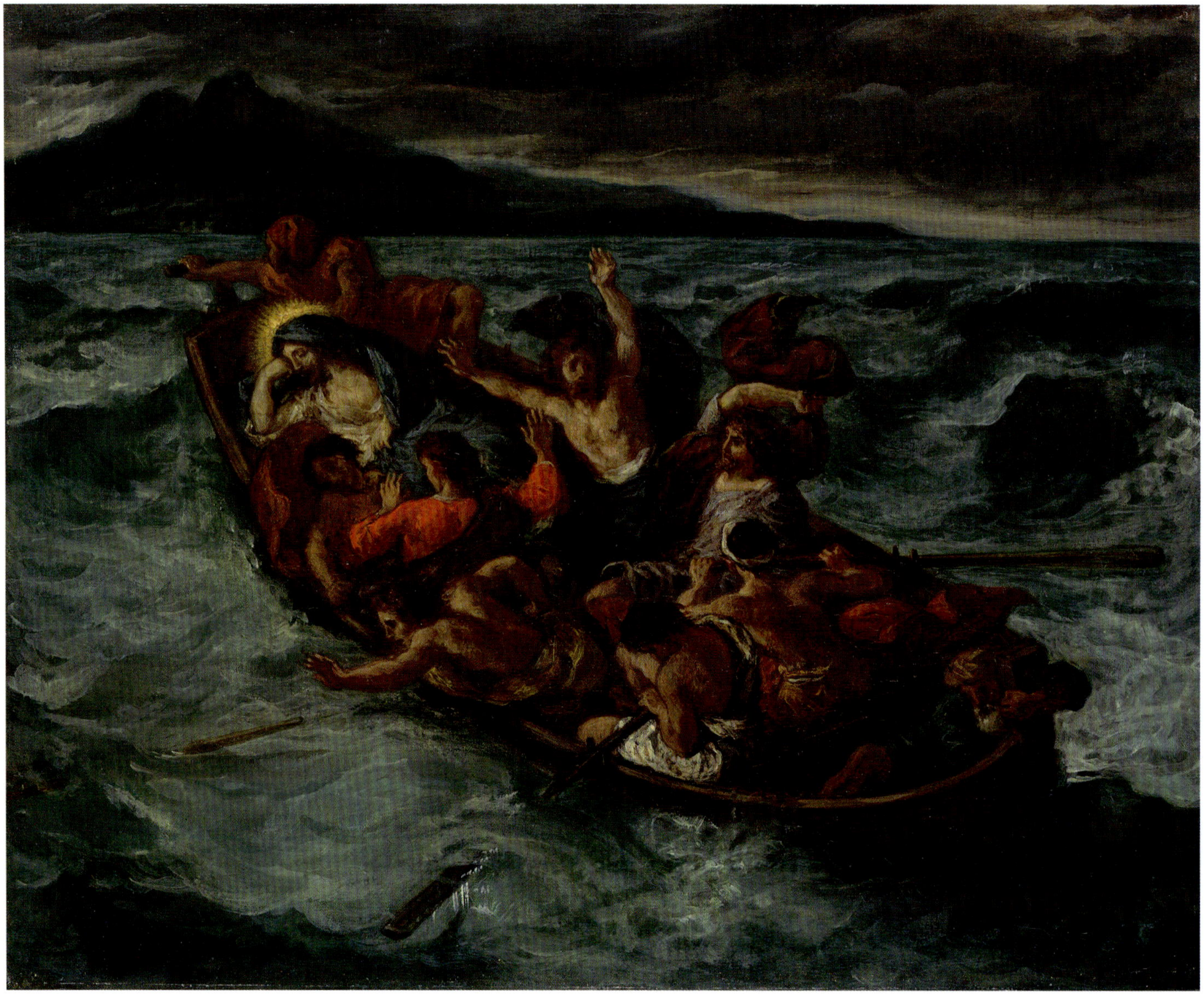

Fig. 28
Eugène Delacroix (1798–1863),
Christ Asleep during the Tempest,
ca. 1853, oil on canvas,
20 × 24 in. (50.8 × 61 cm),
The Metropolitan Museum of
Art, H. O. Havermeyer Collection,
Bequest of Mrs. H. O. Havermeyer,
1929, 29.100.131

but it took the sojourn in Paris, the direct encounter with his art, and discussions with avant-garde painters to grasp Delacroix's full impact on contemporary painting.[16] Because the French master was widely acknowledged as the father of modern art, Van Gogh, more than ever before, felt justified in relying on him as a reference while developing his own palette. Delacroix had traveled to North Africa to experience the intense light of the South, and Van Gogh followed this example by moving to Provence. While the rural surroundings of Arles provided him with the opportunity to depict the countryside and peasant life that in the Netherlands had so impassioned him, he recognized that it now had to be done differently. Like Delacroix, Van Gogh set out to employ color to create emotion in his paintings (fig. 28). He wrote to his brother:

> Yesterday and today I worked on the sower, which has been completely reworked. The sky is yellow and green, the earth purple and orange. There's definitely a painting like that to be made of this splendid subject, and I hope it will be done one day, either by someone else or by me. The question remains this—Christ's boat by Eugène Delacroix and Millet's sower are of entirely different workmanship. Christ's boat—I'm talking about the blue and green sketch with touches of purple and red and a little lemon yellow for the halo, the aureole speaks a symbolic language through colour itself. Millet's sower is colourless *grey*—as are Israëls's paintings too. Can we now paint the sower with colour, with simultaneous contrast between yellow and purple for example (like Delacroix's Apollo ceiling, which is precisely yellow and purple), yes or no? *Yes*—definitely. So do it then![17]

And so he did, growing more and more confident throughout the year that he could actually contribute something new to modern art by pursuing this direction: "I believe that a new *colourist* school will take root in the south, seeing increasingly that those from the north rely more on skill with the brush and the so-called picturesque effect than on the desire to express something through colour itself."[18]

Van Gogh also built on other experiences from Paris, in particular on the great appreciation for Japanese art he had encountered there.[19] He had come to realize how the aesthetic qualities of Japanese woodcut prints had revolutionized modern painting, with their bird's-eye views, dramatic angles, high horizon lines, and flat areas of intense color. All avant-garde artists incorporated some or all of these elements into their work and experimented with these aesthetic possibilities to create new forms of expression. Van Gogh decided to take his move south as an opportunity to cultivate this tendency and identify his work, as well as his persona, with Japan.[20] He declared Arles and its surroundings the equivalent of Japan, thus anchoring his own depictions of the landscape firmly within this premise. Accordingly, he wrote in his first letter from Arles to his friend and colleague Émile Bernard:

> I want to begin by telling you that this part of the world seems to me as beautiful as Japan for the clearness of the atmosphere and the gay colour effects. The stretches of water make patches of a beautiful emerald and a rich blue in the landscapes, as we see it in the Japanese prints. Pale orange sunsets making the fields look blue—glorious yellow suns. However, so far I've hardly seen this part of the world in its usual summer splendour.[21]

Beyond Delacroix's guidance, Van Gogh reasoned that his move to the South connected him intimately to Japan, and as such to the future of modern art. "Look, we love Japanese painting, we've experienced its influence—all the Impressionists have that in common—and we wouldn't go to Japan, in other words, to what is the equivalent of Japan, the south? So I believe that the future of the new art still lies in the south after all."[22]

Having claimed the South as the place to be, Van Gogh argued that he actually experienced landscape differently than in the North and hence was obliged to present it in a new manner. Nature and rural subject matter were now viewed through a lens of Japonisme that enabled him to forge his individuality as an artist. "After some time your vision changes, you see with a more Japanese eye, you feel colour differently. I'm also convinced that it's precisely through a long stay here that I'll bring out my personality. The Japanese draws quickly, very quickly, like a flash of lightning, because his nerves are finer, his feeling simpler."[23] As a result of this change, Van Gogh could write to Bernard a few weeks later: "Have made large pen drawings—*2*—an immense flat expanse of country—seen in bird's-eye view from the top of a hill—vineyards, harvested fields of wheat, all of it multiplied endlessly, streaming away like the surface of a sea towards the horizon bounded by the hillocks of La Crau. It *does* NOT look Japanese, and it's *actually* the most Japanese thing that I've done."[24]

By this time Van Gogh's essential peasant was no longer a figure toiling in the fields painted with the colors of the earth, but a man defined by the intensity of the South. Describing his new image of a peasant, the *Portrait of Patience Escalier* (Norton Simon Museum, California, F 443), he wrote: "But imagining the terrific man I had to do, in the very furnace of harvest time, deep in the south. Hence the oranges, blazing like red-hot iron, hence the old gold tones, glowing in the darkness. Ah, my dear brother—and the good folk will see only caricature in this exaggeration."[25]

From seeking the picturesque and empathy in nature during his earlier years, Van Gogh moved to compose with the willingness to "exaggerate," as he called it, both in color and form. The painter felt the need to justify this excessiveness, but at the same time he was fully aware that he was pushing the boundaries of art to new heights. This attitude highlights the self-confidence that the artist had achieved by this time. In contrast to his years in the Netherlands, during which he aimed to work within a recognized tradition, in Provence Van Gogh wanted to capitalize on his connection with modern art in order to surpass it. In Arles it was no longer Millet but the Japanese artist who could teach him how to interpret nature (fig. 29).

> If we study Japanese art, then we see a man, undoubtedly wise and a philosopher and intelligent, who spends his time—on what?—studying the distance from the earth to the moon?—no; studying Bismarck's politics?—no, he studies a single blade of grass.
>
> But this blade of grass leads him to draw all the plants—then the seasons, the broad features of landscapes, finally animals, and then the human figure. He spends his life like that, and life is too short to do everything.
>
> Just think of that; isn't it almost a new religion that these Japanese teach us, who are so simple and live in nature as if they themselves were flowers?
>
> And we wouldn't be able to study Japanese art, it seems to me, without becoming

much happier and more cheerful, and it makes us return to nature, despite our education and our work in a world of convention.[26]

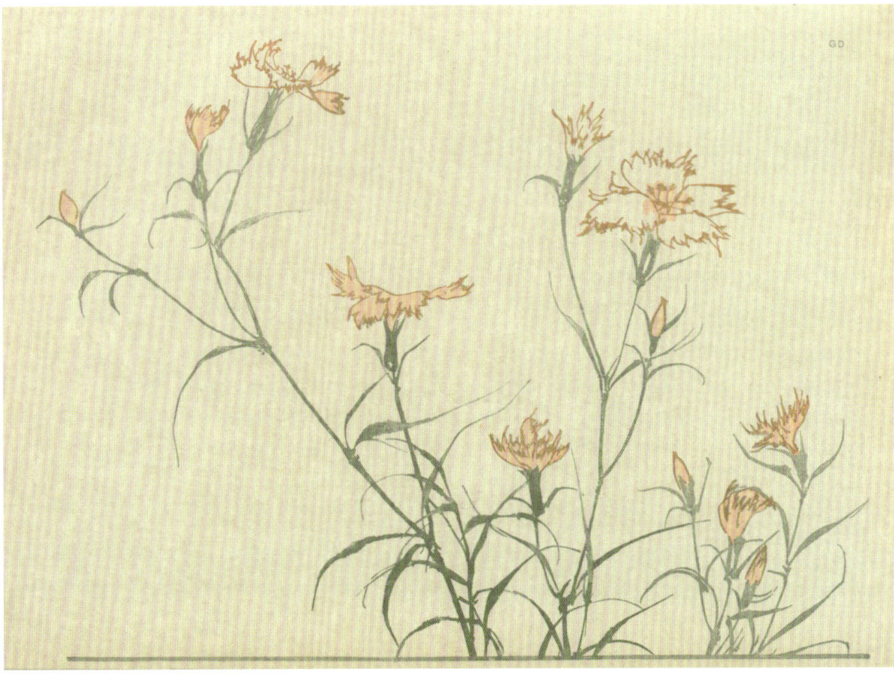

Fig. 29
After Kawamura Bumpo, *Study of Carnations*, 1800, reproduced in *Le Japon Artistique Documents d'Art et d'Industrie*, June 1888, Van Gogh Museum Library, Amsterdam, bvg5372_75b

By taking his cue from the Japanese artists, Van Gogh argued that he was able to return to the fundamentals and find a way to rise above the conventions of life and art—two concerns much discussed among his artist friends in Paris, who all sought to break the molds of tradition and argued for a renewed appreciation of the primitive in art. Van Gogh's study of Japanese art became a guiding principle that had far-reaching consequences for his choices in depicting nature. His close-up views of plants and flowers, as well as the dramatic downward view in his later *sous-bois* compositions, cannot be considered without this new impetus. Paintings such as *Undergrowth* (cat. 7), painted in the Saint-Rémy asylum garden in 1889, and the celebration of spring in *Tree Trunks in the Grass* (cat. 8) the following year, are intimately tied to this approach to nature.[27]

Working in Series

Other motifs, such as the orchards in the South of France, became a focus of Van Gogh's work that has to be examined in the context of this new position. In the spring of 1888 the artist, enchanted by the splendor of the flowering fruit trees at Arles, decided to render their abundance in a group of images.[28] This extensive focus on a specific subject was not new to Van Gogh's manner of working. In Paris, for example, he had painted innumerable floral still lifes to teach himself the use of bright color and modern brushstrokes. In the Netherlands he had expressed the desire to execute at least fifty portraits of peasant heads in his quest to master the genre.[29]

In Arles, however, the decision to present a series of images based on a specific aspect of nature was framed by new references (fig. 30). Now Van Gogh was familiar with the Impressionists' ambition to capture a given motif under changing light and weather conditions. He also had collected Japanese woodcuts with flowering trees, a motif popular in Japanese art,[30] and he greatly admired the Japanese tradition of making series of woodcuts, such as Hokusai's series of Mount Fuji and Hiroshige's views of Edo, both of which were well known and much sought after by collectors.[31] For Van Gogh this concept of creating series fit well within his ambitions, and the link to Japanese art contributed an explicitly modern flavor. As such, the series became an additional element with which to characterize his oeuvre. The painter elaborated on this idea, first in Arles, and later in Saint-Rémy, with spectacular results.

After the initial series of spring 1888, when he had presented the flowering fruit trees in a variety of styles, Van Gogh in early 1889 executed a smaller number of orchards in a firmly Japonist

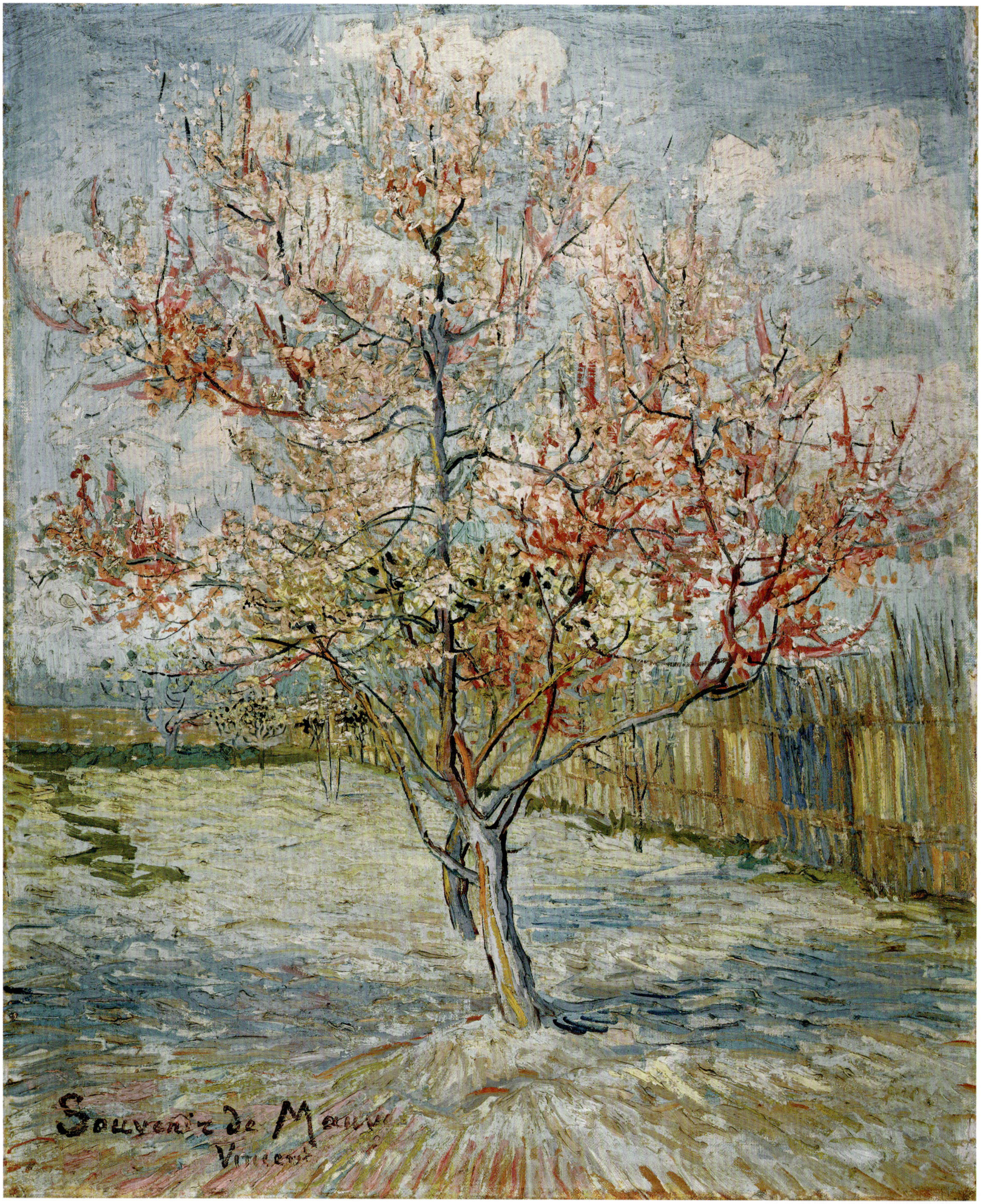
Souvenir de Mauve
Vincent

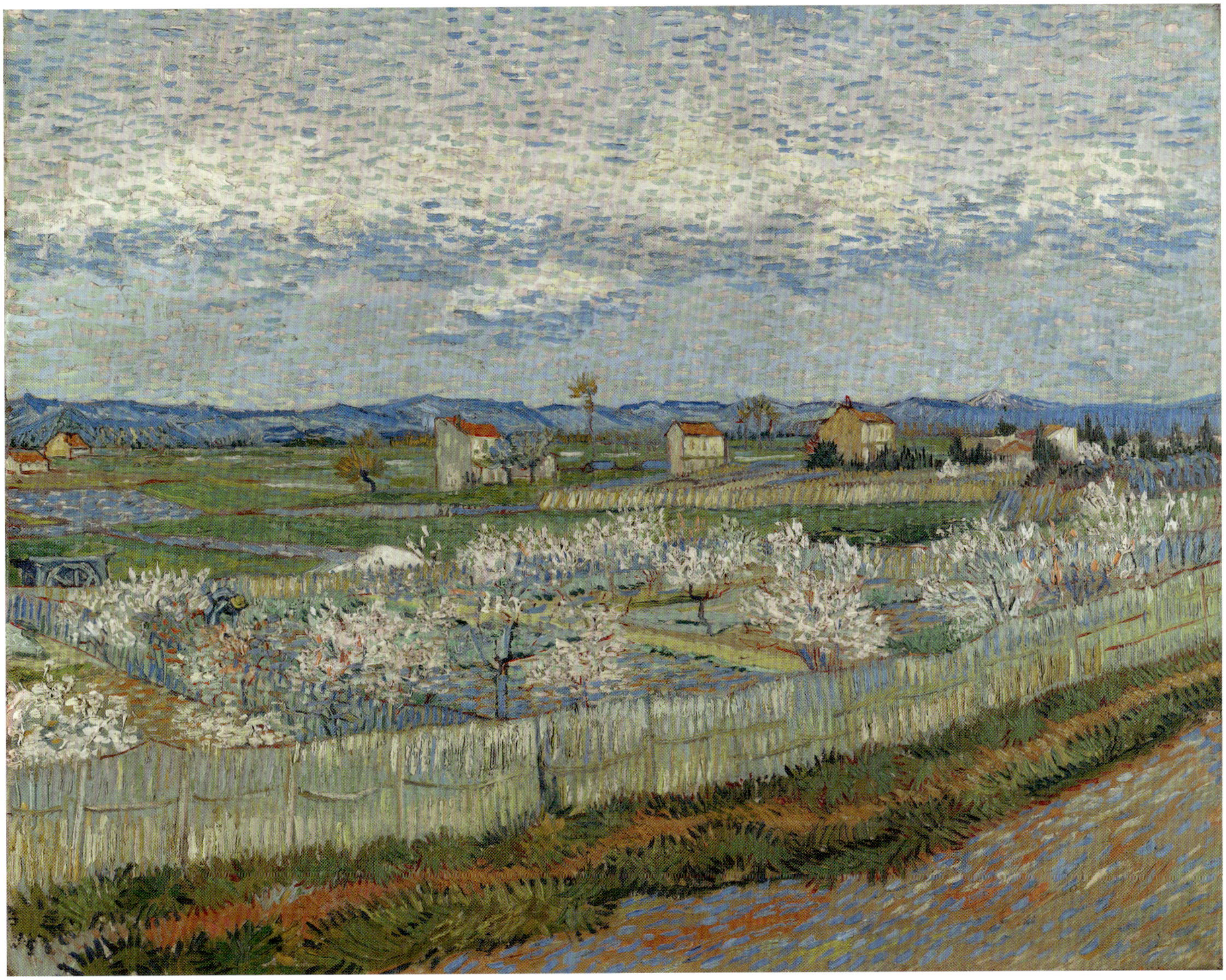

vocabulary.[32] In a letter to the artist Paul Signac, who visited him in Arles at the time, Van Gogh explained how he wanted these orchards to be understood in a Japanese context (fig. 31):

> I've just brought back two studies of orchards. Here's a hasty croquis of them—the largest is a poor green countryside with little cottages, blue line of the Alpilles, white and blue sky. The foreground, enclosures with reed hedges where little peach trees are in blossom—everything there is *small*, the gardens, the fields, the gardens, the trees, even those mountains, as in certain Japanese landscapes, that's why this subject attracted me.[33]

In addition to using the bird's-eye view, Van Gogh argued that the small size of the featured motifs together with the blossoming trees constituted an approach *a la Japonaise*. He introduced this combination of subject matter and technique in each of his compositions in that group.

In the fall of that same year Van Gogh returned to painting series of orchards. This time he chose the olive groves that were a prominent feature of the landscape around Saint-Rémy:

Fig. 30 (opposite)
Vincent van Gogh (1853–1890), *Pink Peach Trees (Souvenir de Mauve)*, March 1888, oil on canvas, 28¾ × 23⁷⁄₁₆ in. (73 × 59.5 cm), Collection Kröller-Müller Museum, Otterlo, KM 108.317, F 394

Fig. 31 (above)
Vincent van Gogh (1853–1890), *Peach Trees in Blossom*, 1889, oil on canvas, 25⁹⁄₁₆ × 31⅞ in. (65 × 81 cm), The Courtauld Gallery, London, The Samuel Courtauld Trust, P.1932.SC.176, F 514

The olive trees are very characteristic, and I'm struggling to capture that. It's silver, sometimes more blue, sometimes greenish, bronzed, whitening on ground that is yellow, pink, purplish or orangeish to dull red ochre. But very difficult, very difficult. But that suits me and attracts me to work fully in gold or silver. And one day perhaps I'll do a personal impression of it, the way the sunflowers are for yellows.[34]

Fig. 32
Vincent van Gogh (1853–1890), *Olive Grove with Two Olive Pickers*, December 1889, oil on canvas, 28⅞ × 36$\frac{5}{16}$ in. (73.3 × 92.2 cm), Collection Kröller-Müller Museum, Otterlo, KM 1040.796, F 587

Like the first series of fruit trees in Arles, the olive orchards offered a range of stylistic interpretations, thus enticing Van Gogh to present the manifold aspects of the motif in a series of images (fig. 32). Even more than the fruit orchards, the olive trees were typical of Provence and constituted—together with the cypresses—a quintessential motif of the South, and as such provided an association the artist considered important for his artistic identity.[35]

The olive tree also presented ideal subject matter in terms of content. In an 1882 letter to Theo, Vincent argued that trees had a soul (see p. 60). Later, during the time he lived in France, the

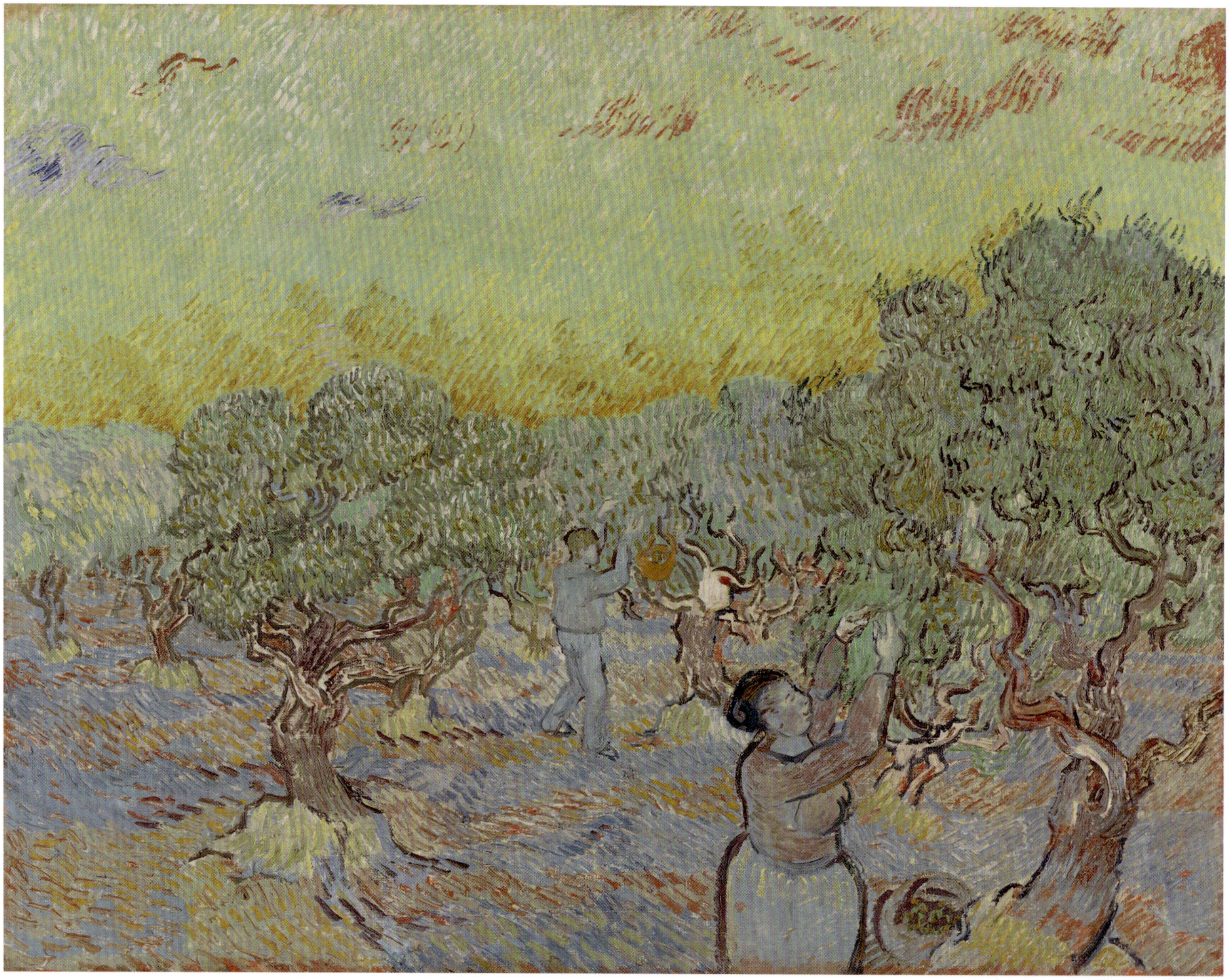

symbolic content of a painting had become increasingly relevant for him. During the late 1880s this topic was hotly debated and promoted in avant-garde circles in Paris, and Van Gogh participated in such discussions through his ongoing exchange of letters with Paul Gauguin and Émile Bernard. In the fall of 1889 they told him about their forays into painting biblical subject matter and Gauguin sent him a sketch of his *Self-Portrait as Christ in the Garden of Olives* (fig. 33).[36] Van Gogh objected to such symbolic inventions or abstractions. Instead he proposed what he saw as a better alternative: by painting olive orchards in his own manner he could evoke the emotional impact of the biblical Garden of Olives and Christ's suffering, but remain firmly anchored in nature.[37]

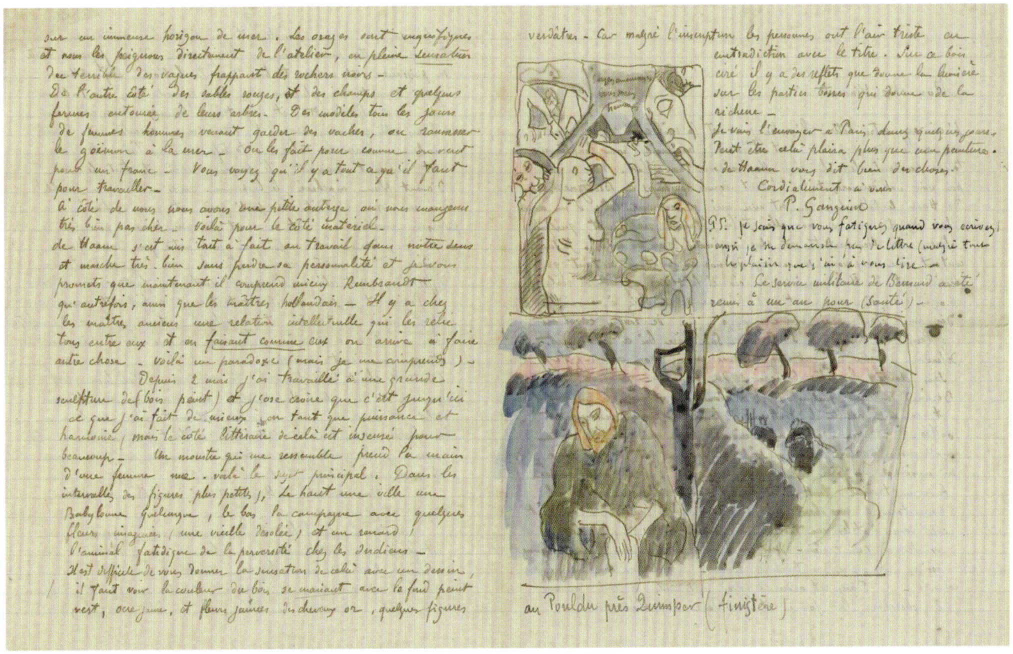
sur un immense horizon de mer. Les orages sont magnifiques et nous les peignons directement de l'atelier, en pleine sensation du terrible des vagues frappant des rochers noirs –
De l'autre côté des sables rouges, et des champs et quelques fermes entourées de leurs arbres. Des modèles tous les jours de femmes hommes venant garder des vaches, ou ramasser le goëmon à la mer – On les fait poser comme on veut pour un franc – Vous voyez qu'il y a tout ce qu'il faut pour travailler –
À côté de nous nous avons une petite auberge où nous mangeons très bien pas cher – Voilà pour le côté matériel –
de Haan s'est mis tout à fait au travail dans notre sens et marche très bien sans perdre sa personnalité et je vous promets que maintenant il comprend mieux Rembrandt qu'autrefois, ainsi que les maîtres hollandais – Il y a chez les maîtres anciens une relation intellectuelle qui les relie tous entre eux et en faisant comme eux on arrive à faire autre chose – Voilà un paradoxe (mais je me comprends) –
Depuis 2 mois j'ai travaillé à une grande sculpture (bois peint) et j'ose croire que c'est jusqu'ici ce que j'ai fait de mieux en tant que puissance et harmonie, mais le côté littéraire de cela est inconnu pour beaucoup – Un monstre qui me ressemble prend la main d'une femme nue – voilà le sujet principal. Dans les intervalles des figures plus petites, le haut une ville une Babylone quelconque, le bas la campagne avec quelques fleurs imaginées (une vieille désolée) et un renard l'animal fatidique de la perversité chez les Indiens –
Il est difficile de vous donner la sensation de cela avec un dessin, il faut voir la couleur du bois se mariant avec le fond peint vert, ocre jaune, et fleurs jaunes, des cheveux or, quelques figures verdâtres – Car malgré l'inscription les personnes ont l'air triste en contradiction avec le titre. Sur ce bois ciré il y a des reflets que donne la lumière sur les parties bosses qui donne de la richesse –
Je vais l'envoyer à Paris dans quelques jours. Peut être cela plaira plus que ma peinture.
de Haan vous dit bien des choses.
Cordialement à vous
P. Gauguin
P.S. je sais que vous fatiguez quand vous écrivez, aussi je ne demande pas de lettre (malgré tout le plaisir que j'ai à vous lire) –
Le service militaire de Bernard a été remis à un an pour (santé) –
au Pouldu près Quimper (Finistère)

Fig. 33
Paul Gauguin to Vincent van Gogh with sketch of *Self-Portrait as Christ in the Garden of Olives*, Le Pouldu, between about 10 and 13 November 1889, pen and ink on paper, 10⅝ × 16½ in. (27 × 41.9 cm), Van Gogh Museum, Amsterdam (Vincent van Gogh Foundation), b866V/1962

Composing Nature

By the late 1880s Van Gogh no longer claimed that he needed to rely on nature as his only model. Even if he argued that nature had to be the starting point of his pictures, he no longer stuck strictly to what he saw in front of him, and he developed other means to evoke the suggestive impact of nature.

The two-month-long collaboration of Van Gogh and Gauguin in the fall of 1888 had generated intense discussions and vivid competition between the two artists. It had also highlighted a fundamental difference in the way in which they used nature as inspiration for their painting. While Gauguin believed he needed to "dream before nature" to arrive at the synthesis he intended to express on canvas,[38] Van Gogh argued that he required nature as a model in order to create a picture. While he wanted to interpret what he saw, at that time he found painting from memory difficult. Nevertheless, these discussions with Gauguin, in addition to exchanges with other colleagues, had a lasting impact on his work in 1889 and 1890.

During the summer of 1888 Van Gogh already had created some compositions in which he had adjusted observed reality to emphasize a specific point of view, such as the contrast between nature and city.[39] Now, under the influence of Gauguin, he painted *Memory of the Garden* (The State Hermitage Museum, St. Petersburg, F 496), in which he referred to earlier compositions from the Netherlands and refashioned earlier figures and the shapes of his parents' garden. The painting gave him a lot of trouble and in the end he felt dissatisfied with the result.[40]

Over the course of 1889, however, Van Gogh began to compose views of nature more freely. His interest in the detailed study of an individual plant from close by led to a number of spectacular paintings in the summer of that year. For at least one of them, *Giant Peacock Moth* (fig. 34), we know that he created a composition of his own invention and are able to reconstruct the process. Van Gogh reported to Theo that he had admired a moth in the asylum garden at Saint-Rémy, but was hesitant to kill it in order to paint it.[41] Instead, he made a detailed drawing, which he transferred to canvas. He then created a context that was inspired by another large drawing representing flowers (*Arums*, Van Gogh Museum, Amsterdam, F 1613). While Van Gogh had found the plants in the garden, he introduced a striped background that most likely referred to Japanese *crepons*, prints on wrinkled paper that he admired. The resulting painting is a small canvas of extraordinary expressiveness in which the insect is presented against a profusion of flowers and berries with a striped backdrop.[42] This work highlights how deliberately Van Gogh selected his subject matter and the manner he felt was most effective in portraying it.

The most famous example of the painter's construction of a landscape is *Starry Night* (Museum of Modern Art, New York, F 612), in which Van Gogh combined motifs from the North, such as the church steeple, with imagery from the South, like the cypresses. *Mountains at Saint-Rémy* (fig. 35), painted the same summer, is based in part on observation of nature and in part on invention. In September 1889 Van Gogh wrote to his brother that he was pleased with the effect of this painting and explained once more his inspiration for executing it.

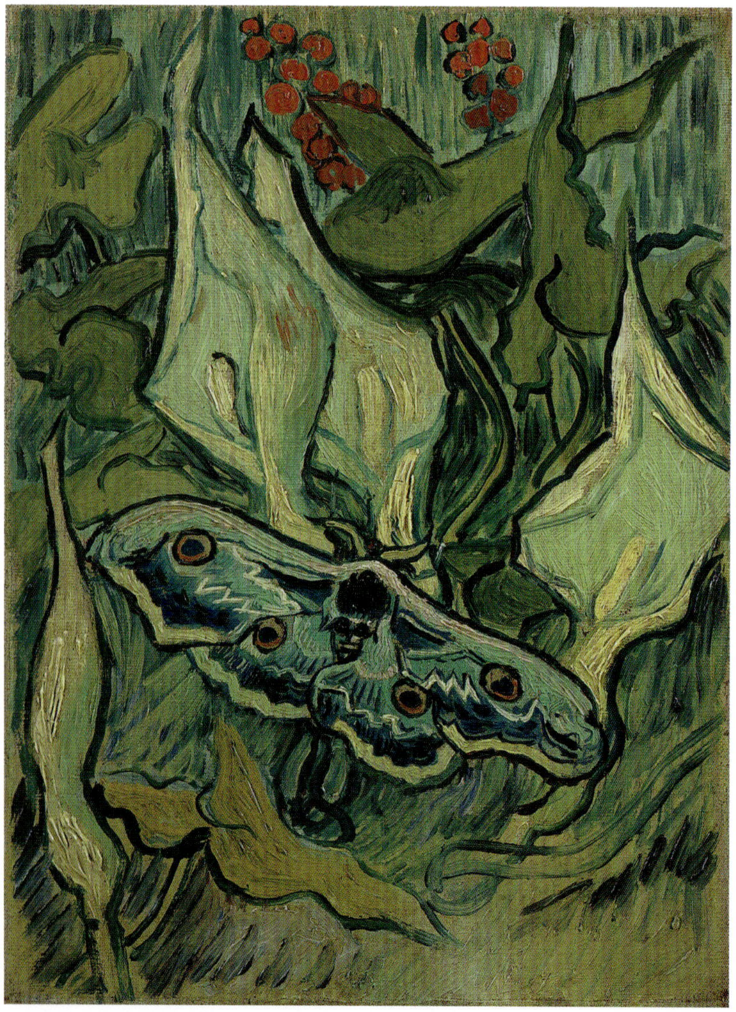

Fig. 34
Vincent van Gogh (1853–1890), *Giant Peacock Moth*, May–June 1889, oil on canvas, 13 3/16 × 9 5/8 in. (33.5 × 24.5 cm), Van Gogh Museum, Amsterdam (Vincent van Gogh Foundation), s189V/1962, F 610

> People will tell me that mountains aren't like that, and that there are black contours as wide as a finger. But anyway it seemed to me that it expressed the passage in Rod's book—one of the very rare passages of his in which I find something good—on a lost land of dark mountains in which one noticed the darkish huts of goatherds, where sunflowers bloomed.[43]

The exaggerated outlines of the Alpilles mountains near Saint-Rémy represented the painter's personal interpretation of what he could see and study, while the hut and sunflowers were inspired by *Le sens de la vie* (1889), a novel by the Swiss author Édouard Rod.[44] With this text as impulse, both the cottage and the flowers hark back to favorite subject matter: the little homes of the peasants Van Gogh had portrayed so often in the Netherlands, and the sunflowers that had become an important motif, culminating in the 1888 still lifes. In a letter to Gauguin he had claimed the sunflowers were intimately identified with his oeuvre.[45] Here, once more, Van Gogh introduced imagery into his composition that could be recognized as characterizing his identity as a painter.

During a long bout of illness in the early spring of 1890, in the asylum of Saint-Rémy, Van Gogh reminisced about his life and work in the North and painted from memory: "And while

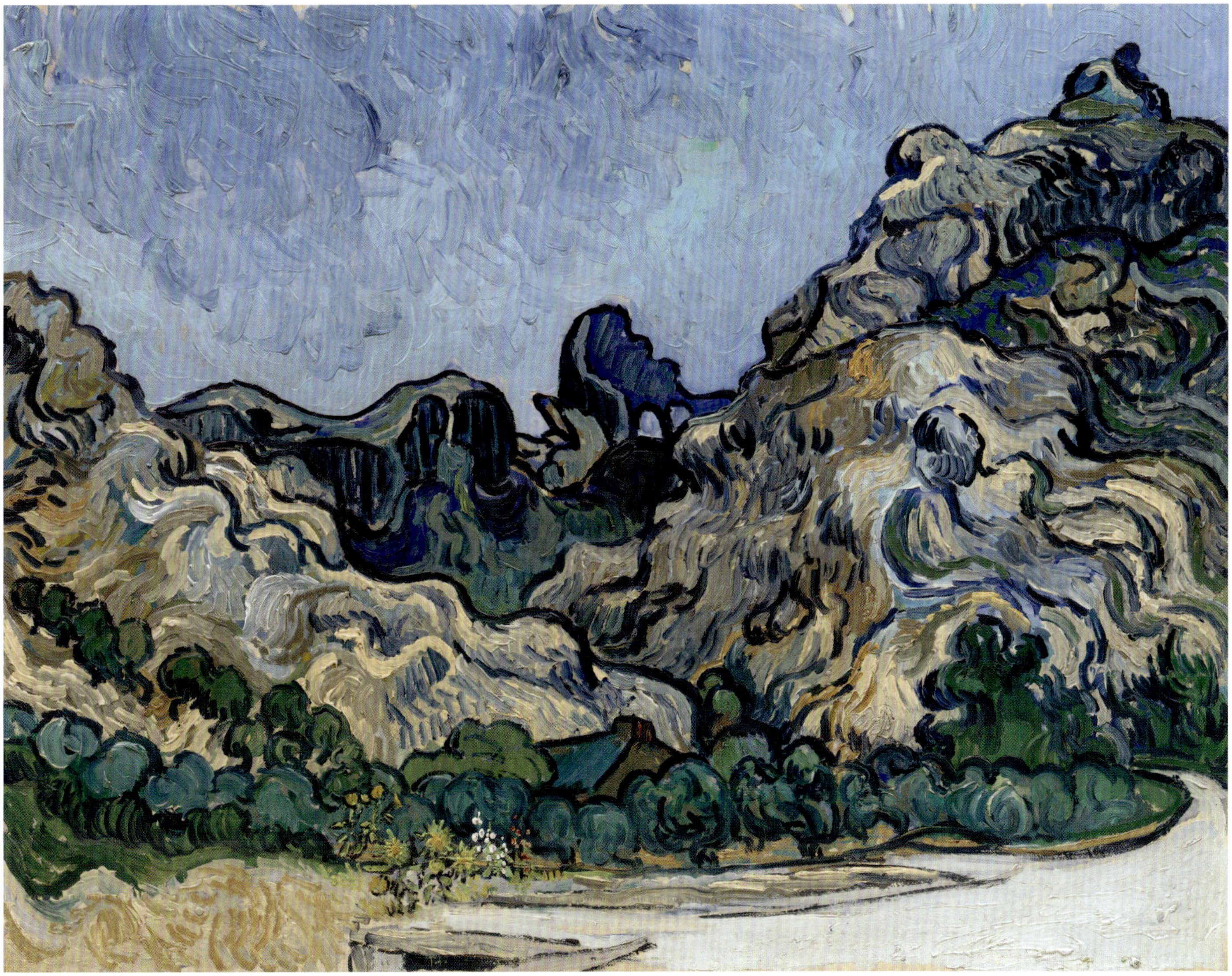

my illness was at its worst, I still painted, among other things a reminiscence of Brabant, cottages with mossy roofs and beech hedges on an autumn evening with a stormy sky, the sun setting red in reddish clouds. And a turnip field with women lifting turnips in the snow."[46] These paintings would have had a consoling function in Van Gogh's times of distress, but they also testified to the artist's attempt to consolidate his most recent oeuvre from the South with the earlier one from the North. The subject matter was executed in intense color and exaggerated brushwork, while the huts recalled those from his childhood, and the women lifting turnips were modeled on Millet's figures.

One of the very last paintings from Saint-Rémy, *Country Road in Provence at Night* (Kröller-Müller Museum, Otterlo, F 683), was an invention. Van Gogh intended it as a memory of Provence, a farewell, but also a résumé of his time there in which he brought together those elements that defined his artistic identity: intense color contrast, exaggerated shapes, the cottage, and the human figures, workers going home. In a letter to Gauguin he called it "reminiscences of Provence, . . . a rather deliberate and studied summary."[47] While Van Gogh emphasized his intention to characterize the South with this work, the imagery—in particular the hut—is also related to the North, to which he returned in May 1890.

Fig. 35
Vincent van Gogh (1853–1890), *Mountains at Saint-Rémy*, 1889, oil on canvas, 28¼ × 35¾ in. (71.8 × 90.8 cm), The Solomon R. Guggenheim Museum, Thannhauser Collection, Gift of Justin K. Thannhauser, 1978, F 622

The introduction of a human element remained vital for Van Gogh and allowed him to underscore the emotional charge of his compositions, and he found ever more effective ways to do so. He invented the lovers in *Couple among Olive Trees* (Museu de Arte de São Paulo, Assis Chateaubriand, F 704), in which the red-headed man was most likely intended as a self-portrait. The couple in *Undergrowth with Two Figures* (cat. 9) was also probably imagined, intended to underscore the melancholic atmosphere of the painting.

While Van Gogh never lost his admiration for Millet and his colleagues, during his time in France he began to realize that if he wanted to play a role on the stage of modern art, the great tradition of Barbizon landscape painting could only represent a limited part of his artistic identity. Motifs from nature would reappear throughout Van Gogh's oeuvre, but they were characterized differently via intense—often excessive—color, dramatic viewpoints, and expressive brushstroke. New references, in particular to Japanese art, began to play a vital role. Such elements and concepts became a major part of the vocabulary with which Van Gogh hoped to build a place for himself among his contemporaries. The severe attacks of illness that the artist suffered during the last years of his life often led him to doubt and despair, but they did not thwart his ambition to establish his place as an avant-garde painter. Van Gogh's interpretations of nature were intimately linked to this motivation.

Notes

1 For Van Gogh's literary inspiration, see Judy Sund, *True to Temperament: Van Gogh and French Naturalist Literature* (Cambridge: Cambridge University Press, 1992); Wouter van der Veen, *Van Gogh, a Literary Mind: Literature in the Correspondence of Vincent van Gogh* (Zwolle: Waanders; Amsterdam: Van Gogh Museum, 2009).

2 Vincent van Gogh to Theo van Gogh, 22 June 1885, letter 509.

3 Jenny Reynaerts, "On the Edge: Van Gogh's Early Ideas on City and Countryside," in *Vincent van Gogh: Timeless Country—Modern City,* ed. Cornelia Homburg (Rome: Complesso Monumentale des Vittoriano; Milan: Skira, 2010), 37–53; see also the essays by Jenny Reynaerts and Simon Kelly in this volume.

4 Alfred Sensier and Paul Mantz, *La vie et l'oeuvre de Jean-François Millet* (Paris: A. Quantin, 1881). Van Gogh had read Alfred Sensier's romanticized biography of Millet in 1882 with deep interest. The book served as a reference for him on many levels. For Van Gogh's admiration for Millet, see Louis van Tilborgh et al., eds., *Van Gogh & Millet* (Amsterdam: Van Gogh Museum, 1988; Paris: Musée d'Orsay, 1998).

5 See the paintings of church (F 25), parsonage (F 182), and garden (F 185, F 194). Van Gogh executed a small number of compositions of the parsonage garden, but these were generally not intended to capture the garden per se, instead serving to highlight the changing of the seasons or as a backdrop for depictions of an old church tower from a distance.

6 Van Gogh wrote earlier: "I imagine it as being like North Brabant *when I was young*, about 20 years ago. I remember as a boy seeing the heath and the small farmhouses, the looms and the spinning wheels exactly as I see them now in drawings by Mauve and Ter Meulen. The part of Brabant I know well has since changed enormously through land reclamation and industry. It isn't without a certain nostalgia that I now see a new tavern with a red tiled roof at many places where I remember seeing a wattle-and-daub hut with a moss-covered, thatched roof. Since then have come sugar-beet factories, railways, heath reclamations, &c., which are much less picturesque." Vincent van Gogh to Anthon van Rappard, 13 August 1882, letter 256.

See also Evert van Uitert et al., *Van Gogh in Brabant: Schilderijen en tekeningen uit Etten en Nuenen* (Zwolle: Waanders, 1987); Carol Zemel, *Van Gogh's Progress: Utopia, Modernity, and Late Nineteenth Century Art* (Berkeley: University of California Press, 1997), chap. 2; and Carol Zemel, "The 'Spook' in the Machine: Van Gogh's Pictures of Weavers in Brabant," *Art Bulletin* 67 (March 1985): 123–37.

7 ". . . those *human* nests, those cottages on the heath and their inhabitants." Vincent van Gogh to Theo van Gogh, 4 October 1885, letter 533.

8 *The Cottage* (fig. 27, F 83) was the painting of this type that he considered most successful and shows such a hut in the glow of evening, providing a warm and peaceful atmosphere. He gave it a French title, *La chaumière*, and sent it to Theo in Paris with the hope of selling it on the art market.

9 See, e.g., Sund, *True to Temperament*, 64ff.; see also Chris Stolwijk, "Van Gogh's Nature," in *Vincent's Choice: The Musée Imaginaire of Van Gogh*, ed. Chris Stolwijk, Sjraar van Heugten, Leo Jansen, and Andreas Blühm (Amsterdam: Van Gogh Museum, 2003).

10 Vincent van Gogh to Theo van Gogh, 10 December 1882, letter 292.

11 Vincent van Gogh to Theo van Gogh, 21 April 1885, letter 495.

12 Vincent van Gogh to Theo van Gogh, 2 July 1884, letter 451.

13 Ibid.: ". . . one isn't at liberty to depart from the colours of the costume, since the effect lies in the analogy of the broken indigo tone and the

broken cobalt tone, heightened by the mysterious elements of orange in the ruddy bronze of the wheat. It would be something that expresses *Summer* well—in my view summer isn't easy to express. Usually, or often at least, a summery effect is either impossible or ugly that's my feeling, at least—it's offset by the twilights, though. But I mean it isn't easy to find the effect of a summer sun that's as lush and as simple and as pleasant to look at as the characteristic effects of the other seasons."

14 Ibid.

15 Given the limited scope of this essay, I have chosen to focus on only two aspects that are particularly relevant in the context of this project. Van Gogh composed his identity via several concepts and models.

16 Van Gogh had seen Delacroix's work in Paris in 1875 but not with the eyes of an artist.

17 Vincent van Gogh to Theo van Gogh, 28 June 1888, letter 634.

18 Vincent van Gogh to Theo van Gogh, 17 October 1888, letter 707.

19 For the interest in Japanese art in France, see, among others, Galeries Nationales du Grand Palais, *Le Japonisme* (Paris: Ministère de la Culture et de la Communication, Editions de la Réunion des Musées Nationaux; Tokyo: National Museum of Western Art, 1988), and most recently, Sandra Gianfreda et al., eds., *Monet, Gauguin, Van Gogh . . . : Inspiration Japan* (Göttingen: Edition Folkwang/Steidl, 2014).

20 For Van Gogh's fascination with Japan, see in particular Tsukasa Kōdera, *Vincent van Gogh: Christianity versus Nature* (Amsterdam; Philadelphia: John Benjamins, 1990), and Kōdera, "Van Gogh's Utopian Japonisme," in *Catalogue of the Van Gogh Museum's Collection of Japanese Prints*, ed. Charlotte van Rappard-Boon (Zwolle: Waanders, 1991), 11–45; Elizabeth C. Childs, "Seeking the Studio of the South: Van Gogh, Gauguin, and Avant-Garde Identity," in *Vincent van Gogh and the Painters of the Petit Boulevard*, ed. Cornelia Homburg (Saint Louis: Saint Louis Art Museum in association with Rizzoli, 2001), 113–58. In 2017/18 a major exhibition in Japan and the Netherlands will be dedicated to Van Gogh's relationship with Japan. Curators and authors of this catalogue are Nienke Bakker, Cornelia Homburg, Tsukasa Kōdera, and Louis van Tilborgh.

21 Vincent van Gogh to Émile Bernard, 18 March 1888, letter 587.

22 Vincent van Gogh to Theo van Gogh, 5 June 1888, letter 620.

23 Ibid.

24 Vincent van Gogh to Émile Bernard, 15 July 1888, letter 641. Van Gogh is referring to the drawings *La Crau Seen from Montmajour* (F 1420) and *Landscape near Montmajour with a Train* (F 1424). Compare also Colta Ives, "A Visit to the Sea," in *Vincent van Gogh: The Drawings*, by Colta Ives et al., exh. cat. (New York: The Metropolitan Museum of Art; Amsterdam: Van Gogh Museum, 2005), 165.

25 Vincent van Gogh to Theo van Gogh, 18 August 1888, letter 663.

26 Vincent van Gogh to Theo van Gogh, 24 September 1888, letter 686. This characterization, which Van Gogh distilled largely from his readings about Japanese art, had a fundamental impact on his views of nature. This particular quote is most likely inspired by his reading of Siegfried Bing's "Programme," *Le Japon Artistique* 1 (May 1888), and earlier, "Le caractère du Japonais," by Tadamasa Hayashi in *Paris Illustré* (May 1886). For these sources, see also Kōdera, *Christianity versus Nature*.

27 Cornelia Homburg, ed., *Van Gogh: Up Close*, exh. cat. (Ottawa: National Gallery of Canada; Philadelphia: Philadelphia Museum of Art; New Haven: Yale University Press, 2012).

28 Compare Van Gogh's enthusiastic letters of March and April 1888.

29 This was a plan he did not fully complete.

30 See also Janet A. Walker, "Van Gogh, Collector of 'Japan,'" *Comparatist* 32 (May 2008): 82–114.

31 See, e.g., Hokusai, *Thirty-Six Views of Mount Fuji (Fugaku sanjûrokkei)*, and Hiroshige, *One Hundred Famous Views of Edo (Meisho Yedo Hiakkei)*.

32 See, e.g., F 514, F 515, F 516, and F 575. This time there were fewer paintings, as Van Gogh's time had been restricted due to repeated stays in hospital.

33 Vincent van Gogh to Paul Signac, 10 April 1889, letter 756.

34 Vincent van Gogh to Theo van Gogh, 28 September 1889, letter 806.

35 See Vojtěch Jirat-Wasiutyński, "Vincent van Gogh's Paintings of Olive Trees and Cypresses from St.-Rémy," *Art Bulletin* 75 (December 1993): 647–70; Cornelia Homburg, "Vincent van Gogh's Avant-Garde Strategies," in Homburg, *Painters of the Petit Boulevard*, 21–56.

36 Gauguin sent a sketch of his self-portrait as *Christ in the Garden of Olives*, 1889 (Norton Museum of Art, West Palm Beach, Florida, W326); Paul Gauguin to Vincent van Gogh, between about 10 and 13 November 1889, letter 817.

37 Vincent van Gogh to Theo van Gogh, 19 November 1889, letter 820.

38 Paul Gauguin to Émile Schuffenecker, 14 August 1888, letter 159 in Victor Merlhès, *Paul Gauguin et Vincent Van Gogh, 1887–88: Lettres retrouvées, sources ignores* (Taravao: Avant et après, 1989).

39 For an extensive discussion of the particular work, see Roland Dorn, "Vincent van Gogh: Soir d'été," in *Texte zu Werken im Kunstmuseum Winterthur*, ed. Dieter Schwarz (Düsseldorf: Richter, 1999), 11–41. See also Cornelia Homburg, "Imaging City and Country," in Homburg, *Timeless Country—Modern City*, 19–35.

40 For a detailed discussion of this picture, see Douglas Druick and Peter Zegers, eds., *Van Gogh and Gauguin: The Studio of the South*, exh. cat. (Chicago: The Art Institute of Chicago; New York: Thames & Hudson, 2001), 202ff.

41 Vincent van Gogh to Theo van Gogh, 23 May 1889, letter 776.

42 See also the analysis in Marije Vellekoop and Roelie Zwikker, *Vincent van Gogh Drawings*, vol. 4, *Arles, Saint-Rémy & Auvers-sur-Oise, 1888–1890* (Amsterdam: Van Gogh Museum, 2007), part I, 182ff. and 195ff.; and Cornelia Homburg, "Nature So Close," in Homburg, *Van Gogh: Up Close*, 19ff.

43 Vincent van Gogh to Theo van Gogh, 20 September 1889, letter 805.

44 See, among others, Anabelle Kienle on this painting in Homburg, *Timeless Country—Modern City*, 265.

45 Vincent van Gogh to Paul Gauguin, 21 January 1889, letter 739.

46 Vincent van Gogh to Anna van Gogh-Carbentus and Willemien van Gogh, 29 April 1890, letter 864. There are three paintings of cottages at sunset (*Reminiscence of Brabant*), F 673, F 674, and F 675. The painting of the field with women lifting turnips is F 695.

47 Vincent van Gogh to Paul Gauguin, 17 June 1890, letter draft RM 20.

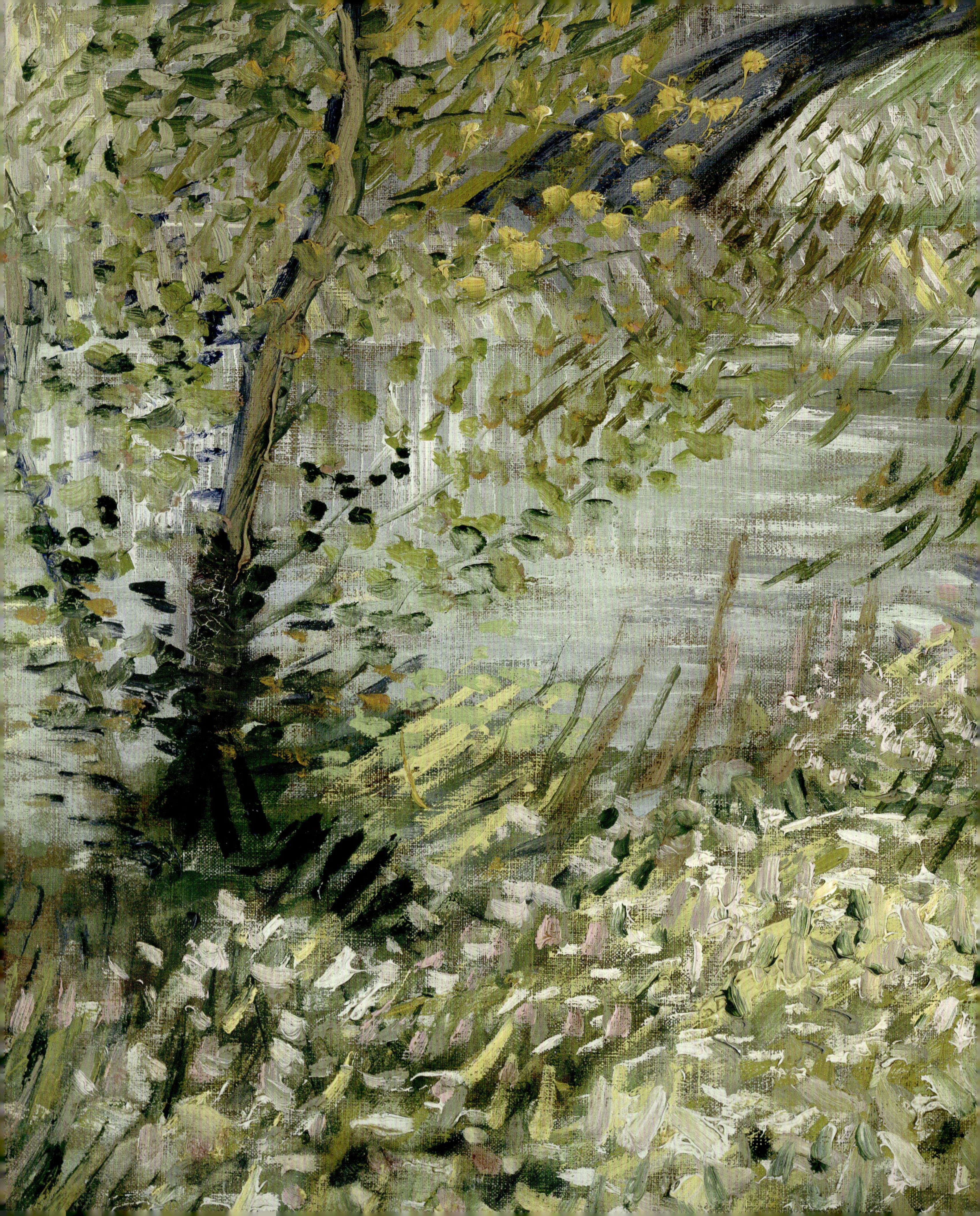

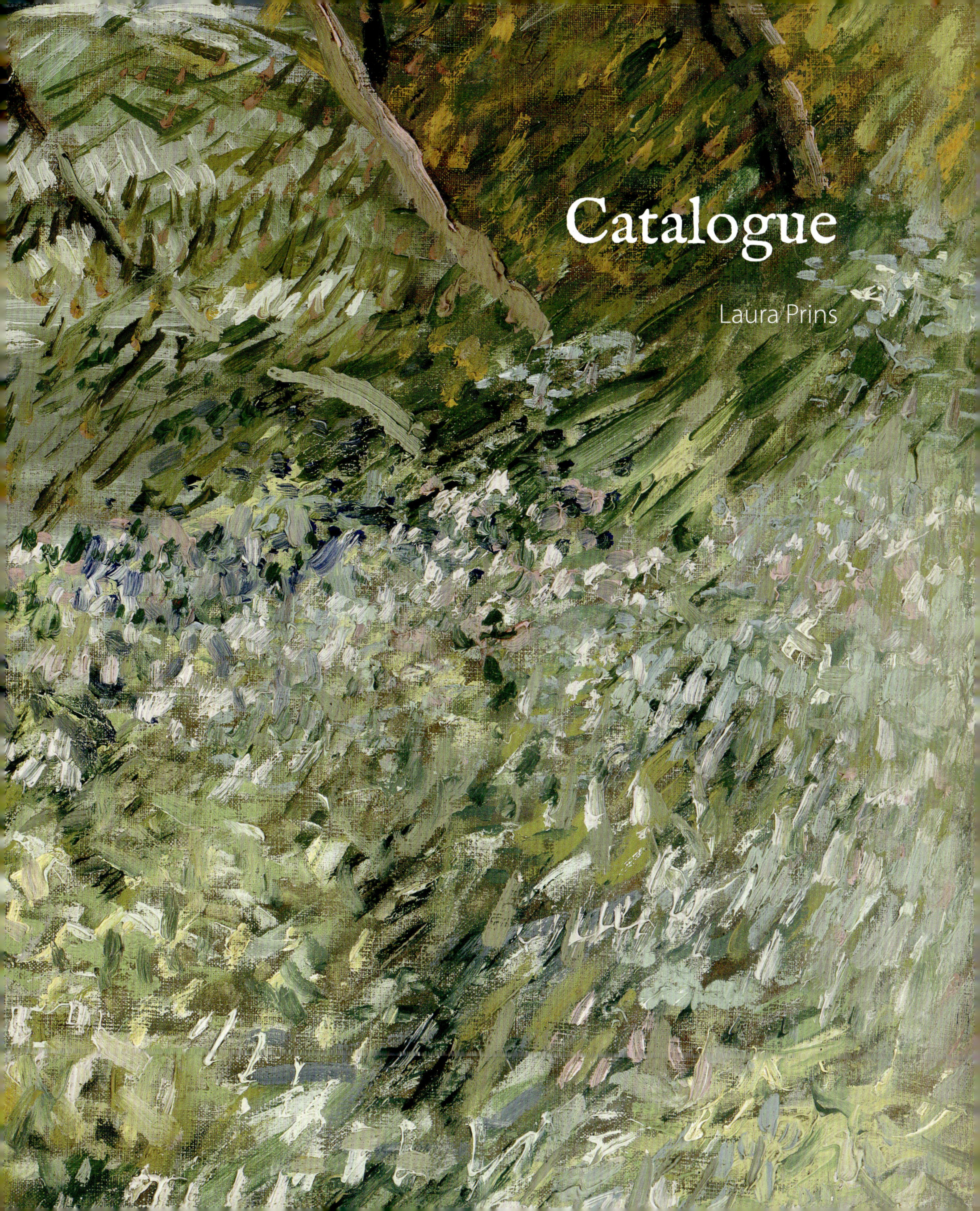

Catalogue

Laura Prins

1

VINCENT VAN GOGH (1853–1890)

Girl in the Woods

August 1882/83

oil on canvas laid down on cradled panel

13 5/8 × 18 5/8 in. (34.7 × 47.3 cm)

Lent by Parkview

F 8a

The star of this composition is the large trunk in front of a heavy curtain of trees, with roots that are almost human, about to embrace a little girl. The trees flanking the path figure like bystanders in the middle ground. Van Gogh was not yet an experienced painter, but he was able to produce "an echo of what struck me, I see that nature has told me something, has spoken to me," as he explained to his brother.[1] Van Gogh constructed the composition wet-in-wet, starting with the foreground trees in different tones of brown and defining the girl in a simple touch. He then colored in the rather monochromatic brown ground, working deftly around the contours. The trees in the background he composed in simplified long strokes. With green accents, he brightened up the trunks and ground, indicating moss and grass. As final touches, Van Gogh created a misty view in the far distance in grayish blue and white, and in a stroke added a path in the middle ground.

The subject was probably derived from one of the English black-and-white wood engravings that Van Gogh collected fanatically in his Dutch period (fig. 36), but he went into the woods to make his personal version.[2] In the summer of 1882 he had admired the Barbizon painters at an exhibition in The Hague and, inspired, he started to paint *en plein air* in a comparable brown palette (see cats. 10, 14, 15, and 16).[3]

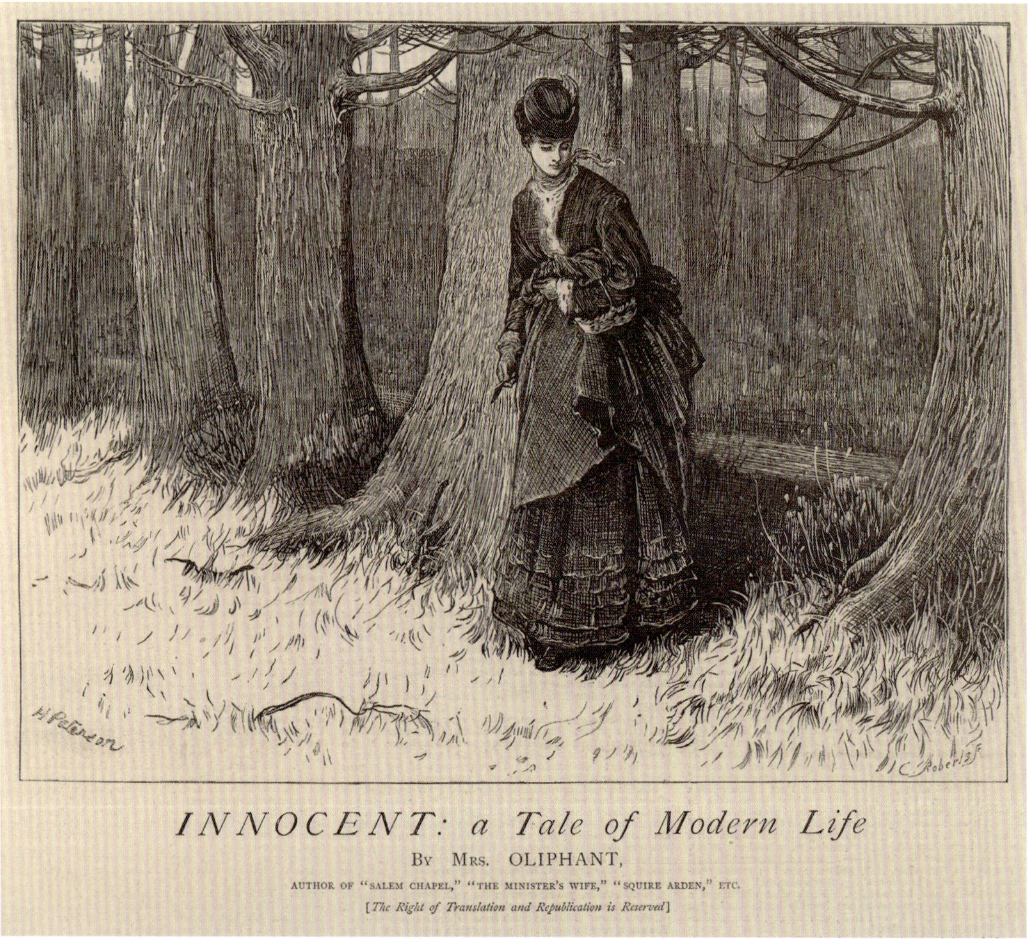

Fig. 36
"Helen Paterson, Innocent: A Tale of Modern Life," by Mrs. Oliphant, reproduced in *The Graphic: An Illustrated Weekly Newspaper*, 11 January 1873, The Pierpont Morgan Library, New York, Bequest of Gordon N. Ray, 1987, 146558-92

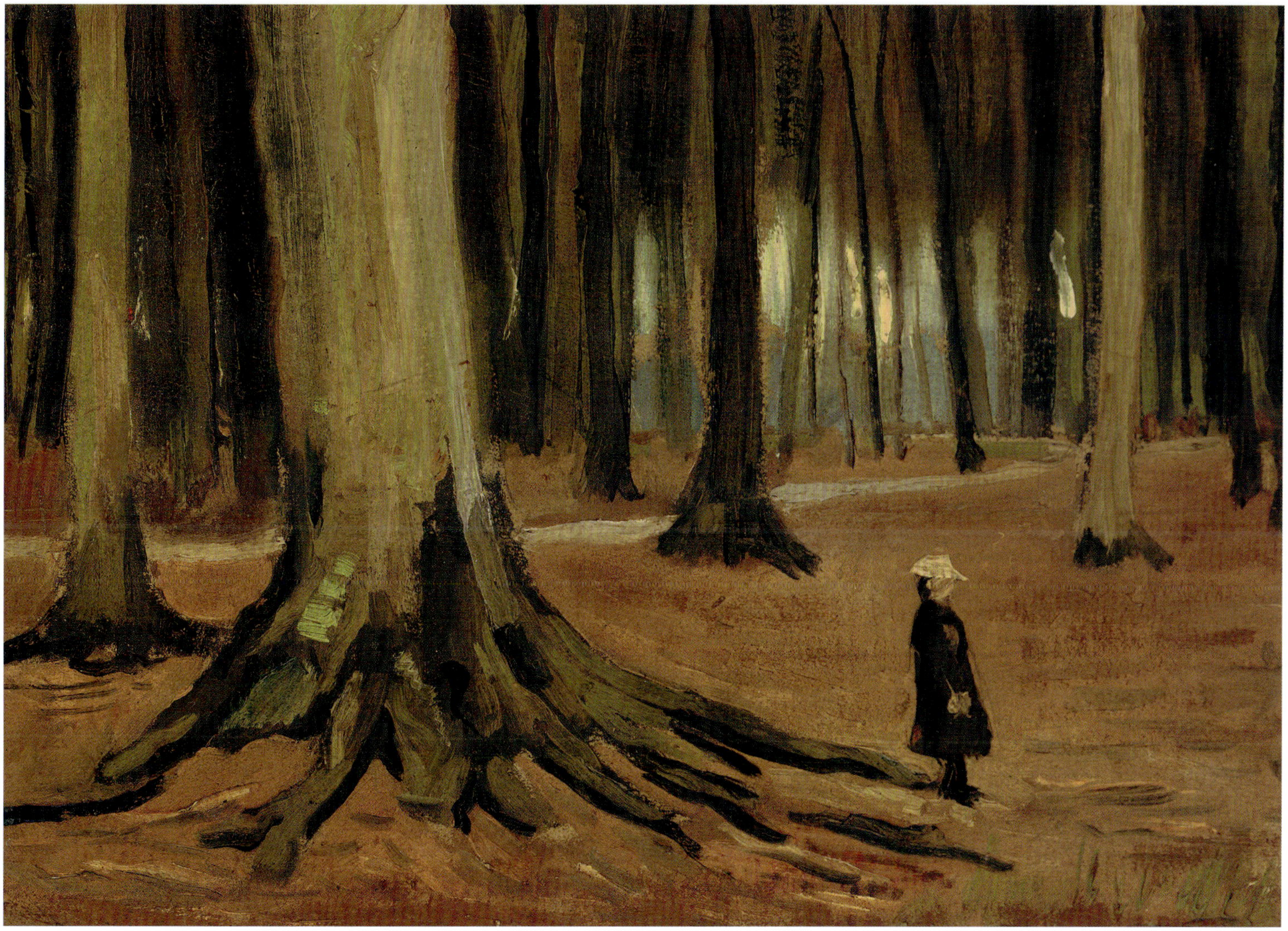

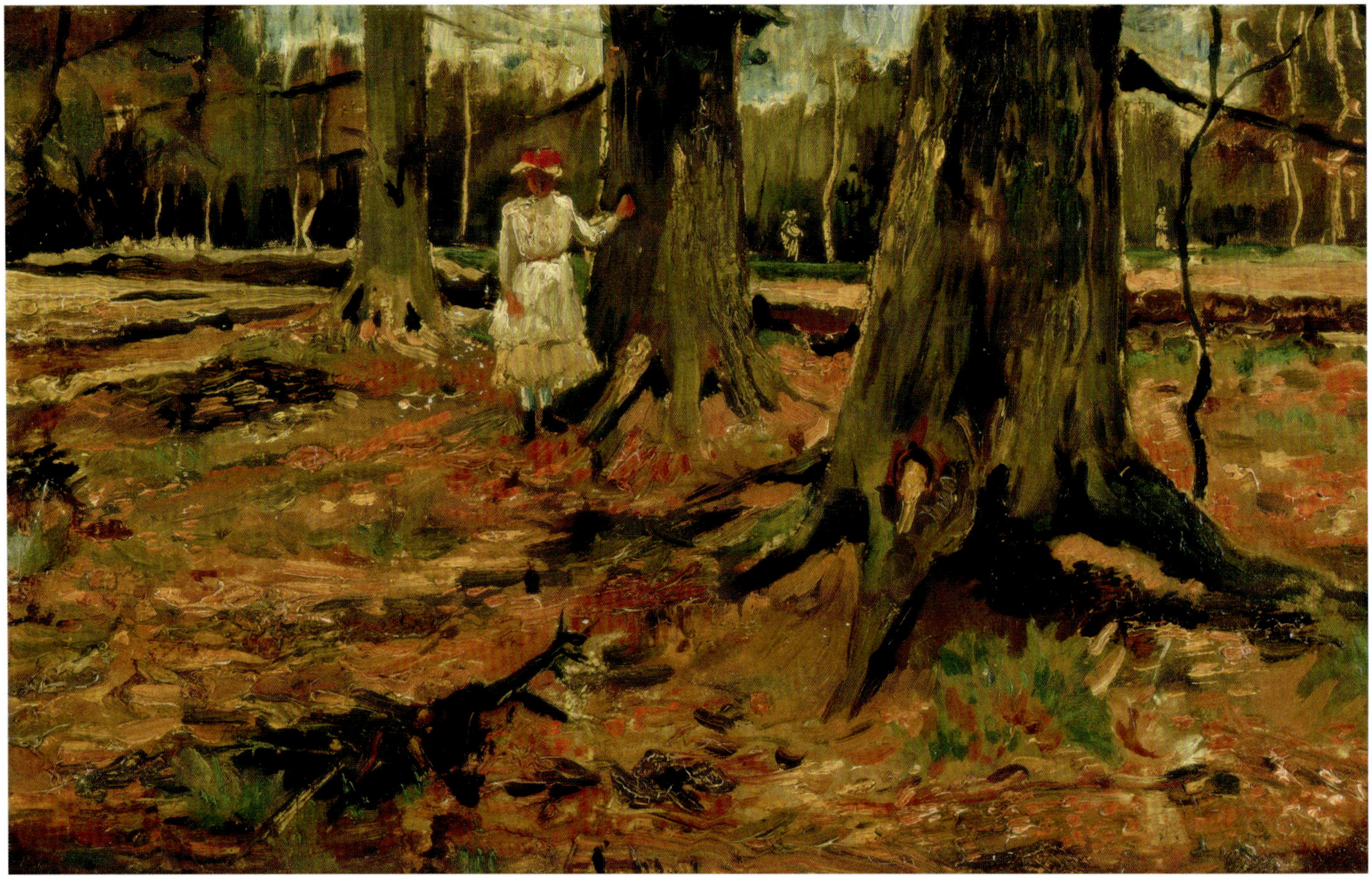

During this period, Van Gogh created a similar work of a young girl, dressed in white, and also staged in the Hague forest (fig. 37). He was well equipped to work outside in a "tough, warm pair of trousers, and, since I bought a pair of sturdy shoes just before you came, I'm now fully prepared to face the elements."[4] Van Gogh did not yet own a field easel, so he was forced to sit on the ground; evidently, the perspective is from a sitting position. Traces of leaves have been found in the paint layer.[5]

The present painting has never been thoroughly analyzed, but because of its similar appearance to the one described in the correspondence, it has been dated August 1882 as well. Furthermore, the painting has been recognized from a fragment in a letter in which Van Gogh described a woodland scene, noting the girl was "there simply and solely for the size" and "to provide an accent." He justified the painting's lack of finish to Theo: "Like me, you will no doubt have reservations about the background in particular. The only explanation I can offer about this is that the study was done as a study of the foreground, namely the tree roots; a lot of work had already gone into them, and as usual I wasn't sitting peacefully because of passers-by, and so when I had got the study to the point you see I couldn't bear it any more."[6] The painting of the girl in brown indeed has its focus in the foreground and shows a rushed simplicity in the background. However, there are arguments for dating this painting 1883. First, the perspective does not appear to be from a sitting position; unless he was sitting on a hill, Van Gogh must have painted it on an easel, which he did not acquire until the following year. In addition, Van Gogh painted the work on canvas, but this too he did not yet have in 1882.[7] These were the exact arguments made in the collection catalogue of the Kröller-Müller Museum for dating another woodland scene a year later (fig. 38).[8] It may be that Van Gogh, endlessly possessed by nature's presence, retried this motif of a girl in the woods in the summer of 1883.

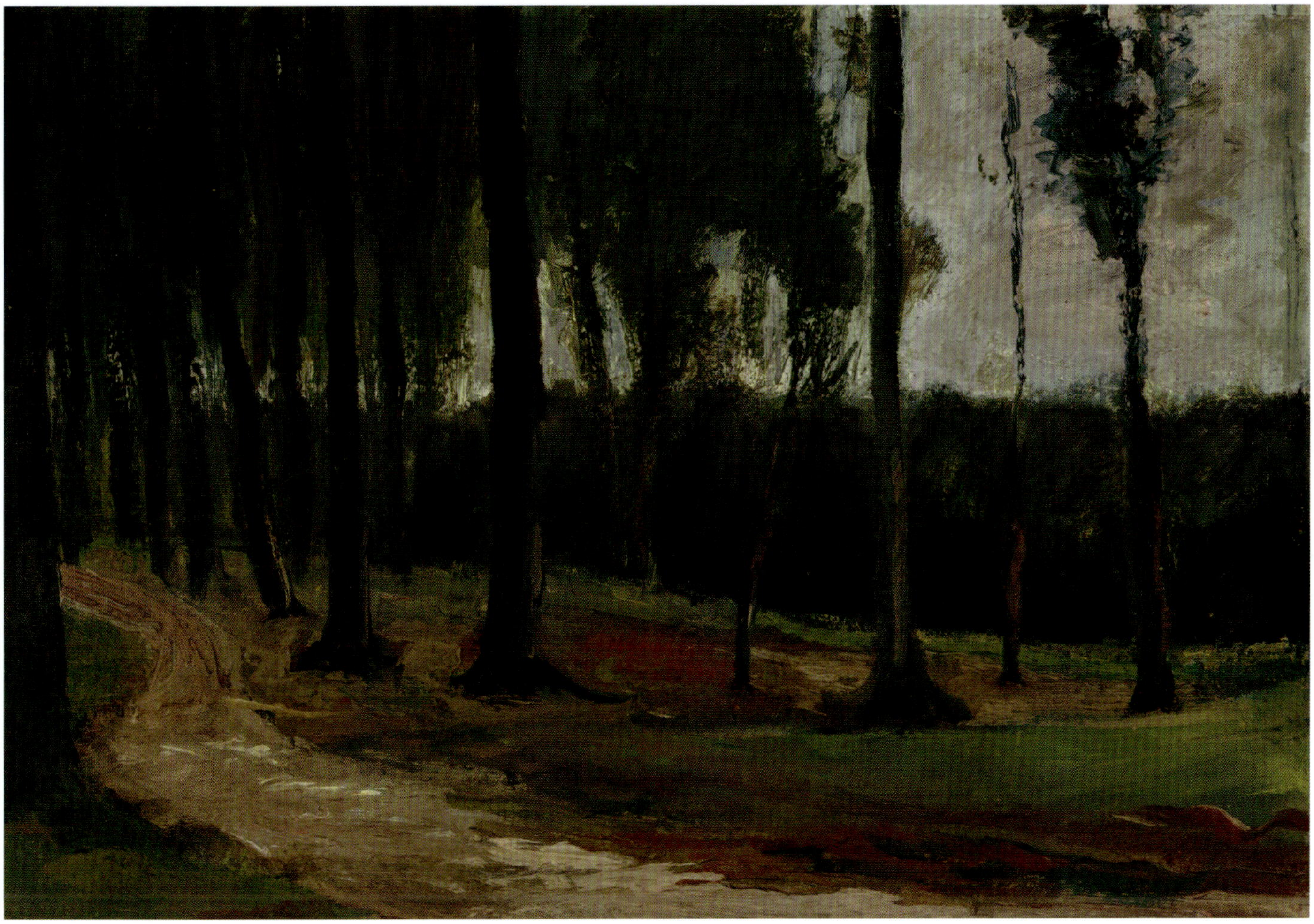

Notes

1 Vincent van Gogh to Theo van Gogh, 3 September 1882, letter 260.

2 Jos ten Berge, Teio Meedendorp, and Aukje Vergeest, *The Paintings of Vincent van Gogh in the Collection of the Kröller-Müller Museum* (Otterlo: Kröller-Müller Museum, 2003), 32–33 (entry by Teio Meedendorp); see also Jenny Reynaerts, "Close Encounters with the Earth," in *Van Gogh: The Man and the Earth*, ed. Kathleen Adler et al. (Milan: 24 ORE Cultura, 2014), 43–44.

3 Nienke Bakker and Maite van Dijk, "Van Gogh in 'The Country of Paintings': An Overview of His Visits to Museums and Exhibitions," in *Van Gogh's Studio Practice*, ed. Marije Vellekoop et al. (Amsterdam: Van Gogh Museum; Brussels: Mercatorfonds, 2013), 58–60.

4 Vincent van Gogh to Theo van Gogh, 5 or 6 August 1882, letter 254.

5 Ten Berge, Meedendorp, and Vergeest, *Van Gogh in the Kröller-Müller Museum*, 32 (entry by Meedendorp).

6 Vincent van Gogh to Theo van Gogh, 25 September 1882, letter 269.

7 According to the condition report of Christie's New York (auction 8 May 2002).

8 Ten Berge, Meedendorp, and Vergeest, *Van Gogh in the Kröller-Müller Museum*, 39–41 (entry by Meedendorp).

Fig. 37 (opposite)
Vincent van Gogh (1853–1890),
Girl in a Wood, August 1882,
oil on paper mounted on canvas,
$14\frac{9}{16} \times 23\frac{1}{8}$ in. (37 × 58.8 cm),
Collection Kröller-Müller Museum,
Otterlo, KM 107.592, F 8

Fig. 38 (above)
Vincent van Gogh (1853–1890),
Edge of a Wood,
August–September 1883,
oil on canvas mounted on panel,
$13\frac{5}{16} \times 19\frac{1}{8}$ in. (33.8 × 48.5 cm),
Collection Kröller-Müller Museum,
Otterlo, KM 109.023, F 192

2

VINCENT VAN GOGH (1853–1890)

River Bank in Springtime

April–May 1887

oil on canvas, 19 × 22½ in. (48.3 × 57.2 cm)

Dallas Museum of Art, gift of Mr. and Mrs. Eugene McDermott in memory of Arthur Berger, 1961.99, F 352

A fresh breeze rustles through the leaves of the trees, the bushes, and the long grass, revealing just a glimpse of the river and the bridge in the background. The wealth of greenery and blossoms in soft colors of pink, purple, and blue, bathed in sunlight, show us spring in the suburbs of Paris. Van Gogh was standing here on the banks of the Seine at Asnières, a commune northwest of Paris, facing the Pont de Clichy, which connected the suburb to the city (fig. 39).[1] During the nineteenth century, Asnières had become a popular recreational spot for young city-dwellers. Artists, too, visited Asnières to paint there in the open air, as Renoir and Monet had in the 1870s and Seurat, Signac, and Bernard in the 1880s.[2]

Much had happened since Van Gogh's Hague painting (cat. 1). After living a few years with his parents in the Dutch village of Nuenen, where he inexhaustibly studied all the aspects of impoverished peasant life, Van Gogh moved to Antwerp in late 1885, then to Paris in early 1886. For two years, he lived with his brother Theo in a small apartment in Montmartre, finally grasping the new directions in art about which Theo had been writing. While in that first year Van Gogh's subjects mainly concerned the surroundings of Montmartre, his attention shifted to Asnières sometime in the spring of 1887.[3] There, he painted some of his first ambitious landscapes, which benefited from his previous year's painstaking studies in color and style, influenced

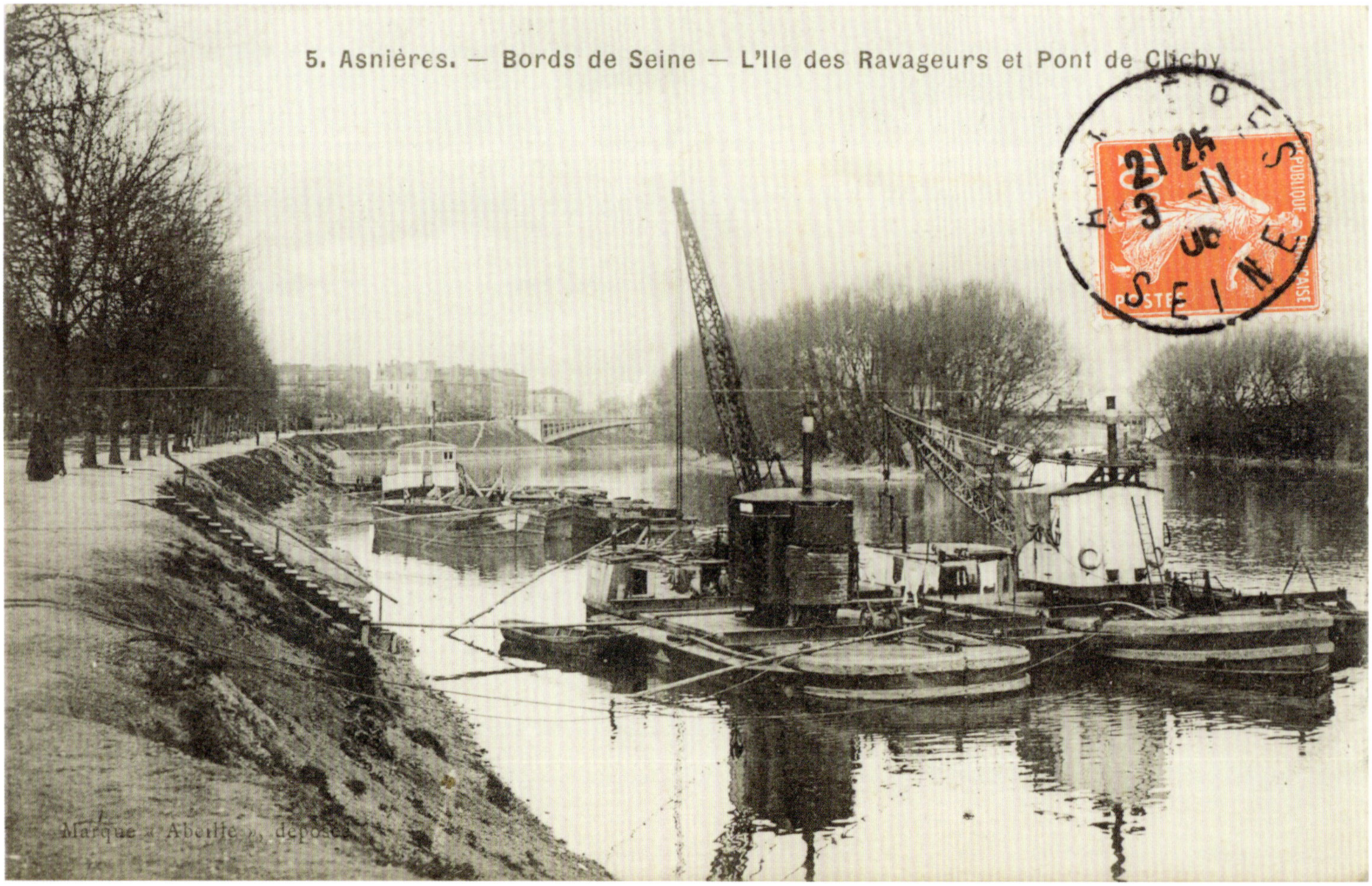

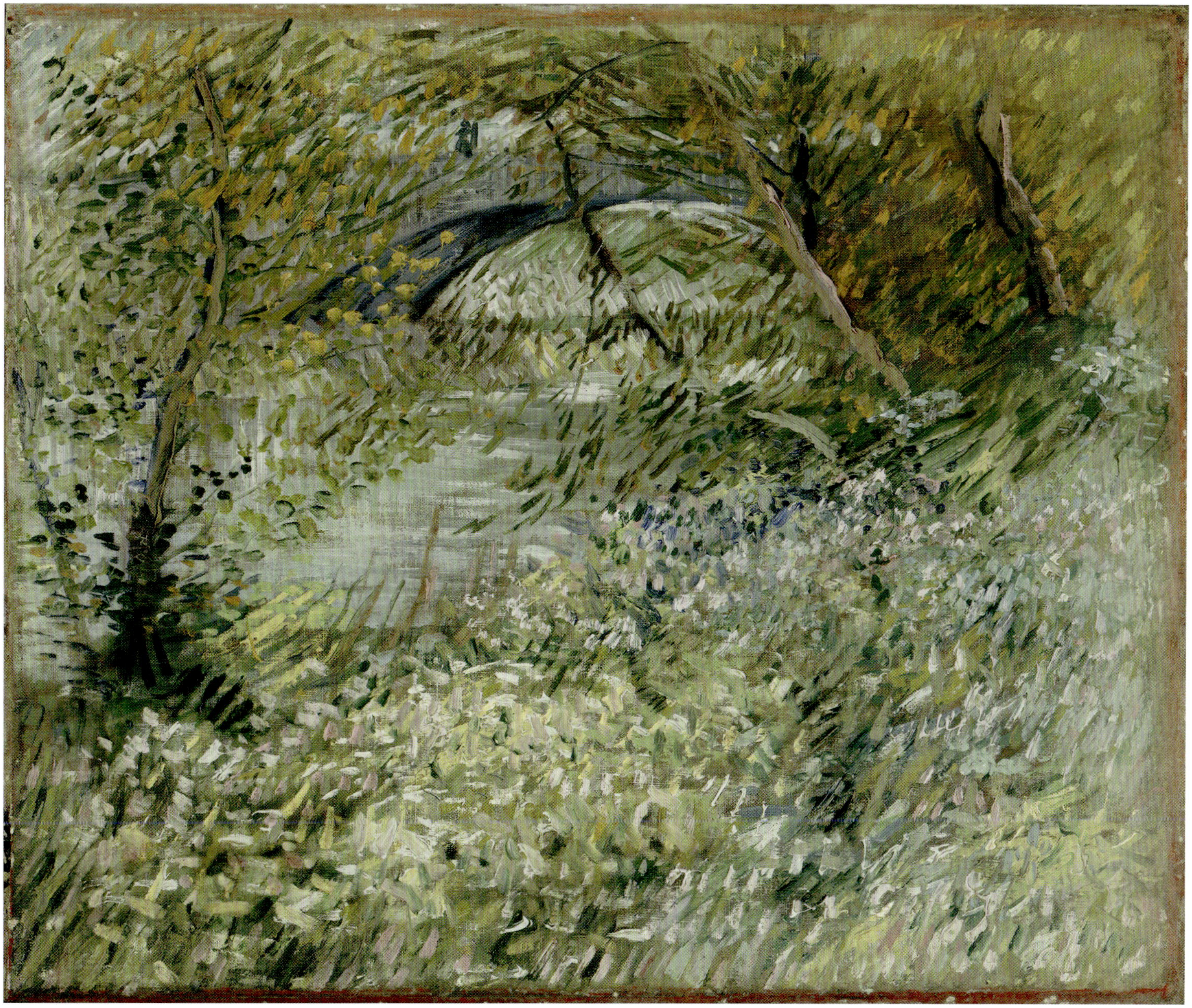

Fig. 39 (opposite)
Asnières, Bords de Seine, L'Ile des Ravageurs et Pont de Clichy,
ca. 1908, postcard,
private collection

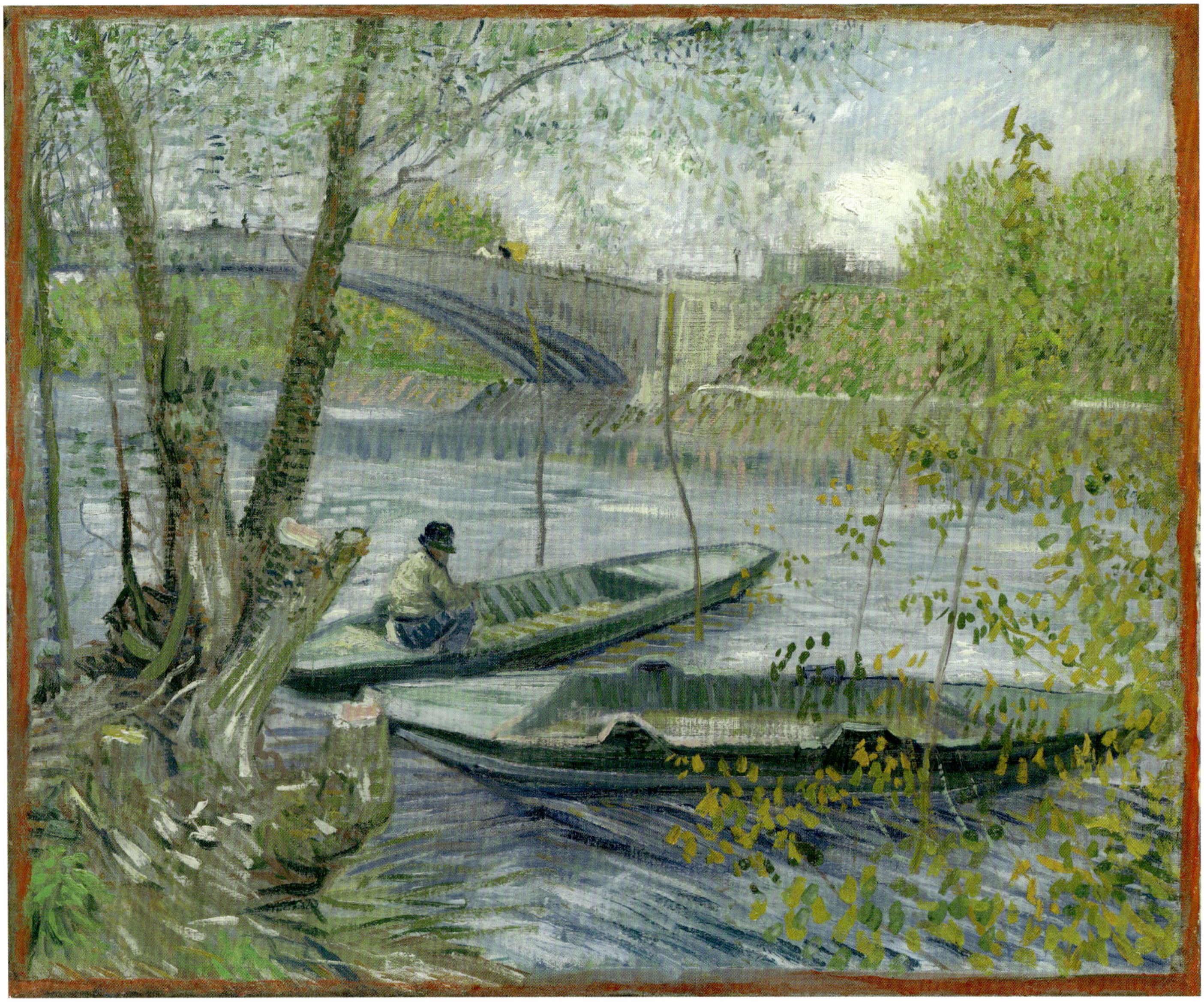

Fig. 40
Vincent van Gogh (1853–1890), *Fishing in Spring, the Pont de Clichy (Asnières)*, 1887, oil on canvas, 19⅞ × 23⅝ (50.5 × 60 cm), Art Institute of Chicago, Gift of Charles Deering McCormick, Brooks McCormick, and Roger McCormick, 1965.1169, F 354

by his encounters with Impressionism and Neo-Impressionism. Van Gogh visited the site several times with Signac, whose advice about applying and juxtaposing unmixed colors directly on the canvas had proven to be a major influence. But in this painting the motif and dynamic brushstrokes especially recall the 1870s work of Monet.

Because of its abundance of spring blossoms, Van Gogh must have made this painting on one of his early Asnières visits (see also cat. 3). Compared to the other paintings he made there, his colors are relatively cautious, reminiscent of pastel. It is possible that Van Gogh painted this work on the same day as *Fishing in Spring, the Pont de Clichy (Asnières)* (fig. 40), in which a spring palette also dominates. Analysis of the canvas weave reveals that the two works were painted close together on the same roll.[4] Possibly Van Gogh took with him on a *plein air* trip a large piece of canvas on which he painted different compositions that he separated with a red border; after finishing the paintings, he cut them apart as single works.[5]

Considering the depth in the painting, hidden behind the foliage, Van Gogh must have used a perspective frame, a tool he had frequently used since 1882 to help him adapt his subject to the canvas in the right proportion. With confidence, he built up his composition: the thinly painted geometric structure of the bridge and the calm, gently rippling river make an exciting contrast with the dense and lively brushstrokes of the foliage in the foreground.

Notes

1 This bridge, constructed in 1866 and rebuilt in 1874 after the Franco-Prussian war, no longer exists; it was replaced in 1973 by the present structure.

2 See, e.g., John Leighton and Richard Thomson, *Seurat and the Bathers* (London: National Gallery, 1997), 132–45.

3 According to Louis van Tilborgh and Ella Hendriks, *Vincent van Gogh Paintings*, vol. 2, *Antwerp & Paris 1885–1888* (Amsterdam: Van Gogh Museum; Zwolle: Waanders, 2011), 387, it must have been at the end of April or beginning of May at the earliest that Van Gogh went to Asnières for the first time, but they have reason to believe that he started to work there in the middle of May.

4 Ella Hendriks et al., "Automated Thread Counting and the Studio Practice Project," in *Van Gogh's Studio Practice*, ed. Marije Vellekoop et al. (Amsterdam: Van Gogh Museum; Brussels: Mercatorfonds, 2013), 169–72.

5 The red border is clearly visible in *Fishing in Spring* (fig. 40), and may have functioned here both practically and aesthetically. In the present painting, traces are found of a red border. For more information, see Louis van Tilborgh, "Framing Van Gogh," in *In Perfect Harmony: Picture + Frame 1850–1920*, ed. Eva A. Mendgen, exh. cat. (Amsterdam: Van Gogh Museum; Zwolle: Waanders, 1995), 164–68; Marieke Jooren, "Finishing Touches: Varnish, Signatures, Frames and Painted Borders," in Vellekoop et al., *Van Gogh's Studio Practice*, 302–4. It has been suggested that these paintings functioned together as a triptych. See Ronald Pickvance, *Van Gogh* (Martigny: Fondation Pierre Gianadda, 2000), 296–97; Nina Zimmer, "Serial Van Gogh: Cycles, Groups, Triptychs," in *Vincent van Gogh: Between Earth and Heaven: The Landscapes*, exh. cat. (Basel: Kunstmuseum Basel; Ostfildern: Hatje Cantz, 2009), 102–5.

3

VINCENT VAN GOGH (1853–1890)

Trees on a Slope

April–May 1887

oil on canvas, 14¾ × 18⅛ in. (37.5 × 46 cm)

P. and N. de Boer Foundation, Amsterdam

F 291

At the Ile des Ravageurs, the quay of Asnières near Pont de Clichy, Van Gogh painted this view of the banks of the Seine (compare fig. 39).[1] In contrast to the lush vegetation that dominates the foreground of *River Bank in Springtime* (cat. 2), here the bare sandy ground, which absorbs the sun, takes up two-thirds of the composition. As viewers, we are still aware of the city's presence because of the two large apartment buildings in the background, where the working class lived packed together in the suburbs.[2]

Like *River Bank in Springtime*, *Trees on a Slope* was painted in the spring of 1887, when Van Gogh first set foot in Asnières.[3] He was in his final stages of experimentation with *peinture à l'essence*, a technique that he briefly applied during his Paris experiments.[4] This thinned, fluent paint resulted in matte, transparent layers, reminiscent of Renaissance frescoes and completely opposed to the thick application of paint Van Gogh had used until that moment. The reason for this sudden shift must be found in his encounter with Henri de Toulouse-Lautrec, who was then still in the early stages of his own experiments with *peinture à l'essence*. Van Gogh must also have learned about this age-old technique from the paintings of Edgar Degas, who had reintroduced it in the 1870s. Its modern aesthetic appealed to Van Gogh at a time when he was still hungry to learn everything about the new directions in art and needed to develop his personal style.

With his back to the Seine, Van Gogh worked on an easel, looking through a perspective frame to grasp his surroundings.[5] The grid is still visible in some areas underneath the paint. Van Gogh did not apply the paint in thin layers all through the composition; he used it mainly for the purple shades in the foreground. In the sky and the areas of bright sand, he worked with thicker strokes, but the ground shimmers through in numerous places. Because the paint dried quickly, Van Gogh could work fast without the colors mixing too much on the canvas: see, for instance, the pink branch in the middle with thick leaves of green and yellow (fig. 41). By combining different techniques, Van Gogh created an exciting contrast between the matte landscape and the sparse vegetation making up the undergrowth. He enlivened the canvas by finishing the undergrowth in thick, colored touches.

Trees on a Slope already shows a glimpse of the expressive use of color in thick applications of paint that Van Gogh would further develop in the summer of 1887. Not long after creating this painting, he ended his experiments with the technique of *peinture à l'essence*; its cautious palette and thin layers of paint did not match Van Gogh's expressive character.[6]

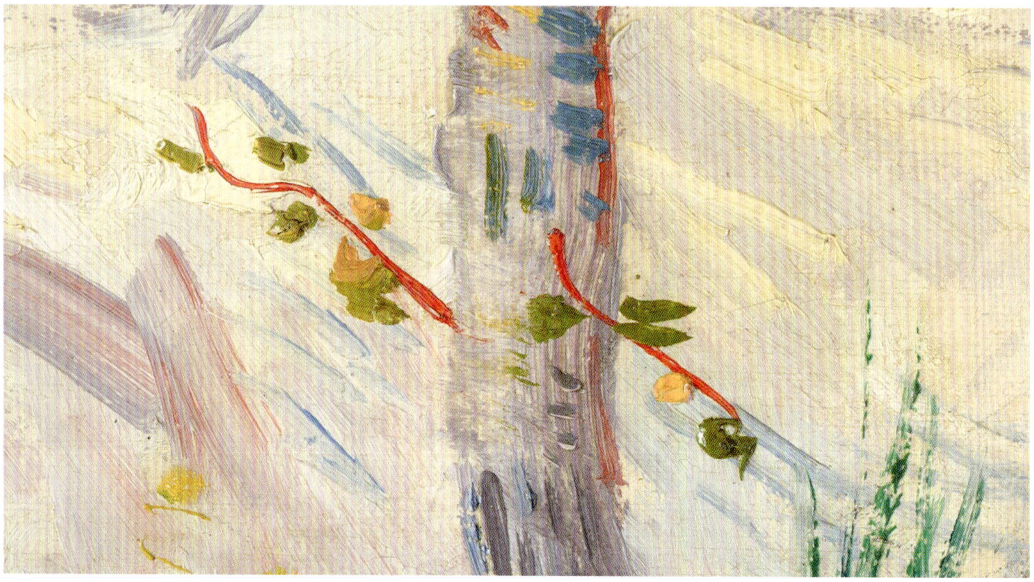

Fig. 41
Vincent van Gogh (1853–1890),
Trees on a Slope (detail),
April–May 1887,
P. and N. de Boer Foundation,
Amsterdam, F 291

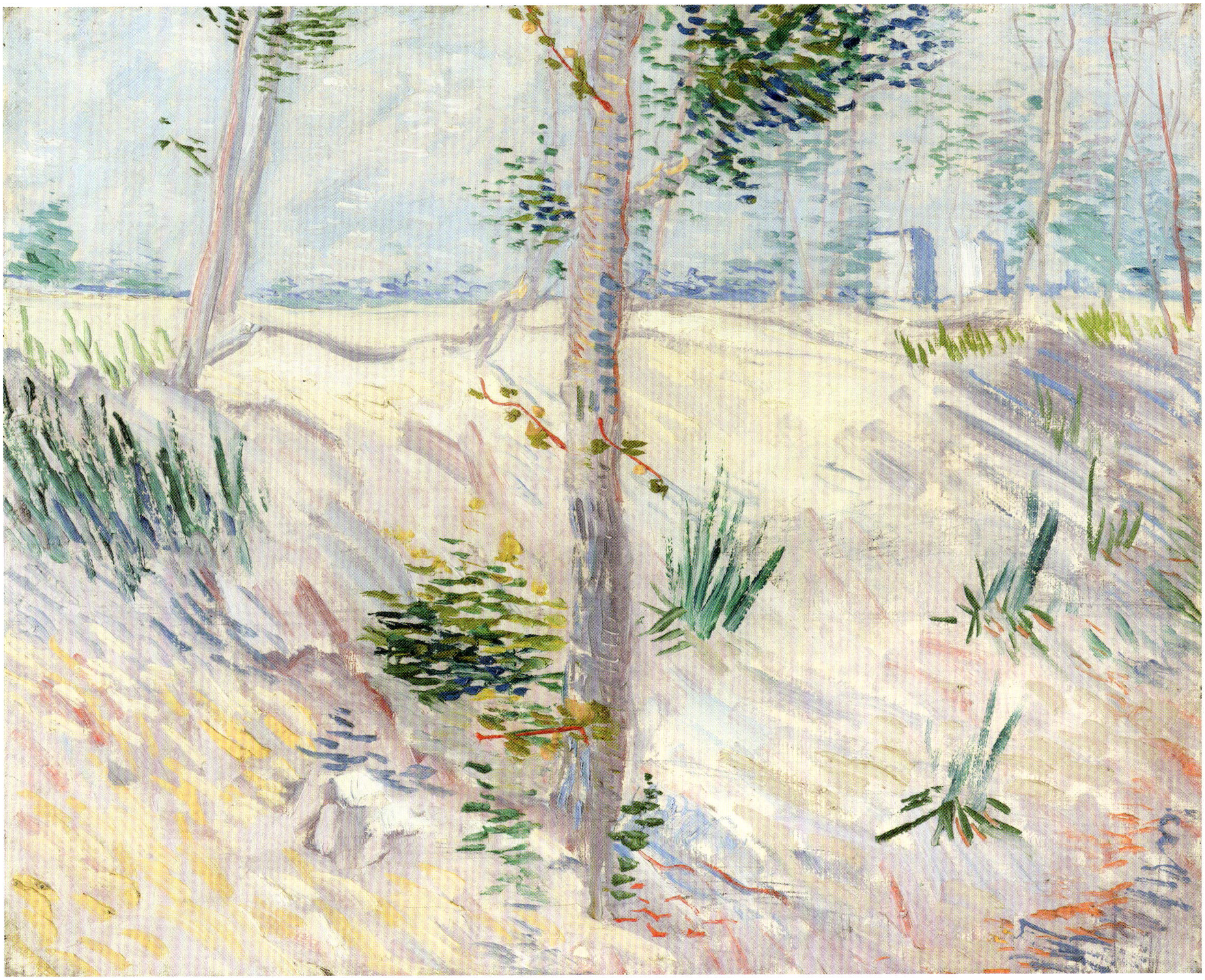

Notes

1 Louis van Tilborgh and Ella Hendriks, *Vincent van Gogh Paintings*, vol. 2, *Antwerp & Paris 1885–1888* (Amsterdam: Van Gogh Museum; Zwolle: Waanders, 2011), cat. 106, note 2.

2 Richard Kendall, "Nature and the City: Paris, 1886–88," in *Van Gogh and Nature*, ed. Richard Kendall, Sjraar van Heugten, and Chris Stolwijk, exh. cat. (Williamstown: Clark Art Institute; New Haven: Yale University Press, 2014), 116.

3 See cat. 2, note 3.

4 With *peinture à l'essence*, the oil is extracted from the paint and replaced by turpentine or lavender spike oil. On this subject, see especially Fleur Roos Rosa de Carvalho, "Degas, Toulouse-Lautrec and Van Gogh: The Use of Diluted Paint," in *Van Gogh's Studio Practice*, ed. Marije Vellekoop et al. (Amsterdam: Van Gogh Museum; Brussels: Mercatorfonds, 2013), 330–49.

5 Klaus Albrecht Schröder et al., *Van Gogh: Heartfelt Lines*, exh. cat. (Cologne: Dumont; Vienna: Albertina, 2008), 220 (entry by Heinz Widauer).

6 Marije Vellekoop, *Van Gogh at Work*, exh. cat. (Amsterdam: Van Gogh Museum; Brussels: Mercatorfonds, 2013), 125.

4

VINCENT VAN GOGH (1853–1890)

Trees

second half of July 1887

oil on canvas, 18⁵⁄₁₆ × 14³⁄₁₆ in. (46.5 × 36 cm)

Van Gogh Museum, Amsterdam (Vincent van Gogh Foundation), s78V/1962

F 307

A number of factors explain Van Gogh's use of the pinkish-brown ground layer, visible here between the thickly applied strokes depicting the trees, foliage, blossom, and bits of summer sky and sunshine. Stylistically, it functions both as earth and as the darkness of a wooded landscape, as well as a perfect complementary contrast with the greens. It was also useful that the brown corresponded to the color of the artist's palette. It simplified the work process, in that Van Gogh knew the effect of color before applying it to the canvas.[1] Using this dark ground was not a typical modern choice, nor a feature found among the paintings of Van Gogh's Impressionist and Neo-Impressionist colleagues, although we see something similar in the early work of Seurat (cat. 22).

The main reason for using this dark ground, however, was practical. Around 18 July 1887 Vincent wrote to his brother that he had little money left, "and I fear I won't know how to get through the days from now till you get back. Because remember when I started working at Asnières I had lots of canvases and Tanguy was very good to me." *River Bank in Springtime* and *Trees on a Slope* (cats. 2 and 3) were painted on these prepared canvases, given to Van Gogh by Tanguy, but because the art dealer's "old witch of a wife" put a stop to this, Van Gogh was forced to reuse his canvases on his following trips to Asnières.[2] With an opaque ground, he covered up earlier compositions, in this case probably a Montmartre landscape from 1886.[3] Because the letter to Theo is from mid-July, we can date *Trees* to later in July.[4]

Van Gogh painted six of these woodland scenes in Asnières (see also cat. 5).[5] The density of foliage and richness of vegetation provided a perfect exercise with which to develop his new color scheme and techniques he had eagerly absorbed from the Impressionists and Neo-Impressionists. He applied his unmixed colors in short brushstrokes directly on the canvas, with the green and red-purple tones strengthening each other. In this way, he brought a fresh and spontaneous appeal to the painting. Van Gogh did not have the patience of Seurat or Signac, whose meticulous methods resulted in carefully constructed compositions of tiny dots; he adapted their techniques in his own expressive manner.

In this composition, Van Gogh used a perspective frame not to achieve depth, but to translate the structure of the foliage onto the canvas. Without sketching first, he applied his brushstrokes directly. The three trees, positioned in a triangle, function as the framework of the composition, carrying the overload of greens. By keeping the foreground somber in earth tones, here and there brightened with red flowers, Van Gogh intensified the refreshing feeling of forest shade on a warm summer day. Playfully, he added yellows and blues between the foliage wet-in-wet (see fig. 42) to suggest the flickering of a sunny summer sky within a wood. With its zoomed-in composition, freely applied paint strokes, and lack of a distant view, this small study has a modern character, despite the rather traditional brown ground.[6]

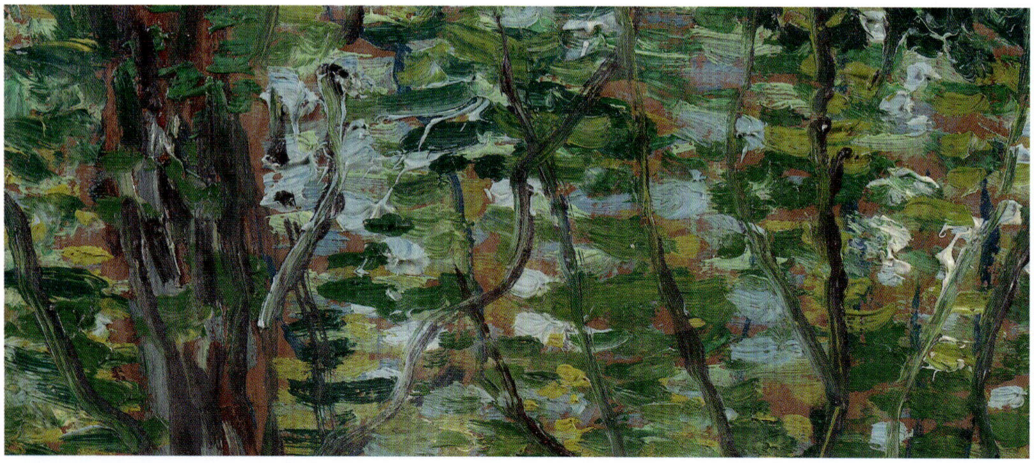

Fig. 42
Vincent van Gogh (1853–1890), *Trees* (detail), 1887, Van Gogh Museum, Amsterdam (Vincent van Gogh Foundation), s78V/1962, F 307

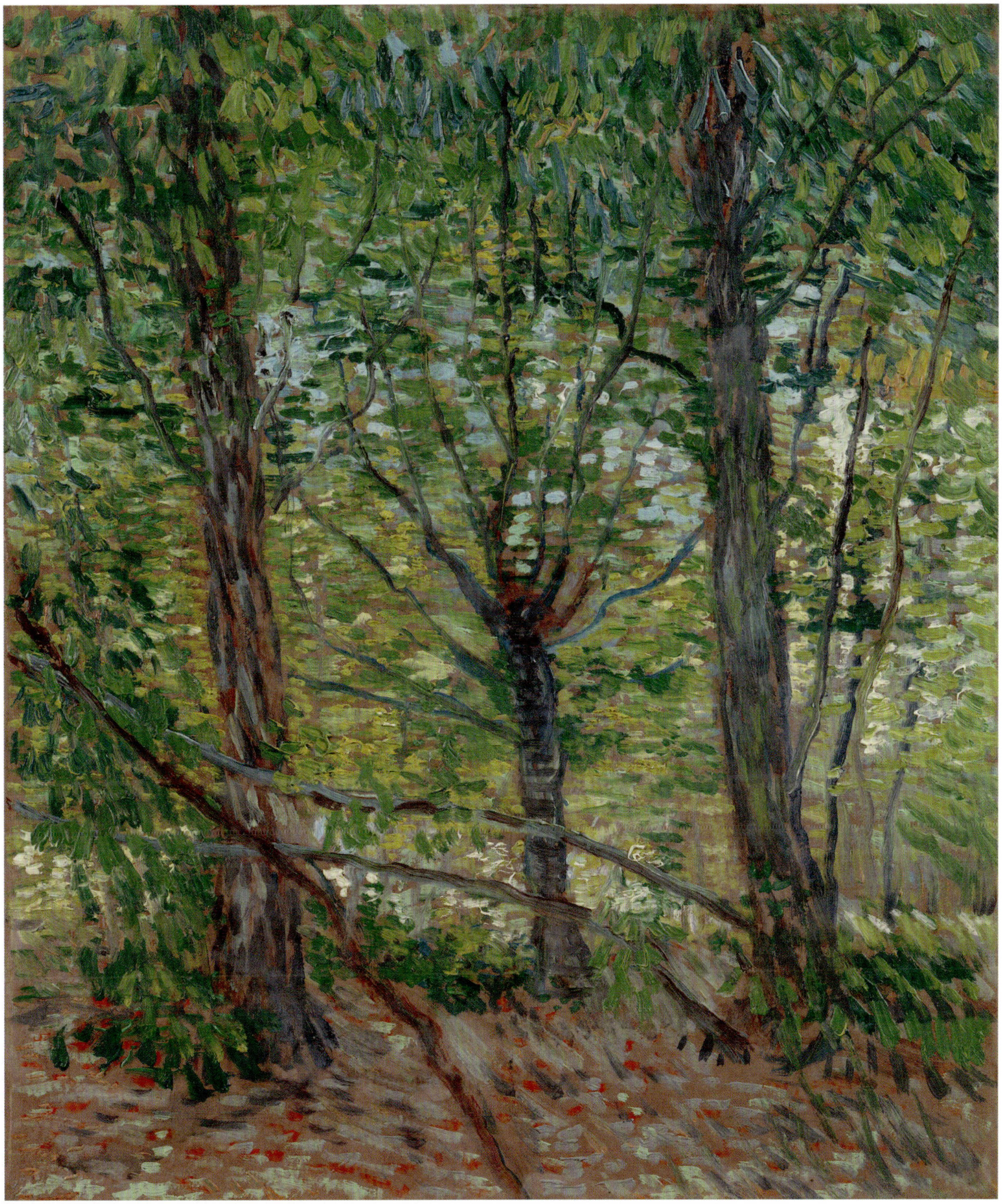

Notes

1 Louis van Tilborgh and Ella Hendriks, *Vincent van Gogh Paintings*, vol. 2, *Antwerp & Paris 1885–1888* (Amsterdam: Van Gogh Museum; Zwolle: Waanders, 2011), 410.

2 Vincent van Gogh to Theo van Gogh, between about 17 and 19 July 1887, letter 571.

3 Van Tilborgh and Hendriks, *Vincent van Gogh Paintings*, 2:403, 410.

4 Ibid.

5 Four are in the Van Gogh Museum (F 309, F 307, F 309a, and F 308), one in Centraal Museum, Utrecht (cat. 5; F 306), and one in a private collection (F 362).

6 See also Jennifer A. Thompson, "Sous-Bois," in *Van Gogh: Up Close*, ed. Cornelia Homburg (New Haven: Yale University Press, 2012), 206.

5

VINCENT VAN GOGH (1853–1890)

Undergrowth

second half of July 1887

oil on canvas, 13 × 18⁵⁄₁₆ in. (33 × 46.5 cm)

Centraal Museum, Utrecht (on loan from the Van Baaren Museum Foundation, Utrecht), inv. 22123

F 306

"Last year I painted almost nothing but flowers to accustom myself to a colour other than grey, that's to say pink, soft or bright green, light blue, violet, yellow, orange, fine red. And when I painted landscape in Asnières this summer I saw more colour in it than before," Van Gogh wrote in the autumn of 1887 to his sister in the Netherlands.[1] He saw so much color that he could eliminate all depth and sight-lines through to the rich Seine landscape, and simply look at the ground of the Parisian suburb's wooded areas. In *Undergrowth*, Van Gogh focused on the base of a tree trunk that itself was already composed of multiple tones of purple, hidden in even more colorful undergrowth. Van Gogh created a strong contrast between the deeply shaded grass and the sunlit background, suggesting a clearing in the woods. Some of this warmth catches the small shrubs and the trunk as well. It all adds up to a colorful composition in which viewers can almost smell the wood and forget that they are in fact surrounded by a city.[2] Van Gogh had come a long way from his dark Dutch paintings, heavy with browns.

As was the case with *Trees* (cat. 4), Van Gogh reused one of his canvases for the present painting. Consequently, this painting can be dated to the second half of July as well. This time, Van Gogh covered the existing composition with a light pinkish-gray ground.[3] In contrast to *Trees*, the ground is less visible through the lively foliage and grasses. Van Gogh covered his whole canvas with a density of quickly applied brushstrokes in all colors, probably in a hurry before the sun moved to another part of the woods and altered his subject. Another of Van Gogh's Asnières wood scenes, also titled *Undergrowth*, has a similar focus (fig. 43). Because his brushstrokes are much more carefully arranged in that version, Van Gogh must have painted it right after the present painting. He even dared to eliminate any suggestion of a far distance.

A painting such as *Undergrowth* combines Van Gogh's different sources of inspiration over the previous years. The heavily cut composition was something he had already learned in The Hague by looking at English black-and-white wood engravings from his collection (see, e.g., fig. 36).[4] The omitted horizon recalls Japanese woodcuts, which he actively began to collect in Paris. The isolation of the expressive trunk is reminiscent of Barbizon painter Jules Dupré, who, according to Van Gogh, depicted trees as if painting a figure (see fig. 14).[5] In addition, Van Gogh must have been aware of his contemporaries' wood scenes, such as Monet's representations of Fontainebleau (cat. 18).[6]

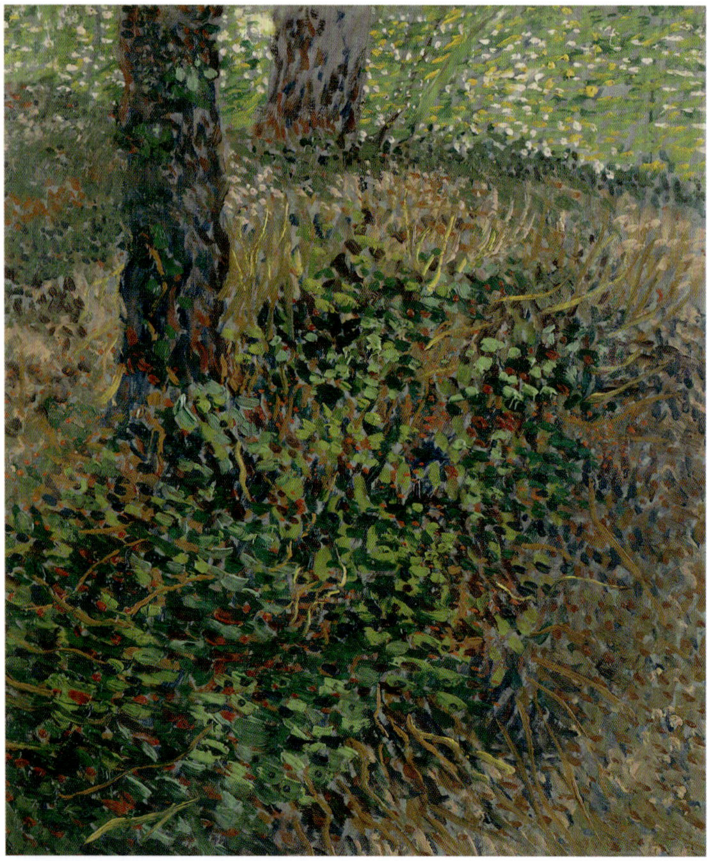

Fig. 43
Vincent van Gogh (1853–1890),
Undergrowth, July 1887,
oil on canvas,
18⅛ × 14¹⁵⁄₁₆ in. (46 × 38 cm),
Van Gogh Museum, Amsterdam
(Vincent van Gogh Foundation),
s79V/1962, F 308

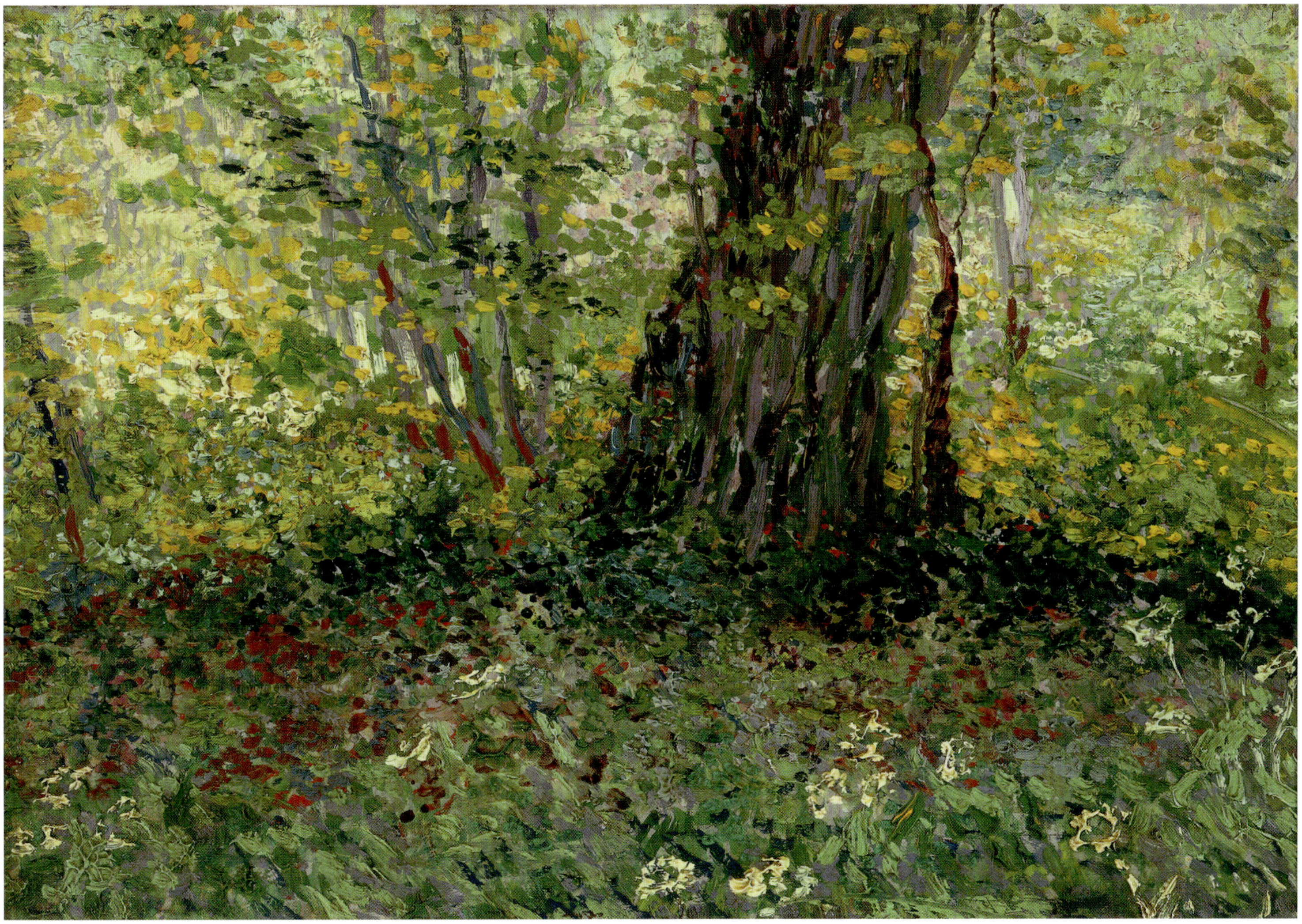

Notes

1 Vincent van Gogh to Willemien van Gogh, late October 1887, letter 574.

2 Carel Blotkamp, "Ruisdael in Provence," in *Vincent van Gogh: Between Earth and Heaven: The Landscapes*, exh. cat. (Basel: Kunstmuseum Basel; Ostfildern: Hatje Cantz, 2009), 71.

3 Louis van Tilborgh and Ella Hendriks, *Vincent van Gogh Paintings*, vol. 2, *Antwerp & Paris 1885–1888* (Amsterdam: Van Gogh Museum; Zwolle: Waanders, 2011), 410.

4 Ibid., 416.

5 Van Gogh expressed this twice (see letters 361 and 483), quoting the Hague School painter Jozef Israëls: "I think what Israëls said about a Dupré is a mighty clever saying—it's just like a painting of a figure." Vincent van Gogh to Theo van Gogh, between about 5 and 26 February 1885, letter 483.

6 Jenny Reynaerts, "Close Encounters with the Earth," in *Van Gogh. The Man and the Earth*, Kathleen Adler et al. (Milan: 24 ORE Cultura, 2014), 49–50.

6

VINCENT VAN GOGH (1853–1890)

Tree Trunks with Ivy

July 1889

oil on canvas, 19 15/16 × 25 1/2 in. (49 × 64.7 cm)

Collection Kröller-Müller Museum, Otterlo, KM 100.398

F 747

After his stay in hectic Paris, an overly agitated Van Gogh traveled to the peaceful South. Here he was able to consolidate all he had learned during the previous years and arrive at his personal style. In Arles, he mastered the landscape, developed his figure painting, and created some of his most iconic paintings, such as *Sunflowers* and *The Bedroom* series. Most of his landscapes are extensive views of the rich surroundings of Arles, breathing freedom and delight. Then Van Gogh fell ill.

In consultation with his brother, Van Gogh decided to have himself admitted to the asylum of Saint-Rémy, some fifteen miles (twenty-four kilometers) northeast of Arles. Although Theo could not promise that the doctor would allow Vincent to go outside, he was sure "that after seeing you there's no doubt that he'll leave you free to go out to go and work."[1] It turned out that Theo was right, as Vincent reported in one of his first letters that he had already painted in the confinement of the hospital's garden "thick tree-trunks covered with ivy, the ground also covered with ivy and periwinkle, a stone bench and a bush of roses, blanched in the cold shadow. In the foreground a few plants with white calyxes. It's green, violet and pink."[2] This painting, now lost, was a vertical composition focused on a detail of the landscape, reminiscent of his woodland scenes in Paris (figs. 44 and 45).[3]

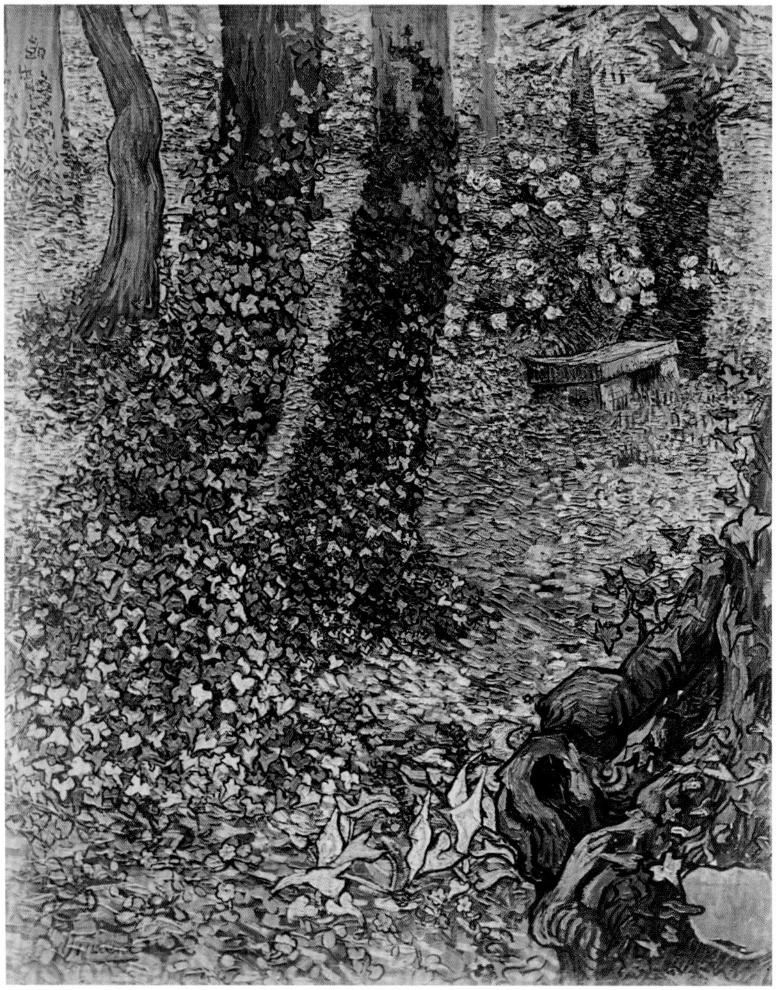

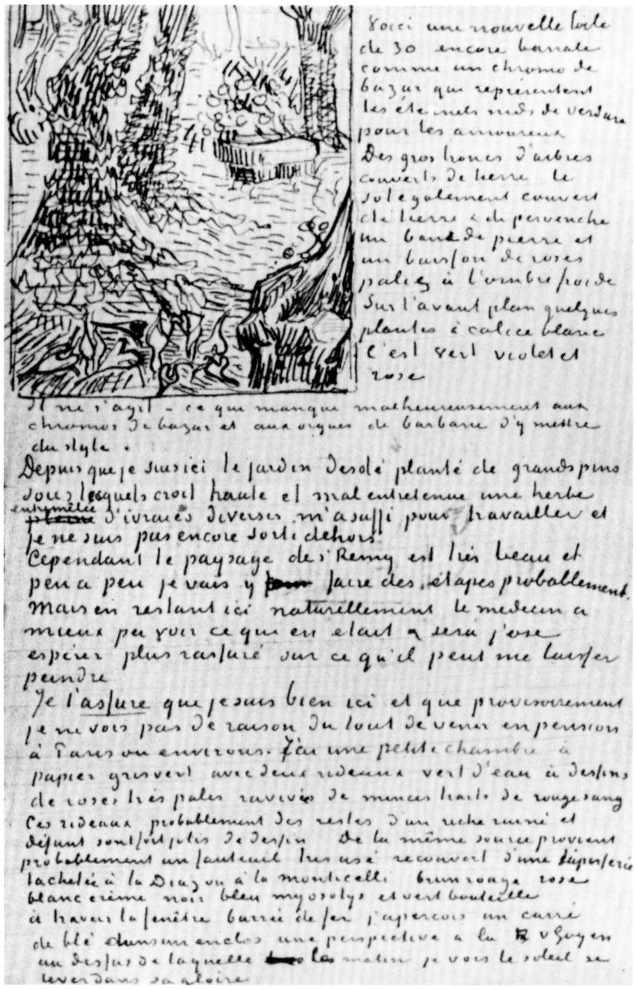
Voici une nouvelle toile
de 30 encore banale
comme un chromo de
bazar qui représentent
les éternels nids de verdure
pour les amoureux
Des gros troncs d'arbres
couverts de lierre le
sol également couvert
de lierre & de pervenche
un banc de pierre et
un buisson de roses
pâlies à l'ombre froide
Sur l'avant plan quelques
plantes à calice blanc
C'est vert violet et
rose
Il ne s'agit – ce qui manque malheureusement aux
chromos de bazar et aux orgues de barbarie d'y mettre
du style.
Depuis que je suis ici le jardin désolé planté de grands pins
sous lesquels croît haute et mal entretenue une herbe
entremêlée d'ivraies diverses m'a suffi pour travailler et
je ne suis pas encore sorti dehors.
Cependant le paysage de St Remy est très beau et
peu à peu je vais y faire des étapes probablement.
Mais en restant ici naturellement le médecin a
mieux pu voir ce qui en était & sera j'ose
espérer plus rassuré sur ce qu'il peut me laisser
peindre
Je t'assure que je suis bien ici et que provisoirement
je ne vois pas de raison du tout de venir en pension
à Paris ou environs. J'ai une petite chambre à
papier gris vert avec deux rideaux vert d'eau à dessins
de roses très pâles ravivés de minces traits de rouge sang
Ces rideaux probablement des restes d'un riche ruiné et
défunt sont fort jolis de dessin De la même source provient
probablement un fauteuil très usé recouvert d'une tapisserie
tachetée à la Diaz ou à la Monticelli brun rouge rose
blanc crème noir bleu myosotys et vert bouteille
à travers la fenêtre barrée de fer j'aperçois un carré
de blé dans un enclos une perspective à la v Goyen
au dessus de laquelle le matin je vois le soleil se
lever dans sa gloire

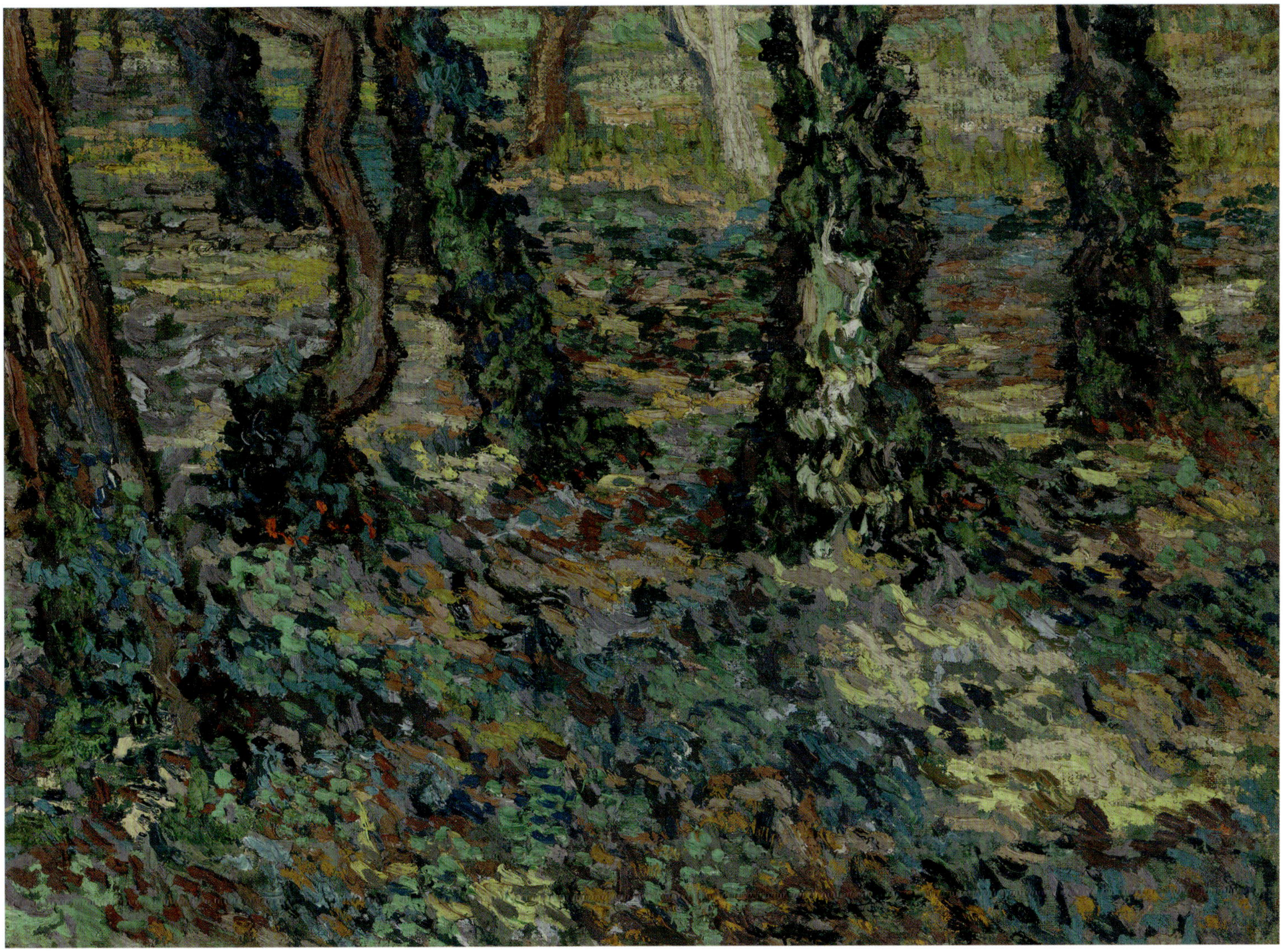

Fig. 44 (opposite, left)
Vincent van Gogh (1853–1890),
A Corner in the Garden of the Asylum at Saint-Rémy, 1889, oil on canvas,
36¼ × 28¼ in. (92 × 72 cm),
location unknown, F 609

Fig. 45 (opposite, right)
Vincent van Gogh to Theo van Gogh with sketch of *Trees with Ivy in the Garden of the Asylum*,
Saint-Rémy-de-Provence,
on or about 23 May 1889,
pen and ink on paper,
8¼ × 10⅝ in. (21 × 27 cm),
page location unknown

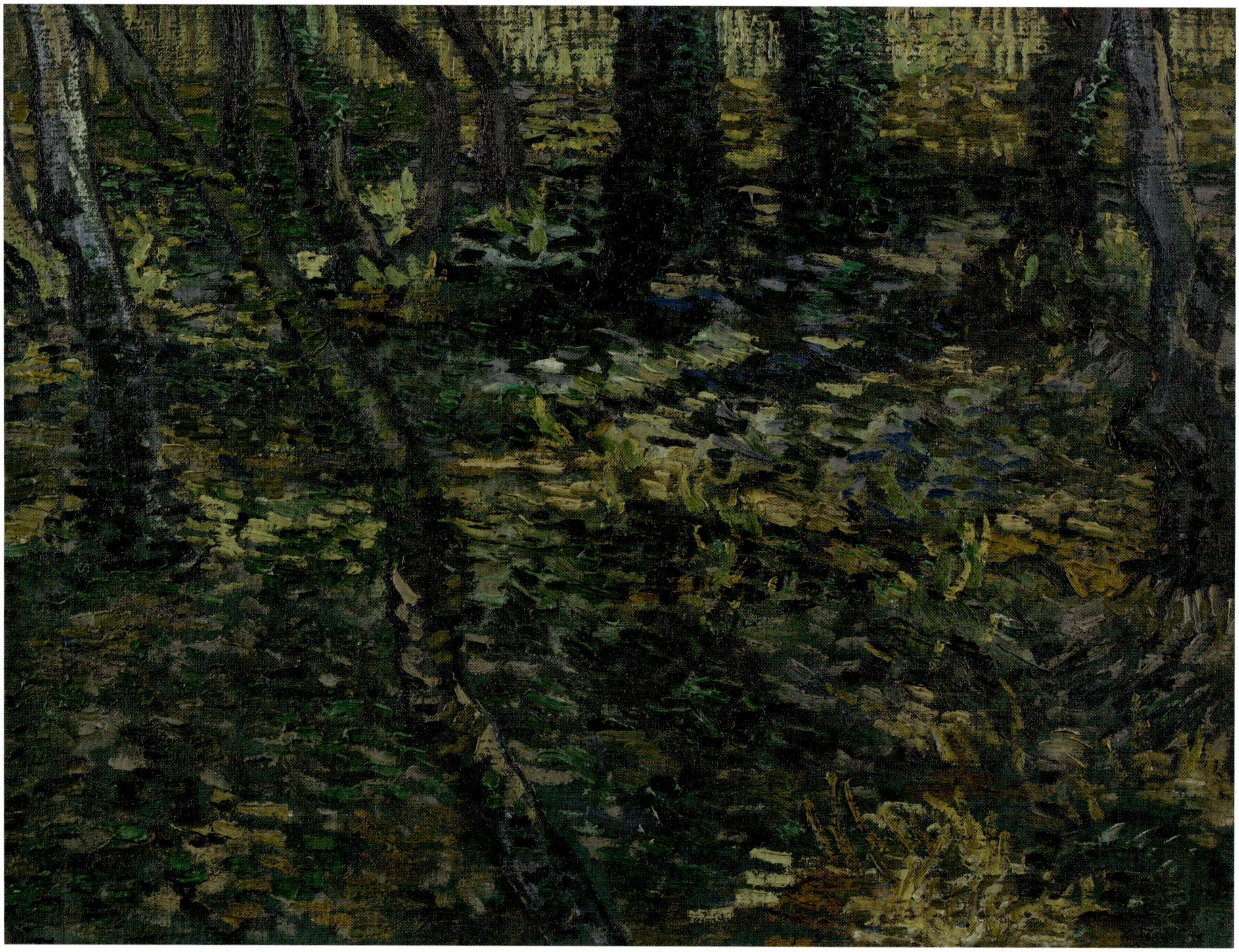

Fig. 46
Vincent van Gogh (1853–1890),
Undergrowth, July 1889,
oil on canvas,
19 15⁄16 × 25 5⁄16 in. (49 × 64.3 cm),
Van Gogh Museum, Amsterdam
(Vincent van Gogh Foundation),
s111V/1962, F 745

Two months later, still feeling optimistic about his hospital treatment, Van Gogh worked on this motif again. Around 14 July, he reported that he had another painting with ivy on the go (cat. 7). The present painting was initially considered a smaller copy made for his mother and sister after the final painting of undergrowth, something he did more often when he was happy with a composition.[4] *Tree Trunks with Ivy* is, however, more likely to be a second study for the actual painting.[5] The first study was a rough sketch in which he figured out the arrangement of the trunks and color scheme of the vegetation (fig. 46). In the background, Van Gogh added grayish-green vertical strokes, clearly different from the structure of the undergrowth, with which he seemed to indicate the hospital's garden wall.[6] In the second study, the wall is no longer visible, because Van Gogh lowered the perspective even closer to the ground. He eliminated the diagonal trunk that floated in the foreground and positioned himself closer to the bases of the trunks instead. This time, he practiced with the different structures of the undergrowth, which he constructed with excessive impasto brushstrokes in a gamut of colors. The final composition (cat. 7) corresponds mostly to the second study, but because much detail is lacking in *Tree Trunks with Ivy*, it is unlikely to have functioned as a copy. Since Vincent was afraid the canvas could not hold the weight of such thick layers of paint, he probably felt the need to experiment in more than one study.[7]

Notes

1 Theo van Gogh to Vincent van Gogh, 2 May 1889, letter 766.

2 Vincent van Gogh to Theo van Gogh, on or about 23 May 1889, letter 776.

3 See, e.g., Cornelia Homburg, "Gardens of Love and Suffering," in *The Painter's Garden: Design, Inspiration, Delight*, ed. Sabine Schulze, exh. cat. (Frankfurt: Städel Museum; Ostfildern: Hatje Cantz, 2006), 246–47.

4 See Evert van Uitert, Louis van Tilborgh, and Sjraar van Heugten, in *Vincent van Gogh: Paintings*, exh. cat. (Amsterdam: Van Gogh Museum; Milan: Mondadori, 1990), 218.

5 On 28 September 1889 (letter 806) Van Gogh wrote to Theo that he had made several copies after his paintings for his mother and sister to start a small collection. In the paintings he listed here, there is no mention of this *Tree Trunks with Ivy*. See also Jos ten Berge, Teio Meedendorp, and Aukje Vergeest, *The Paintings of Vincent van Gogh in the Collection of the Kröller-Müller Museum* (Otterlo: Kröller-Müller Museum, 2003), 312–13 (entry by Teio Meedendorp).

6 This wall is clearly visible in the drawing with the same motif, F 1505, now in the Kröller-Müller Museum, which he probably made before starting with the painted studies.

7 Ten Berge, Meedendorp, and Vergeest, *Van Gogh in the Kröller-Müller Museum*, 313 (entry by Meedendorp).

7

VINCENT VAN GOGH (1853–1890)

Undergrowth

July 1889

oil on canvas, 28¾ × 36⁵⁄₁₆ in. (73 × 92.3 cm)

Van Gogh Museum, Amsterdam (Vincent van Gogh Foundation), s51V/1962

F 746

Rich greens and blues, combined with touches of yellow, orange, and white, cover the whole surface of this canvas. After carefully examining this motif both in drawn and painted studies (see cat. 6), Van Gogh confidently constructed the lush vegetation of the hospital garden. He painstakingly followed the different structures of the tree trunks, grass, and ivy with his brush. In elongated strokes, he built up the trunks, while he added in short, curly, and extremely thick touches the ivy climbing the tree. The shaded undergrowth is depicted in an assortment of dark greens and blues, highlighted here and there in bright colors where the sunlight is scattered through the foliage. Depth is created by the positioning of the trees and the increasingly lighter color in the background. In the upper part, Van Gogh recreated from his first study a small strip of vertical strokes representing the wall around the hospital garden. The variety of textures is something he must have studied in detail from his Barbizon examples (see cats. 14 and 16), while the play of light and dark is reminiscent of Monet's depictions of Fontainebleau (cat. 18).

Van Gogh is completely in control here of his impasto technique; never before had he applied paint in such an excessive manner, as if the undergrowth were literally growing on the canvas. And never before had he rendered the motif of *sous-bois* with such perfection. Once in Arles, he had experimented with this impasto technique, and aspired to eternalize the richness of brushwood in the recently discovered landscape *Sunset at Montmajour* (fig. 47): "The sun was pouring its very yellow rays over the bushes and the ground, absolutely a shower of gold. . . . I brought back a study of it too, but it was well below what I'd wished to do."[1] Largely as a result of the mistral, he could not control his brushstrokes, which were all over the canvas. Van Gogh did not try this motif of undergrowth with this kind of impasto technique again until his hospitalization. Soon, however, he would stop painting this thickly in Saint-Rémy as well, as it exhausted his paint supplies too quickly.[2]

When Van Gogh was working on *Undergrowth*, he wrote to Theo: "Anyway, in the meantime I can do nothing but fiddle with my paintings a little. . . . I also have a new one with ivy on the go. Above all, dear fellow, I beg of you, don't fret or worry or be melancholy on my account, the idea that you would do so, certainly in this necessary

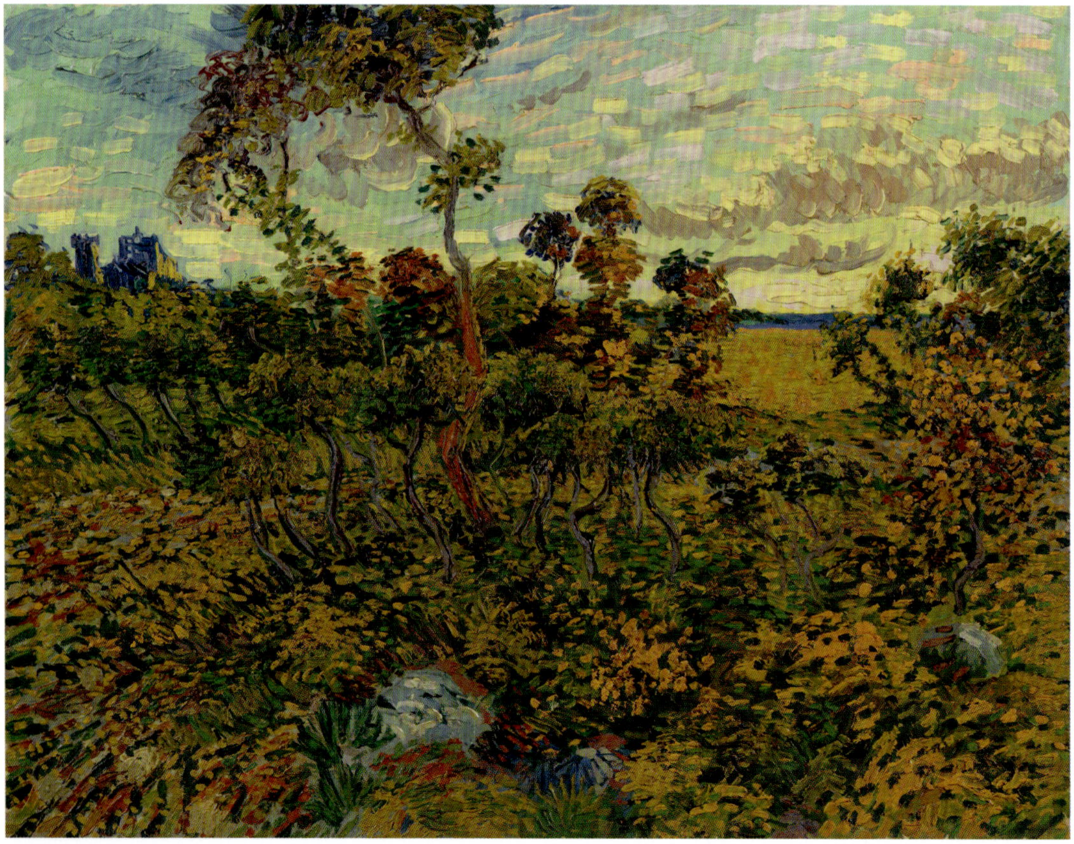

Fig. 47
Vincent van Gogh (1853–1890), *Sunset at Montmajour*, July 1888, oil on canvas, 36¾ × 28⅞ in. (93.3 × 73.3 cm), private collection

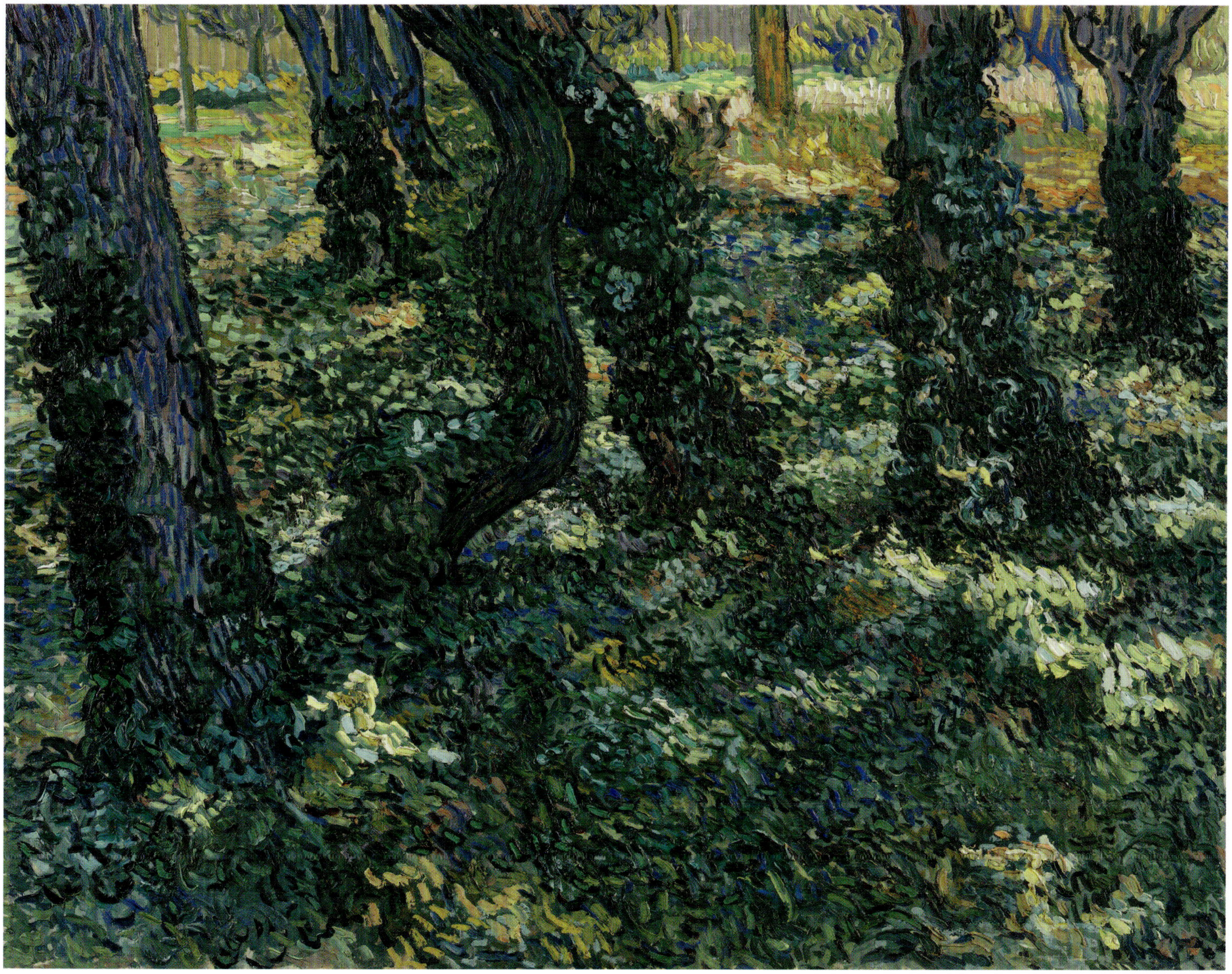

and salutary quarantine, would have little justification when we need a slow and patient recovery."[3] Van Gogh felt calm his first few weeks in the hospital. He knew he needed a structured environment before he was able to take care of himself again. It gave Theo, father-to-be, who of course was worried about his brother, some relaxation as well. Van Gogh was likewise excited to become an uncle. And as long as he could work, he was satisfied. *Undergrowth* may have been intended to symbolize comfort. Just before he left Arles for the hospital, Vincent had written to Theo, "I would try to console myself about it by thinking that illnesses like that are perhaps to man what ivy is to the oak."[4] He repeated a similar saying to his sister as words of encouragement. "Ivy loves the old lopped willows each spring, ivy loves the trunk of the old oak tree."[5] With this he meant that the worst things could happen to the best people, but their inner selves would still remain untouched.

Notes

1 Vincent van Gogh to Theo van Gogh, 5 July 1888, letter 636. This painting has only recently been discovered. See Louis van Tilborgh, Teio Meedendorp, and Oda van Maanen, "'Sunset at Montmajour': A Newly Discovered Painting by Vincent van Gogh," *The Burlington Magazine* 155 (October 2013): 696–705.

2 Jos ten Berge, Teio Meedendorp, and Aukje Vergeest, *The Paintings of Vincent van Gogh in the Collection of the Kröller-Müller Museum* (Otterlo: Kröller-Müller Museum, 2003), 313 (entry by Teio Meedendorp).

3 Vincent van Gogh to Theo van Gogh, 14 or 15 July 1889, letter 790.

4 Vincent van Gogh to Theo van Gogh, 28 April 1889, letter 763.

5 Vincent van Gogh to Willemien van Gogh, between about 28 April and 2 May 1889, letter 764.

8

VINCENT VAN GOGH (1853–1890)

Tree Trunks in the Grass

late April 1890

oil on canvas, 28⁹⁄₁₆ × 36 in. (72.5 × 91.5 cm)

Collection Kröller-Müller Museum, Otterlo, KM 100.189

F 676

Van Gogh's sense of calm in the hospital of Saint-Rémy did not last long. During his first weeks, he produced an impressive number of paintings and drawings, but shortly after his consolatory depictions of undergrowth (cats. 6 and 7), he experienced another crisis while working in the fields.[1] It took him weeks to recover, precious time in which he could not work. "You can imagine that I'm very deeply distressed that the attacks have recurred when I was already beginning to hope that it wouldn't recur," he wrote to Theo a month later.[2]

For the next couple of months Van Gogh was able to work again. He expanded his oeuvre with ambitious paintings, and even achieved public recognition in an article by the critic Albert Aurier, but another major crisis occurred the next February.[3] This time he could hardly work for two months. In late April, after his recovery, he was in a hurry to produce again and badly in need of painting supplies, as his letter to Theo shows. Yet, distracted by the recognition, he preferred to work in isolation: "Please ask Mr Aurier not to write any more articles about my painting, tell him earnestly that first he is wrong about me, then that really I feel too damaged by grief to be able to face up to publicity."[4] One of the first works Van Gogh produced in the garden again was *Tree Trunks in the Grass*: "[N]ow I've just finished a sunlit corner of a meadow which I think is fairly vigorous."[5] A week later, he showed Theo a "hasty croquis" of the painting in his letter (fig. 48), "The trunk of a pine tree violet pink, and then grass with white flowers and dandelions, a little rose bush and other tree-trunks in the background, in the uppermost part of the canvas. I'll be out of doors there. I'm sure that the desire to work will devour me and make me insensible to everything else and in a good mood. And I'll let myself go there, not without consideration but without dwelling on regrets for things that might have been."[6] It was clear that working helped the troubled artist a great deal.

The optimism that Van Gogh tried to muster in his somber mood radiates from this good-sized canvas. In a spring palette, with fresh greens and light blue, he recorded another part of the hospital's garden. With confidence, Van Gogh rendered the different structures in the landscape: in the richly colored foreground, he used long, vertical strokes for the trunks and short ones for the flowered grass, while he outlined the garden in the back with horizontal touches in more uniform greens.[7] While reminiscent of his earlier *Undergrowth* (cat. 7), the differences are evident. Instead of shade, Van Gogh chose an area of sunbathed grass lushly covered with flowers. Instead of emphasizing the confinement of the garden, he depicted a path in the background, suggesting there was a way out. Only few weeks later, Van Gogh left the hospital. Though he was not completely recovered, he knew he would suffer another crisis in the hospital anyway and then would not be able to work again for an indefinite period. Theo had therefore arranged for him to come to live near Paris, in Auvers, where he would be taken care of by Doctor Gachet.

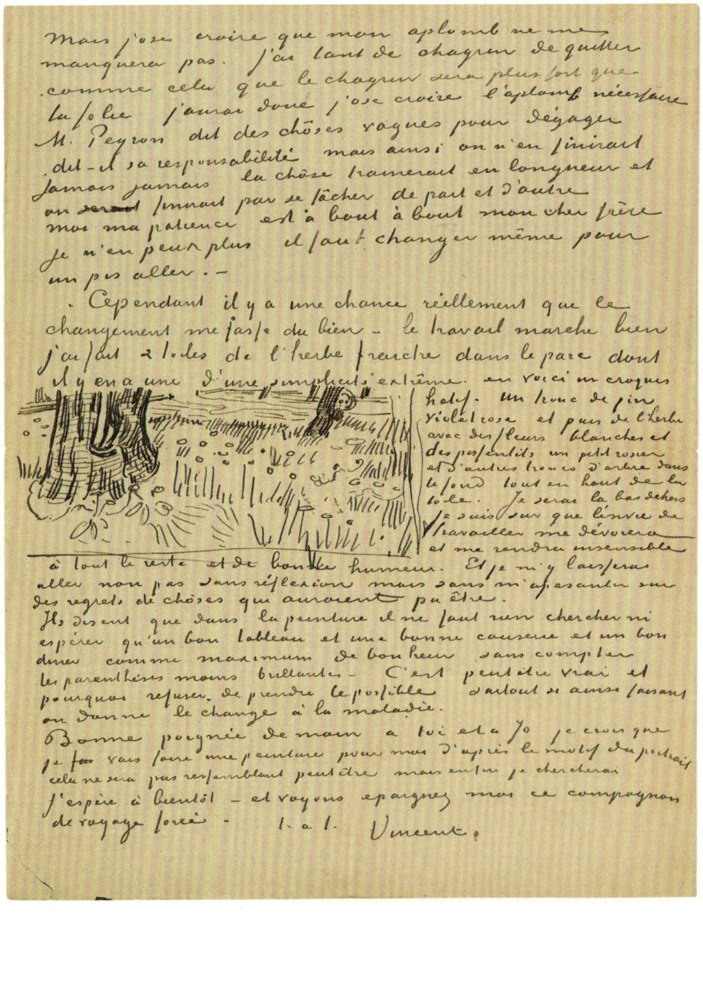
mais j'ose croire que mon aplomb ne me manquera pas. J'ai tant de chagrin de quitter comme cela que le chagrin sera plus fort que la folie j'aurai donc j'ose croire l'aplomb nécessaire. M. Peyron dit des choses vagues pour dégager dit-il sa responsabilité mais ainsi on n'en finirait jamais jamais la chose traînerait en longueur et on finirait par se fâcher de part et d'autre. Moi ma patience est à bout à bout mon cher frère je n'en peux plus il faut changer même pour un pis aller. –

Cependant il y a une chance réellement que le changement me fasse du bien – le travail marche bien j'ai fait 2 toiles de l'herbe fraîche dans le parc dont il y en a une d'une simplicité extrême. en voici un croquis hâtif. un tronc de pin violet rose et puis de l'herbe avec des fleurs blanches et des pissenlits, un petit rosier et d'autres troncs d'arbre dans le fond tout en haut de la toile. Je serai là bas dehors je suis sûr que l'envie de travailler me dévorera et me rendra insensible à tout le reste et de bonne humeur. Et je m'y laisserai aller non pas sans réflexion mais sans m'appesantir sur des regrets de choses qui auraient pu être.

Ils disent que dans la peinture il ne faut rien chercher ni espérer qu'un bon tableau et une bonne causerie et un bon dîner comme maximum de bonheur sans compter les parenthèses moins brillantes. C'est peut-être vrai et pourquoi refuser de prendre le possible surtout si ainsi faisant on donne le change à la maladie.

Bonne poignée de main à toi et à Jo je crois que je vais faire une peinture pour moi d'après le motif du portrait cela ne sera pas ressemblant peut être mais enfin je chercherai. J'espère à bientôt – et voyons épargnez moi ce compagnon de voyage forcé – t. à t. Vincent.

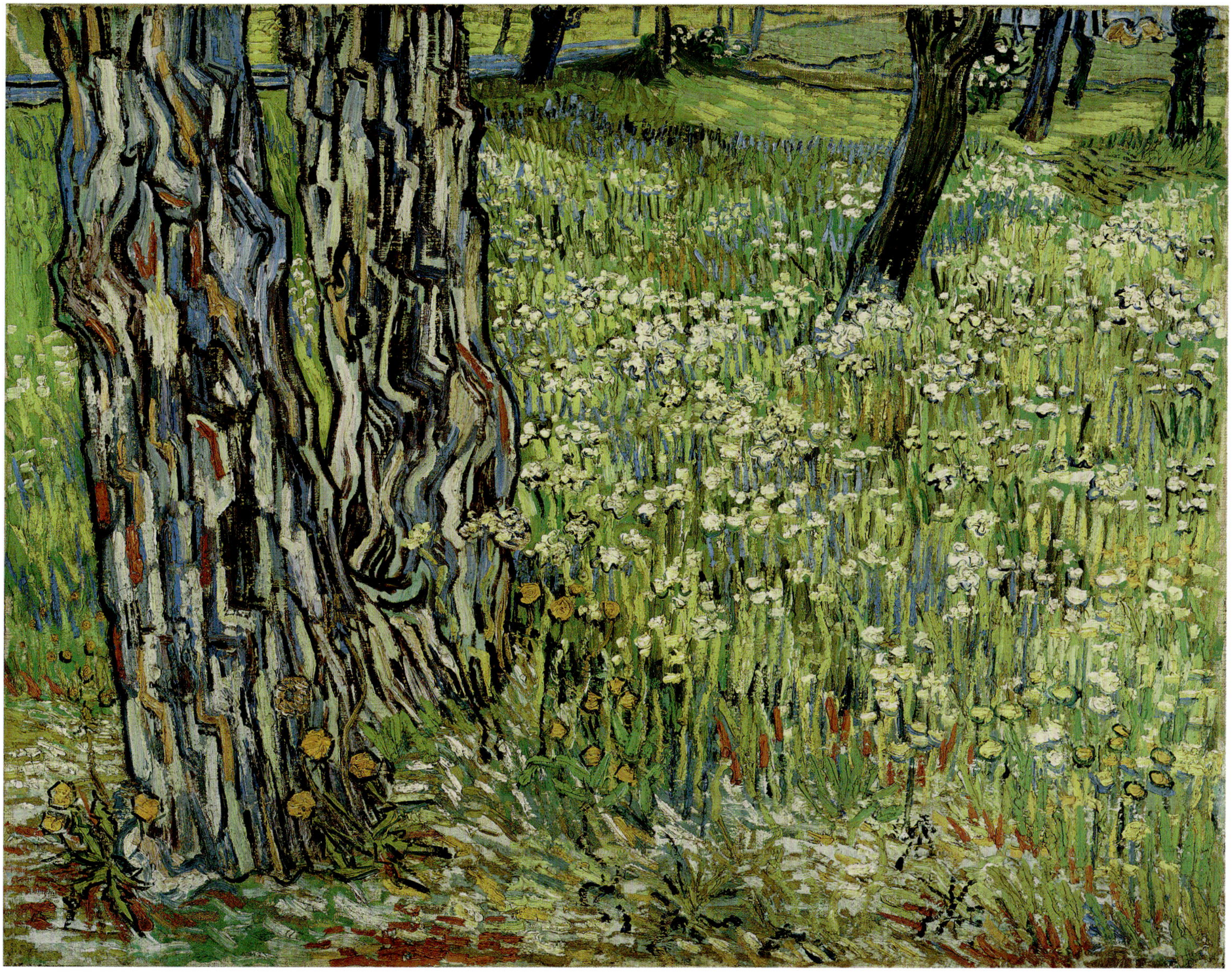

Fig. 48 (opposite)
Vincent van Gogh to Theo van Gogh with sketch of the *Asylum Garden with Dandelions and Tree Trunks*, Saint-Rémy-de-Provence, 4 May 1890, pen and ink on paper, 10$^{11}/_{16}$ × 16$^{9}/_{16}$ in. (27.1 × 42 cm), Van Gogh Museum, Amsterdam (Vincent van Gogh Foundation), b680V/1962

Notes

1 Van Gogh was painting *Entrance to a Quarry* (F 744, Van Gogh Museum, Amsterdam). See Vincent van Gogh to Theo van Gogh, 22 August 1889, letter 797.

2 Ibid.

3 Van Gogh had two more crises, in December and January, but these were relatively light—he did not work then for about a week.

4 Vincent van Gogh to Theo van Gogh, 29 April 1890, letter 863.

5 Ibid.

6 Vincent van Gogh to Theo van Gogh, 4 May 1890, letter 868.

7 See also Jos ten Berge, Teio Meedendorp, and Aukje Vergeest, *The Paintings of Vincent van Gogh in the Collection of the Kröller-Müller Museum* (Otterlo: Kröller-Müller Museum, 2003), 346 (entry by Teio Meedendorp).

9

VINCENT VAN GOGH (1853–1890)

Undergrowth with Two Figures

second half of June 1890

oil on canvas, 19½ × 39¼ in. (49.5 × 99.7 cm)

Cincinnati Art Museum, Bequest of Mary E. Johnston, 1967.1430, F 773

In Auvers, Van Gogh did not have much time to write to Theo; he had to make up the time lost in the hospital. Although he was nostalgic about leaving the Provence landscape that had offered him endless inspiration, he was not disappointed when he arrived in the North of France: "Auvers is decidedly very beautiful. So much so that I think it'll be more advantageous to work than not to work."[1] And productive he was. In the seventy days he spent there until his death, Vincent created an average of one painting a day.

In late June, Van Gogh started to work on a peculiar size of canvas, "one metre long by only 50 centimetres high." Among his first paintings was *Undergrowth with Two Figures*.[2] In early July he sent Theo a sketch of the painting (fig. 49), explaining that the purple poplars function as "columns" that "cross the landscape perpendicularly."[3] The alien atmosphere of the painting is emphasized by a strip of dark blue in the background, suggesting the depth of the forest, while the grass is overgrown with flowers. As in his other *Undergrowth* paintings, Van Gogh outlined the trees in long, vertical strokes that he painted directly on the ground layer, while he constructed the rich vegetation in short, thick touches. In the middle, two faceless figures stand confined between the trunks. Van Gogh had not intended to paint the figures in the beginning, or he would have left space in the paint layers. Instead, the figures have been directly added wet-in-wet to the thick layers of the undergrowth. Van Gogh did not mention the couple in the description in his letters, but he did clearly show them in the sketch.[4] This motif of "lovers" had been used previously in some of Van Gogh's landscapes, in Paris as well as in Arles.[5]

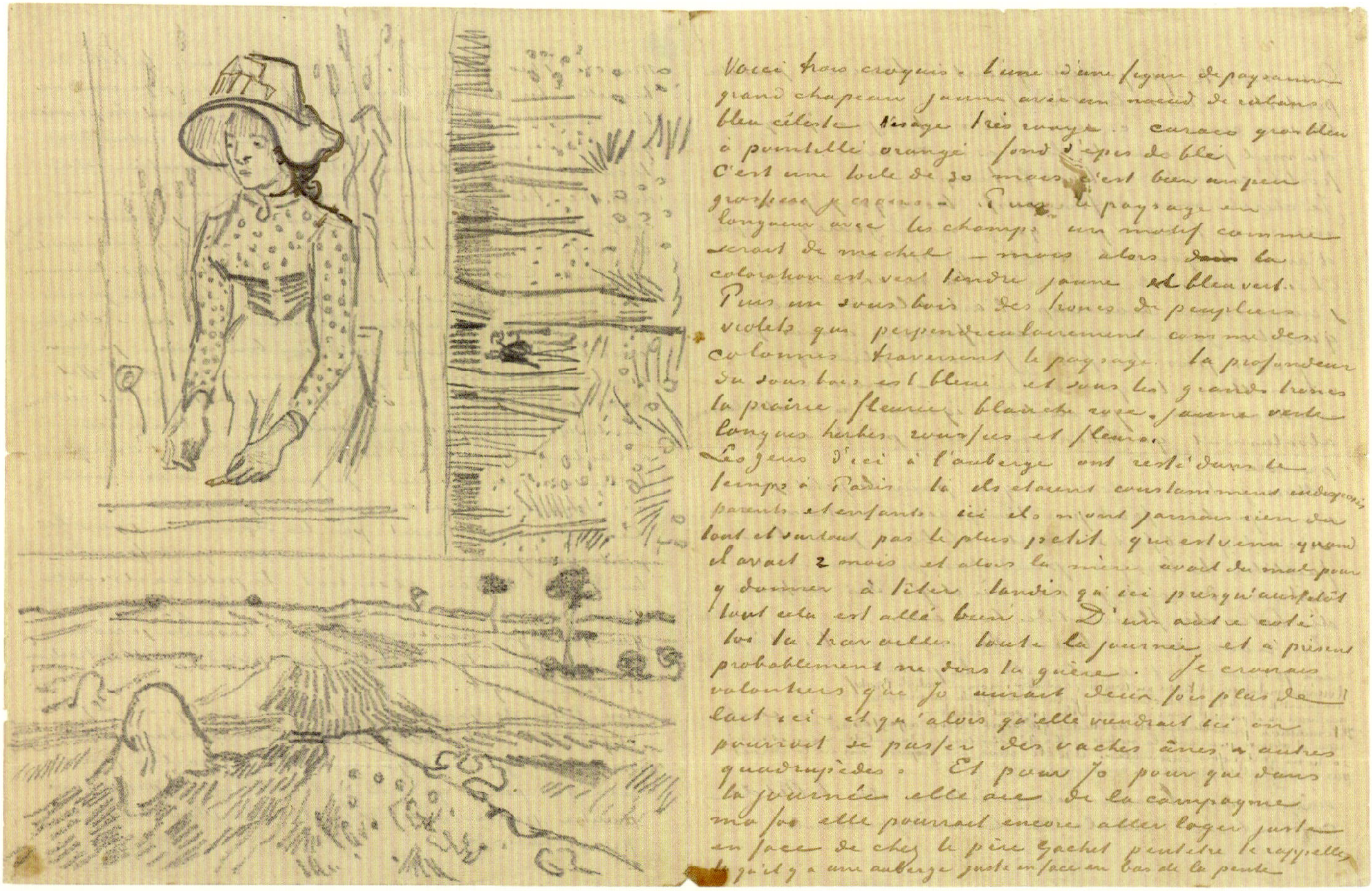
Voici trois croquis – l'une d'une figure de paysanne grand chapeau jaune avec un noeud de rubans bleu céleste visage très rouge caraco gros bleu à pointillé orangé fond d'épis de blé
C'est une toile de 30 mais c'est bien un peu grossier
Puis un sous bois des troncs de peupliers violets qui perpendiculairement comme des colonnes traversent le paysage. la profondeur du sous bois est bleue et sous les grands troncs la prairie fleurie blanche rose, jaune verte longues herbes rousses et fleurs.
Les gens d'ici à l'auberge ont resté dans le temps à Paris là ils étaient constamment indisposés parents et enfants ici ils n'ont jamais rien du tout et surtout pas le plus petit qui est venu quand il avait 2 mois et alors la mère avait du mal pour y donner à téter tandis qu'ici presqu'aussitôt tout cela est allé bien. D'un autre côté
toi tu travailles toute la journée et à présent probablement ne dors tu guère. Je croirais volontiers que Jo aurait deux fois plus de lait ici et qu'alors qu'elle viendrait ici on pourrait se passer des vaches ânes & autres quadrupèdes. Et pour Jo pour que dans la journée elle ait de la compagnie ma foi elle pourrait encore aller loger juste en face de chez le père Gachet peutêtre te rappelles tu qu'il y a une auberge juste en face en bas de la pente

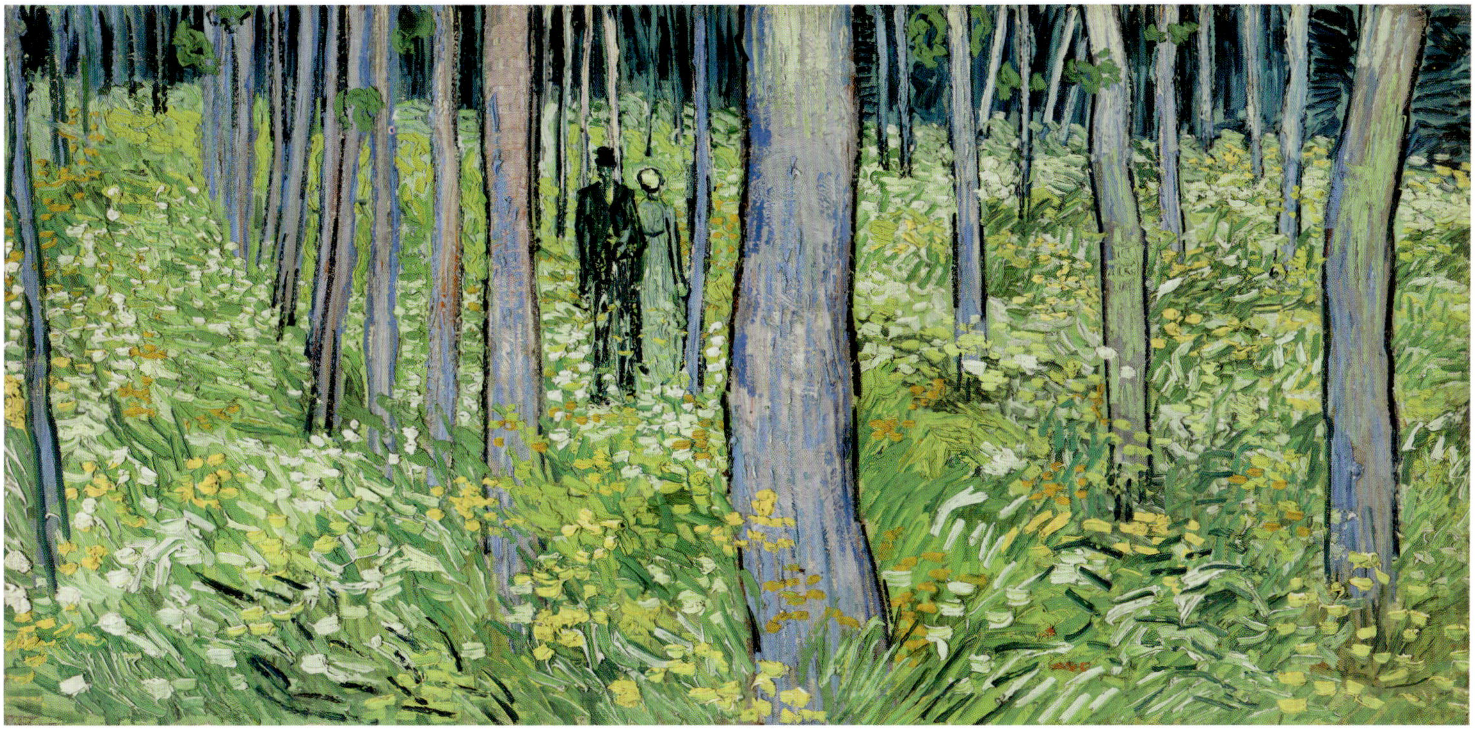

Fig. 49 (opposite)
Vincent van Gogh to Theo van Gogh and Jo van Gogh-Bonger with sketches of *Girl against a Background of Wheat*, *Couple Walking between Rows of Poplars*, and *Wheatfields*, Auvers-sur-Oise, 2 July 1890, pen and ink on paper, 10⅝ × 16⁷⁄₁₆ in. (27 × 41.8 cm), Van Gogh Museum, Amsterdam (Vincent van Gogh Foundation), b694V/1962

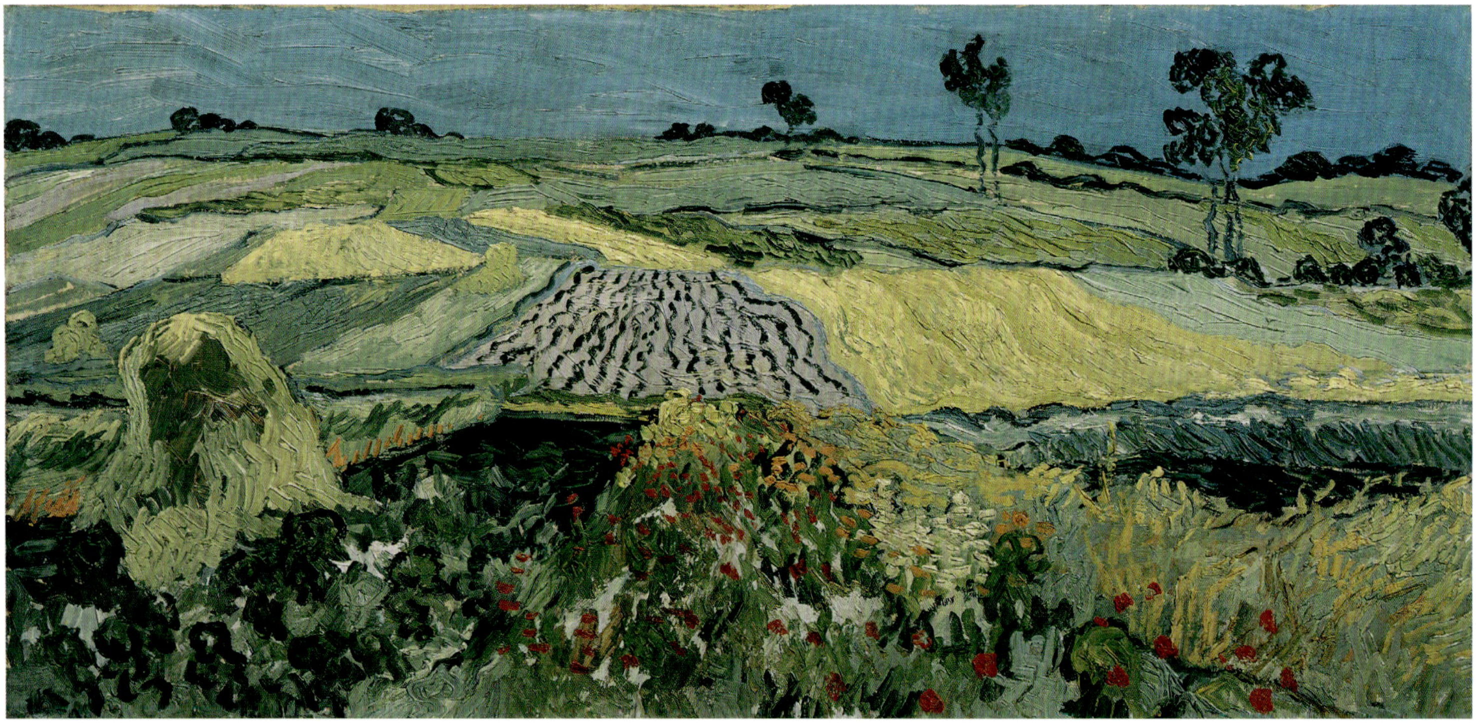

Fig. 50
Vincent van Gogh (1853–1890),
The Plain of Auvers, 1890,
oil on canvas,
19 11/16 × 197 1/4 in. (50 × 50.1 cm),
Österreichische Galerie Belvedere,
Vienna, 1007, F 775

It is tempting to read Van Gogh's mental condition into this claustrophobic painting of undergrowth with the ghostlike couple. Although he was working frantically, producing a succession of masterworks, Van Gogh was in a somber state of mind. He was worried about Theo and his young family's health, and about their financial position as well. He realized that he was too dependent on his brother. However, he created at the same time a painting of "fields of wheat . . . that makes a pendant of undergrowth" (fig. 50).[6] This extensive landscape, which breathes optimism, forms an exciting contrast with the enclosed view of the forest. Van Gogh loved to create combinations like this, based on color and decorative compositions, because they intensified the individual paintings. "But we're still a long way from people understanding the curious relationships that exist between one piece of nature and another, which however explain and bring each other out."[7] The feeling of estrangement in *Undergrowth with Two Figures* may have been enhanced over time, moreover, because we know that a certain red pigment Van Gogh frequently used has faded with the years: some of the white flowers in the grass were in fact originally pink.[8] The way Van Gogh described the work to Theo reveals nothing of a somber mood. "The depths of the undergrowth are blue, and under the big trunks the flowery meadow, white, pink, yellow, green, long russet grasses and flowers."[9] For Van Gogh, the landscape was consoling, and he hoped to bring solace with his paintings, too.

Notes

1 Vincent van Gogh to Theo van Gogh and Jo van Gogh-Bonger, on or about 21 May 1890, letter 874.

2 Vincent van Gogh to Theo van Gogh, 24 June 1890, letter 891.

3 Vincent van Gogh to Theo van Gogh and Jo van Gogh-Bonger, 2 July 1890, letter 896.

4 See also Jennifer A. Thompson, "Sous-Bois," in *Van Gogh: Up Close*, ed. Cornelia Homburg (New Haven: Yale University Press, 2012), 208.

5 See Vincent van Gogh to Theo van Gogh, on or about 3 April 1888, letter 592, on the Paris painting *Couples in a Montmartre Garden* (F 314, Van Gogh Museum, Amsterdam), and letter 709, 21 October 1888, for the Arles paintings titled *The Poet's Garden* (F 485, location unknown; F 479, private collection).

6 Vincent van Gogh to Theo van Gogh, 24 June 1890, letter 891.

7 Vincent van Gogh to Theo van Gogh, 28 June 1890, letter 893. See also Cornelia Homburg, "Nature So Close," in Homburg, *Van Gogh: Up Close*, 32.

8 Gregory Smith, "Conservation Science: Van Gogh and the Case of Geranium Lake," *IMA Magazine* (August–October 2012): 4–7.

9 Vincent van Gogh to Theo van Gogh and Jo van Gogh-Bonger, 2 July 1890, letter 896.

10

KARL BODMER (1809–1893)

Fontainebleau in Autumn
(or Interior of the Forest During Winter)

1850–51

oil on canvas, 35⁵⁄₁₆ × 39¾ in. (82 × 101 cm)

Musée du Louvre, Paris, France,

RF 63

In January 1874, when Van Gogh worked in the London branch of the art gallery Goupil, he wrote to Theo about the artists he liked best.[1] It is a long list of names—all testifying to Van Gogh's rather conservative taste, as well as to Goupil's core business—and it includes Karl Bodmer. This autumn view of a forest with a group of deer resting in the middle is a good example of what in the Swiss artist's work attracted him. From a low perspective, as if sitting on the ground with the deer, Bodmer depicted truthfully and with respect the diversity of Fontainebleau's forest.

Van Gogh carried on in his letter to Theo with the advice to "always continue walking a lot and loving nature, for that's the real way to learn to understand art better and better. Painters understand nature and love it, and *teach us to see*." Van Gogh tirelessly shared his ideas on art. A few years later, when he had decided to become an artist himself, he put these ideas into practice.

Van Gogh saw this Bodmer painting at the Musée du Luxembourg in 1875, when he worked for the Paris branch of Goupil, but he may already have known the print after the painting (fig. 51) when he worked in London.[2] Goupil had created a worldwide brand by publishing high-quality black-and-white reproductions of their paintings. These popular prints enabled many households to hang art on their walls. Van Gogh's small apartment was no exception, and he regularly sent family and friends copies from the works he admired, including this one by Bodmer.[3] The copy Vincent had given to his father in 1875 decorated the latter's study, as Van Gogh recalled on 8 April 1877: "On Saturday evening I left on the last train from Dordrecht to Oudenbosch and walked from there to Zundert. It was so beautiful there on the heath, even though it was dark one could make out the heath and the pine-woods and the marshes stretching far and wide, it reminded me of that illustration by Bodmer that's hanging in Pa's study."[4]

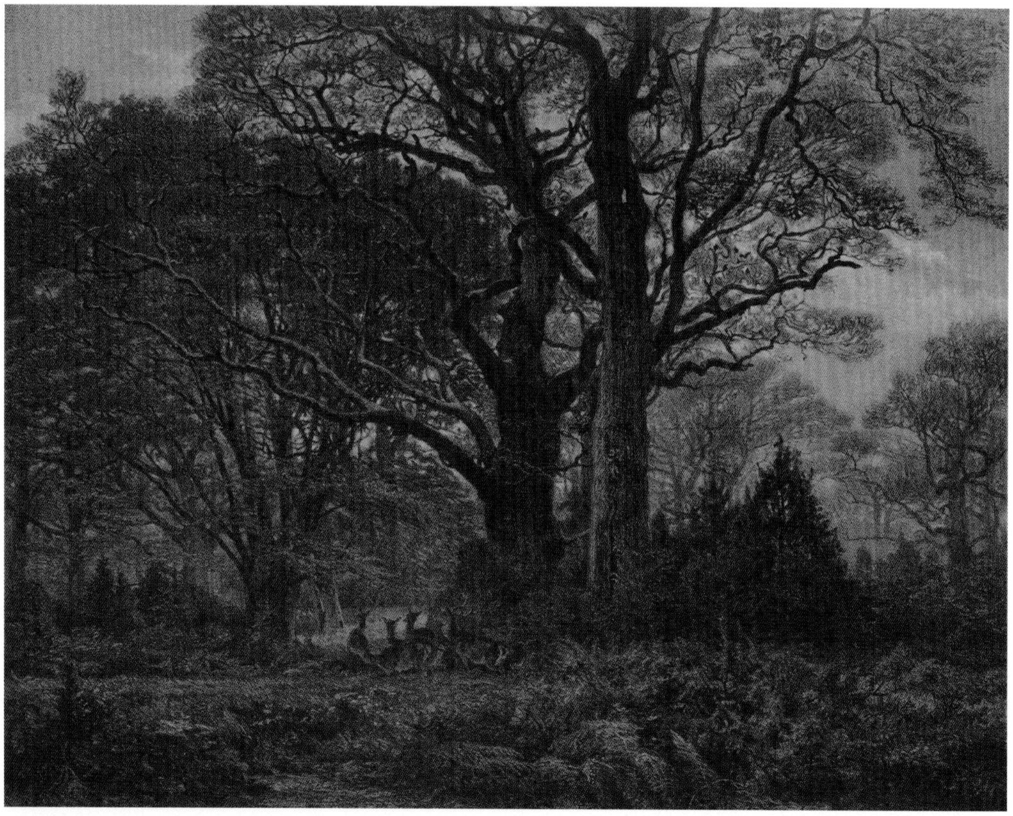

Fig. 51
Eugène Leroux (1807–1863) after Karl Bodmer (1809–1893),
Fôret de Fontainebleau, 1850–51,
lithograph,
9 × 11¼ in. (23 × 28.5 cm),
Rijksmuseum, Amsterdam,
RP-P-OB-40.651

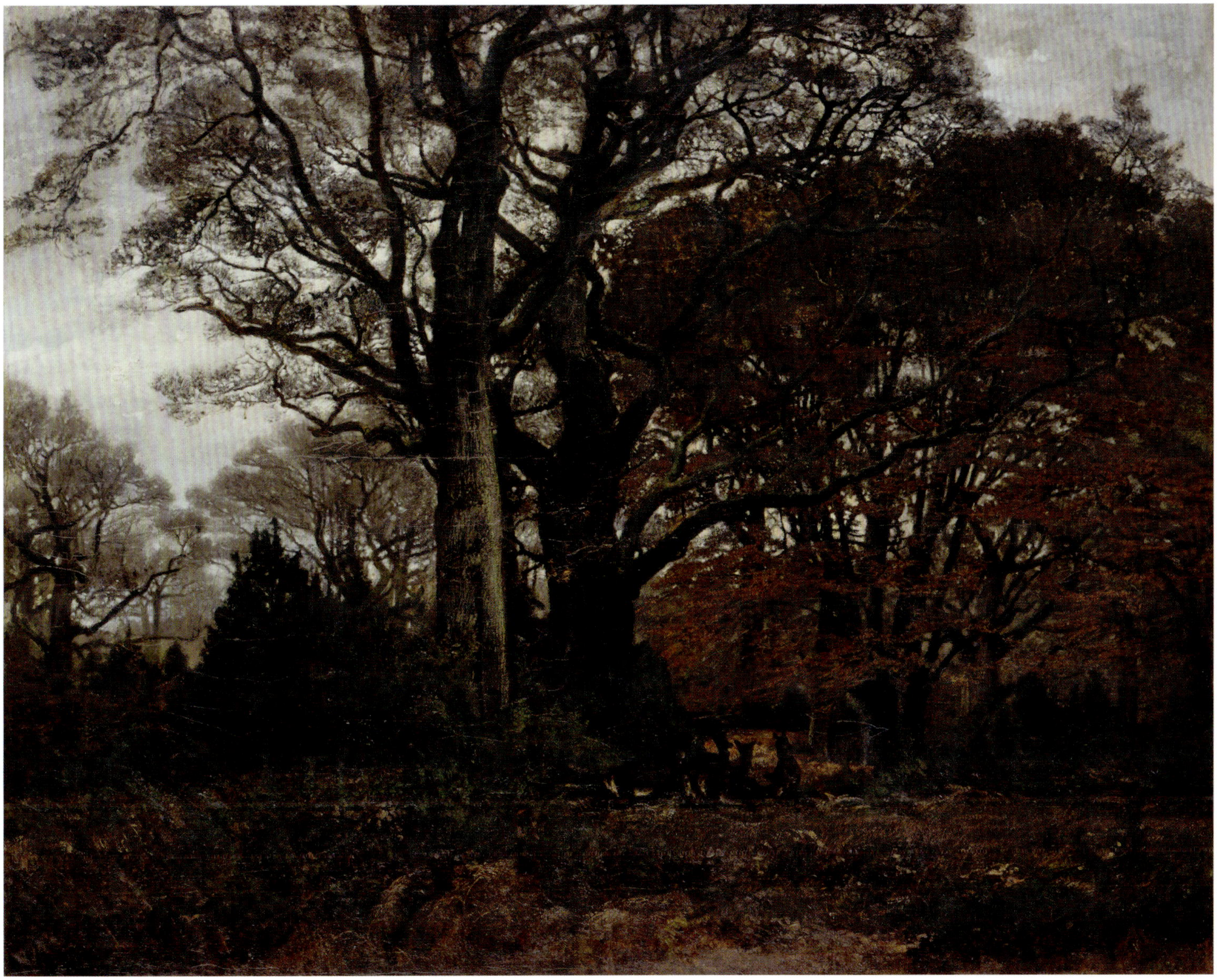

Today Karl Bodmer is nearly forgotten, except for the documentary illustrations he made of Native Americans in the 1830s. In his productive years, however, especially the 1850s and 60s before he suffered severe health and financial problems, Bodmer was a respected painter and printmaker connected to the Barbizon School.[5] He exhibited regularly at the Paris Salon and had these paintings reproduced at the same time, providing him a great deal of exposure. Bodmer's painting of an oak in the Forest of Fontainebleau, exhibited at the 1850 Salon, is a famous example. Both painting and tree became known as "The Bodmer Oak" (see cat. 18).[6] As the Barbizon oeuvre of Bodmer is only sketchily inventoried, it is not clear precisely which one of his paintings was responsible for this hype, but it may well be this view of Fontainebleau that Van Gogh loved so much.

Notes

1 Vincent van Gogh to Theo van Gogh, beginning of January 1874, letter 17.

2 Vincent van Gogh to Theo van Gogh, 11 October 1875, letter 55. It is assumed that Van Gogh meant this present painting by Bodmer. We know that Van Gogh had this print on his wall in Paris; see letter 37.

3 See letters 37, 54, 55, and 66.

4 Vincent van Gogh to Theo van Gogh, 8 April 1877, letter 110.

5 David C. Hunt, "A Publication History of Karl Bodmer's North American Atlas," in *Karl Bodmer's Studio Art: The Newberry Library Bodmer Collection*, ed. W. Raymond Wood, Joseph C. Porter, and David C. Hunt (Urbana: University of Illinois Press, 2002), 111–12.

6 Kimberly Jones, ed., *In the Forest of Fontainebleau: Painters and Photographers from Corot to Monet* (Washington: National Gallery of Art; Houston: Museum of Fine Arts; New Haven: Yale University Press, 2008), 65.

11

KARL BODMER (1809–1893) and
JEAN-FRANÇOIS MILLET (1814–1875)

In the Forest (En forêt ou haute futaie)

1852

lithograph, 23½ × 18¼ in. (59.7 × 46.4 cm)
Cincinnati Art Museum, Anonymous Gift,
1940.845

In the midst of the untamed forest, a small peasant figure drags a heavy pile of brushwood. The representation of the working class is a recurrent characteristic in the oeuvre of Millet, the artist Van Gogh admired most. It was especially by studying and copying the peasants of Millet that Van Gogh learned his figure painting.[1] Millet rarely depicted this type of wooded landscape; the few examples show his interest in evoking a certain atmosphere rather than rendering the trees in detail (fig. 52). It was Bodmer—the other artist Van Gogh admired all his life—who was responsible for this forest landscape. As late as 1889 Vincent wrote to Theo, "Let's take good Bodmer for example. Was he not able to study nature as a hunter, a savage, did he not love it and know it with experience of an entire long manly life . . . ?"[2] The skills of the Swiss artist lay precisely in depictions of the forest and its inhabitants. Van Gogh knew many of Bodmer's lithographs and reproductions from early on. Their "lithographic spectrum of colours, or rather spectrum of greys" influenced him greatly. Van Gogh, who was still practicing his drawing skills, considered these works "prints finished like paintings."[3] This lithograph, for which Bodmer asked Millet to draw the figure, thus combined the strengths of Van Gogh's two heroes.

There is little documentation of the Bodmer-Millet cooperation. In the 1850s and 60s, Bodmer was commissioned several times to create lithographs or etchings, for instance for the journal *L'Illustration*, which published a series of animal scenes in limited edition. In 1851 an American publisher requested a series of scenes of early American colonial life. Bodmer asked Millet to participate, but in the end only four lithographs were realized, titled *Annals of the United States Illustrated: The Pioneers*.[4] The present lithograph is not part of this series, but must have been made in the same period. Whether it was intended for a different series or is simply the result of a friendly collaboration cannot be determined.

In 1849, Bodmer and Millet had become good friends when they both settled in Barbizon, a rural village southeast of Paris, bordering Fontainebleau. This ancient forest had been the royal hunting ground for centuries, but by the mid-nineteenth century, especially with the development of the railway, Fontainebleau had become a popular tourist retreat for Parisians. Many artists, attracted to this unique forest, had begun in the 1820s to visit it. In the late 1840s, Rousseau, Diaz, Millet, and Bodmer rented cottages on the Grand Rue to settle there on a more permanent basis. Known as the Barbizon School, they scrupulously depicted the extraordinary variety of vegetation at different moments of the day and in different seasons (see cats. 10, 14, 15, and 16).[5]

Van Gogh had never visited the forest of Fontainebleau, but through the works of the Barbizon painters and his own experience of nature he could relate to this landscape. "Now take the Barbizon painters, not only do I understand them as people, but in my view *everything*, the tiniest, most intimate particulars, sparkles with spirit and life. . . . It has a certain good will in its favour, a certain sincerity, a certain genuinely human quality."[6]

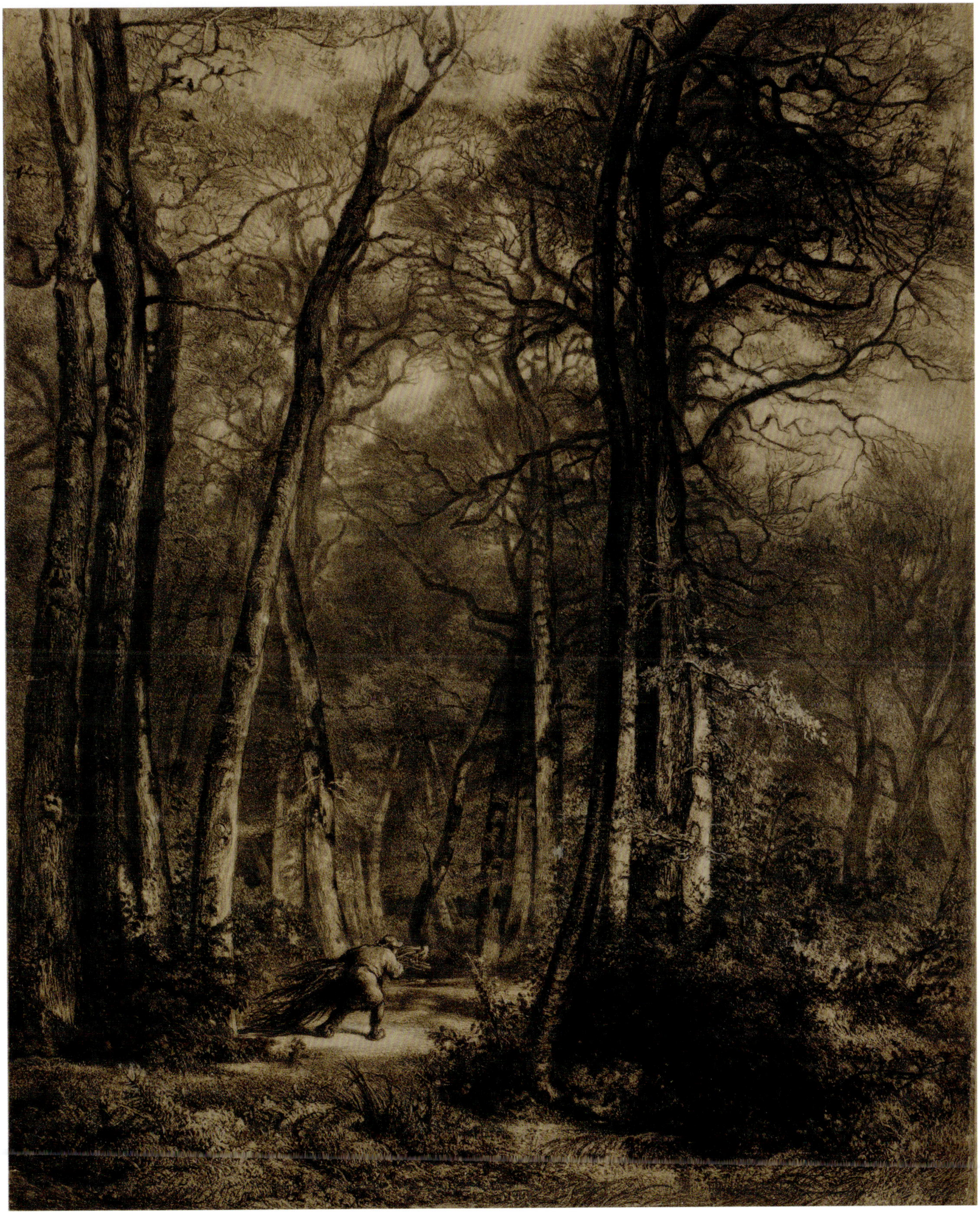

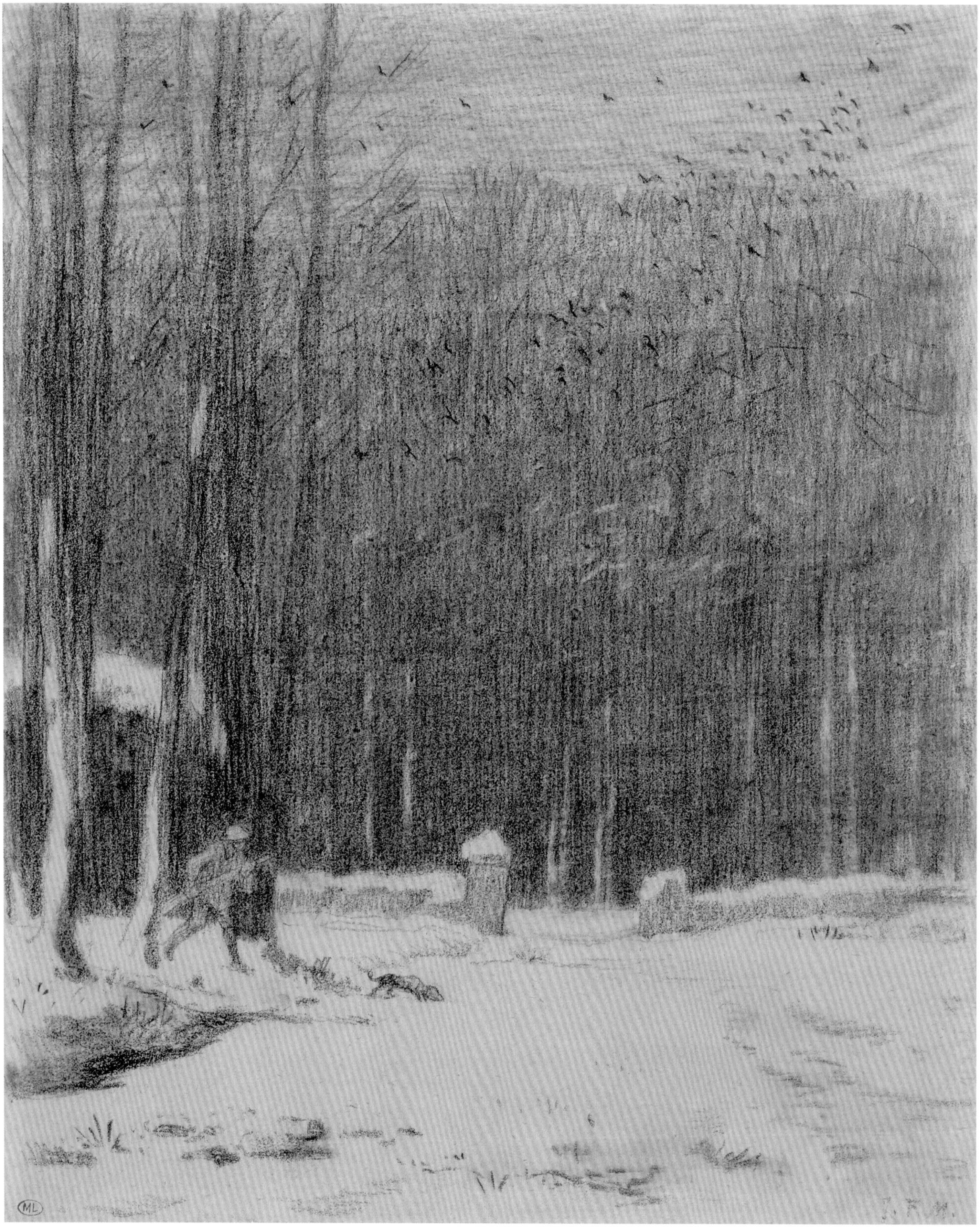

Notes

1 On this subject, see especially Louis van Tilborgh et al., *Van Gogh & Millet*, exh. cat. (Amsterdam: Van Gogh Museum; Zwolle: Waanders, 1988; Paris: Musée d'Orsay, 1998).

2 Vincent van Gogh to Theo van Gogh, on or about 2 September 1889, letter 798.

3 Vincent van Gogh to Theo van Gogh, on or about 29 March and 1 April 1883, letter 333.

4 David C. Hunt, "A Publication History of Karl Bodmer's North American Atlas," in *Karl Bodmer's Studio Art: The Newberry Library Bodmer Collection*, ed. W. Raymond Wood, Joseph C. Porter, and David C. Hunt (Urbana: The University of Illinois Press, 2002), 111.

5 See especially Nicholas Green, *The Spectacle of Nature: Landscape and Bourgeois Culture in Nineteenth-Century France* (Manchester: Manchester University Press, 1990), 116–17; Kimberly Jones, ed., *In the Forest of Fontainebleau: Painters and Photographers from Corot to Monet* (Washington: National Gallery of Art; Houston: Museum of Fine Arts; New Haven: Yale University Press, 2008), 4–14. See also the essay by Jenny Reynaerts.

6 Vincent van Gogh to Theo van Gogh, 28 October 1883, letter 400.

Fig. 52
Jean-François Millet (1814–1875),
L'entrée de la forêt enneigée à Barbizon (*Entrance to the Forest of Barbizon; Effect of Snow*), 1853,
charcoal on beige paper,
11⅛ × 8⅞ in. (28.3 × 22.5 cm),
Musée d'Orsay, Paris, France,
RF 4159

12

JEAN-BAPTISTE-CAMILLE COROT (1796–1875)

The Large Oak with Three Peasants (Tower in the Distance)

ca. 1860–65

oil on canvas, 19 11/16 × 24 1/16 in. (50 × 61.1 cm)

Cincinnati Art Museum, Gift of John B. Hollister, 1975.375

As a young artist still in his apprenticeship, Corot had already visited Fontainebleau. After a period of study in Italy, he returned numerous times to record the forest in all its natural wealth. Corot became one of the first painters to elevate the study directly derived from nature into a finished work worthy of exhibition.[1] At the Salon, his somber palette and lack of finish were often criticized, but to his colleagues of the Barbizon School (see cats. 14, 15, and 16), he was extremely influential.[2]

As he matured, Corot changed his strategy and began to create landscapes largely from memory.[3] This painting is a wonderful view of massive oaks and lush meadow, where two peasants labor as a woman approaches them. Behind the figures a distant sunlit town is visible through the woods. Possibly Corot depicted Ville-d'Avray, where his family owned property.[4] In his typical late style, with tones of silvery gray, Corot created an exciting contrast between the dark shade of the trees and the blue sky in the background. The humid atmosphere suggests that a rain shower has just freshened the landscape. Carefully, the sun touches the small figures of the peasants and reveals itself in the darkness through bright dots of blue and red.

Next to the tall oak in the middle, the figures look insignificant. Oaks were a favorite subject for artists, because their expressive trunks with diverging limbs gave them human-like features, while their longevity emphasized human mortality. According to the critic Théophile Thoré, the oak was "the sacred tree . . . the national tree which served our ancestors as natural cathedral in the celebration of their mysteries."[5] With Corot, we feel as if the oak is here to protect the figures, because its vast shade is inviting rather than mysterious.

Such paintings with a typical "Corot atmosphere" must have spoken to Van Gogh, who may have seen this painting when he visited the large 1875 Corot retrospective in Paris.[6] Van Gogh not only admired Corot's work, but by reading his biography he was drawn to Corot's character as well. When he lived in Antwerp, sensitive to all the misery he observed in the city, Vincent wrote to Theo: "One may not be able to cure or save, but one can nonetheless sympathize and share in it. Corot, who had serenity if anyone did, who truly felt the spring, wasn't he as simple as a working man and thus sensible of all the misfortunes of others all his life? And something that struck me in a biography of him—when he was already very old in 70–71, he certainly still looked up into the clear sky, but—at the same time he visited the ambulances where the wounded lay dying. Illusions may fade—but what *endures* is the sublime . . . . And I think that in moments when one doesn't care about nature any more, one still cares about people."[7]

Notes

1 See the essay by Jenny Reynaerts in this volume.

2 Simon Kelly, "The Mystery of the Forest," in *In the Forest of Fontainebleau: Painters and Photographers from Corot to Monet*, ed. Kimberly Jones (Washington: National Gallery of Art; Houston: Museum of Fine Arts; New Haven: Yale University Press, 2008), 142–44.

3 See Gary Tinterow, "Le père Corot: Le patriarche des paysagistes; Le poète même du paysage," in *Corot 1796–1875*, ed. Vincent Pomarède, Michael Pantazzi, and Gary Tinterow, exh. cat. (Paris: Réunion des Musées Nationaux et al., 1996), 325.

4 Compared to, e.g., Corot's painting *A Woman Gathering Faggots at Ville-d'Avray*, ca. 1871–74 (Metropolitan Museum of Art, New York); see Gary Tinterow et al., *Masterpieces of European Painting in the Metropolitan Museum of Art (1800–1920)* (New York: Metropolitan Museum of Art; New Haven: Yale University Press, 2007), 39.

5 Thoré in 1847, quoted in Jones, *In the Forest of Fontainebleau*, 65.

6 In a letter to Theo on 29 and 30 July 1883 (letter 369), Van Gogh spoke about a "Corot atmosphere." For his visit to the 1875 Corot exhibition, see Van Gogh's letter to Theo on 31 May 1875, letter 34. It is unknown if the present painting was in this exhibition but, according to a newspaper article in the documentation of the Cincinnati Art Museum, in September 1875 the work had only recently arrived in Cincinnati. Its owner, Mr. Baker, bought a Corot landscape from Goupil in 1875, which could be this one.

7 Vincent van Gogh to Theo van Gogh, 14 February 1886, letter 562.

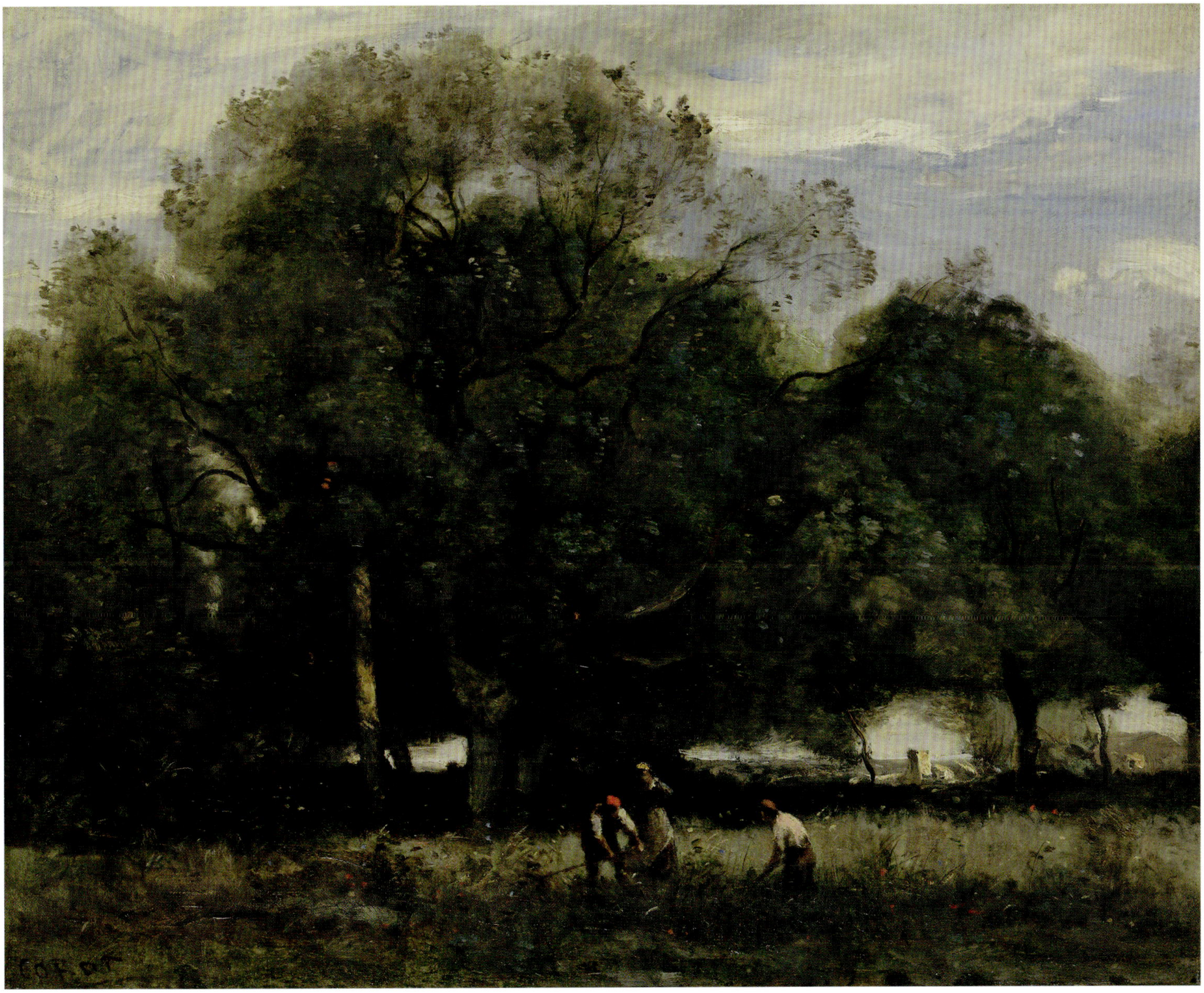

13

JEAN-BAPTISTE-CAMILLE COROT (1796–1875)

The Dreamer (Le songeur)

From the portfolio Maurice Le Garrec, *Quarante clichés-glace*, 1921
January 1854
cliché-verre, 4⅛ × 6⅛ in. (10.5 × 15.6 cm)
Cincinnati Art Museum, Gift of Herbert Greer French,
1940.563

Two large, overhanging trees offer protection to a small figure who sits on a rock, staring into the brightly lit distance. The lone figure in contemplation is completely in harmony with his natural surroundings. To the viewer, the dreamer represents the artist's experience of nature.[1] Corot created this little composition in the experimental technique of the *cliché-verre*, to which he was introduced in 1853 in Arras. In this village in northern France, Corot worked together with a group of artists, led by Constant Dutilleux, who explored both the calm surroundings of the region and different forms of printmaking and photography.[2]

The *cliché-verre* is a combination of drawing, print, and photograph: it is made on a transparent (glass) support coated with an opaque substance. By scratching away the coating with a needle, pencil, finger, or brush, a drawing takes form. The result is printed through exposure to light, as with a photographic negative. The *cliché-verre* was not widely popular, having neither the sophisticated look of etching, nor the advantages of mass production, due to its rather high costs and unpredictable character. But its accessible and experimental quality was attractive to artists like Corot.[3] The French master mainly worked in the dry technique, using a sharp object, which resulted in a drawing consisting of harsh lines, reminiscent of a drypoint (fig. 53). In *The Dreamer*, however, Corot achieved a tonal effect that he created with the wet technique. With a brush or stick, and perhaps a piece of cloth, he worked in the wet coating, as if painting in negative.[4] Corot worked from dark to light, first modeling the different elements in the composition, and then using something sharp to outline the contours of the trees and figure. The result is an intimate, mysterious black-and-white scene that perfectly suits the dream state of the isolated figure at the mercy of Mother Nature.

Corot made this *cliché-verre* in 1854 in only a few impressions. In 1921, Maurice Le Garrec reprinted the glass plates from his collection in a portfolio titled *Quarante clichés-glace* in a limited edition of 150. Because Le Garrec used twentieth-century paper and chemicals, which had a different light sensitivity than the albumen paper used in Corot's time, the modern impressions unintentionally differed from the originals. The compositions had become black, instead of brown, and much more darkened. This darkening is especially evident in *The Dreamer*, and numerous nuances have been lost.[5]

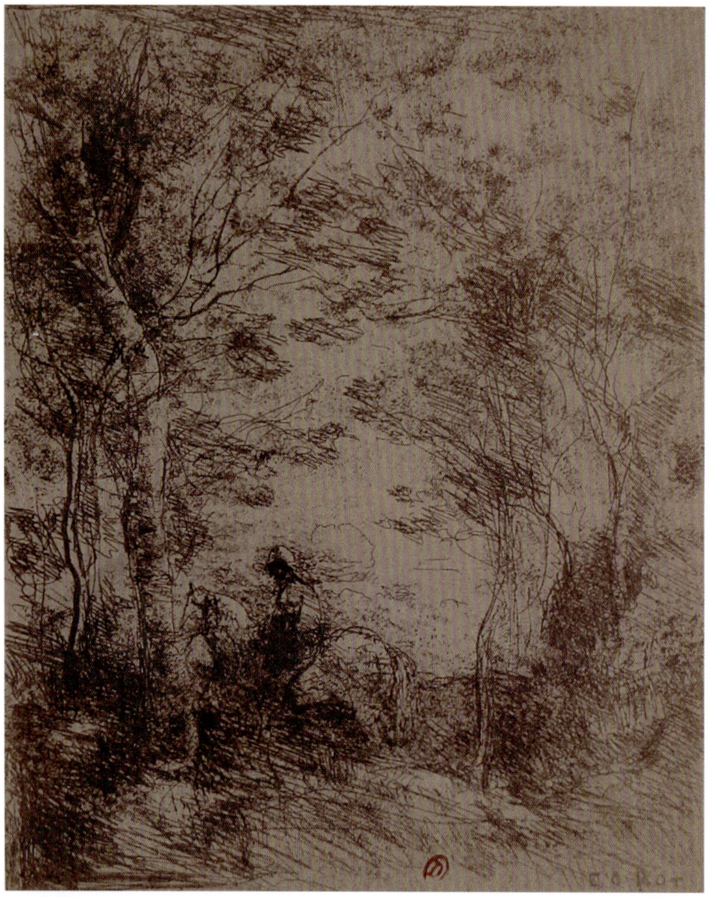

Fig. 53
Jean-Baptiste-Camille Corot
(1796–1875),
Le petit cavalier sous bois, 1854,
cliché-verre,
7¼ × 5¾ in. (18.4 × 14.6 cm),
Bibliothèque de l'Institut national
d'histoire de l'art, Paris, France,
Collections Jacques Doucet,
Mfilm347_05_084

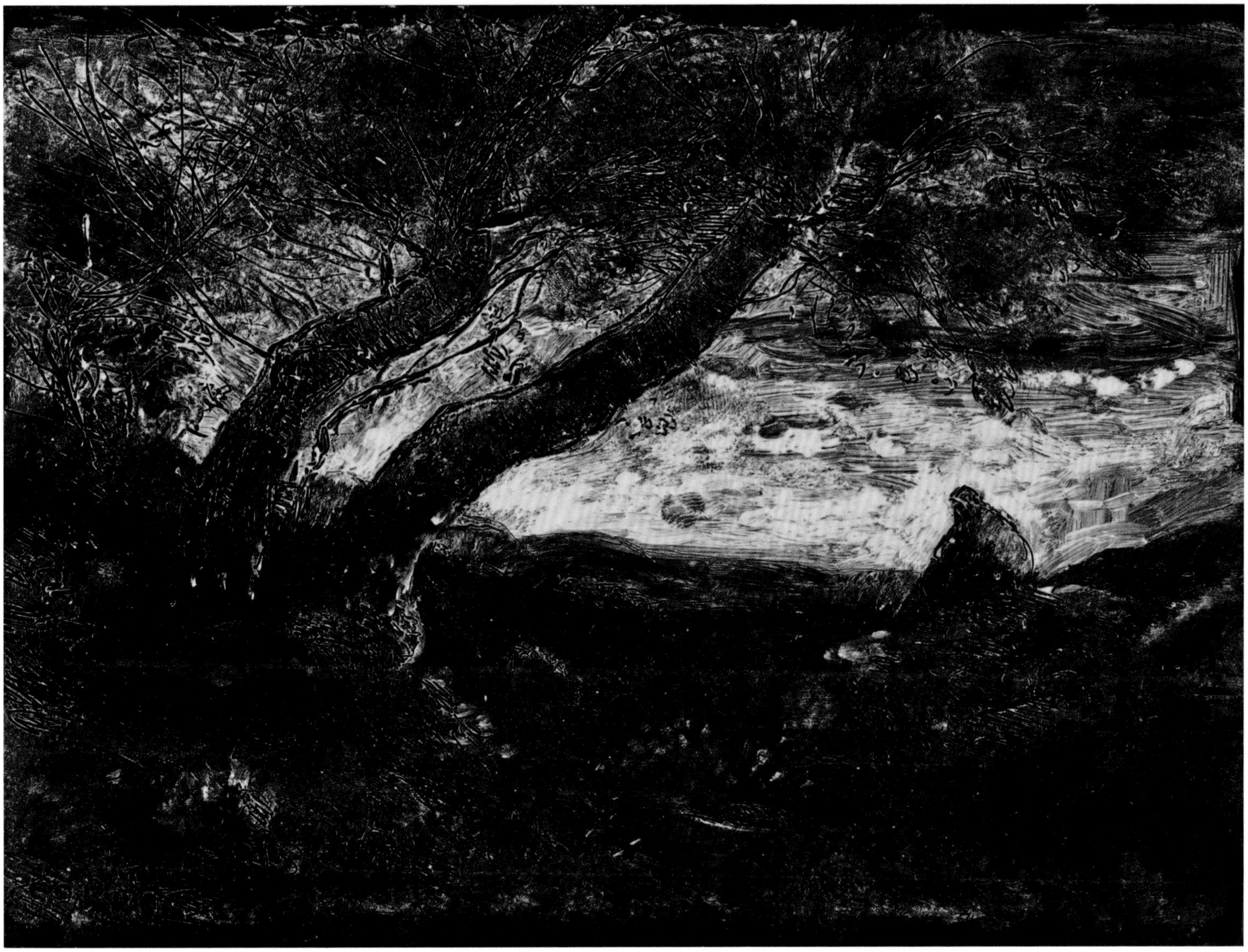

Notes

1 See the essay by Jenny Reynaerts in this volume.

2 Elizabeth Glassman and Marilyn F. Symmes, *Cliché-verre, Hand-Drawn, Light-Printed: A Survey of the Medium from 1839 to the Present* (Detroit: Detroit Institute of Arts, 1980), 36.

3 Ibid., 29–30. Corot had made 66 plates, by far the most of all artists who practiced the technique. See also *Gravure ou photographie? Une curiosité artistique: Le cliché-verre* (Montreuil: Gourcuff Gradenigo; Arras: Musée des Beaux-Arts, 2007), 65.

4 Glassman and Symmes, *Cliché-verre,* 52–55.

5 Ibid., 43–44, 55.

14

THÉODORE ROUSSEAU (1812–1867)

Leaving the Forest, Fontainebleau: Setting Sun

1851–60

oil on fabric, 42 15/16 × 51 1/4 in. (109.1 × 130.2 cm)

Cleveland Museum of Art, John L. Severance Fund, 1983.70

"How good it feels to see a fine Rousseau that has been laboured over in order to be faithful and honest," Van Gogh wrote to Theo in December 1882.[1] According to Van Gogh, Théodore Rousseau did not simply copy nature, but understood it, which effect he rendered truthfully on his canvas. Van Gogh knew the paintings of Rousseau from his Goupil period, as well as from visits to the Louvre and the remarkable collection of Hendrik Willem Mesdag in The Hague. In July 1883, Vincent recalled a forest painting by Rousseau and explained to his brother, "The dramatic effect of these paintings is something that helps us to understand 'a corner of nature seen through a temperament' and that helps us understand that the principle of 'man added to nature' is needed more than anything else in art . . . it's more than nature, more like a revelation."[2]

During his lifetime, Rousseau's artistic reputation suffered under the conventions of academic taste. After receiving some critical acclaim early in his career, Rousseau's paintings began to be rejected at the Salon in the late 1830s, because of his lack of finish. This gave him the nickname "Le grand refusé." In 1842, the dispirited Rousseau stopped sending works to the Salon. It was in these years of refusal that he traveled increasingly to the savage Forest of Fontainebleau, rather than to the more idyllic Normandy and Auvergne.[3] In 1847, Rousseau settled in a Barbizon cottage and, from the dead of winter to the height of summer, painted woodland scenes from sunrise to sunset. In 1849, Rousseau returned to the Salon. This time, his critical success lasted a bit longer, culminating at the 1855 Exposition Universelle.

It was in this later period that Rousseau painted *Leaving the Forest, Fontainebleau: Setting Sun*.[4] At first glance, it comes across as an *ébauche*, a preliminary sketch in oil, since large parts appear to be unfinished. This effect was most likely the artist's intention.[5] The painting, which Rousseau probably worked on for a couple of years, does appear to be experimental, as he combined different techniques. He first applied the browns and grays thinly, then added the green foliage, and with thicker strokes brought out the trunks of the trees and the distant sunset. He scratched away paint in some places to bring back the ground layers, marvelously done in the foreground with the rocks.[6] As such, Rousseau achieved an exciting composition of thin and impasto paint strokes, rendering the edge of the forest in the evening, when the setting sun adds a mysterious atmosphere. The first owner of this painting, Charles Edwards, expressed this perfectly in his 1870 auction catalogue: "A bleak melancholy reigns in the landscape of the *Great Forest*. It is a crumbling mass of stripped and barren trees, falling into ruins. You can almost hear dull cracking sounds coming out of the canvas."[7]

This painting is only one of many examples that almost breathe Rousseau's respect for the forest. In real life, he became a fervent petitioner to protect the wild forest, which, due to increasing tourism, suffered from human interference. To Napoleon III, together with critic Alfred Sensier, he wrote in a long petition: "I ask you for protection, Monseigneur, for these old trees which for artists are the source from which they draw their inspiration."[8] Rousseau succeeded in his conservation efforts when, in 1861, the emperor signed a decree to preserve several parts of the forest.[9]

Notes

1 Vincent van Gogh to Theo van Gogh, between 4 and 9 December 1882, letter 291.

2 Vincent van Gogh to Theo van Gogh, on or about 11 July 1883, letter 361. Van Gogh is discussing here the painting *Edge of the Forest of Fontainebleau, Setting Sun* of ca. 1850, which he saw in the Musée du Luxembourg (now in the Musée du Louvre, see fig. 12). Van Gogh is quoting Émile Zola, the famous naturalist writer, and Francis Bacon, the English philosopher.

3 Nicholas Green, *The Spectacle of Nature: Landscape and Bourgeois Culture in Nineteenth-Century France* (Manchester: Manchester University Press, 1990), 117–18.

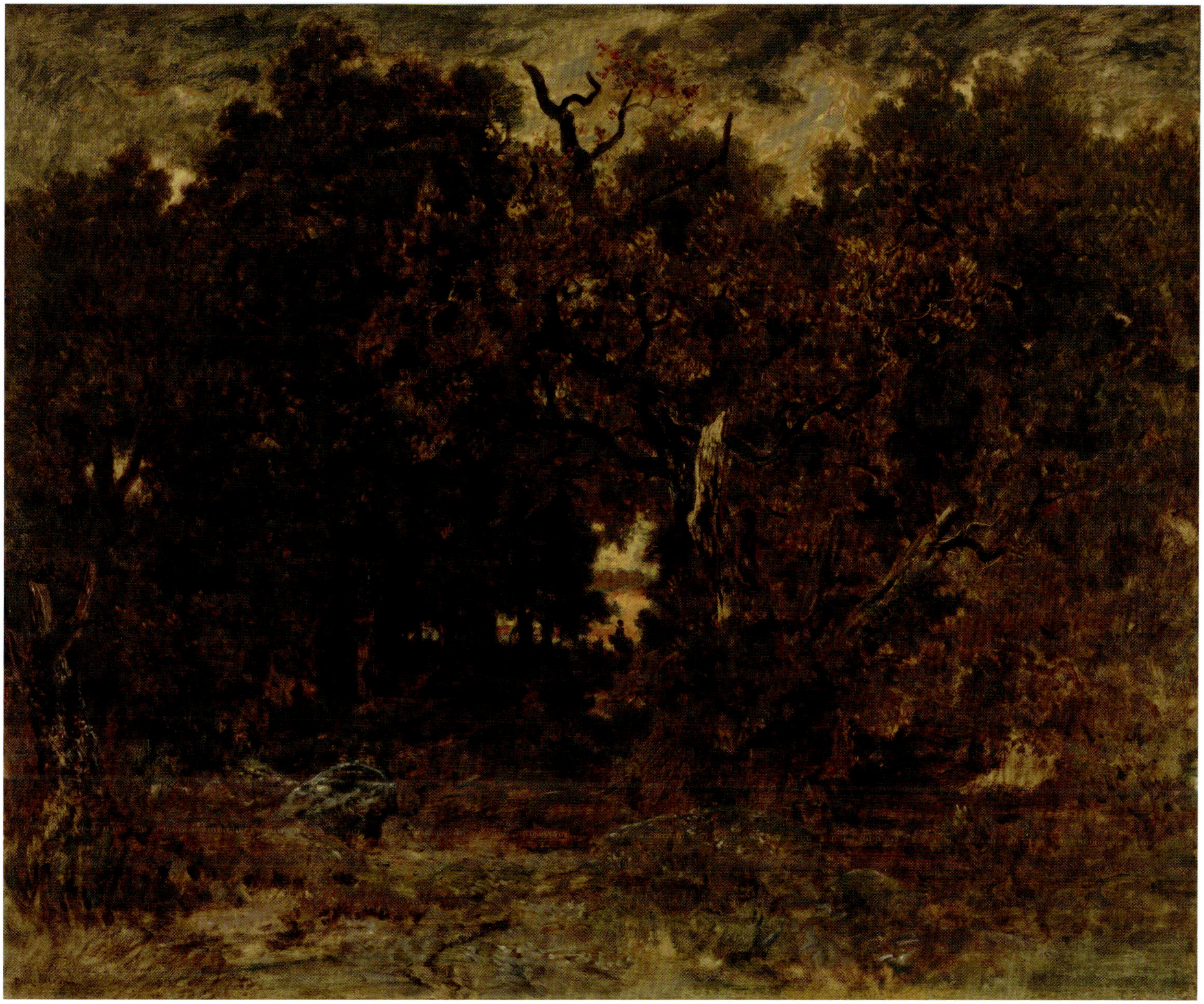

4 Louise d'Argencourt et al., "European Paintings of the 19th Century," in *The Cleveland Museum of Art Catalogue of Paintings* (Cleveland: Cleveland Museum of Art, 1999), 2:562. In the Cleveland collection catalogue, the painting is dated 1851 and is recognized as one of the works that Rousseau exhibited at the 1855 Exposition Universelle (no. 3931). In the main literature, including the catalogue raisonné by Michel Schulman and Marie Bataillès, *Théodore Rousseau 1812–1867: Catalogue raisonné de l'oeuvre peint* (Paris: Éditions de l'Amateur, 1999), the painting now in the Louvre (no. 325) was ascribed to this entry. Schulman even dates the present painting (no. 605) 1860.

5 Rousseau had signed the painting and sold it during his lifetime to Durand-Ruel; D'Argencourt et al., "European Paintings of the 19th Century," 2:562.

6 Unfortunately, the varnish has yellowed; ibid.

7 Quoted in ibid.

8 Greg M. Thomas, *Art and Ecology in Nineteenth-Century France: The Landscapes of Théodore Rousseau* (Princeton: Princeton University Press, 2000), 217.

9 Ibid., 175–76; Kimberly Jones et al., *In the Forest of Fontainebleau: Painters and Photographers from Corot to Monet* (Washington: National Gallery of Art, Houston: Museum of Fine Arts; New Haven: Yale University Press, 2008), 23.

15

JULES DUPRÉ (1811–1889)

Plateau de Belle-Croix, Fontainebleau Forest

1830s–40s

oil on canvas, 68 × 58 in. (172.7 × 147.3 cm)

Cincinnati Art Museum, Bequest of Mary M. Emery, 1927.391

"Approach full of confidence these beautiful landscapes so clear and so solid, do not be afraid that a breath will cause them to evaporate. You can sit down at the feet of the trees, the branches will not collapse on you; you can walk along these sandy paths, they will not sink beneath your step; you can plunge into the lake, the water is limpid and deep."[1] The critic Jules Janin recorded this poetical experience when he looked at the paintings of Jules Dupré, exhibited at the 1839 Salon. In contrast to the detached academic renderings of nature that represented the majority of Salon paintings, the Barbizon artists invited their viewers to immerse themselves in the compositions: to feel the fresh air, smell the vegetation, and hear the murmuring water. Of course, not all critics greeted these paintings with praise—their sketchy, unfinished quality looked realistic rather than idealistic, and was incongruent with the Academy's rules—but from the beginning, Dupré's irregular submissions to the Salon were well received.[2]

Plateau de Belle-Croix, Fontainebleau Forest is quite impressive, not only because of its substantial dimensions, but also because of the clever arrangement of its composition. Dupré emphasized the painting's verticality by placing the large trees on the left, balancing them with the water coming in from the right. Such ponds were a rarity in the dry forest of Fontainebleau.[3] Dupré skillfully played with the contrast of the dark reflections of the surrounding trees and of the calmness of the dull sky in the water surrounded by the fresh green and yellow tones of the shore. The sun catches the left side of the trees and grass, highlighting the remains of the summer greens, and suggesting that autumn is approaching.

The painting has been dated 1830 based on the recording of the original signature and date as *Jules Dupré '30* on various documents in the Cincinnati Art Museum curatorial files that predate Mary Emery's 1927 bequest of the work to the collection. Unfortunately, the last name and date that once appeared on the painting have disappeared over time, and it cannot now be verified whether the date was in fact 1830. According to the same documentation, this painting was exhibited at the 1831 Salon, but no work of this title is mentioned in the Salon catalogue. If 1830 is correct, it means that the painting was one of Dupré's first that he must have made shortly before he left for London as protégé of Lord Graves.[4] Both the dimensions and composition are rather ambitious for an eighteen-year-old beginner, however.[5] It is more likely that Dupré made this painting well after his London trip, because his admiration for Constable can easily be recognized.[6] It was in London that Dupré was introduced to the work of the English painter, whose somber depictions of the Suffolk landscape, derived from nature, were diametrically opposed to academic paintings (e.g., fig. 54).[7] Constable's work made a lasting impact on Dupré.

In addition, *Plateau de Belle-Croix* relates to the Barbizon School. Dupré met his Barbizon fellows no earlier than 1836. It can be assumed that Dupré was introduced to the Forest of Fontainebleau by his good friend Rousseau, with whom he frequently traveled. In the present painting, Dupré depicted one of the sites Rousseau would later succeed in protecting from human impact. Dupré painted similar wooded scenes in the late 1830s and 40s.[8] After his close friendship with Rousseau ended in 1850, Dupré sadly retreated to his native village of L'Isle-Adam, where he started to paint largely from memory.[9]

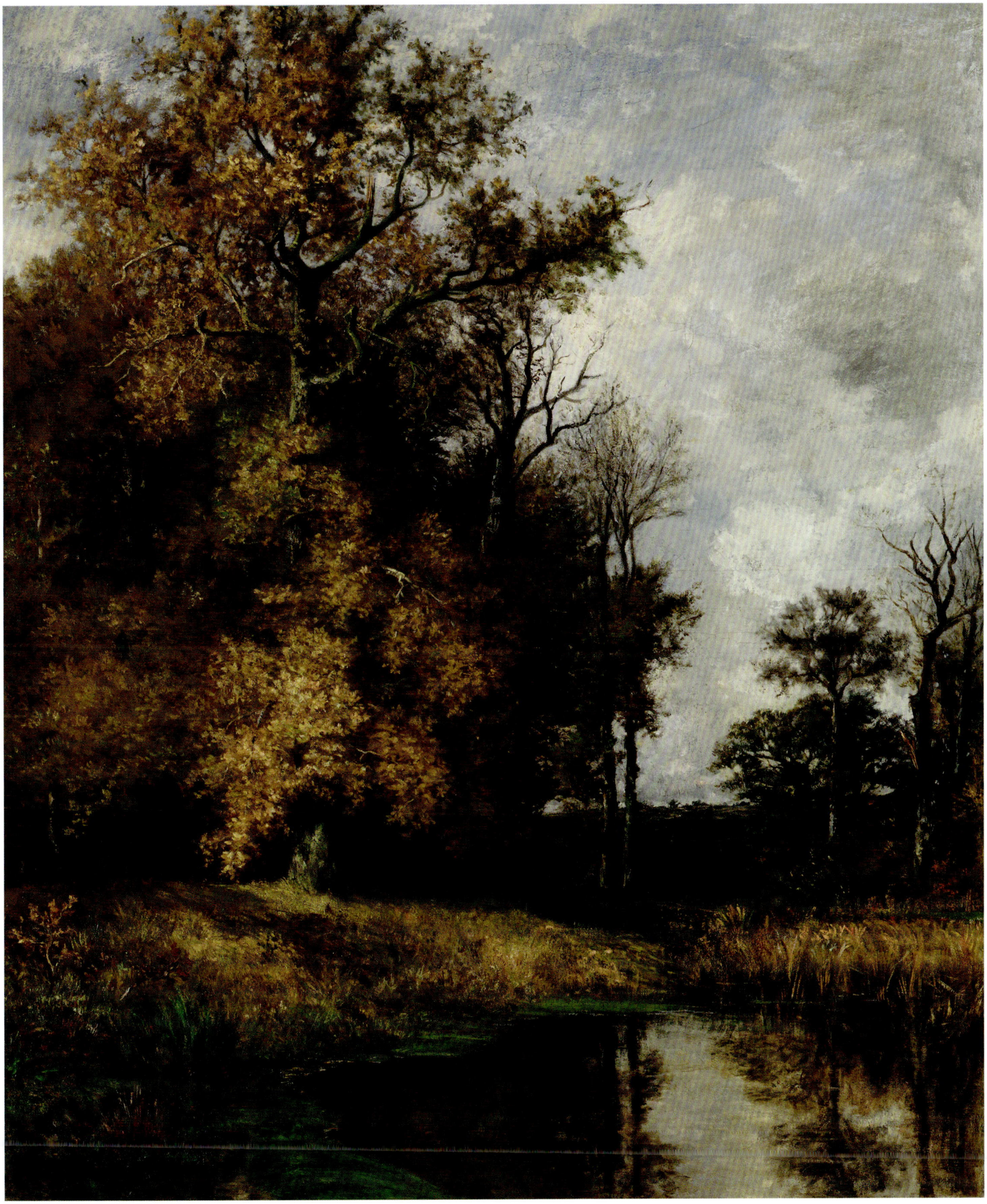

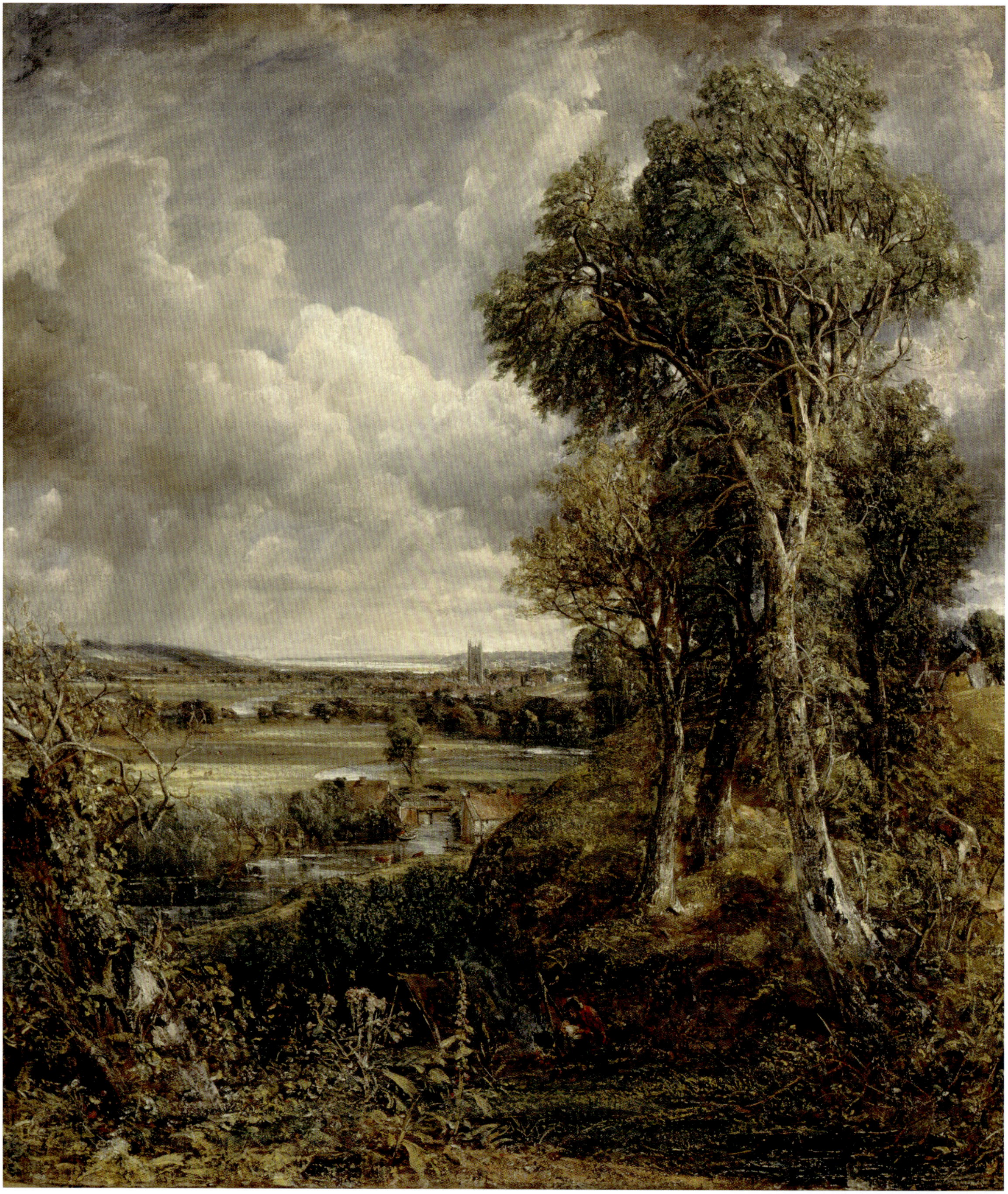

Notes

1 Janin in *L'Artiste* (1839), quoted in Nicholas Green, *The Spectacle of Nature: Landscape and Bourgeois Culture in Nineteenth-Century France* (Manchester: Manchester University Press, 1990), 109.

2 Michael Milkovich, *Jules Dupré 1811–1889* (Memphis: Dixon Gallery, 1979), 6–7.

3 Kimberly Jones et al., *In the Forest of Fontainebleau: Painters and Photographers from Corot to Monet* (Washington: National Gallery of Art; Houston: Museum of Fine Arts; New Haven: Yale University Press, 2008), 42.

4 It is, in fact, number one in the catalogue raisonné: Marie-Madeleine Aubrun, *Jules Dupré 1811–1889: Catalogue raisonné de l'oeuvre* (Paris: L. Laget, 1974).

5 In Aubrun, *Jules Dupré*, there are only a few paintings from the 1830s with large dimensions (1 meter or more), and not until 1835 are any paintings listed with dimensions similar to the present work. In the Cincinnati Art Museum's documentation, two scholars, Nicholas Green and Hans-Peter Buhler, have already questioned the date of 1830, but so far as is known they did not discuss this specific painting in any of their publications.

6 I thank Jenny Reynaerts for this tip.

7 Constable had already exhibited successfully in France—e.g., with *The Hay Wain* at the 1824 Salon—so it could be that the young Dupré was already familiar with Constable's art. But it was in London, where Dupré saw a group of Constable's works, that Constable made a major impression on him.

8 See, e.g., Aubrun, *Jules Dupré*, nos. 131–41.

9 Milkovich, *Jules Dupré 1811–1889*, 7.

Fig. 54
John Constable (1776–1837),
The Vale of Dedham, 1828,
oil on canvas,
56⅞ × 48¹⁄₁₆ in. (144.5 × 122 cm),
Scottish National Gallery of
Modern Art, Edinburgh,
Purchased with the aid of
The Cowan Smith Bequest and the
Art Fund 1944, NG 2016

16

NARCISSE VIRGILE DIAZ DE LA PEÑA (1807–1876)

Forest of Fontainebleau

1868

oil on canvas, 33¼ × 43¾ in. (84.5 × 111.1 cm)

Dallas Museum of Art, Munger Fund,

1991.14.M

Narcisse Virgile Diaz de la Peña was one of the first artists to settle in Fontainebleau, probably just before Rousseau.[1] Diaz became known for his cropped, close-up views of the forest, concentrating on the bases of the trunks covered in moss and surrounded by grass and rocks. He became a specialist in the *sous-bois*, of which this version is a perfect example.[2] Despite their unfinished look, Diaz's paintings were greeted with much praise in the Salon throughout his entire career.[3]

In this detail of Fontainebleau, Diaz emphasized the density of the forest by applying his brushstrokes thickly and rapidly onto the canvas. Only at some points can we glimpse individual trees further within the wood, suggesting the immensity of the forest. The sunlight penetrates the composition from the left, highlighting the upper parts of the grasses, the white bark of the trunks, and some of the foliage of the trees back within the wood. In this way, he achieved depth in the middle ground. Diaz had positioned himself in a small clearing in front of a hill, but the heavy shade indicates that dense woodland surrounded him as well. As viewers we feel similarly immersed in this wooded landscape. With so many motifs to look at, the eye can barely rest at any one point of the composition. Diaz painted this large *sous-bois* scene in 1868, when there was already an international demand for Barbizon paintings.[4]

As he did the other Barbizon painters, Van Gogh had admired Diaz since his time at Goupil. At one time in Arles, only a few weeks before Gauguin visited him, Van Gogh even compared himself to Diaz: "I feel that [Gauguin]'s more Millet than I am, but I'm more Diaz than he is, and like Diaz, I'll try to please the public so that some sous may come into the community." Through Millet's biographer, Van Gogh knew that because of his financial success, Diaz could support his Barbizon colleagues—something Van Gogh hoped to achieve as well, when he aspired to turn the Yellow House into an artists' community. At that moment Van Gogh began to believe that he managed to create "more saleable [works], and I feel that I can continue to make more. I have confidence in that, at last."[5]

In his Paris days, Van Gogh had intended, like Diaz, to create works for the market. These were particularly cheerful flower still lifes. Yet, when looking at his Asnières paintings of trees (cats. 4 and 5), in which he increasingly achieved a personal style, Van Gogh certainly must have had Diaz's *sous-bois* paintings in mind as well.

Notes

1 Nicholas Green, *The Spectacle of Nature: Landscape and Bourgeois Culture in Nineteenth-Century France* (Manchester: Manchester University Press, 1990), 117.

2 Jennifer A. Thompson, "Sous-Bois," in *Van Gogh: Up Close*, ed. Cornelia Homburg (New Haven: Yale University Press, 2012), 202.

3 Simon Kelly, "The Mystery of the Forest," in *In the Forest of Fontainebleau: Painters and Photographers from Corot to Monet*, Kimberly Jones et al. (Washington: National Gallery of Art; Houston: Museum of Fine Arts; New Haven: Yale University Press, 2008), 144.

4 See the entry for this work in Stephen F. Eisenmann, ed., *From Corot to Monet: The Ecology of Impressionism* (Milan: Skira, 2010), 164. The provenance of this painting does not extend back before 1914, when it was in the hands of Knoedler Gallery in New York: see Pierre Miquel and Rolande Miquel, *Narcisse Diaz de la Peña (1807–1876): Monographie et catalogue raisonné de l'oeuvre peint* (Paris: ACR Édition, 2006), 259, no. 1625 (here, the painting is titled *En forêt, éclats de soleil sur le troncs*).

5 Vincent van Gogh to Theo van Gogh, 4 or 5 October 1888, letter 697.

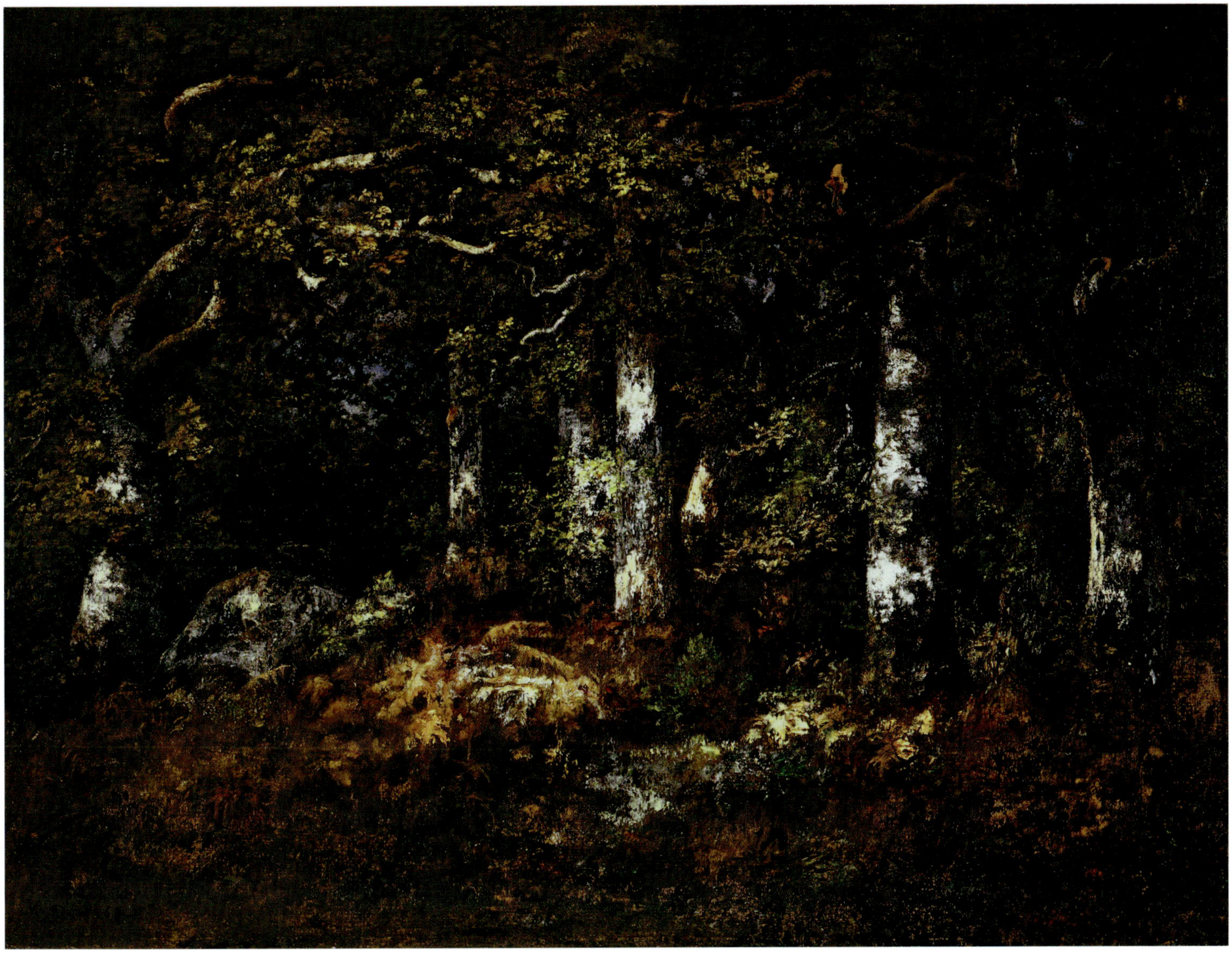

17

ALEXANDRE CALAME (1810–1864)

The Sycamores

1854

oil on canvas, 21½ × 27⅛ in. (54.6 × 68.9 cm)

Cincinnati Art Museum, Bequest of Mary M. Emery, 1927.383

Alexandre Calame was a reasonably successful artist. Throughout his career, he drew and painted the same motifs from Swiss and French landscapes, in compositions that he knew would sell to his well-to-do international clientele. Calame, a native Swiss, was known for his mountain views, but the forest also was one of his favorite subjects. According to Calame's biographer, the forest "had been his first love, to which he would never be unfaithful."[1] Calame created the present painting of trees in 1854 and sold it to a Cincinnati collector that same year.[2] He had made repeated studies of every motif in the composition, as can be seen in his numerous sketchbooks.[3] *The Sycamores* shows the typical refined style of Calame's mature oeuvre.[4] As a pragmatic artist, wanting to sell, he was able to achieve maximum results with minimal resources. Calame played with a limited palette and varied the applications of paint, thick to thin. Here, the mountains in the background are depicted thinly in brown, while the green of the foliage and moss appear almost tangible on the canvas. By removing parts of the paint layers, he allowed the soft ground layer to shimmer through, enhancing the earthy tones in the foreground, and enlivening the sky.[5]

Van Gogh may have seen some of Calame's paintings in museum collections or at exhibitions, but he probably knew his work especially from lithographic reproductions.[6] Goupil, for instance, is known to have successfully reproduced Calame's landscape drawings as original lithographs.[7]

Van Gogh once mentioned Calame in a letter, at the time when Vincent was drawing fanatically, practicing his artist's skills. He considered the Swiss a draughtsman who "used [charcoal] to great advantage," naming him along with the old Dutch masters Jacob van Ruisdael and Jan van Goyen, and Van Gogh's modern Hague School colleague Willem Roelofs.[8] Calame's name arose when Van Gogh made two drawings: a female figure representing sorrow and a study of tree roots (fig. 55). "I've tried to imbue the landscape with the same sentiment as the figure," Van Gogh wrote to Theo. Looking at the blackness of the roots and branches, which Van Gogh heavily accentuated with his pencil, we can feel that he was indeed portraying this element of nature as if looking at a human model. "I wanted to express something of life's struggle, both in that white, slender female figure and in those gnarled black roots with their knots. Or rather, because I tried without any philosophizing to be true to nature, which I had before me, something of that great struggle has come into both of them almost inadvertently."[9]

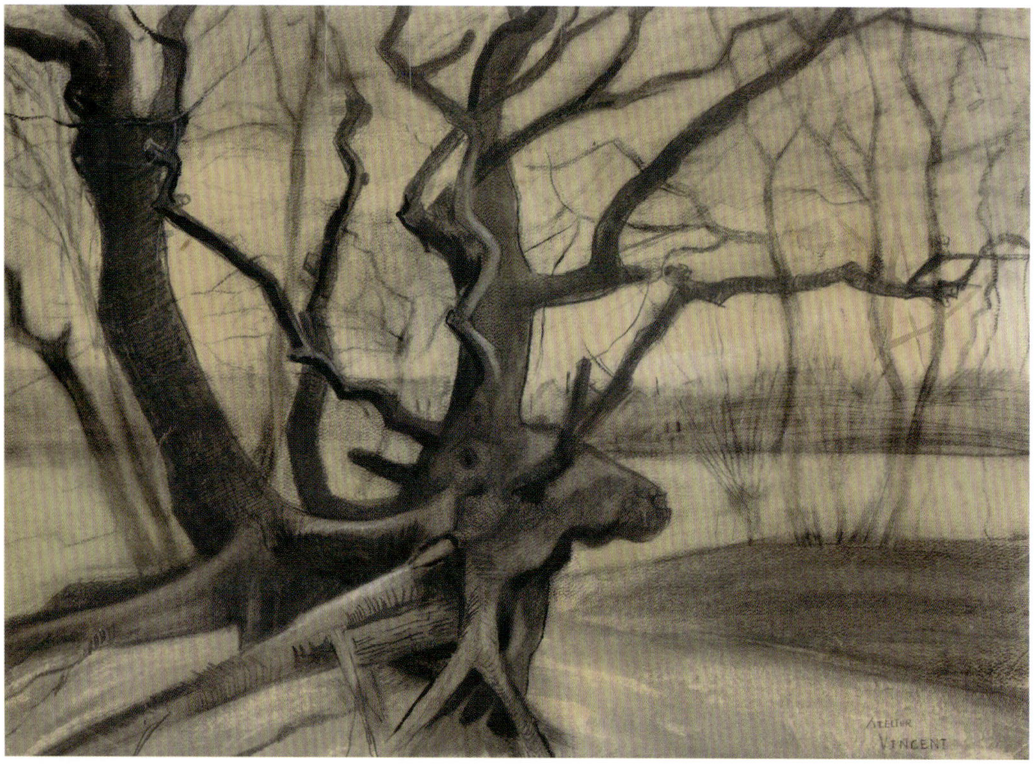

Fig. 55
Vincent van Gogh (1853–1890), *Tree Roots in a Sandy Ground (Les racines)*, April–May 1882, pencil, black chalk, brush in ink, brown and gray wash, opaque watercolor on watercolor paper, 20¼ × 27$^{13}/_{16}$ in. (51.5 × 70.7 cm), Collection Kröller-Müller Museum, Otterlo, KM 117.091, F 933 (recto)

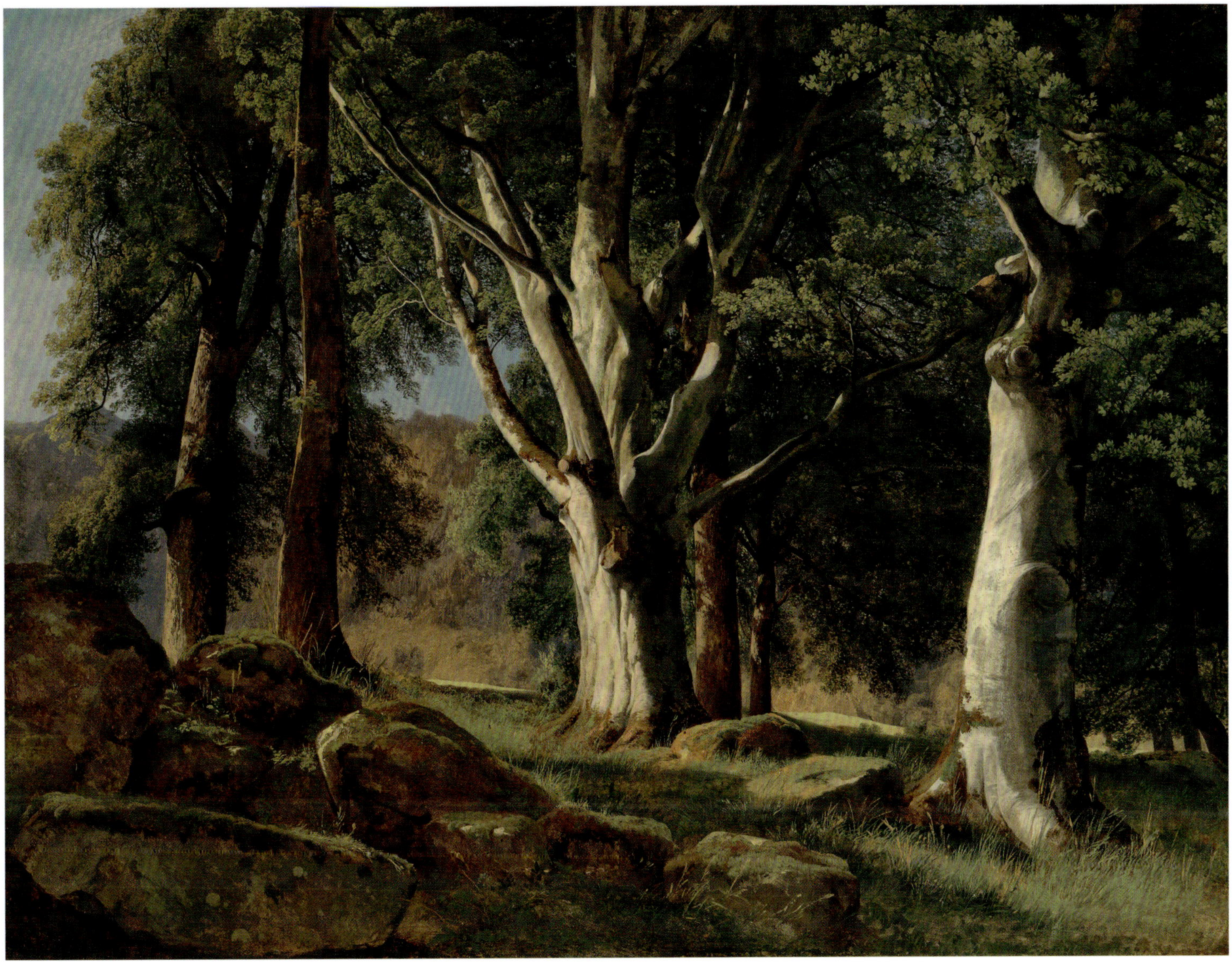

Notes

1 E. Rambert, *Alexandre Calame: Sa vie et son oeuvre d'après les sources originales* (Paris: Librairie Fischbacher, 1884), 337.

2 Valentina Anker, *Calame: Vie et oeuvre; Catalogue raisonné de l'oeuvre peint* (Fribourg: Office du Livre, 1987), no. 584.

3 Valentina Anker, *Alexandre Calame (1810–1864): Dessins, catalogue raisonné* (Bern: Benteli, 2000), see, e.g., sketchbook 3 to compare the moss-clad rocks in the painting to those in his sketchbook made in Isenfluh, Switzerland. Despite Calame's extensive practice, the trees are not interpreted unambiguously. The painting is titled here *The Sycamores*—probably by the first American owners—but according to Anker, *Calame: Vie et oeuvre*, no. 584, the trees are probably beeches (*Hêtres*).

4 Anker, *Calame: Vie et oeuvre*, no. 584; also in a 12 March 1981 letter from Anker to Frances R. Martindale at the Cincinnati Art Museum in the museum's curatorial file.

5 Ann Hoenigswald, "Manipulating Paint: The Shorthand of Plein-Air Technique," in *Studying Nature: Oil Sketches from the Thaw Collection*, ed. Jennifer Tonkovich (New York: Morgan Library & Museum, 2011), 18–19.

6 Van Gogh visited, for instance, the Van der Hoop Collection in 1877 and the Rijksmuseum in 1885. At the time, both collections had a Calame in their collection (I thank Jenny Reynaerts for this tip). Van Gogh probably did not see Calame's work during his time as an art dealer, because the Swiss artist sold the majority of his paintings straight to his clientele; a gallery such as Goupil was not likely to have dealt in his paintings. There is no mention of Goupil in Anker, *Calame: Vie et oeuvre*; see 94–110 on Calame's clientele.

7 Anker, *Alexandre Calame (1810–1864)*, 131ff.

8 Vincent van Gogh to Theo van Gogh, 1 May 1882, letter 222.

9 Ibid.

18

CLAUDE MONET (1840–1926)

Forêt de Fontainebleau

1863–65

oil on canvas, 19 11/16 × 25 9/16 in. (50 × 65 cm)

Kunstmuseum Winterthur, Donated by the Galerievereins, 1934, 632

Smitten by the work of the Barbizon School as a young artist still in training, Monet visited the Forest of Fontainebleau in April 1863. He was joined by Frédéric Bazille, Pierre-Auguste Renoir, and Alfred Sisley, whose names would later be connected to Impressionism, but who then were Monet's fellow students at the studio of history painter Charles Gleyre. They stayed at Chailly, a larger village that bordered on Bas-Préau, just above Barbizon. This area, famous for its expressive oaks and beeches, was one of the sites that Rousseau eventually succeeded in protecting from human interference (see cat. 14). Monet's friends left after their break was over, but he stayed on for another month, amazed by the rich motifs the forest had to offer.[1]

For the next couple of years, Monet returned repeatedly to Fontainebleau to make numerous *plein air* studies of the wooded landscape. By 1865, these studies were mainly intended for his first ambitious project, the figure piece *Luncheon on the Grass*, which he hoped to exhibit at the 1866 Salon. As the painting was larger than life, Monet had to construct the piece, based on his sketches, in his Paris studio.[2] The site he chose for his picnic was in Bas-Préau, where the celebrated Bodmer Oak still stood proudly (see cat. 10). Honoring his Barbizon predecessor, Monet portrayed this oak twice.[3]

In the present study, Monet examined a field with trees that would be the perfect stage for a summer picnic in the shade. With simple brushstrokes in fresh greens and orange tones, Monet constructed this sophisticated composition in the open air. With the examples of his Barbizon predecessors etched in his memory, Monet chose a composition similar to those by Rousseau and Diaz, cropping the upper part of the tree. He intensified the density of the foliage and its heavy shade on the grass by showing a strip of the sunbathed field in the back. The blue sky shimmers through the leaves here and there, scattering a play of sunlight on the grass.[4]

Monet never succeeded in finishing his ambitious figure painting, but the numerous studies he made of the Forest of Fontainebleau are a beautiful foreshadowing of the Impressionist style he would develop a few years later.[5] Most of these studies remained in the private sphere. Monet kept this *Forest of Fontainebleau* in his studio until he gave it to his daughter-in-law, the painter Blanche Hoschedé-Monet, in 1897.[6]

Notes

1 Daniel Wildenstein, *Claude Monet: Biographie et catalogue raisonné*, vol. 1, *Monet or the Triumph of Impressionism* (Paris: Wildenstein Institute; Cologne: Taschen, 1996), 48; Helga Aurisch, "The Impressionists at Fontainebleau," in *In the Forest of Fontainebleau: Painters and Photographers from Corot to Monet*, Kimberly Jones et al. (Washington: National Gallery of Art; Houston: Museum of Fine Arts; New Haven: Yale University Press, 2008), 173.

2 Wildenstein, *Claude Monet*, 58; Aurisch, "Impressionists at Fontainebleau," 173–75.

3 There are two paintings of the Bodmer Oak by Monet, one in the Metropolitan Museum of Art (inv. 64.210; Wildenstein, *Claude Monet*, no. 60) and one in a private collection (Wildenstein, *Claude Monet*, no. 60a). See also Jennifer A. Thompson, "Van Gogh and Close-Up Techniques in Nineteenth-Century French Painting," in *Van Gogh: p Close*, ed. Cornelia Homburg (New Haven: Yale University Press, 2012), 77.

4 See the essay by Jenny Reynaerts in this volume.

5 Aurisch, "Impressionists at Fontainebleau," 170. The composition of this figure painting is known only from a painted sketch now in the Pushkin Museum (Wildenstein, *Claude Monet*, no. 62) and two fragments now in the Musée d'Orsay (Wildenstein, *Claude Monet*, nos. 63-1 and 63-2).

6 Dieter Schwarz and Astrid Näff, *Kunstmuseum Winterthur: Katalog der Gemälde und Skulpturen 2* (Düsseldorf: Richter Verlag, 2008), 38, no. 9.

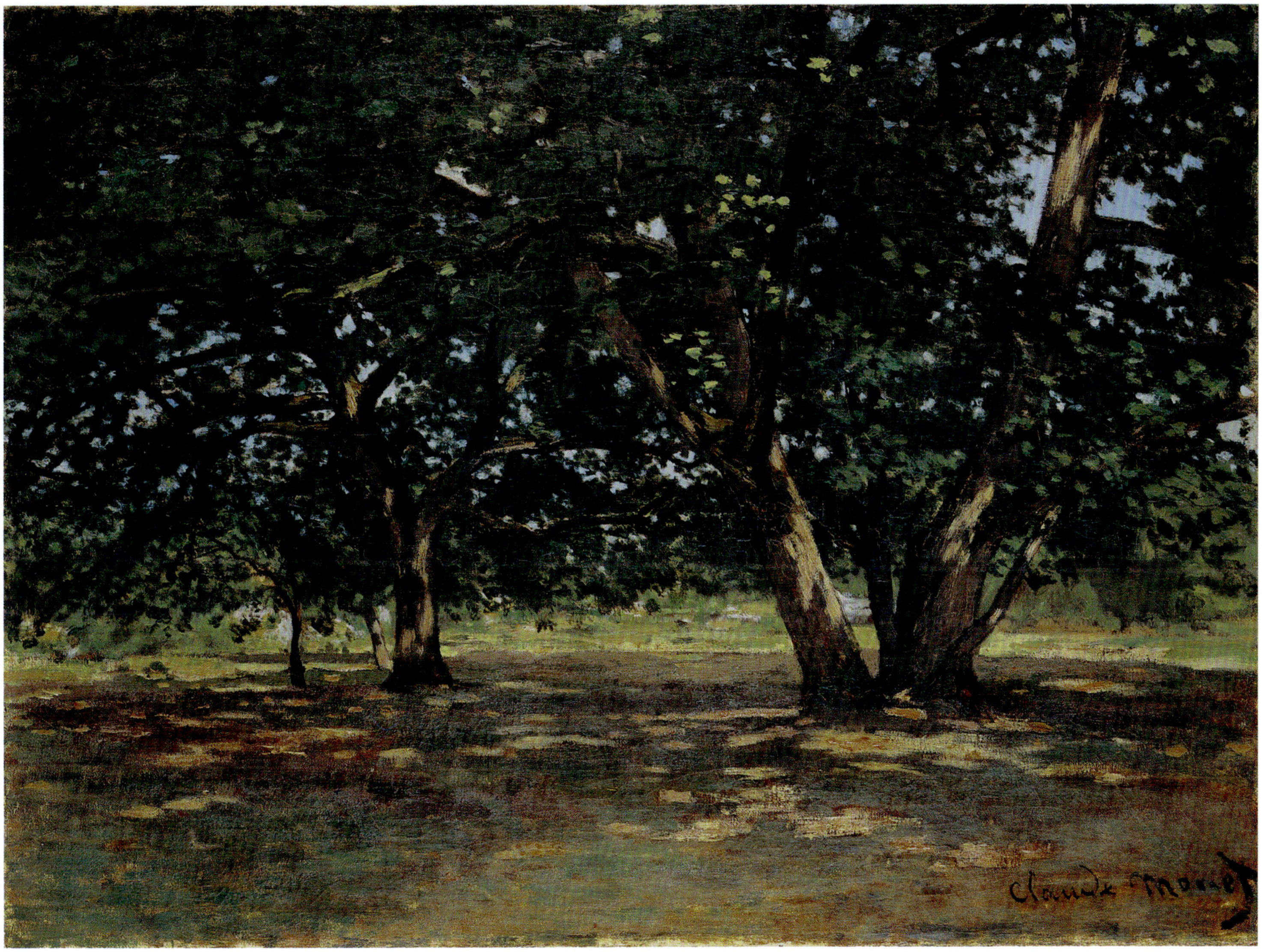

19

CAMILLE PISSARRO (1830–1903)

Road in the Woods in Summer (Chemin sous bois, en été)

1877

oil on canvas, 32 1/16 × 25 7/8 in. (81.5 × 65.8 cm)

Musée d'Orsay, Paris, France

RF 2731

In the peaceful surroundings of Pontoise, a village northwest of Paris, Camille Pissarro carefully positions himself with his easel in the shaded woods, along a meandering path, and begins to paint. A dynamic depth exists through the sun-drenched greenery on the hill and the path, but the dense foliage dominating both foreground and background interrupts any kind of grand view. The crisscross of nervous strokes representing the leaves, tree trunks, sandy path, and bits of sky complicates the legibility of the composition; it almost literally overshadows the encounter between two locals. Pissarro captures the exact moment of village geniality between a peasant, leading his donkey, and a female neighbor, passing by in their daily routine. Unbothered by the painter observing them, they are completely at ease in their environment.

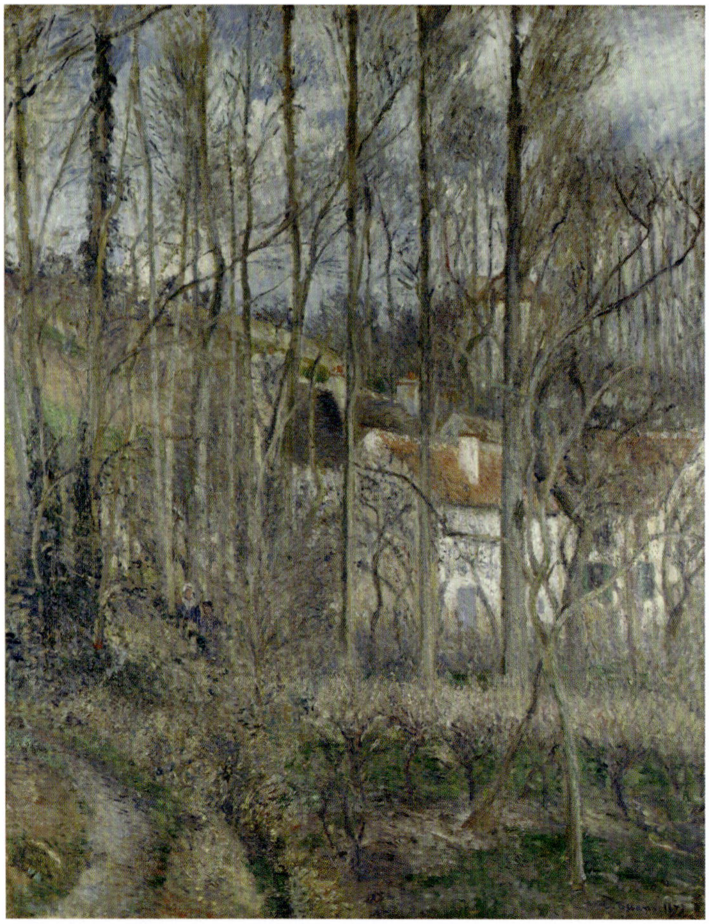

Pissarro came to Pontoise, a rural site that had largely been "untouched" by artists, in 1866. At a time when almost the entire French countryside, including the surroundings of Paris, was represented in landscape painting, Pissarro seems to have chosen Pontoise specifically for its unfamiliarity, although its scenery was nothing exceptional.[1] Until 1882, Pissarro lived with his family in this area where time seemed to stand still, endlessly exploring its surroundings in his work (fig. 56 and cat. 20).[2] Pissarro was known as a loving husband and father and a generous friend to his fellow artists, but also as a well-read social anarchist. While his paintings do not overtly portray any of his political sympathies, he did ignore the industrial developments that marked even Pontoise, and instead immortalized the simple peasant life remote from modernity. To the Paris viewer, *Road in the Woods in Summer* represented this tranquil harmony of rural life, when Pissarro's Impressionist style was at its height.[3]

Pissarro was an important figure—one could say a father figure—for many of the young avant-garde artists. He worked with the Impressionists Cézanne (see cat. 23) and Gauguin (see cat. 24), and regularly visited Theo van Gogh, as well as Vincent when he lived in Paris. After Vincent's move to the South of France, Theo kept his brother informed about Pissarro's wellbeing. In September 1889, when Van Gogh had just recovered from a severe crisis in Saint-Rémy, Theo wrote: "There's old *père* Pissarro, who has all the same done some really fine things lately, and it's precisely there that one also finds these qualities of rusticity which show immediately that the man is more at his ease in a pair of clogs than in polished boots."[4] It is not surprising that Van Gogh, when he was sick and tired of his stay in the asylum, would have loved to have boarded with this elder artist, who, just like him, preferred the simple life. Pissarro, however, already had a large family to take care of. He did introduce Theo to Doctor Gachet, who was to become Van Gogh's caretaker in Auvers, only four miles (six kilometers) northeast of Pontoise. By that time, Pissarro already had moved to Éragny-sur-Epte, Picardy.

Fig. 56
Camille Pissarro (1830–1903),
The Côte des Boeufs at L'Hermitage,
1877, oil on canvas,
45 1/4 × 34 1/2 in. (114.9 × 87.6 cm),
The National Gallery, London,
Presented by C. S. Carstairs to the
Tate Gallery through The Art Fund,
1926, transferred, 1950, NG4197

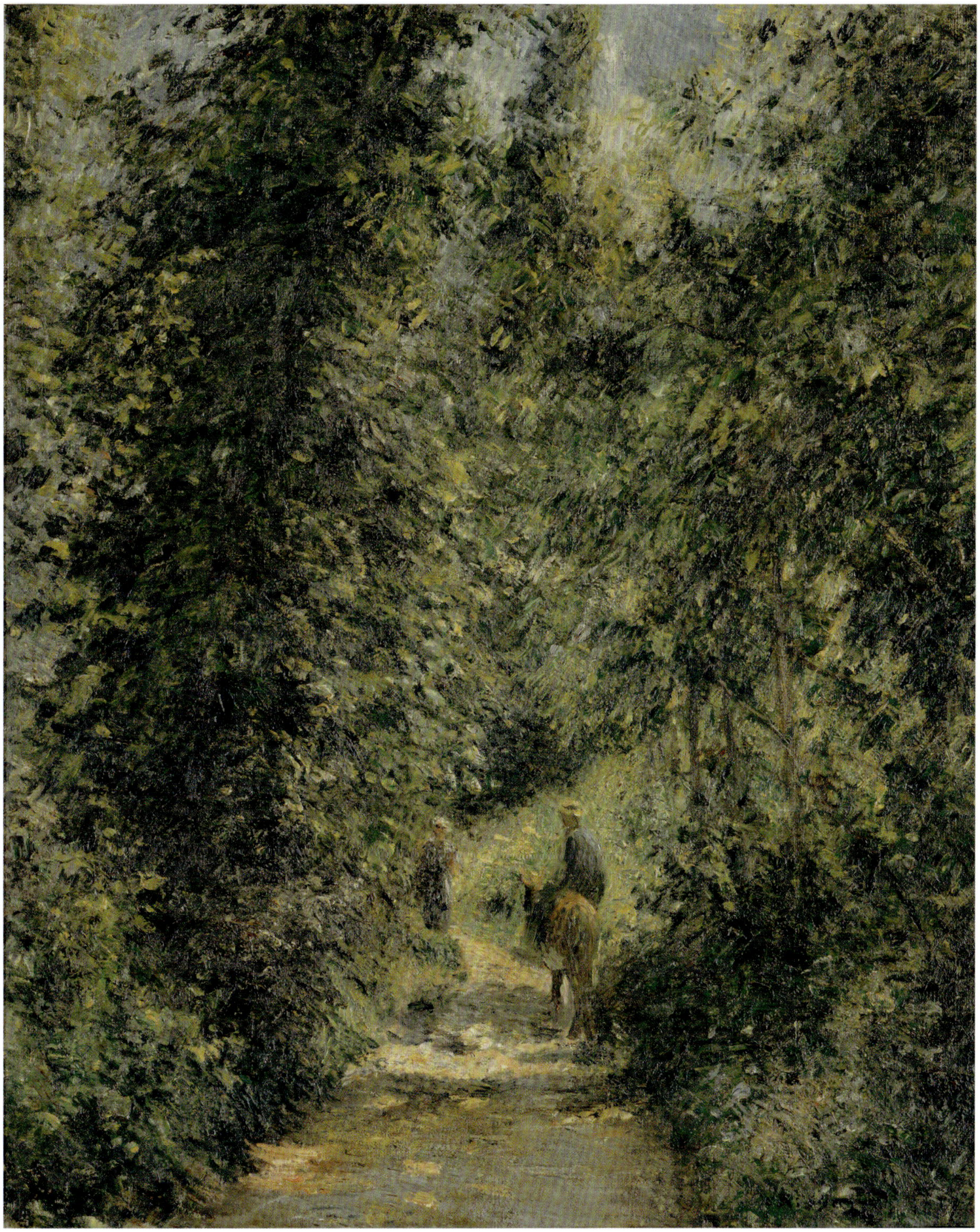

Notes

1 Richard R. Brettell, *Pissarro and Pontoise: The Painter in a Landscape* (New Haven: Yale University Press, 1990), 2–3.
2 With the exception of 1869–72, when Pissarro lived in Louveciennes, Montfoucault, and, during the Franco-Prussian War, in London.
3 This painting was exhibited at the fourth Impressionist exhibition in 1879.
4 Theo van Gogh to Vincent van Gogh, 5 September 1889, letter 799.

20

CAMILLE PISSARRO (1830–1903)

Wooded Landscape at the Hermitage, Pontoise (Paysage Sous Bois, à L'Hermitage (Pontoise))

1879

soft ground, aquataint, dry point, and scraping

platemark 8⅝ × 10⁹⁄₁₆ in. (21.9 × 26.8 cm)

sheet 10⁹⁄₁₆ × 14 in. (26.8 × 35.6 cm)

Cincinnati Art Museum, Gift of Herbert Greer French, 1940.425

The process of printmaking inevitably creates a disconnect between seeing the subject and producing its image. Thus, it would seem to be an unsuitable medium for the Impressionists, who sought to spontaneously capture the world around them. Yet it was exactly the experimentation in the process of printmaking that attracted Camille Pissarro and Edgar Degas.[1] In 1879, the two worked side by side, achieving some of the most innovative etchings of the time. Pissarro and Degas transformed the art of reproduction into experimental drawing series. There was no final outcome: each state of one composition, reproduced in only a few proofs, was a bit different and a result on its own, while the series as a whole beautifully represented the artistic process as it developed.

For his etchings, as for his paintings, Pissarro chose the rural areas surrounding Paris as subjects. He generally presented a stilled view of traditional peasant life untouched by industrialization. In *Wooded Landscape at the Hermitage, Pontoise*, we glimpse, through a drapery of trees, the village where Pissarro lived. An unidentifiable peasant figure emerges from the rich vegetation in the foreground, at ease in his environment like the locals in cat. 19. In the first state, the composition is still an abstraction of dark, slender trunks against the vague contours of the figure and of the town in the distance. In each state, Pissarro increased its legibility. Up to the fourth state, the composition became more monotone (fig. 57). He combined different etching techniques—aquatint, soft-ground, and drypoint—to achieve a variety of tonal and drawing effects. In the fifth state he even began to scrape parts of the plate to bring back bright areas (fig. 58).[2] As such, the trees and figure alike have become more distinguishable from their surroundings. The *sous-bois* subject lent itself perfectly to Pissarro's experimental approach to etching technique.

The present state is the sixth, which closely resembles the fifth.[3] While most Impressionist etchings were experiments in the private sphere, this work was intended for a portfolio of original prints titled *Le jour et la nuit*. Degas had been the mastermind behind this publication, intending to turn his printmaking activities into a lucrative business. Of course, Impressionist printmaking was too experimental to be suitable for commercial publication, thus the portfolio never materialized. Nonetheless, Pissarro must have believed in the project, as the printer Salmon made fifty impressions of his sixth state.[4]

Notes

1 Antonia Lant, "Purpose and Practice in French Avant-Garde Printmaking of the 1880s," *The Oxford Art Journal* 6, no. 1 (1983): 18–21.

2 George T. M. Shackelford and Fronia E. Wissman, *Impressions of Light: The French Landscape from Corot to Monet* (Boston: Museum of Fine Arts, 2002), 164 (entry by Barbara Stern Shapiro).

3 Loys Delteil, Jean Cailac, and Alan Hyman, *Camille Pissarro: L'oeuvre gravé et lithographié: Catalogue raisonné /Camille Pissarro: The Etchings and Lithographs: Catalogue Raisonné* (San Francisco: Alan Wofsy Fine Arts, 1999), no. 16; Barbara Stern Shapiro, *Camille Pissarro: The Impressionist Printmaker*, exh. cat. (Boston: Museum of Fine Arts, 1973), no. 11.

4 For more information on *Le jour et la nuit*, see, e.g., Michel Melot, *The Impressionist Print* (New Haven: Yale University Press, 1996), 151–59; Douglas Druick and Peter Zegers, "Degas and the Printed Image," in *Edgar Degas as Printmaker*, ed. Sue Welsh Reed and Barbara Stern Shapiro, exh. cat. (Boston: Museum of Fine Arts; Philadelphia: Philadelphia Museum of Art, 1984), xlv.

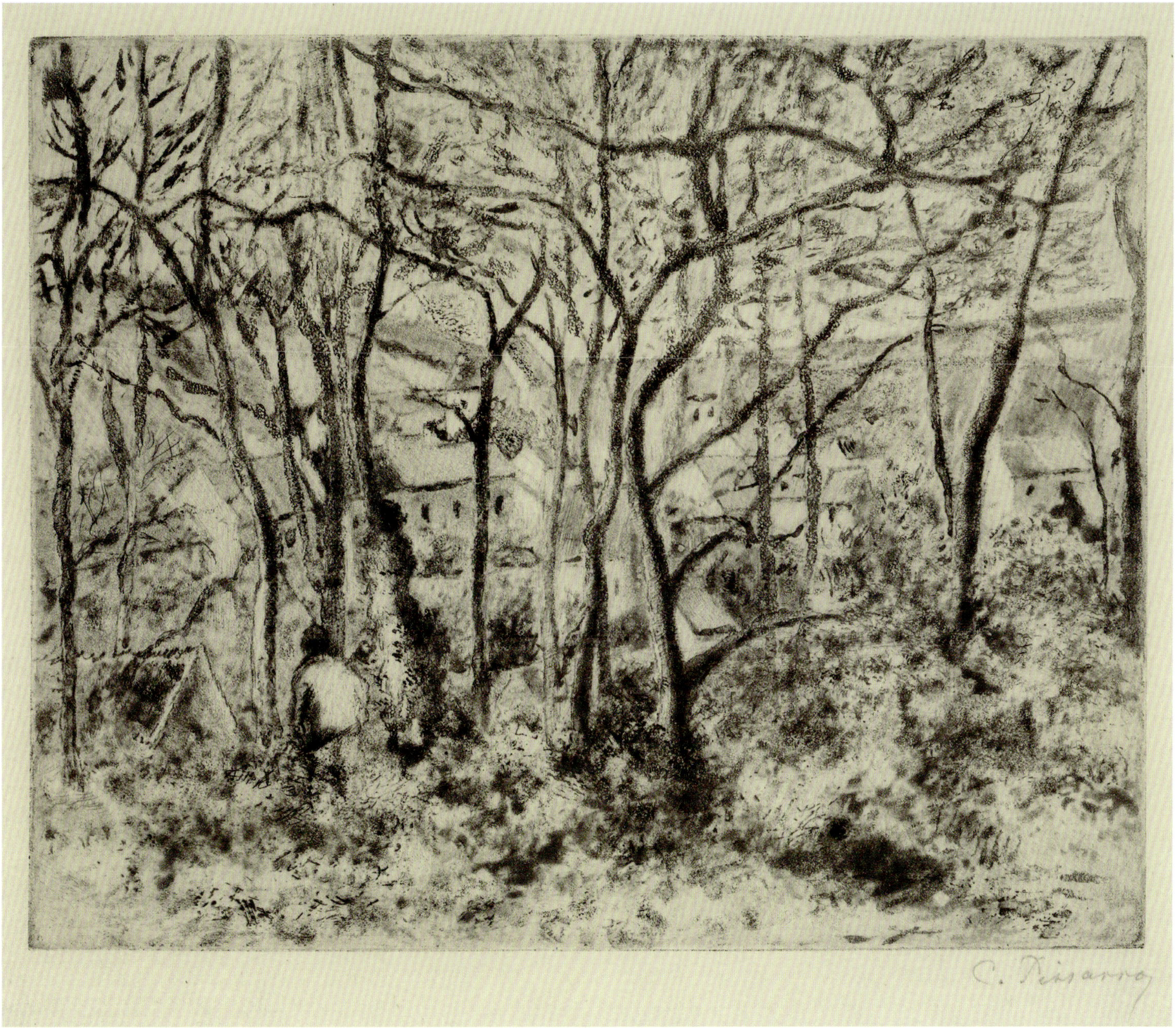
C. Pissarro

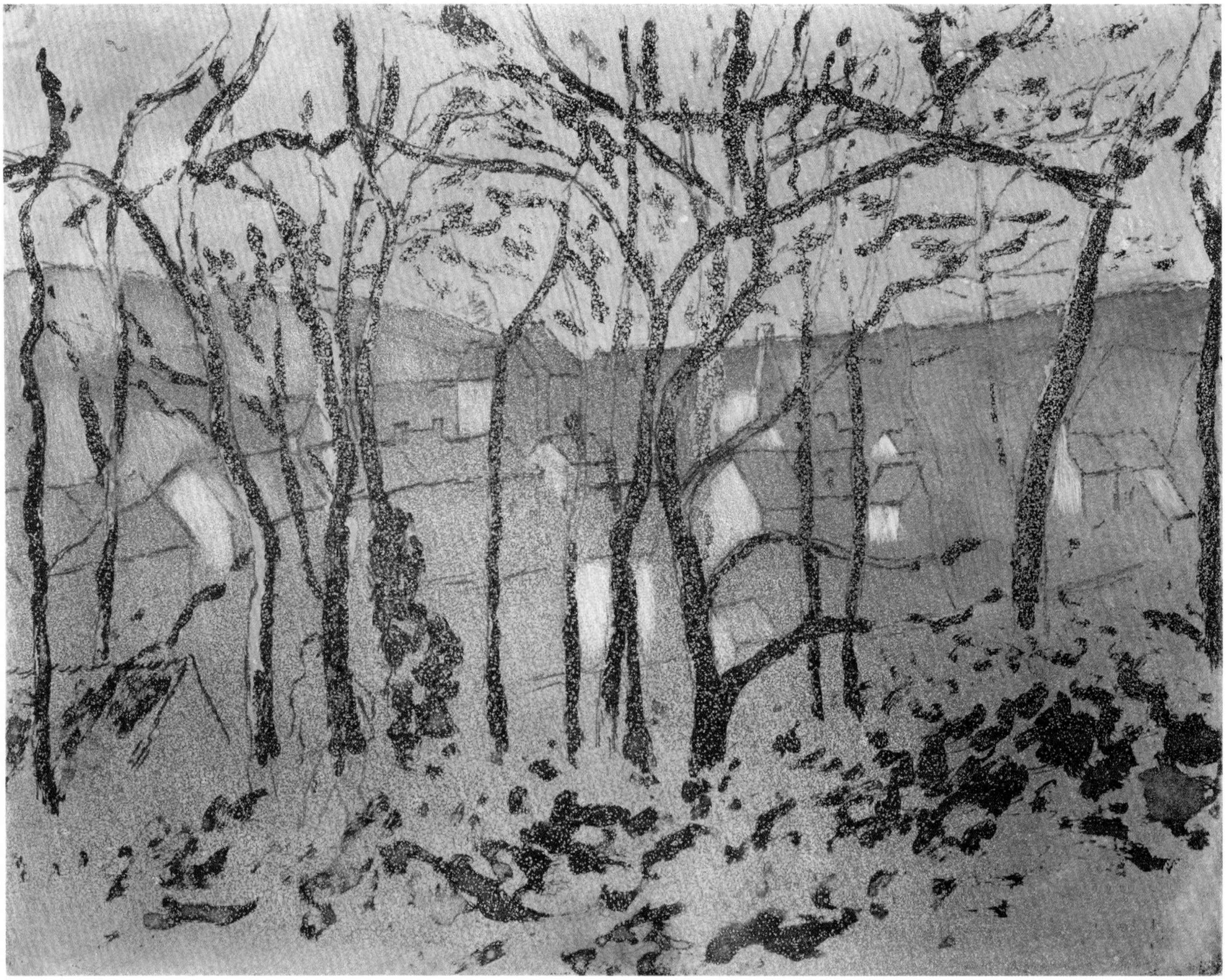

Fig. 57
Camille Pissarro (1830–1903),
Wooded Landscape at the Hermitage, Pontoise, 1879,
soft-ground etching and aquatint on cream wove paper, first state,
platemark 8½ × 10 ½ in.
(21.6 × 26.7 cm),
Museum of Fine Arts, Boston,
Lee M. Friedman Fund, 1971.267

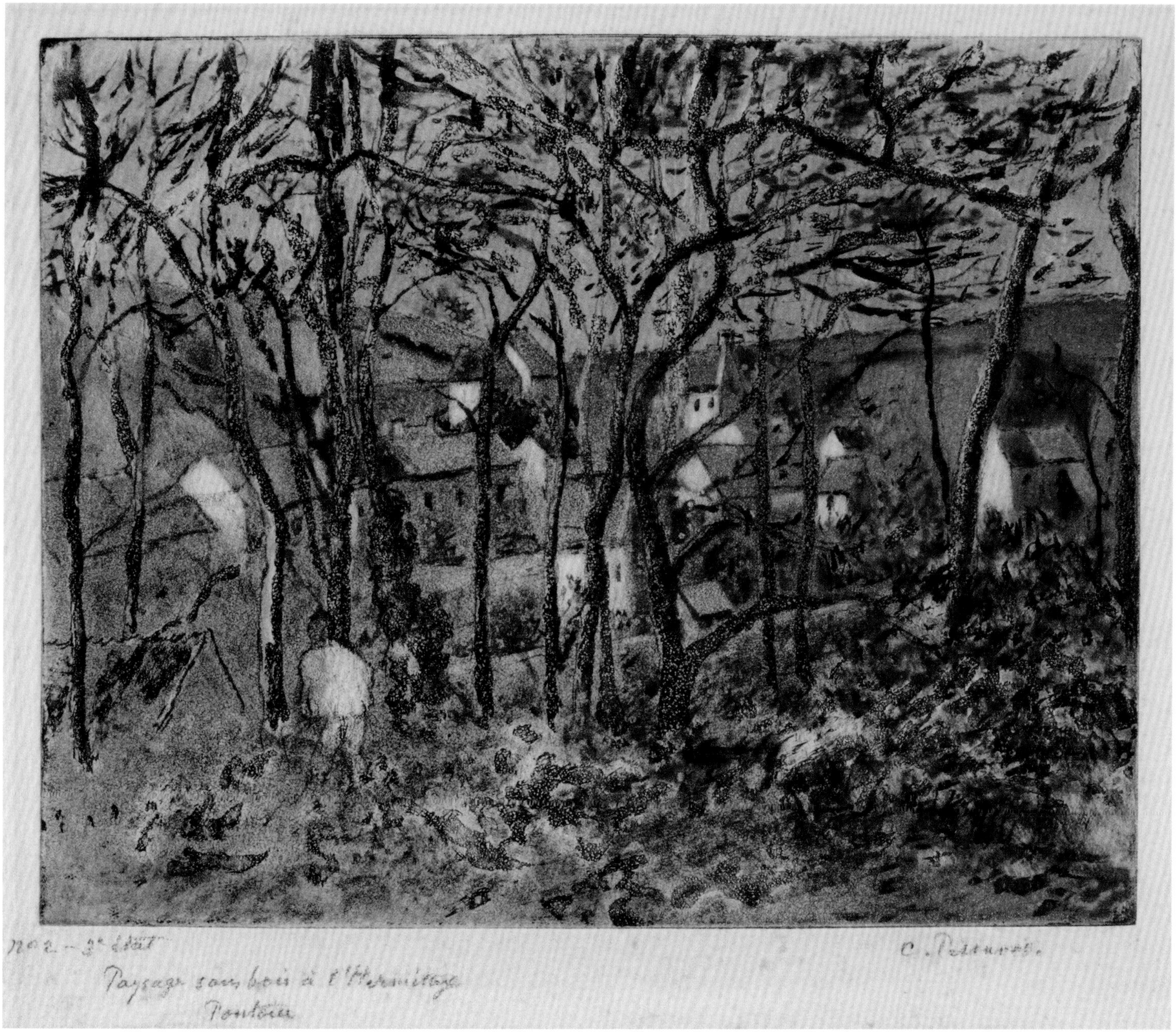

Fig. 58
Camille Pissarro (1830–1903),
Wooded Landscape at the Hermitage, near Pontoise, 1879,
soft-ground etching, lift-ground etching and spit-bite aquatint, and drypoint with scraping and burnishing, fifth state, platemark $8\frac{9}{16} \times 10\frac{1}{2}$ in. (21.8 × 26.7 cm),
Philadelphia Museum of Art,
Purchased with the John D. McIlhenny Fund, 1941, 1941-8-105

21

PIERRE-AUGUSTE RENOIR (1841–1919)

In the Woods

ca. 1880

oil on canvas, 21¹⁵⁄₁₆ × 18¼ in. (55.8 × 46.3 cm)

The National Museum of Western Art, Tokyo, Matsukata Collection, P.1959-183

For Van Gogh, Renoir was one of the representatives of the "Impressionists of the Grand Boulevard," modern artists whose reputations were already established and who were thus able to improve the position of the younger generation, such as Seurat and Toulouse-Lautrec. It is uncertain if Renoir and Van Gogh ever met in Paris, but they moved in the same circles and had similar interests: for example, their love of nature and aspiration to paint it honestly. Even though Renoir was, unlike his fellow Impressionists, rather more of a figure painter—especially of young, blushing women—than a landscapist, he regularly positioned his figures in fresh, colorful garden settings (fig. 59). This peaceful *sous-bois* scene, however, remote from human presence, is an exception, and therefore difficult to date.[1] Because he signed the work, Renoir must have intended to exhibit it, which rules out the possibility that it was simply a study. It was likely made in a period when Renoir worked intensively with the Impressionists.[2]

The Impressionists are often accused of being ignorant of politics in their art, but the late John House made a convincing argument that there was a relation between their work in the later 1870s and the social unrest of the French Republic at that time. According to House, it was in these years that the Impressionists challenged themselves to work that was more experimental.[3] This *sous-bois* painting by Renoir is probably one of his most freely arranged landscapes, in which he experiments with small touches of paint and color juxtapositions. The scene is clearly a forest in summer, painted *en plein air*, but Renoir managed to give the suggestion of greenery almost without using green tones; yellow, blue, and pink dominate his palette instead. This makes it an interesting painting to compare with an early Seurat (cat. 22), in which the greens are overpowering.

According to Renoir, his landscapes were inferior to his figures, yet "useful for the painter of figures. In the open air you are inspired to use colours that would have been unimaginable in the attenuated lighting of the studio."[4] Nature held a more prominent place, however, in his unpublished drafts on art in which he mainly discussed decorative arts. In one draft, Renoir elaborated extensively on "irregularity [as] Nature's essential principle." According to him: "The irregular is he who, loving nature above all else, has understood that he must slavishly copy her without trying to correct her."[5] In another draft headed "Grammar Dedicated to all those who love art and those who wish to make a career out of it," Renoir wrote, "if you want to create a new style, go to the inexhaustible source of nature, but as long as you keep yourself cooped up in the silence of your room, endlessly going over how to arrange what's already been done, it's useless labor."[6]

One can imagine that such statements would have spoken to Van Gogh—if he had known them. It is possible that he heard about Renoir's drafts in the Paris art scene, but unfortunately no record is made of this.[7] Van Gogh was familiar with Renoir's work. From Arles he even wrote to Theo, "I very often think of Renoir here and his pure, clean drawing. That's just the way objects or figures are here, in the clear light."[8]

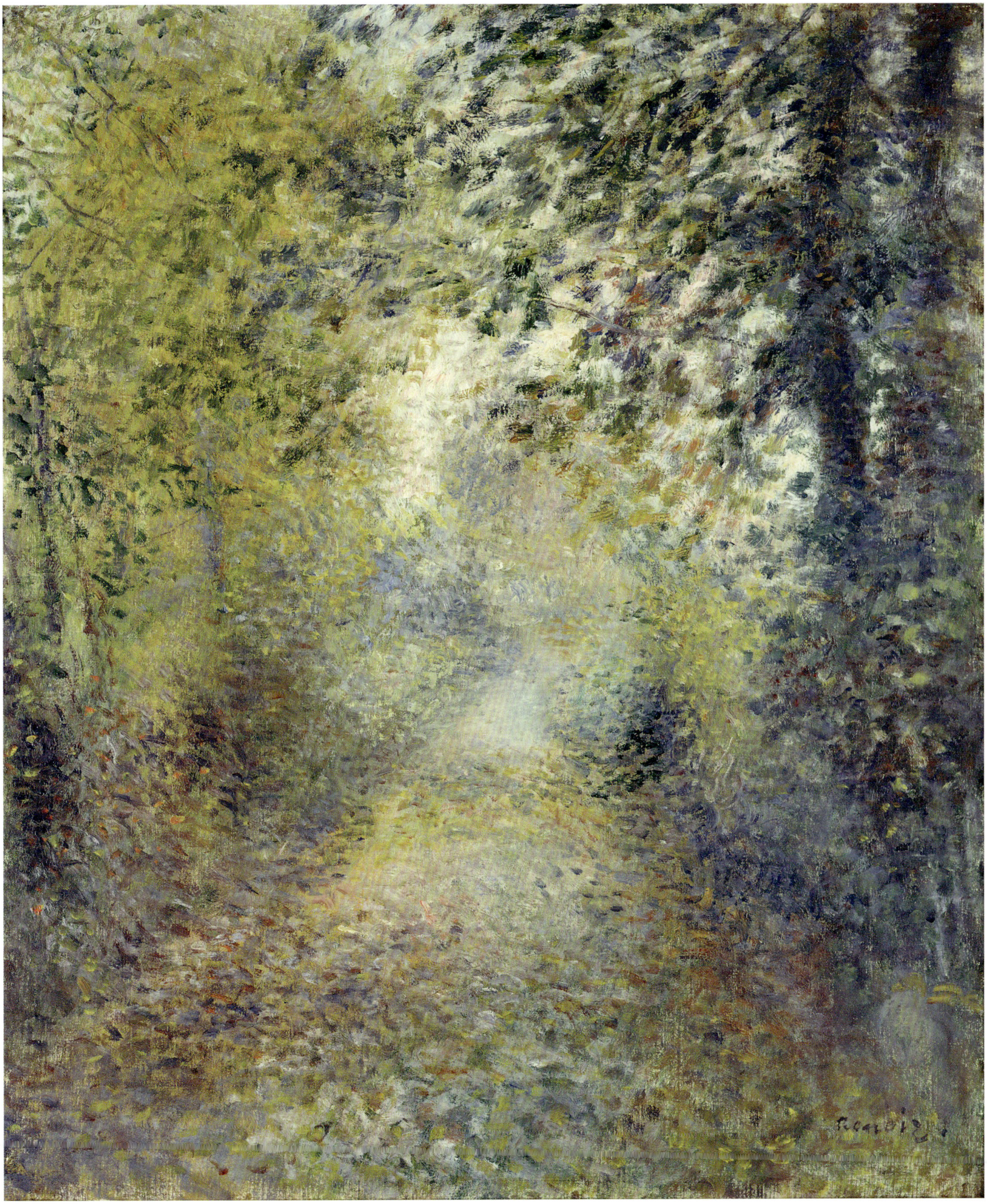

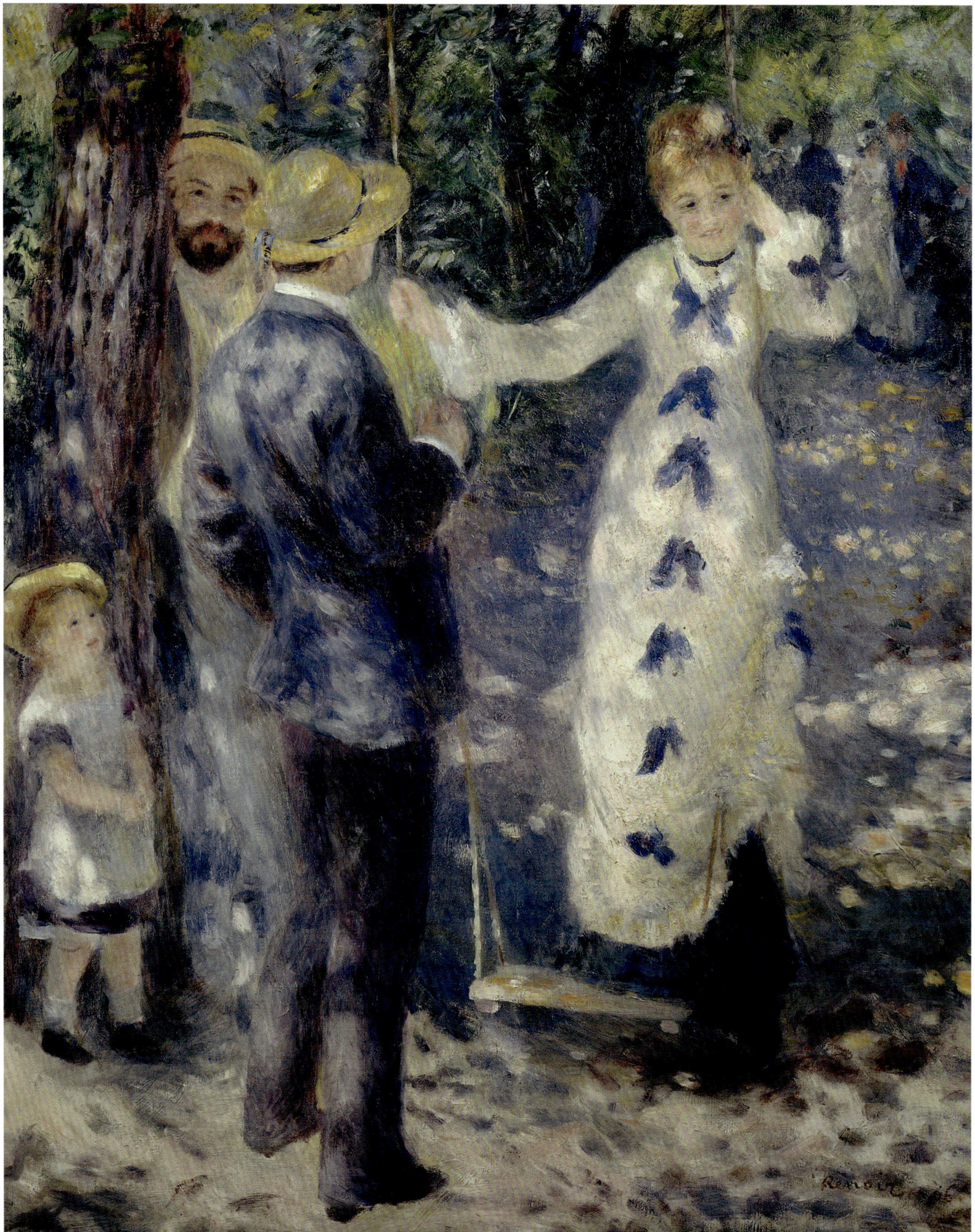

Notes

1 In Guy-Patrice Dauberville and Michel Dauberville, *Renoir: Catalogue raisonné des tableaux, pastels, dessins et aquarelles* (Paris: Éditions Bernheim Jeune, 2007), vol. 1, only a few examples of these "simple landscapes" are inventoried. Interestingly, most of them appear to be in private collections, and are therefore rather unknown to the general audience. In the catalogue raisonné the painting is dated ca. 1880. In Colin B. Bailey and Robert McDonald Parker, *Renoir Landscapes 1865–1883* (London: National Gallery, 2007), the work is dated ca. 1877, because of Renoir's signature (following John House, *Renoir: Master Impressionist* (Sydney: Art Exhibitions Australia, 1994)).

2 Bailey and Parker, *Renoir Landscapes*, 62.

3 John House, *Impressionism: Paint and Politics* (New Haven: Yale University Press, 2004).

4 Pierre-Auguste Renoir to Georges Rivière, 1921, quoted in Colin B. Bailey, "'The Greatest Luminosity, Colour and Harmony': Renoir's Landscapes, 1862–1883," in Bailey and Parker, *Renoir Landscapes*, 52.

5 Published in Robert L. Herbert, *Nature's Workshop: Renoir's Writings on the Decorative Arts* (New Haven: Yale University Press, 2000), 104.

6 Ibid., 143.

7 See also Jennifer A. Thompson, "Van Gogh and Close-Up Techniques in Nineteenth-Century French Painting," in *Van Gogh: Up Close*, ed. Cornelia Homburg (New Haven: Yale University Press, 2012), 81.

8 Vincent van Gogh to Theo van Gogh, 4 May 1888, letters 603 and 604.

Fig. 59
Pierre-Auguste Renoir (1841–1919),
The Swing (La balançoire), 1876,
Oil on canvas,
36¼ × 28¾ in. (92 × 73 cm),
Musée d'Orsay, Paris, RF 2738

22

GEORGES SEURAT (1859–1891)

The Forest at Pontaubert

1881

oil on canvas, 31⅛ × 24⅝ in. (79.1 × 62.5 cm)

The Metropolitan Museum of Art, New York,
Purchase, Gift of Raymonde Paul, in memory of her brother,
C. Michael Paul, by exchange, 1985,
1985.237

No sound of rustling leaves nor the smell of a late summer shower interrupts the utter silence of this forest scene. Seurat instead shows the quiescent, almost ethereal effect of a sun-drenched forest in this early painting. The young artist had recently fulfilled his military service and, moving away from his training at the École des Beaux-Arts, followed the example of the Barbizon painters. Seurat visited the Forest of Fontainebleau, which already had started to lose its earlier reputation as an artistic Valhalla, and in the summer of 1881 continued further south, to Pontaubert in Burgundy. There, Seurat constructed *The Forest at Pontaubert*, one of his first paintings larger than his small-scale studies. He probably finished it the following winter in his studio.[1]

On a brown ground, Seurat applied multiple tones of green, varied with yellow and blue, to create a rich tapestry of vegetation. He clearly accentuated the trunks on the right in brown and dark blue dots, highlighting them with white where they are touched by the sun. The trees in the distance are much more slender and disappear in the mist of greens. Both the brown ground and weave of the canvas are visible through the paint layers, with which Seurat added to the density of the forest. It is difficult to believe that Seurat made such a mature painting in 1881, just before he adopted the Impressionist technique, and well before he began his Neo-Impressionist experiments.[2] The brown ground, the mixing of his colors, the irregular use of the dotted brushstroke—all indicate that this painting was an early masterpiece that anticipates his Neo-Impressionist style.[3] According to Robert L. Herbert in the 1991 retrospective of Seurat's work, it was "the largest and most ambitious of his canvases until the *Baignade* [*Bathers at Asnières*]," his first large-scale figure painting, exhibited at the 1884 Salon des Indépendants.[4]

Apart from the obvious Barbizon connection, another source of inspiration for Seurat is often mentioned as well: the fifteenth-century Italian painter Piero della Francesca.[5] Seurat knew Piero's mural *The Resurrection of Christ*, which shows an ethereal, timeless forest in green tones (fig. 60).[6] Whether Seurat had this fresco particularly in mind when he painted his forest scene is difficult to determine, but the comparison is nonetheless striking.[7]

In the years that followed, Seurat's attention shifted to the city and he began to develop his systematic Neo-Impressionist style. It was during this period that Van Gogh met Seurat, whom he considered "the leader of the Petit Boulevard."[8] The personal expressive style that Van Gogh developed in his later years is, in part, indebted to the art of Seurat.

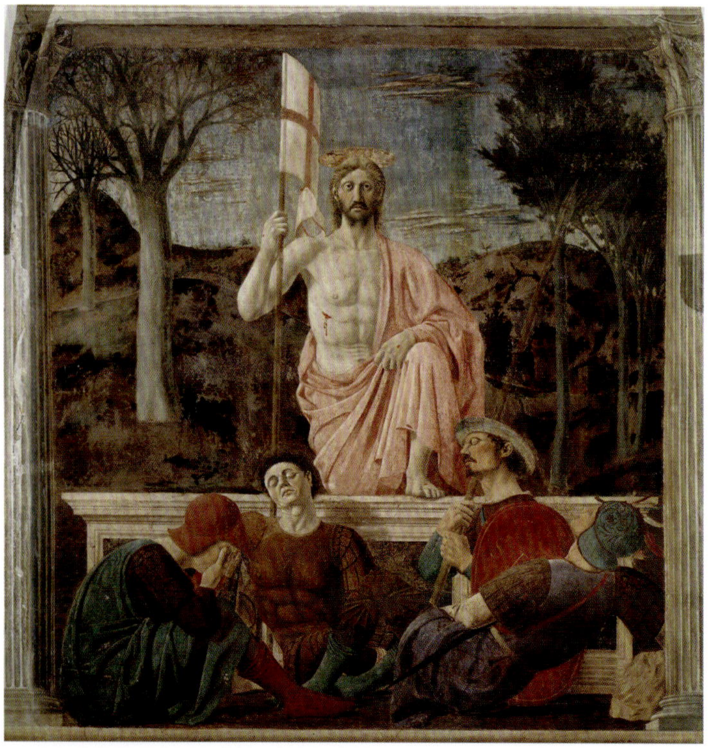

Fig. 60
Piero della Francesca
(ca. 1415–1492),
The Resurrection of Christ, 1463–65,
fresco,
88⁹⁄₁₆ × 78 ¾ in. (225 × 220 cm),
Museo Civico, Sansepolcro

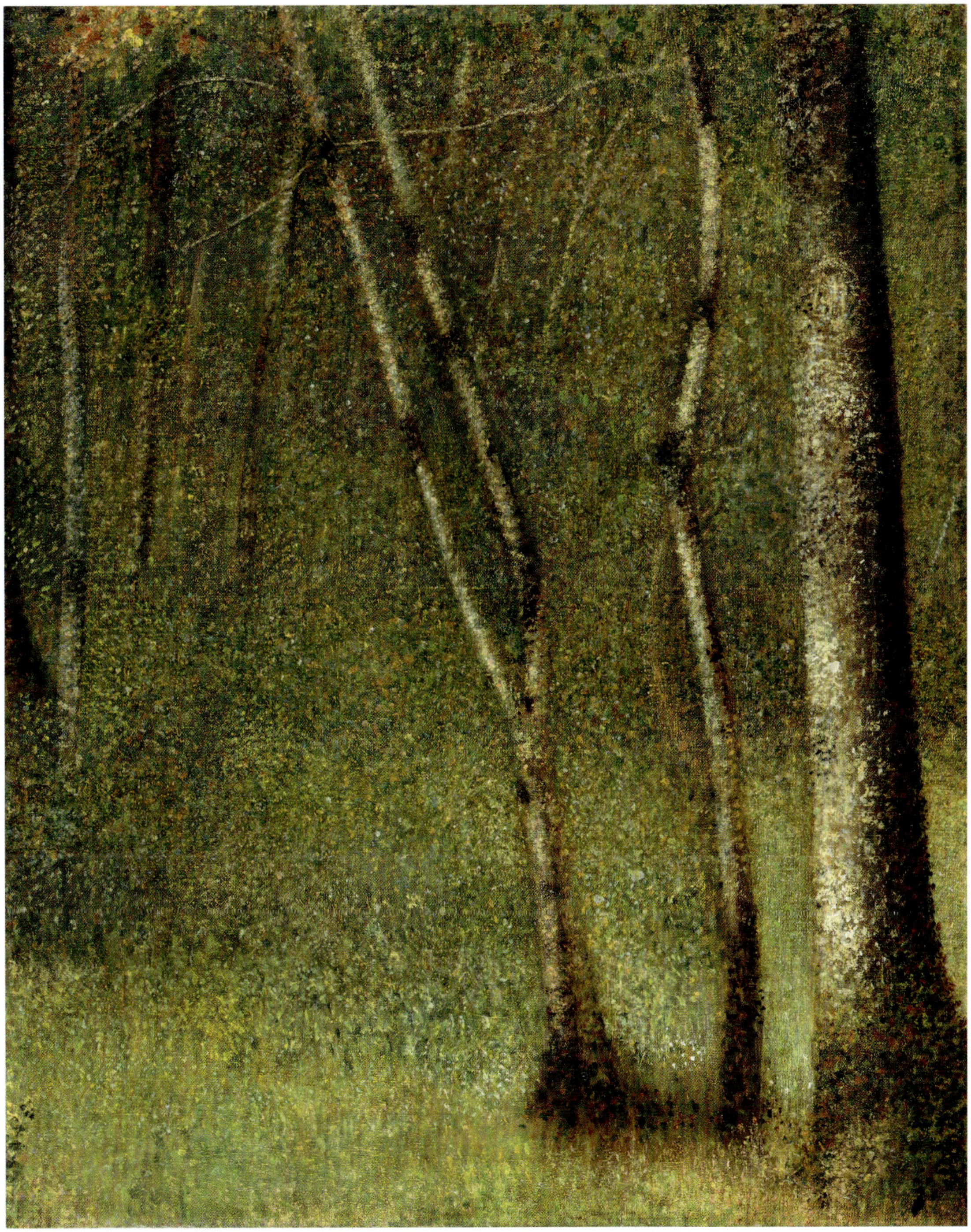

Notes

1 Gary Tinterow et al., *Masterpieces of European Painting in the Metropolitan Museum of Art (1800–1920)* (New York: Metropolitan Museum of Art; New Haven: Yale University Press, 2007), 176 (entry by Susan Alyson Stein).

2 Robert L. Herbert et al., *Georges Seurat, 1859–1891* (New York: Metropolitan Museum of Art, 1991), 104, 113–14.

3 Herbert et al., *Georges Seurat*, 113; Tinterow et al., *Masterpieces of European Painting*, 176 (entry by Stein).

4 Herbert et al., *Georges Seurat*, 113.

5 See Nancy Ireson, "The Pointillist and the Past: Three English Views of Seurat," *The Burlington Magazine* 152 (December 2010): 802–3. Albert Boime, "Seurat and Piero della Francesca," *Art Bulletin* 47, no. 2 (1965): 265–71, was one of the first to point this out, but he does not mention this painting by Seurat specifically.

6 Paul Smith, *Seurat and the Avant-Garde* (New Haven: Yale University Press, 1997), 12–13.

7 According to Herbert et al., *Georges Seurat*, 174, no theory on this relation has convincingly been proven.

8 Vincent van Gogh to Theo van Gogh, on or about 5 June 1888, letter 620.

23

PAUL CÉZANNE (1839–1903)

Interior of a Forest

ca. 1885

oil on canvas, 18¼ × 22¹⁄₁₆ in. (46.4 × 56.1 cm)

Collection of Art Gallery of Ontario, Canada, Given in loving memory of Saidye Rosner Bronfman by her family, 1996, 96/321

After experimenting with Impressionism for a decade, Cézanne began to develop his mature style around 1880. He continued to paint onsite, but instead of giving an impression of the landscape, Cézanne built up his paintings with short, parallel strokes. He dissected each of his motifs, whether in a landscape, still life, or figure painting, into facets that he carefully constructed layer by layer. His works therefore do not look spontaneous, as the Impressionists' do, but they never become static either, as with the Neo-Impressionists. How Cézanne observed the world around him, and the way he eternalized it on the canvas, was unique. He taught his viewers to look at objects in the real world differently, and at the same time created awareness that they were looking at a plane surface of paint. This tension between two- and three-dimensionality is what makes Cézanne a modern artist, extremely influential on his contemporaries and for generations to follow.

Interior of a Forest shows Cézanne in the midst of his experiments, in his search to master his technique.[1] His dissected strokes lend themselves perfectly to rendering the varieties of dense foliage. Cézanne freely and thickly applied the greens in a tapestry of touches, encircling the crisscross of trunks. Some of the trunks he painted almost in one stroke directly on the ground; others he painted in thick browns over the heavy greens. The sky is nowhere to be seen, but depth is created by the shrubs in the foreground, caught by the light, while the background is covered in shade. In addition, Cézanne added a path in the foreground, simply indicated with a brown plane. Yet the closer we come to the painting, the more we are aware of the paint strokes, applied in numerous tones of green on the two-dimensional surface.

Van Gogh greatly admired "le père Cézanne." They probably never met, but Van Gogh had seen a few of Cézanne's paintings at the gallery of the Paris art dealer Portier.[2] In Provence, near the regions where Cézanne lived and worked most of his life, Van Gogh recognized scenes from the master's paintings. He was well aware of Cézanne's uniqueness, marveling, "One must feel the wholeness of a country—isn't that what distinguishes a Cézanne from something else."[3] Whether Cézanne was familiar with the works of Van Gogh is unknown; nonetheless, the similarities between the two artists are striking. Apart from the isolation they both sought in the South of France, both evolved from Impressionism to a personal, innovative style. While they both used a similar impasto application of confident and accurate brushstrokes and chose similar subjects to paint, their outcomes were completely different. This *sous-bois* scene of Cézanne's, for instance, recalls those by Van Gogh in his Paris and Saint-Rémy periods, although, as Richard Shiff writes, "Cézanne proved to be more extreme than Van Gogh, who retained an unambiguously mimetic sense of specific features of his subjects." Van Gogh remained more true to nature in a sense, whereas Cézanne's pictures "amount to abstractions of a *material* sort" and "record the painter's sensory response to his experience (of both the scene and the work in process)."[4]

Notes

1 Because Cézanne rarely dated his paintings and could sometimes work for years on one canvas, or occasionally revert to old habits, his oeuvre is difficult to date. According to the 1996 catalogue raisonné, this painting has always proven difficult, and scholars' dates have ranged from 1872 to 1894. Because this painting and similar works relate to another group of paintings known to have been created around 1885 and 1886, this painting is dated ca. 1885 as well: see John Rewald, Walter Feilchenfeldt, and Jayne Warman, *The Paintings of Paul Cézanne: A Catalogue Raisonné* (New York: Abrams, 1996), 367–68, no. 543.

2 See Vincent van Gogh to Theo van Gogh, 13 June 1888, letter 624.

3 Vincent van Gogh to Theo van Gogh, on or about 3 November 1889, letter 816; see also letters 610 (14 May 1888) and 624 (13 June 1888).

4 Richard Shiff, "Matière très Matière," in *Van Gogh: Up Close*, ed. Cornelia Homburg exh. cat. (New Haven: Yale University Press, 2012), 130–32.

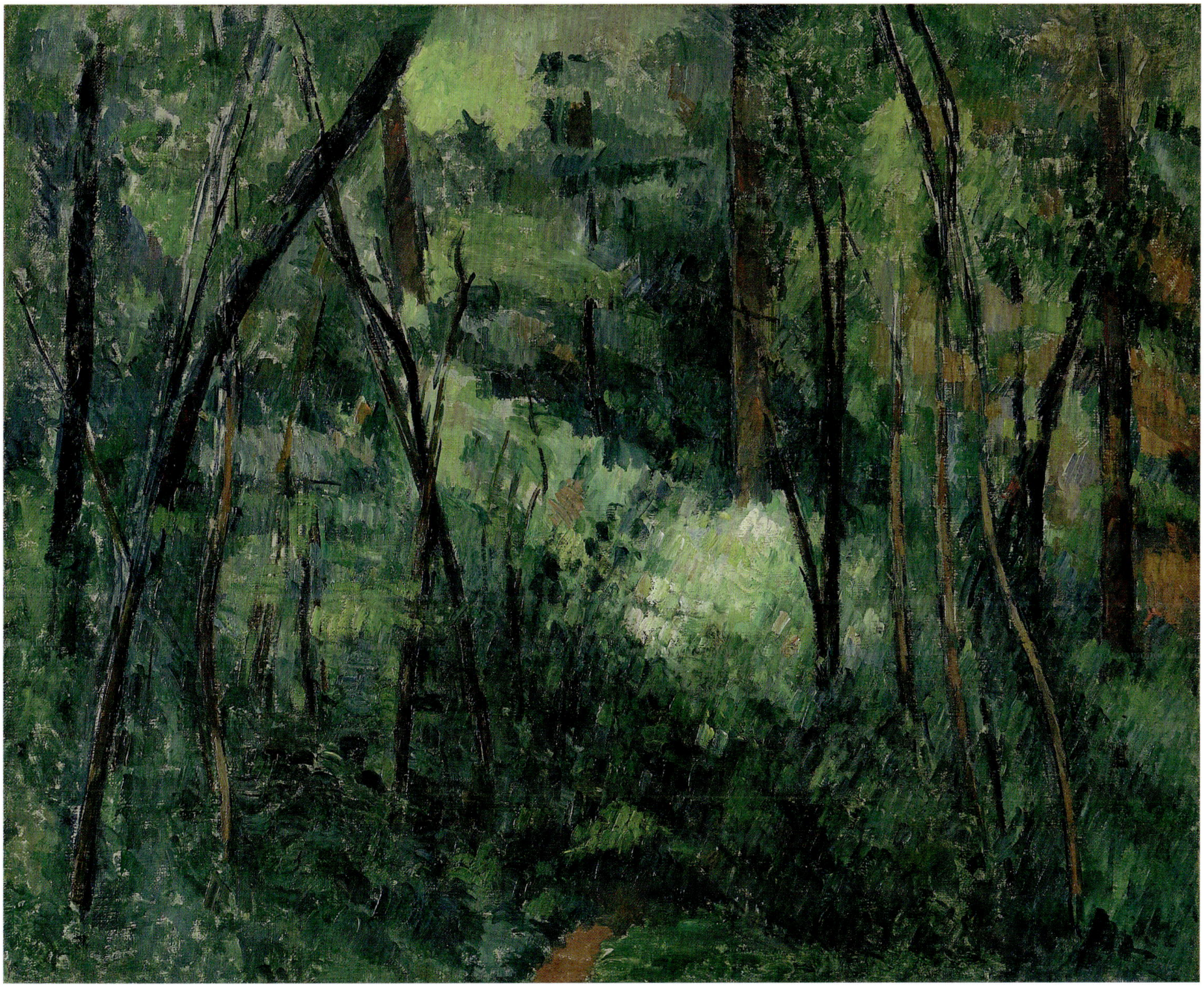

24

PAUL GAUGUIN (1848–1903)

Sunken Path, Wooded Rise

1884

oil on canvas, 23¼ × 18⅛ in. (59.5 × 46 cm)

Lent by Ananda Foundation N.V.

On 13 August 1883, Gauguin wrote to his friend Camille Pissarro, "You're so lucky, being able to paint every day. I am bored to death in the office. I do nothing all day long when I could be spending the time studying my art."[1] Gauguin began his professional life as a stockbroker, but in the years following the 1882 market crash he decided to dedicate his life completely to art, despite the large family he needed to support. Prior to this decision, Gauguin already painted as an amateur and, at Pissarro's invitation, had even exhibited with the Impressionists. During these first years of his career, Gauguin, still in search of his own style, was working with Impressionist techniques. Because these works are far from the innovative Symbolist paintings he produced after he left for Pont-Aven in 1886, Gauguin's early career as a "temporary Impressionist" is often dismissed as irrelevant.[2] In a 2005 exhibition catalogue by Richard Brettell and Anne-Birgitte Fonsmark, proper attention is given to the Impressionist works of Gauguin, whose "emotional and artistic range is much greater than that of Sisley, or even Renoir or Monet, although the latter two are undeniably greater as Impressionist painters."[3] Like Van Gogh and Cézanne, Gauguin came through Impressionism to a completely personal style.

This painting, *Sunken Path, Wooded Rise,* was created by Gauguin in 1884, when he had left Paris for Rouen to cut his expenses.[4] Life was difficult: he failed to take care of his family and, isolated from the Parisian art world, he struggled in his development as a painter. Gauguin gained inspiration from his art collection, however, and, once accustomed to the Normandy landscape, he did manage to create some paintings he was happy with.[5] Both Pissarro and Cézanne proved to be major sources of inspiration, which is clearly visible in *Sunken Path, Wooded Rise*. The toned-down palette and viewpoint looking down into a valley, where a peasant woman stands at the bottom by the stream, is similar to Pissarro's Impressionist oeuvre, while the elimination of the horizon and the deconstruction of the foliage into different facets was inspired by Cézanne.[6] The tapestry of leaves covering most of the canvas is broken up by the verticals of the tree trunks. Gauguin suggests a limited sense of depth with the stream that zigzags down the slope. Nevertheless, with the movement of the stream in and out of the hill's rich vegetation, he creates an overall vagueness and asserts the two-dimensionality of the picture plane.

Van Gogh met Gauguin in Paris late in 1887. The men came from completely different backgrounds, yet they shared both the decision to become an artist at a rather late age and the will to develop a personal style: everyone and everything in their lives had to yield to their art. This was what probably attracted them to each other, when they met that first time, both in the early stages of developing their signature styles. In the years to come, they would keep each other informed about their progress, exchange works, and endlessly discuss art. With such strong-willed characters, it was not surprising that an estrangement would soon follow, resulting in their flaming row in Arles, when Van Gogh in a rage cut off part of his ear and had to be admitted to a hospital.

Notes

1 Quoted in Richard R. Brettell and Anne-Birgitte Fonsmark, *Gauguin and Impressionism*, exh. cat. (New Haven: Yale University Press, 2005), 196.

2 See overview in Brettell and Fonsmark, *Gauguin and Impressionism*, 4 (quote from Gauguin's biographer David Sweetman).

3 Ibid., 6.

4 Daniel Wildenstein et al., *Gauguin: Premier itinéraire d'un sauvage: Catalogue de l'oeuvre peint (1873–1888)* (Milan: Skira; Paris: Wildenstein Institute, 2001), no. 135.

5 Brettell and Fonsmark, *Gauguin and Impressionism*, 203–7.

6 Ibid., 207.

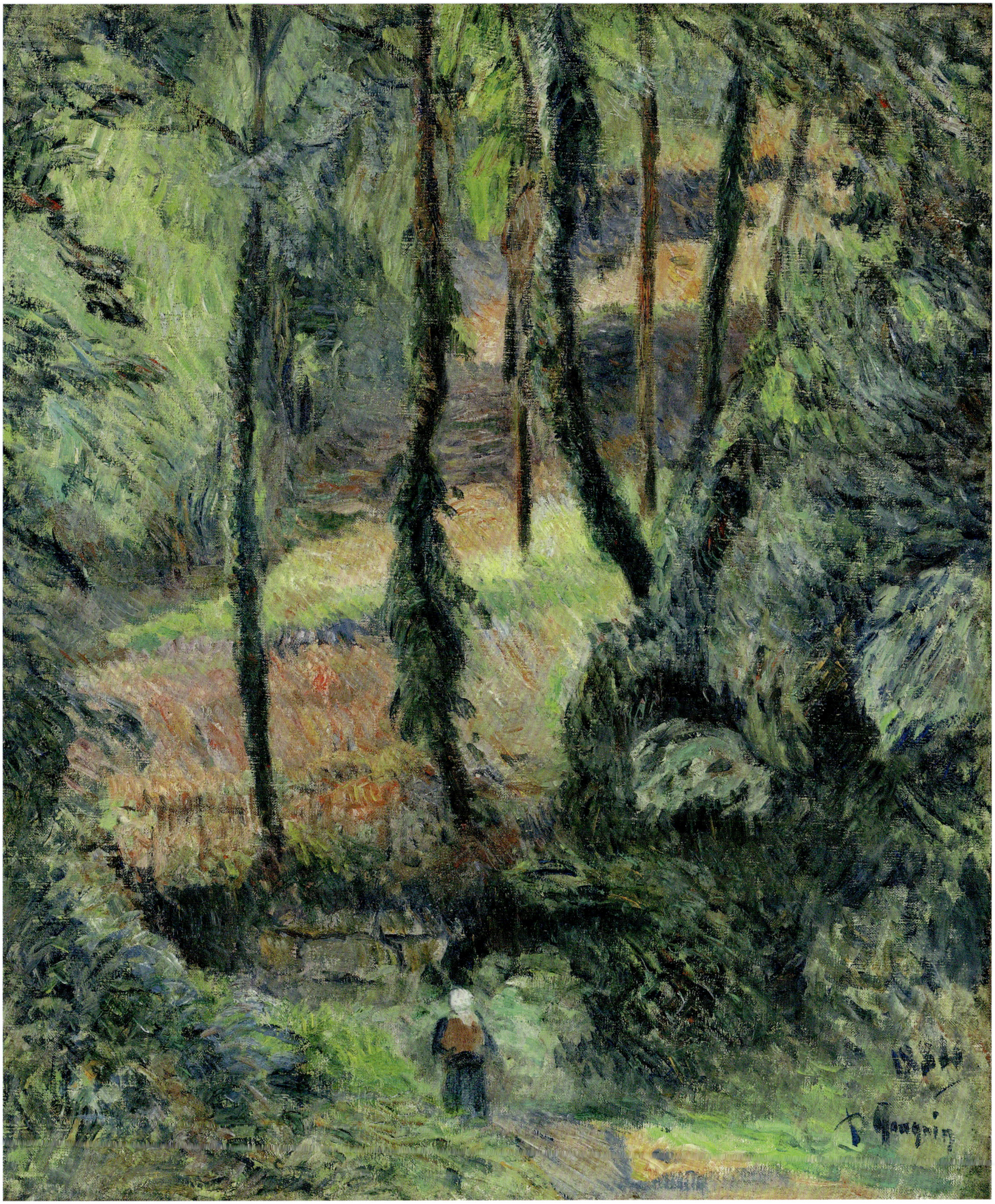

25

ÉMILE BERNARD (1868–1941)

Madeleine au Bois d'Amour

1888

oil on canvas, 54⁵⁄₁₆ × 64³⁄₁₆ in. (138 × 163 cm)

Musée d'Orsay, Paris, France,

RF 1977 8

"Last year, from what Gauguin was telling me, you were doing a painting more or less like this, I imagine [fig. 61]. Against a foreground of grass, a figure of a young girl in a blue or white dress, lying full length. Behind that: edge of a beech wood, the ground covered in fallen red leaves, the verdigrised trunks crossing it vertically—I imagine the hair a colourful note in the tone required as complementary to the white dress: black if the clothing was white, orange if the clothing was blue. But anyway, I said to myself, what a simple subject, and how he knows how to create elegance with nothing," Van Gogh wrote to Émile Bernard in late November 1889.[1] In Arles in late 1888, Gauguin had described this painting, which Bernard had made earlier that year in Pont-Aven. It clearly made an impression on Van Gogh.

The compliments from Van Gogh certainly must have pleased Bernard, possibly even more because Gauguin had been the one to describe the work. When Van Gogh's letters to Bernard were published in 1911, Bernard added a footnote: "The exactitude of the description shows how much Gauguin had appreciated the painting."[2] This meant a lot to Bernard, who had worked throughout his career to strengthen his position as the Symbolist artist ranked alongside Gauguin. He tried to upgrade his reputation from that of a young, impressionable artist to Gauguin's artistic equal.[3]

When Bernard painted this life-size depiction of his younger sister Madeleine, he was only twenty years old. Together with Madeleine, Bernard joined Gauguin in Pont-Aven in the summer of 1888, where he absorbed lessons from the older artist. For example, Gauguin inspired Bernard to paint nature from personal experience with an emotional use of color. Paul Sérusier's *The Talisman* (Musée d'Orsay, Paris) had become the perfect representation of such new ideas in art. In *Madeleine au Bois d'Amour*, Bernard carefully adopted the lessons from his elder, although he did not go as far yet as Sérusier. Bernard built up his composition as a decorative pattern and used a color scheme partly from his imagination to evoke an emotional reaction. He constructed the painting in his studio from different sketches, which explains the awkward position of Madeleine in the foreground, as if she is pasted onto the canvas. Madeleine's horizontal posture mirrors the river in the background, contrasting with the rhythmic, vertical tree trunks. With this "simple" arrangement, Bernard managed to intensify the dreamy appearance of his innocent young sister and favorite model.[4]

The color scheme and structure of the composition was what attracted Vincent; he did not like overly Symbolist work, such as Bernard's religious-themed pictures. Van Gogh always wished to stay true to nature, and that was exactly what had caused his passionate arguments with Gauguin, who exhorted his friend to work from memory. To Bernard, Vincent explained, "When Gauguin was in Arles, I once or twice allowed myself to be led into abstraction, as you know . . . . But that's enchanted ground,—my good fellow—and one soon finds oneself up against a wall."[5] Probably the loving portrayal of the young sister was what had spoken to Gauguin when he described the painting to Van Gogh. Twice Bernard's age, Gauguin had fallen madly in love with the young Madeleine.[6]

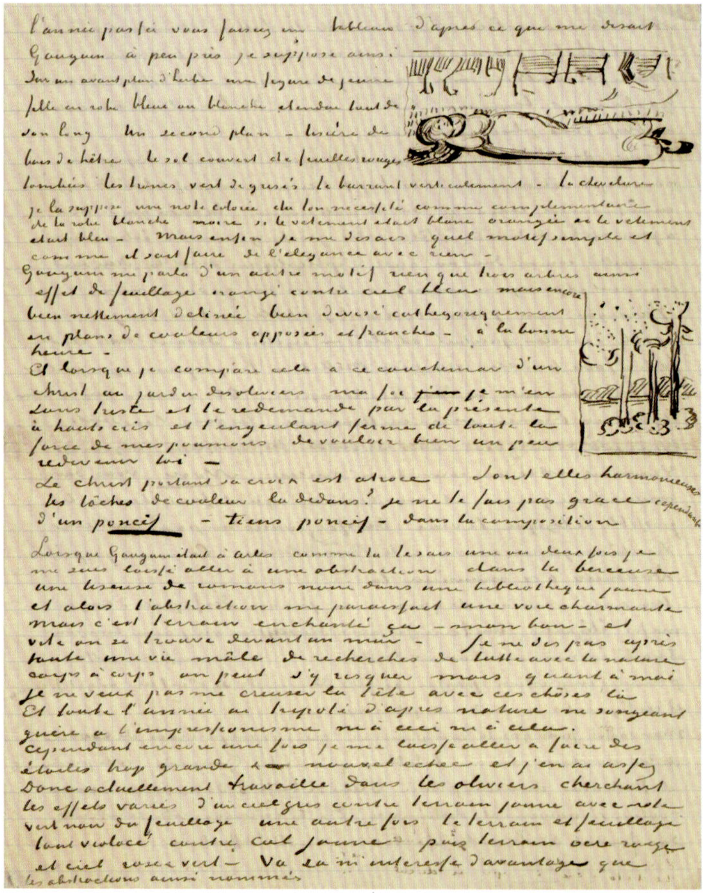

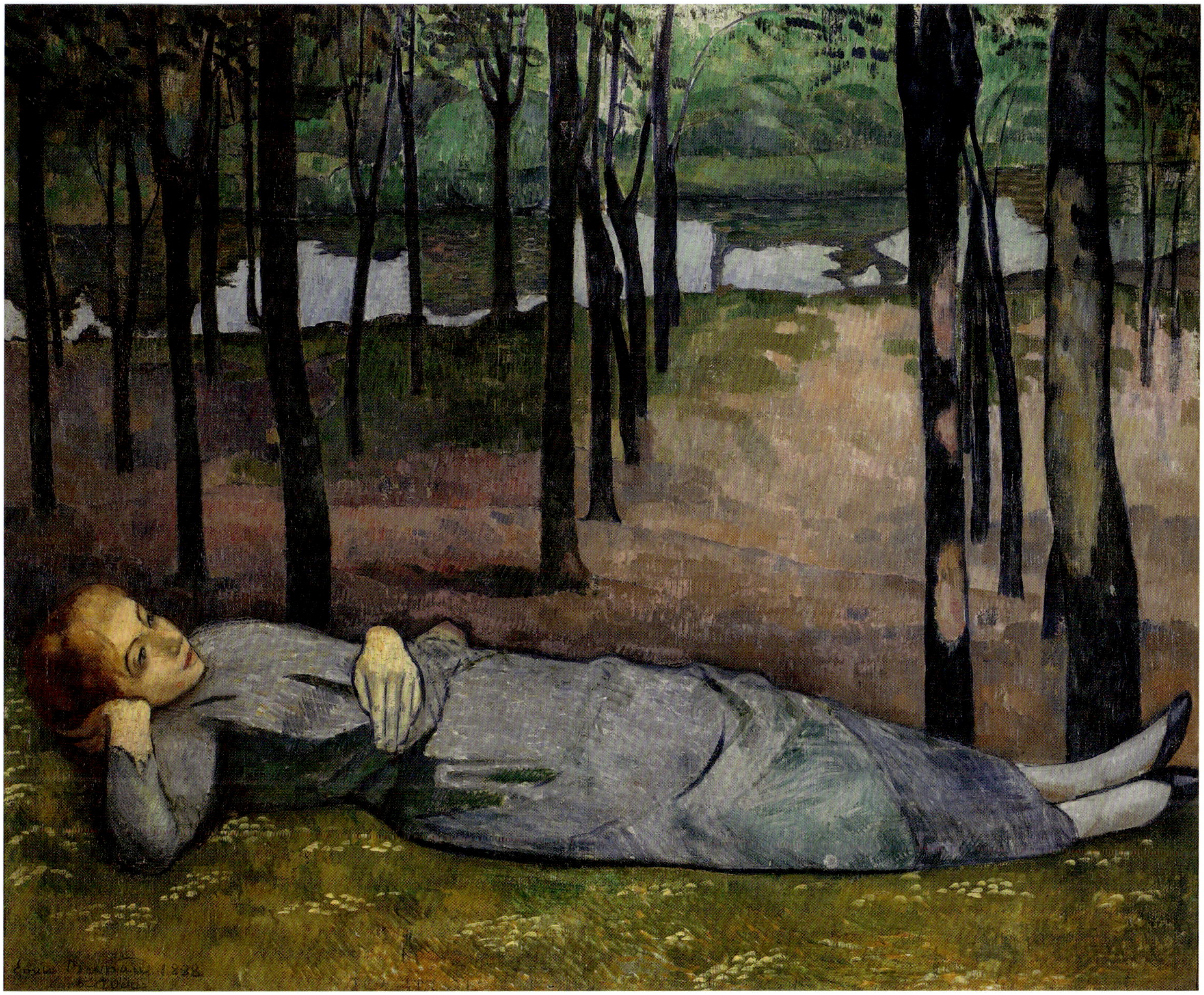

Fig. 61 (opposite)
Vincent van Gogh to Émile Bernard, with sketches after É. Bernard, *Madeleine in the Bois d'Amour*, Arles, on or about 26 November 1889, The Pierpont Morgan Library, New York, Thaw Collection, MA 6441.19

Notes

1 Vincent van Gogh to Émile Bernard, on or about 26 November 1889, letter 822.

2 Ambroise Vollard and Émile Bernard, *Lettres de Vincent van Gogh à Émile Bernard* (Paris: Vollard, 1911), 144.

3 See, e.g., Douglas W. Druick and Peter Kort Zegers, *Van Gogh and Gauguin: The Studio in the South* (Chicago: Art Institute of Chicago, 2001), 336.

4 See Fred Leeman et al., *Émile Bernard (1868–1941)* (Paris: Wildenstein Institute, 2013), 126–32; Dorothée Hansen, ed., *Émile Bernard 1868–1941*, exh. cat. (Paris: Flammarion and Musée d'Orsay, 2014), 80 (entry by Fred Leeman).

5 Vincent van Gogh to Émile Bernard, on or about 26 November 1889, letter 822.

6 See Paul Gauguin to Vincent van Gogh, 17 January 1889, letter 737, note 4.

Artist Biographies

Anne Buening

Émile Bernard (Lille, France 1868–1941 Paris, France)

Émile Bernard arrived in Paris when his family moved to the western suburb of Asnières in 1881. Within three years Bernard was a student at the Atelier Cormon, where he met and became friends with Henri de Toulouse-Lautrec (1864–1901). An avant-garde artist at heart, Bernard experimented with Impressionism and Pointillism in opposition to Cormon's academic training; this experimentation led to Bernard's expulsion from the studio in 1886. This freed Bernard to travel that same year to Normandy and Brittany, encountering Paul Gauguin (see entry) at Pont-Aven, and meeting Vincent van Gogh in the winter. With his friend Louis Anquetin (1861–1932), Bernard created Cloisonnism, a style of painting in flat colored areas with dark or black contours, in 1887. Delving deeper into the use of color, and inspired by Japanese prints, Bernard developed another new form of painting, called Synthetism. In 1891, however, critics hailed Gauguin, not Bernard, as the creator of Synthetism, and Bernard's friendship with Gauguin suddenly ended, setting Bernard on a new artistic path that diverged from his past painting techniques. Traveling to Italy in 1893 and then to Egypt, where he lived until 1903, Bernard turned to a more realistic representation of volume and classical figures in paintings that increasingly focused on religion.

Bernard was something of a Renaissance man; in addition to his paintings, he embraced printmaking, illustration, tapestry, and wood carving. He was a prolific writer, publishing articles and poems in a number of journals. Bernard also maintained correspondence with Van Gogh, Gauguin, and Paul Cézanne (see entry). He organized the first retrospective exhibition of Van Gogh's work in 1892, eventually publishing his letters to Van Gogh in the mid-1890s.

Karl Bodmer (Riesbach, Switzerland 1809–1893 Barbizon, France)

Karl Bodmer was probably introduced to art by his uncle, the landscape painter and engraver Johann Jakob Meyer (1787–1858). Bodmer moved in 1831 to Paris, where he studied with Sébastien Cornu (1804–1870). After making a name for himself by selling engravings after his own paintings of German scenes, Bodmer was invited by Prince Maximilian of Wied-Neuwied to accompany him on a scientific expedition in North America. Arriving in Saint Louis in 1832, the expedition traveled for seven weeks in the West, with Bodmer making sketches of the peoples and landscapes they encountered. These sketches were published in *Travels in the Interior of North America* (1839).

By 1849 Bodmer had established himself in Barbizon, joining Théodore Rousseau (see entry) and Jean-François Millet (1814–1875), where he created landscapes that often focused on large trees and herds of deer. Bodmer exhibited at the Paris Salons and created illustrations, lithographs, and etchings for a number of publications, including *Monde Illustrée*, *L'Art*, *Magasin Pittoresque*, and *La Chasse Illustrée*.

Alexandre Calame (Vevey, Switzerland 1810–1864 Menton, France)

Apprenticed to a banker in his mid-teens, Alexandre Calame began to paint gouache landscapes in an effort to support his widowed mother. His formal art training began in 1829, in Geneva, under

François Diday (1802–1877). Calame's artistic career was launched in 1835 with his successful exhibition of the paintings *Course of the River Giffre* and *View of Bouveret*. The following year saw Calame furthering his studies in Paris, then the Netherlands and Düsseldorf in 1838, Italy in 1844, and London in 1850.

Calame had success during his lifetime with landscapes that were influenced by Jacob van Ruisdael (1628/29–1682). Calame viewed all his paintings, whether grandiose depictions of mountains or calm and intimate scenes, as expressions of God's divine power. Despite ill health, Calame spent summers in the mountains filling his sketchbooks with drawings and studies that would become fully realized paintings in his studio. Though mainly known for his paintings, Calame was also an active etcher and lithographer.

Paul Cézanne (Aix-en-Provence, France 1839–1906 Aix-en-Provence, France)

The son of a banker, Paul Cézanne initially followed his father's wish that he study law. In 1861, however, he turned to art and entered the Académie Suisse in Paris. There, Cézanne met Camille Pissarro (see entry) and Armand Guillaumin (1841–1927). He was later introduced to Claude Monet (see entry), Alfred Sisley (1839–1899), and Pierre-Auguste Renoir (see entry). During Cézanne's early period, he created works that mix Romanticism and Realism, characterized by dark colors and dramatic, often violent themes.

By the mid-1860s, Cézanne had come under the influence of the Barbizon School and began painting from nature. From 1864 to 1870, Cézanne moved between Aix and Paris, as his paintings were continually refused by the Paris Salon. In 1872 he moved to Pontoise, working alongside Pissarro and Guillaumin, gradually shifting his style toward Impressionism and its brighter palette, and exhibiting in the first and third Impressionist exhibitions. During the late 1870s Cézanne's technique changed to patchwork brushstrokes that used color instead of tonal gradations to model form. He distanced himself from the Paris art world for much of the 1880s, staying for the most part in Provence. At this time his painting style moved away from Impressionism as he sought to represent mass and structure. In 1888 he returned to Paris, where he spent time with Vincent van Gogh, Paul Gauguin (see entry), and Émile Bernard (see entry). In the early 1890s Cézanne traveled to Fontainebleau and then visited Monet in Giverny. He suddenly found success as an artist in 1895, with his first solo exhibition at Ambroise Vollard's Paris gallery. Afterward, Cézanne exhibited widely, and his reputation grew with a younger generation of artists. He is now regarded as one of the most influential artists of the twentieth century.

Jean-Baptiste-Camille Corot (Paris, France 1796–1875 Ville-d'Avray, France)

Jean-Baptiste-Camille Corot's family ran a successful dress shop in Paris. Despite his father's wish that he, too, follow a career in textiles, Corot became a student of Achille Etna Michallon (1796–1822), and then of Jean Victor Bertin (1767–1842) in 1822. Corot's classical training inspired him to make his first trip to Italy, where, during a long stay, from 1825 to 1828, he sought to perfect his rendering of light and atmosphere. From that point on, Corot frequently traveled to better himself as an artist. Returning to Paris in 1828, Corot set out for Fontainebleau, followed by Normandy, Brittany (1829), Chartres (1830), Normandy again, Burgundy, Italy (1834), Switzerland (1841–42), a final visit to Italy (1843), the Netherlands (1854), London (1862), and Auvers-sur-Oise (1868). Over time Corot's early Neoclassicism evolved into a style characterized by its freedom and spontaneity, diffused light, and limited palette. For Corot, harmony in tones, not color, was key in painting. In addition to his works on canvas, Corot also created *cliché-verre* prints, etchings, and decorations for churches and private homes.

Beginning in 1827, Corot regularly exhibited at the Paris Salon, where many of his paintings were purchased by museums and collectors, including the emperor Napoleon III. In 1846 he was named a Chevalier de la Légion d'honneur, and later, in 1867, an officer of the légion. A popular figure, Corot always worked surrounded by a crowd of pupils—including Berthe Morisot (1841–1895), Alfred Sisley (1839–1899), and Camille Pissarro (see entry)—collectors, and tradesmen. As an artist, Corot influenced Charles François Daubigny (1817–1878), Théodore Rousseau (see entry), Jean-François Millet (1814–1875), and Gustave Courbet (1819–1877).

Narcisse Virgile Diaz de la Peña (Bordeaux, France 1807–1876 Menton, France)
Narcisse Virgile Diaz de la Peña's father, Thomas, was a political exile from Spain who moved his family first to Bordeaux and then to England. After Thomas's early death, his widow Maria returned to France, eventually settling in Paris, where she supported herself and her son through teaching. Diaz was ten when his mother died and a Protestant minister took him in. When he was old enough, Diaz worked first with a printer, and then in a Paris porcelain factory. Though he was largely self-taught, Diaz briefly studied with François Souchon (1787–1857). Diaz first exhibited at the Paris Salon in 1831, and then on a regular basis from 1834 to 1859. From 1835, Diaz regularly painted in the Forest of Fontainebleau, eventually becoming a leader of the Barbizon School. His work is characterized by dramatic light effects and impasto brushwork that captures a relatively small area of landscape frozen in a moment of time. Diaz is known for his landscapes, but he also created paintings that appealed to popular taste, with subjects ranging from oriental, mythological, and historical scenes to nudes and florals.

Jules Dupré (Nantes, France 1811–1889 Val-d'Oise, France)
Jules Dupré's early exposure to art was as a decorator in his father's porcelain factories, at Creil, Île de France, and Saint-Yrieix-la-Perche, Limousin. In 1831 Dupré went to Paris, where he studied with Jean-Michel Diébolt (b. 1779) and entered the Paris Salon for the first time, submitting seven paintings. While in Paris, Dupré became friends with the painters Constant Troyon (1810–1865), Charles François Daubigny (1817–1878), Théodore Rousseau (see entry), Jean-François Millet (1814–1875), and Nicolas-Louis Cabat (1812–1893).

Dupré often traveled with Troyon and Cabat to the Indre or Berry regions to paint landscapes. In 1834 Dupré visited England, where he met and was subsequently influenced by John Constable (1776–1837), Joseph Mallord William Turner (1775–1851), and Richard Parkes Bonington (1802–1828). Though considered a member of the Barbizon School, Dupré did not paint in Fontainebleau as much as the others. A successful artist during his lifetime, Dupré was made Chevalier de la Légion d'honneur in 1849. In his later years Dupré painted the coastline of Cayeux-sur-Mer.

Paul Gauguin (Paris, France 1848–1903 Atuona, Marquesas Islands)
Paul Gauguin spent his early childhood in Lima, Peru, returning to France with his widowed

mother when he was six. He joined the merchant marine at age seventeen, then served in the navy through the Franco-Prussian War. When he mustered out in 1871 and returned to Paris, the financier Gustave Arosa, Gauguin's guardian after his mother's death, found the young man a job in a stockbroker's office. Gauguin proved adept in the world of finance; he was a prosperous father of five by 1883.

During this time, Gauguin's interest in art was encouraged by Arosa. In his spare moments, Gauguin worked on paintings and sculpture and collected art by the early Impressionists, whom he came to know. In 1877 one of his landscapes was accepted into the Paris Salon; then, in 1879, Gauguin participated in the fourth Impressionist exhibition. The 1882 French stock-market crash caused Gauguin's income to plummet and led him to decide in 1883 to support his family as a full-time artist. When he was unable to find buyers for his own work, he sold his collection of Impressionist paintings. His wife took their children to her native Denmark, leaving Gauguin to concentrate on his art.

In 1886 Gauguin painted in Pont-Aven for the first time. The following year he traveled to Panama and Martinique, but contracted malaria and returned to Brittany. In October 1888 Gauguin spent two legendary months with Vincent van Gogh in Arles. By 1889 Gauguin, inspired by Émile Bernard (see entry), had turned to Synthetism. His free use of color emphasized the emotional effect of his primitive-based style. Gauguin in 1891 sailed for Tahiti, where his work became simplified as his colors grew more profound. He returned to Paris in 1893 and exhibited at Durand-Ruel's gallery. Unable to sell his paintings, however, Gauguin was back in Tahiti two years later. The art dealer Ambroise Vollard began to provide Gauguin with a stipend in 1901. That same year he moved to the Marquesas Islands, where he remained until his death in 1903.

Claude Monet (Paris, France 1840–1926 Giverny, France)

Claude Monet's artistic talents developed early; at age fifteen he was creating caricatures and portraits of friends. Eugène Boudin (1824–1898) introduced Monet to *plein air* painting in 1856. Shortly afterward, Monet went to Paris to study at the Académie Suisse. This was followed by two years of military service in Algiers. Monet joined the teaching atelier of Charles Gleyre (1808–1874) in 1862, where Pierre-August Renoir (see entry), Alfred Sisley (1839–1899), and Frédéric Bazille (1841–1870) were also students.

By 1864 Monet was working in Barbizon, creating landscapes. He first exhibited with the Paris Salon in 1865 and then, for the rest of the decade, regularly sent work for display. With Renoir, Monet spent 1869 painting along the river Seine, creating works with informal compositions that studied the effects of color through loose brushstrokes. These are considered the earliest examples of Impressionism. In 1874 Monet participated in what has since become known as the first Impressionist exhibition. He continued to show work in these exhibitions between 1876 and 1882. Monet last sent work to the Paris Salon in 1880; after that, he exhibited his work through art dealers.

By this time Monet had distanced himself from his scenes of modern life, creating instead series of studies focusing on the changing effects of color and atmosphere. In 1883 Monet moved to Giverny, where his success as an artist allowed him to create an expansive garden that served as his inspiration for paintings until his death in 1926.

Camille Pissarro (Saint Thomas, Danish Virgin Islands 1830–1903 Paris, France)

Camille Pissarro was sent to France by his family to attend boarding school in Passy. Pissarro's artistic talents were encouraged by the headmaster, but Pissarro returned to Saint Thomas at age seventeen to work in his father's hardware business. He continued to draw in his spare time. A chance meeting with the Danish artist Fritz Melbye (1826–1896) influenced Pissarro to devote his life to painting. In 1855 Pissarro visited the Exposition Universelle in Paris. There he saw the work of Eugéne Delacroix (1798–1863), Jean-Baptiste-Camille Corot (see entry), Gustave Courbet (1819–1877), Charles François Daubigny (1817–1878), and Jean-François Millet (1814–1875). Pissarro soon set himself up in Montmartre, painting everything he saw as he learned to reproduce the effects of changing light and seasons. At this time Pissarro became friends with Claude Monet (see entry), Armand Guillaumin (1841–1927), Paul Cézanne (see entry), and Édouard Manet (1832–1883). In 1870 Pissarro traveled to London, where he and Monet were inspired by the works of Joseph Mallord William Turner (1775–1851) and met Daubigny.

Returning to France in 1871, Pissarro moved to Pontoise, where he became an observer of peasant life. With his friends, Pissarro helped organize the first Impressionist exhibition in 1874. Throughout his career, Pissarro experimented with different painting techniques and media. With Cézanne, he worked at applying paint with a palette knife. After this, Pissarro adopted a systematic division of color inspired by Georges Seurat (see entry), but felt this way of painting limited spontaneity, so he returned to his more fluid brushstrokes. Pissarro was also an accomplished engraver and etcher, ultimately creating more than two hundred prints that are known for their tonal lightness and innovative techniques.

Pierre-Auguste Renoir (Limoges, France 1841–1919 Cagnes-sur-Mer, France)

Pierre-Auguste Renoir began his career as a porcelain painter and decorative painter. He attended evening painting classes in Paris and copied eighteenth-century works at the Louvre. In the early 1860s Renoir studied at the École des Beaux-Arts, followed by a period at the teaching studio of Charles Gleyre (1808–1874), where he met Claude Monet (see entry), Alfred Sisley (1839–1899), and Frédéric Bazille (1841–1870). With Monet, Renoir painted in the Forest of Fontainebleau. It was there that Renoir met Narcisse Virgile Diaz de la Peña (see entry), who advised him to lighten his palette.

Between 1869 and 1880 Renoir was an enthusiastic and integral supporter of Impressionism. Painting with Monet along the Seine in 1869, the two artists created some of the earliest Impressionist works. Throughout the 1870s Renoir painted loose, unstructured landscapes and more finished scenes of modern urban life. In the mid-1880s Renoir turned away from Impressionism and began to look back at the paintings of Titian (ca. 1488–1576) and Peter Paul Rubens (1577–1640), which led Renoir to give his figures more massive form and to use a warmer palette.

Théodore Rousseau (Paris, France 1812–1867 Barbizon, France)

Théodore Rousseau's love of forest painting probably began when his cousin Alexandre Pau de Saint-Martin (1782–1850), a landscape artist, took Rousseau to create studies in the forest of Compiègne. Not long after that, around 1826, Rousseau began training with Jean Charles Joseph Rémond (1795–1875), and then with Guillaume Lethiere (1760–1832). The academic approach to landscape did not appeal to Rousseau, who felt that nature scenes needed to be realistic. In 1830, at the age of eighteen, Rousseau traveled to Auvergne, where he spent several months working in the rugged landscape. Beginning in 1836, Rousseau worked mainly at Fontainebleau, which he had first visited ten years earlier. Rousseau's painting was influenced by seventeenth-century Dutch painters like Jacob van Ruisdael (1628/29–1682) and by the work of John Constable (1776–1837). Rousseau constantly sought an elusive perfection in his art. Because of this, he would often rework his paintings over a span of years.

After his initial entry in 1831 to the Paris Salon, Rousseau's subsequent submissions were routinely denied. As a result, in 1836 Rousseau began working at Barbizon, splitting his time between the village and the Forest of Fontainebleau. Despite Rousseau's lack of official academic recognition, many successful contemporary artists appreciated his paintings. Among his strongest supporters were his friends Narcisse Virgile Diaz de la Peña (see entry) and Jules Dupré (see entry). In 1849 Rousseau again submitted work to, and this time was accepted by, the Paris Salon; he was even awarded a first-class medal. This began a period of success for Rousseau, culminating in 1855, when a room at the Exposition Universelle in Paris was devoted to his work. Despite his new popularity, Rousseau preferred solitude, and moved permanently to Barbizon in 1848, where he was often visited by Jean-François Millet (1814–1875) and other friends.

Georges Seurat (Paris, France 1859–1891 Paris, France)

Georges Seurat's formal art training began around 1875, when he took classes at a local municipal school taught by the sculptor Justin Lequien (1826–1882). This was followed by the École des Beaux-Arts, which he entered in February 1878, where he studied with Henri Lehmann (1814–1882). Unhappy with Lehmann's traditional teachings, Seurat looked elsewhere for artistic inspiration. He found it in the work of Piero della Francesca (ca. 1415–1492), Eugène Delacroix (1798–1863), and Pierre Puvis de Chavannes (1824–1898). In April 1879, Seurat visited the fourth Impressionist exhibition and was astounded by the paintings of Claude Monet (see entry) and Camille Pissarro (see entry). Seurat was also influenced by his reading of Michel-Eugène Chevreul's *De la loi du contraste simultané des couleurs* (1839) and Charles Blanc's *Grammaire des arts du dessin* (1867), which introduced the student-artist to color theories. After a year's conscripted service in the military, Seurat decided to continue exploring the expressive nature of color by integrating his accumulated research with painting and drawing techniques. In these early works Seurat used *balayé* (criss-cross) brushstrokes, but by 1883 he employed an Impressionist brushstroke that created varied texture and movement across the canvas.

Seurat's first large-scale painting, *Bathers at Asnières*, was rejected by the jury for the 1884 Paris Salon but subsequently exhibited in the Salon des Indépendants. His next major painting, *A Sunday on La Grande Jatte—1884*, was completed in Seurat's new technique, now referred to as Divisionism. *La Grande Jatte*'s successful exhibition in the eighth Impressionist exhibition (1886) established Seurat as a leader in the avant-garde group that became known as the Neo-Impressionists. Seurat split his time between summer trips to the Normandy coast, where he painted marines, and winters in the studio creating figure paintings. Seurat's life was suddenly cut short when he died in 1891 from an infectious angina, aged thirty-one.

Bibliography

Unless otherwise noted, Van Gogh's letters are quoted from Leo Jansen, Hans Luijten, and Nienke Bakker, eds., *Vincent van Gogh: The Letters* (Amsterdam and The Hague: Van Gogh Museum and Huygens ING, 2009), Version: November 2014, http://vangoghletters.org. All italics are in the originals.

F numbers in the text refer to the catalogue raisonné of Van Gogh's oeuvre: J.-B. de la Faille, *The Works of Vincent van Gogh: His Paintings and Drawings*, rev. ed. (Amsterdam: Meulenhoff International; New York: Reynal, 1970).

All measurements are in inches and centimeters;
height precedes width.

Adler, Kathleen, ed. *Van Gogh: The Man and the Earth*. Milan: ORE Cultura, 2014. An exhibition catalogue.

Anker, Valentina. *Alexandre Calame (1810–1864): Dessins, catalogue raisonné*. Bern: Benteli, 2000.

Anker, Valentina. *Alexandre Calame: Vie et oeuvre; Catalogue raisonné de l'oeuvre peint*. Fribourg: Office du Livre, 1987.

Aubrun, Marie-Madeleine. *Jules Dupré, 1811–1889: Catalogue raisonné de l'oeuvre peint, dessiné, et grave*. Paris: L. Laget, 1974.

Bailey, Colin B., and Robert McDonald Parker. *Renoir Landscapes 1865–1883*. London: National Gallery; Ottawa: National Gallery of Canada; Philadelphia: Philadelphia Museum of Art, 2007. An exhibition catalogue.

Belloli, Andrea P. A., ed. *A Day in the Country: Impressionism and the French Landscape*. Los Angeles: Los Angeles County Museum of Art; New York: Harry N. Abrams Publishers, 1984. An exhibition catalogue.

Berge, Jos ten, Teio Meedendorp, and Aukje Vergeest. *The Paintings of Vincent van Gogh in the Collection of the Kröller-Müller Museum*. Otterlo: Kröller-Müller Museum, 2003.

Bermingham, Peter. *American Art in the Barbizon Mood: A Visual History*. Chicago: University of Chicago Press, 1976.

Bernard, Émile. *Lettres de Vincent van Gogh à Émile Bernard*. Edited by Ambroise Vollard. Paris: A. Vollard, 1911.

Blotkamp, Carel, et al. *Vincent van Gogh: Between Earth and Heaven: The Landscapes*. Basel: Kunstmuseum Basel; Ostfildern: Hatje Cantz, 2009. An exhibition catalogue.

Boime, Albert. "Seurat and Piero della Francesca." *Art Bulletin* 47 (June 1965): 265–71.

Brettell, Richard R. *Pissarro and Pontoise: The Painter in a Landscape*. New Haven: Yale University Press, 1990.

Brettell, Richard R., and Anne-Birgitte Fonsmark. *Gauguin and Impressionism*. New Haven: Yale University Press, 2005. An exhibition catalogue.

Brettell, Richard R., et al. *A Day in the Country: Impressionism and the French Landscape*. New York: Abradale Press, 1990. First published 1984 by the Los Angeles County Museum of Art.

Burty, Philippe. "Camille Corot." In *Exposition de l'oeuvre de Corot á l'École nationale des beaux-arts*, 5. Paris: Typ. Jules-Juteau, 1875.

Burty, Philippe. "N. Diaz." In *Maîtres et petits maîtres*, 358–67. Paris: G. Charpentier, 1877.

Busch, Werner. "Paul Cézanne, Gespräch mit Joachim Gasquet (um 1900)." In *Landschaftsmalerei*. Berlin: Reimer, 1997.

Carus, Carl Gustav. *Nine Letters on Landscape Painting: Written in the Years 1815–1824*. Translated by David Britt, introduction by Oskar Bätschmann. Los Angeles: Getty Research Institute, 2002.

Catalogue general des photographies inalterables au charbon et heliogravures. Paris: A. D. Braun & Cie, 1887.

Cincinnati Art Museum. *The Mary E. Johnston Collection*. Cincinnati: Cincinnati Art Museum, 1972. An exhibition catalogue.

"Cincinnati's New Collectors at Cincinnati Modern Art Society." *ARTnews* 44 (15–30 November 1945): 14–15.

Claretie, Jules. "N. Diaz de la Peña." In *Exposition des oeuvres de N. Diaz de la Peña*, 9–27. Paris: Jules Claye, 1877.

D'Argencourt, Louise, et al. "European Paintings of the 19th Century." Part 4 in *The Cleveland Museum of Art Catalogue of Paintings*. 2 vols. Cleveland: The Cleveland Museum of Art, 1999.

Dauberville, Guy-Patrice, and Michel Dauberville. *Renoir: Catalogue raisonné des tableaux, pastels, dessins et aquarelles*. Paris: Éditions Bernheim Jeune, 2007.

Delteil, Loys, Jean Cailac, and Alan Hyman. *Camille Pissarro: L'oeuvre gravé et lithographié; Catalogue raisonné /Camille Pissarro: The Etchings and Lithographs; Catalogue Raisonné*. San Francisco: Alan Wofsy Fine Arts, 1999.

Dijke, Frouke van, Doede Hardeman, and Gerrit Willems, eds. *Holland op zijn mooist: Op pad met de Haagse School*. Dordrecht: Dordrechts Museum; The Hague: Gemeentemuseum Den Haag, 2015. An exhibition catalogue.

Dorn, Roland. "Vincent van Gogh: Soir d'été." In *Van Gogh, van Doesburg, de Chirico, Picasso, Guston, Weiner, Mangold, Richter: Texte zu Werken im Kunstmuseum Winterthur*, edited by Dieter Schwarz, 11–41. Düsseldorf: Richter, 1999.

Druick, Douglas, and Peter Zegers. "Degas and the Printed Image." In *Edgar Degas as Printmaker*, edited by Sue Welsh Reed and Barbara Stern Shapiro, xv–lxxii. Boston: Museum of Fine Arts, 1984.

Druick, Douglas W., and Peter Kort Zegers. *Van Gogh and Gauguin: The Studio of the South*. Chicago: Art Institute of Chicago; New York: Thames & Hudson, 2001. An exhibition catalogue.

Dumesnil, Henri. *Corot: Souvenirs intimes*. Paris: Rapilly, 1875.

Eisenmann, Stephen F., ed. *From Corot to Monet: The Ecology of Impressionism*. Milan: Skira, 2010. An exhibition catalogue.

Evans, Mark. *John Constable: Oil Sketches from the Victoria and Albert Museum/John Constable—Maler der Natur: Ölskizzen und Zeichnungen aus dem Victoria and Albert Museum, London*. London: V & A Publications; New York: Harry N. Abrams; Ostfildern: Hatje Cantz, 2011. An exhibition catalogue.

Faille, Jacob-Baart de la. *The Works of Vincent van Gogh: His Paintings and Drawings*. Rev. ed. New York: Reynal, 1970.

Feilchenfeldt, Walter. *Vincent van Gogh: The Years in France: Complete Paintings 1886–1890*. London: Philip Wilson Publishers, 2013. First published 2009 in German.

Fermigier, André. *Courbet: Étude biographique et critique*. Geneva: Skira, 1994. First printed 1971 by Skira.

Friesen, Victor Carl. "A Tonic of Wildness: Sensuousness in Henry David Thoreau." In *Empire of the Senses: The Sensual Culture Reader*, edited by David Howes, 251–64. Oxford; New York: Berg, 2005.

Galassi, Peter. *Corot in Italy: Open-Air Painting and the Classical-Landscape Tradition*. New Haven: Yale University Press, 1991.

Galeries nationales du Grand Palais. *Le Japonisme*. Paris: Ministère de la culture et de la communication, Éditions de la Réunion des Musées Nationaux; Tokyo: National Museum of Western Art, 1988. An exhibition catalogue.

Gassner, Hubertus. *Caspar David Friedrich: Die Erfindung der Romantik*. Munich: Hirmer, 2006. An exhibition catalogue.

Gauguin, Paul. *Oviri, écrits d'un sauvage*. Edited by Daniel Guérin. Paris: Gallimard, 1974.

Gianfreda, Sandra, et al., eds. *Monet, Gauguin, Van Gogh . . . : Inspiration Japan*. Göttingen: Edition Folkwang/Steidl, 2014. An exhibition catalogue.

Glassman, Elizabeth, and Marilyn F. Symmes. *Cliché-verre, Hand-Drawn, Light-Printed: A Survey of the Medium from 1839 to the Present*. Detroit: Detroit Institute of Arts, 1980.

Goncourt, Jules de, and Edmond de Goncourt. *Manette Salomon*. Paris: Gallimard, 1996. First published 1867 by Librairie International.

Gravure ou photographie: Une curiosité artistique; Le cliché-verre. Montreuil: Gourcuff Gradenigo; Arras: Musée des Beaux-Arts, 2007. An exhibition catalogue.

Green, Nicholas. "Dealing in Temperaments: Economic Transformations of the Artistic Field in France during the Second Half of the Nineteenth Century." *Art History* 10 (March 1987): 59–78.

Green, Nicholas. *The Spectacle of Nature: Landscape and Bourgeois Culture in Nineteenth-Century France*. Manchester: Manchester University Press, 1990.

Hansen, Dorothée, et al. *Émile Bernard 1868–1941*. Paris: Flammarion; Musée d'Orsay, 2014. An exhibition catalogue.

Hedinger, Bärbel, Inés Richter-Musso, and Ortrud Westheider, eds. *Wolkenbilder: Die Entdeckung des Himmels*. Munich: Hirmer, 2004.

Herbert, Robert L., et al. *Georges Seurat, 1859–1891*. New York: Metropolitan Museum of Art, 1991. An exhibition catalogue.

Herbert, Robert L. *Nature's Workshop: Renoir's Writings on the Decorative Arts*. New Haven: Yale University Press, 2000.

Hildebrecht, Douglas R. "Otto Marseus van Schrieck (1619/20–1678) and the Nature Piece: Art, Science, Religion, and the Seventeenth-Century Pursuit of Natural Knowledge." PhD diss., University of Michigan, 2004.

Hoenigswald, Ann. "Manipulating Paint: The Shorthand of Plein-Air Technique." In *Studying Nature: Oil Sketches from the Thaw Collection*, edited by Jennifer Tonkovich, 9–23. New York: The Morgan Library & Museum, 2011.

Homburg, Cornelia. "Gardens of Love and Suffering." In *The Painter's Garden: Design, Inspiration, Delight*, edited by Sabine Schulze, 244–51. Frankfurt: Städel Museum; Ostfildern: Hatje Cantz, 2006. An exhibition catalogue.

Homburg, Cornelia, ed. *Van Gogh: Up Close*. Ottawa: National Gallery of Canada; Philadelphia: Philadelphia Museum of Art; New Haven: Yale University Press, 2012. An exhibition catalogue.

Homburg, Cornelia. *The Copy Turns Original: Vincent van Gogh and a New Approach to Traditional Art Practice*. Amsterdam and Philadelphia: John Benjamins, 1996.

Homburg, Cornelia, ed. *Vincent van Gogh and the Painters of the Petit Boulevard*. Saint Louis: Saint Louis Art Museum in association with Rizzoli, 2001. An exhibition catalogue.

Homburg, Cornelia, ed. *Vincent van Gogh: Timeless Country, Modern City*. Rome: Complesso Monumentale des Vittoriano; Milan: Skira; New York: Distributed in North America by Rizzoli International, 2010. An exhibition catalogue.

House, John. *Impressionism: Paint and Politics*. New Haven: Yale University Press, 2004.

House, John. *Renoir: Master Impressionist*. Sydney: Art Exhibitions Australia, 1994. An exhibition catalogue.

Howoldt, Jenns E., and Uwe M. Schneede, eds. *Expedition Kunst: Die Entdeckung der Natur von C. D. Friedrich bis Humboldt*. Hamburg: Dölling und Galitz, 2002. An exhibition catalogue.

Hunt, David C. "A Publication History of Karl Bodmer's North American Atlas." In *Karl Bodmer's Studio Art: The Newberry Library Bodmer Collection*, edited by W. Raymond Wood, Joseph C. Porter, and David C. Hunt, 99–122. Urbana: The University of Illinois Press, 2002.

Ireson, Nancy. "The Pointillist and the Past: Three English Views of Seurat." *The Burlington Magazine* 152 (December 2010): 799–803.

Ives, Colta, et al. *Vincent van Gogh: The Drawings*. New York: Metropolitan Museum of Art; Amsterdam: Van Gogh Museum, 2005. An exhibition catalogue.

Jackson, David, and Per Hedström, eds. *The Peredvizhniki: Pioneers of Russian Painting*. Stockholm: Nationalmuseum, 2011. An exhibition catalogue.

Jansen, Leo, Hans Luijten, and Nienke Bakker, eds. *Vincent van Gogh: The Letters*. 6 vols. Brussels: Mercatorfonds; London: Thames & Hudson, 2009.

Jansen, Leo, Hans Luijten, and Nienke Bakker, eds. *Vincent van Gogh: The Letters*. Amsterdam and The Hague: Van Gogh Museum and Huygens ING, 2009. Version: November 2014. http://vangoghletters.org.

Jirat-Wasiutyński, Vojtěch. "Vincent van Gogh's Paintings of Olive Trees and Cypresses from St.-Rémy." *Art Bulletin* 75 (December 1993): 647–70.

Jones, Kimberly, ed. *In the Forest of Fontainebleau: Painters and Photographers from Corot to Monet*. Washington: National Gallery of Art; Houston: Museum of Fine Arts; New Haven: Yale University Press, 2008.

Kelly, Simon. "'A big, good enterprise': Vincent van Gogh and His Markets." In *Becoming Van Gogh*, edited by Timothy Standring and Louis van Tilborgh, 55–69. New Haven: Yale University Press, 2012. An exhibition catalogue.

Kelly, Simon. "'This dangerous game': Rousseau, Diaz and the Uses of the Auction in the Marketing of Landscape." In *Soil and Stone: Impressionism, Urbanism, Environment*, edited by Frances Fowle and Richard Thomson, 33–48. Burlington, VT: Ashgate; Edinburgh: VARIE, 2003.

Kendall, Richard, Sjraar van Heugten, and Chris Stolwijk, eds. *Van Gogh and Nature*. Williamstown: Clark Art Institute; New Haven: Yale University Press, 2015. An exhibition catalogue.

Kōdera, Tsukasa. *Vincent van Gogh: Christianity versus Nature*. Amsterdam; Philadelphia: J. Benjamins Pub. Co., 1990.

Kōdera, Tsukasa. "Van Gogh's Utopian Japonisme." In *Catalogue of the Van Gogh Museum's Collection of Japanese Prints*, edited by Charlotte van Rappard-Boon, Willem R. Gulik, and Keiko van Bremen-Ito, 11–45. Amsterdam: Van Gogh Museum; Zwolle: Waanders, 1991.

Lant, Antonia. "Purpose and Practice in French Avant-Garde Printmaking of the 1880s." *Oxford Art Journal* 6, no. 1 (1983): 18–29.

Leeman, Fred, Béatrice Recchi-Altarriba, and Annie Champié. *Émile Bernard (1868–1941)*. Paris: Wildenstein Institute, 2013.

Leighton, John, and Richard Thomson. *Seurat and the Bathers*. London: National Gallery Publications, 1997. An exhibition catalogue.

Leslie, Charles Robert. *Memoirs of the Life of John Constable*. 3rd ed. London: Phaidon Press, 1995.

Mantura, Bruno, and Geneviève Lacambre, *Pierre-Henri de Valenciennes, 1750–1819*. Naples: Electa Napoli, 1996.

Mantz, Paul. "Jean-François Millet" In *Catalogue descriptif des peintures, aquarelles, pastels, dessins rehaussés, croquis et eaux-fortes de J-F. Millet*, 7–35. Paris: A. Quantin, 1887.

McWilliam, Neil. "Mythologizing Millet." In *Barbizon: Malerei der Natur, Natur der Malerei*, edited by Christoph Heilmann, Andreas Burmester, and Michael Zimmermann, 438–47. Munich: Klinkhardt & Biermann, 1999.

Melot, Michel. *The Impressionist Print*. New Haven: Yale University Press, 1996.

Merlhès, Victor. *Paul Gauguin et Vincent Van Gogh, 1887–88: Lettres retrouvées, sources ignores*. Taravao: Avant et après, 1989.

Milkovich, Michael. *Jules Dupré, 1811–1889*. Memphis: Dixon Gallery, 1979.

Miquel, Pierre, and Rolande Miquel. *Narcisse Diaz de la Peña (1807–1876)*. 2 vols. Paris: ACR Éditions, 2006.

Miquel, Pierre, and Rolande Miquel. *Théodore Rousseau: 1812–1867*. Paris: Somogy, 2010.

Moreau-Nélaton, Etienne. *Corot raconté par lui-même*. Vol. 1. Paris: Henri Laurens, 1924.

Morton, Mary, Charlotte Eyerman and Dominique de Font-Réaulx. *Courbet and the Modern Landscape*. Los Angeles: J. Paul Getty Museum, 2006. An exhibition catalogue.

Museum of Fine Arts, Boston. *Art in New England: Paintings, Drawings, Prints from Private Collections in New England*. Boston: Museum of Fine Arts, 1939. An exhibition catalogue.

Noon, Patrick. *Constable to Delacroix: British Art and the French Romantics, 1820–1840*. London: Tate, 2003. An exhibition catalogue.

Ottani Cavina, Anna, ed. *Paysages d'Italie: Les peintres du plein air, 1780–1830*. Milan: Electa 2001. An exhibition catalogue.

Pickvance, Ronald. *Van Gogh*. Martigny: Fondation Pierre Gianadda, 2000.

Piedagnel, Alexandre. *J.-F. Millet; Souvenirs de Barbizon, avec un portrait et neuf eaux-fortes par Charles Beauverie, Maxime Lalanne, Ad. Lalauze, Piguet, Félicien Rops, Saint-Raymond et Alfred Taiée, et un fac-similé d'autographe*. Paris: Vve A. Cadart, 1876.

Pomarède, Vincent, ed. *L'École de Barbizon: Peindre en plein air avant l'impressionnisme*. Lyon: Réunion des Musées Nationaux, 2002. A Musée des Beaux-Arts de Lyon exhibition catalogue.

Rambert, Eugène. *Alexandre Calame: sa vie et son oeuvre d'après les sources originales*. Paris: Librairie Fischbacher, 1884.

Rewald, John, Walter Feilchenfeldt, and Jayne Warman. *The Paintings of Paul Cézanne: A Catalogue Raisonné*. 2 vols. New York: Harry N. Abrams, 1996.

Reynaerts, Jenny. "Der Ästhetik der Polderlandschaft." In *Der weite Blick: Landschaften der Haager Schule aus dem Rijksmuseum*, edited by Jenny Reynaerts, 39–68. Ostfildern: Hatje Canz, 2008. An exhibition catalogue.

Rosenblum, Robert. *Modern Painting and the Northern Romantic Tradition: Friedrich to Rothko*. London: Thames & Hudson, 1978.

Rousseau, Jean-Jacques. "Septième promenade." Chapter 7 in *Les reveries d'un promeneur solitaire*. Paris: Éditions Flammarion, 1964.

Rousseau, Jean-Jacques. "Seventh Walk." Chapter 7 in *Reveries of the Solitary Walker*. Translated by Russell Goulbourne. Oxford: Oxford University Press, 2011.

Rümelin, Christian, ed. *Die Verzauberung der Landschaft zur Zeit von Jean-Jacques Rousseau/Enchantement du Paysage au temp de Jean-Jacques Rousseau*. Cologne: Wienand; Geneva: Musées d'art et d'histoire de la Ville de Genève, 2012.

Ruskin, John. "Of the Pathetic Fallacy." In *The Works of John Ruskin*, edited by E. T. Cook and A. Wedderburn, vol. 5, *Modern Painters III*. Cambridge: Cambridge University Press, 2010.

Scherf, Guilhem, ed. *Jean-Jacques Rousseau et les arts*. Paris: Éditions du patrimoine, Centre des monuments nationaux, 2012.

Schröder, Klaus Albrecht, et al., eds. *Van Gogh: Heartfelt Lines*. Cologne: Dumont; Vienna: Albertina, 2008. An exhibition catalogue.

Schulman, Michel, and Marie Bataillès. *Théodore Rousseau, 1812–1867: Catalogue raisonné de l'oeuvre peint*. Paris: Éditions de l'Amateur, 1999.

Schwarz, Dieter, and Astrid Näff. *Kunstmuseum Winterthur: Katalog der Gemälde und Skulpturen 2*. Düsseldorf: Richter Verlag, 2008.

Sensier, Alfred, and Paul Mantz. *La vie et l'oeuvre de Jean-François Millet*. Paris: A. Quantin, 1881.

Shackelford, George T. M., and Fronia E. Wissman. *Impressions of Light: The French Landscape from Corot to Monet*. Boston: MFA Publications, 2002. An exhibition catalogue.

Shapiro, Barbara S. *Camille Pissarro: The Impressionist Printmaker*. Boston: Museum of Fine Arts, 1973.

Sillevis, John. "De Haagse School: Sentiment van het alledaagse." In *Holland op zijn mooist: Op pad met de Haagse School*, edited by Frouke van Dijke, Doede Hardeman, and Gerrit Willems. Zwolle: WBOOKS, 2015. An exhibition catalogue.

Smith, Gregory. "Conservation Science: Van Gogh and the Case of Geranium Lake." *IMA Magazine* (August–October 2012): 4–7.

Smith, Paul. *Seurat and the Avant-Garde*. New Haven: Yale University Press, 1997.

Solkin, David H. *Richard Wilson: The Landscape of Reaction*. London: Tate Gallery, 1982. An exhibition catalogue.

Stein, Susan A., ed., *Van Gogh: A Retrospective*. New York: Hugh Lauter Levin Associates, Inc., 1986.

Stevens, Arthur. *Le Salon de 1863*. Paris: La Librairie des Arts, 1863.

Stolwijk, Chris. "Van Gogh and the Pictorial Genre of Evening and Night Scenes." In *Van Gogh and the Colors of the Night*, edited by Sjraar van Heugten, Joachim Pissarro, and Chris Stolwijk, 15–42. Amsterdam: Van Gogh Museum; New York: Museum of Modern Art; Brussels: Mercatorfonds, 2008. An exhibition catalogue.

Stolwijk, Chris, Sjraar van Heugten, Leo Jansen, and Andreas Blühm. "Van Gogh's Nature." In *Vincent's Choice: The "Musée Imaginaire" of Van Gogh*, edited by Chris Stolwijk, Sjraar van Heugten, Leo Jansen, and Andreas Blühm, 25–36. Amsterdam: Van Gogh Museum, 2003. An exhibition catalogue.

Stuffmann, Margret, and Dorit Schäfer, eds. *Camille Corot: Natur und Traum*. Karlsruhe: Staatliche Kunsthalle Karlsruhe, 2012. An exhibition catalogue.

Sumner, Ann, and Greg Smith, eds. *Thomas Jones (1742–1803): An Artist Rediscovered*. New Haven: Yale University Press in association with the National Museums & Galleries of Wales, Cardiff, 2003. An exhibition catalogue.

Sund, Judy. *True to Temperament: Van Gogh and French Naturalist Literature*. Cambridge: Cambridge University Press, 1992.

Temmer, Mark J. *Art and Influence of Jean-Jacques Rousseau: The Pastorale, Goethe, Gottfried Keller, and Other Essays*. Chapel Hill: University of North Carolina Press, 1973.

Thomas, Greg M. *Art and Ecology in Nineteenth-Century France: The Landscapes of Théodore Rousseau*. Princeton: Princeton University Press, 2000.

Thoreau, Henry David. *Walden; or, Life in the Woods*. Edited by Philip Smith. Mineola, NY: Dover Publications, 1995. First published 1854 by Ticknor & Fields.

Tilborgh, Louis van. "Framing Van Gogh." In *In Perfect Harmony: Picture + Frame 1850–1920*, edited by Eva A. Mendgen, 163–80. Amsterdam: Van Gogh Museum; Zwolle: Waanders, 1995. An exhibition catalogue.

Tilborgh, Louis van. "Hetzelfde, maar anders: Van Gogh en zijn leermeester Millet." In *Van Gogh & Millet*, by Louis Van Tilborgh, Sjraar van Heugten, and Philip Conisbee, 9–24. Zwolle: Waanders; Amsterdam: Rijksmuseum Vincent van Gogh, 1988.

Tilborgh, Louis van, and Ella Hendriks. *Vincent van Gogh Paintings*. Vol. 2, *Antwerp & Paris 1885–1888*. Translated by Michael Hoyle. Amsterdam: Van Gogh Museum; Zwolle: Waanders, 2011.

Tilborgh, Louis van, Teio Meedendorp, and Oda van Maanen. "'Sunset at Montmajour': A Newly Discovered Painting by Vincent van Gogh." *The Burlington Magazine* 155 (October 2013): 696–705.

Tilborgh, Louis van, et al., eds. *Van Gogh & Millet*. Amsterdam: Van Gogh Museum, 1988; Paris: Musee d'Orsay, 1998.

Tinterow, Gary, Michael Pantazzi, and Vincent Pomarède. *Corot*. New York: Metropolitan Museum of Art, 1996. An exhibition catalogue.

Tinterow, Gary. "Le père Corot: Le patriarche des paysagistes; Le poète même du paysage." In *Corot 1796–1875*, edited by Vincent Pomarède, Michael Pantazzi, and Gary Tinterow, 321–37. Paris: Réunion des Musées Nationaux et al., 1996.

Tinterow, Gary, et al. *Masterpieces of European Painting in the Metropolitan Museum of Art (1800–1920)*. New York: Metropolitan Museum of Art; New Haven: Yale University Press, 2007.

Uitert, Evert van. *Van Gogh in Brabant: Schilderijen en tekeningen uit Etten en Nuenen*. Zwolle: Waanders, 1987.

Uitert, Evert van, Louis van Tilborgh, and Sjraar van Heugten. *Vincent van Gogh: Paintings*. Amsterdam: Van Gogh Museum; Milan: Mondadori, 1990. An exhibition catalogue.

Valenciennes, Pierre Henri de. *Élémens de perspective pratique, à l'usage des artistes, suivis de reflexions et conseils à un elève sur la peinture et particulierement sur le genre du paysage*. Paris: L'Auteur, 1799–1800. Reprint of the second part, La Rochelle: Rumeur des âges, 2005.

Veen, Wouter van der. *Van Gogh, a Literary Mind: Literature in the Correspondence of Vincent van Gogh*. Zwolle: Waanders; Amsterdam: Van Gogh Museum, 2009.

Vellekoop, Marije. *Van Gogh at Work*. Amsterdam: Van Gogh Museum; Brussels: Mercatorfonds, 2013. An exhibition catalogue.

Vellekoop, Marije, ed. *Van Gogh's Studio Practice*. Brussels: Mercatorfonds; Amsterdam: Van Gogh Museum, 2013.

Vellekoop, Marije, and Roelie Zwikker. *Vincent van Gogh Drawings*. Vol. 4, *Arles, Saint-Rémy & Auvers-sur-Oise, 1888–1890*. Amsterdam: Van Gogh Museum, 2007.

Vellekoop, Marije. "Van Gogh in the Borinage: From Evangelist to Artist, 1880." In *Van Gogh: The Birth of an Artist*, edited by Sjraar Van Heugten, 50–77. New Haven: Yale University Press, 2015. An exhibition catalogue.

Walker, Janet A. "Van Gogh, Collector of 'Japan.'" *Comparatist* 32 (May 2008): 82–114.

Wildenstein, Daniel. *Claude Monet: Biographie et catalogue raisonné*. Vol. 1, *Monet or the Triumph of Impressionism*. Paris: Wildenstein Institute; Cologne: Taschen, 1996.

Wildenstein, Daniel, Sylvie Crussard, and Martine Heudron. *Gauguin: Premier itinéraire d'un sauvage: Catalogue de l'oeuvre peint, 1873–1888*. Milan: Skira; Paris: Wildenstein Institute, 2001.

Zemel, Carol. "The 'Spook' in the Machine: Van Gogh's Pictures of Weavers in Brabant." *Art Bulletin* 67 (March 1985): 123–37.

Zemel, Carol. *Van Gogh's Progress: Utopia, Modernity, and Late Nineteenth-Century Art*. Berkeley: University of California Press, 1997.

Photography Credits

Fig. 1 Courtesy National Gallery of Art, Washington

Laura Prins "Undergrowth with Two Figures"

Fig. 2 Photography © The Art Institute of Chicago

Fig. 3 © RMN-Grand Palais / Art Resource, New York; Photo: Gérard Blot / Christian Jean

Fig. 4 Image copyright © The Metropolitan Museum of Art. Image source: Art Resource, New York

Simon Kelly "The Great Revolution"

Fig. 8 © Belvedere, Vienna

Fig. 10 © S. Riandet

Fig. 12 © RMN-Grand Palais / Art Resource, New York; Photo: Gérard Blot

Jenny Reynaerts "Tree Lovers"

Fig. 17 © RMN-Grand Palais / Art Resource, New York; Photo: Hervé Lewandowski

Fig. 18 Photo © Rheinisches Bildarchive Köln, rba_c005014

Fig. 19 © Victoria and Albert Museum, London

Fig. 20 Courtesy National Gallery of Art, Washington

Fig. 23 Courtesy National Gallery of Art, Washington

Fig. 24 Photo Credit: HIP / Art Resource, New York

Cornelia Homburg, "Van Gogh's Nature–Taking Position"

Fig. 26 © RMN-Grand Palais / Art Resource, New York; Photo: Patrice Schmidt

Fig. 28 Image © The Metropolitan Museum of Art

Fig. 30 © Stichting Kröller-Müller Museum

Fig. 31 © The Samuel Courtauld Trust, The Courtauld Gallery, London

Fig. 32 © Stichting Kröller-Müller Museum

Fig. 35 Photo Credit: The Solomon R. Guggenheim Foundation / Art Resource, New York

Catalogue

Cat. 1 © 2002 Christies Images Limited

Fig. 36 The Pierpont Morgan Library, New York

Fig. 37 © Stichting Kröller-Müller Museum

Fig. 38 © Stichting Kröller-Müller Museum

Cat. 2 Image Courtesy Dallas Museum of Art

Fig. 40 Photography © The Art Institute of Chicago

Cat. 5 Image and Copyright Centraal Museum, Utrecht / Ernst Mortiz

Cat. 6 © Stichting Kröller-Müller Museum

Fig. 45 Image courtesy Van Gogh Museum, Amsterdam

Cat. 8 © Stichting Kröller-Müller Museum

Fig. 50 © Belvedere, Vienna

Cat. 10 © RMN-Grand Palais / Art Resource, New York; Photo: Michel Urtado

Fig. 52 © RMN-Grand Palais / Art Resource, New York

Fig. 53 © INHA, Dist. RMN-Grand Palais / Art Resource, New York

Cat. 15 © The Cleveland Museum of Art

Cat. 16 Image Courtesy Dallas Museum of Art

Fig. 55 © Stichting Kröller-Müller Museum

Cat. 18 © Schweizerisches Institut für Kunstwissenschaft, Zürich, Jean-Pierre Kuhn

Cat. 19 © RMN-Grand Palais / Art Resource, New York; Photo: Hervé Lewandowski

Fig. 56 © National Gallery, London / Art Resource, New York

Fig. 57 Photograph © 2016 Museum of Fine Arts, Boston

Fig. 58 Photograph and Digital Image © Philadelphia Museum of Art

Fig. 59 Photo Credit: Scala / Art Resource, New York

Cat. 22 Image © The Metropolitan Museum of Art

Fig. 60 Photo Credit: Alfredo Dagli Orti / The Art Archive at Art Resource, New York

Cat. 23 © 2015 Art Gallery of Ontario

Cat. 24 Photograph Courtesy of Sotheby's, Inc. © 2011

Cat. 25 © RMN-Grand Palais / Art Resource, New York; Photo: Patrice Schmidt

Fig. 61 The Pierpont Morgan Library, New York

Index

Page numbers in **bold** refer to the illustrations

E

F

G

H

I

J

S

T

V

W

Z